# Sound Diplomacy

# Sound Diplomacy

*Music and Emotions in
Transatlantic Relations,
1850–1920*

JESSICA C. E. GIENOW-HECHT

*The University of Chicago Press    Chicago and London*

**JESSICA C. E. GIENOW-HECHT** is professor of international history/peace and conflict studies at the University of Cologne. She received the Stuart Bernath Prize and the Myrna F. Bernath Prize for her previous book, *Transmission Impossible: American Journalism as Cultural Diplomacy in Postwar Germany, 1945–1955* (1999).

The University of Chicago Press, Chicago 60637
The University of Chicago Press, Ltd., London
© 2009 by The University of Chicago
All rights reserved. Published 2009
Printed in the United States of America
18  17  16  15  14  13  12  11  10  09      1  2  3  4  5

ISBN-13: 978-0-226-29215-1 (cloth)
ISBN-10: 0-226-29215-0 (cloth)

Library of Congress Cataloging-in-Publication Data
Gienow-Hecht, Jessica C. E., 1964–
    Sound diplomacy : music and emotions in transatlantic
relations, 1850–1920 / Jessica C. E. Gienow-Hecht.
        p.    cm.
    Includes bibliographical references and index.
    ISBN-13: 978-0-226-29215-1 (hardcover : alk. paper)
    ISBN-10: 0-226-29215-0 (hardcover : alk. paper) 1. Music—Social aspects—
United States—History. 2. Music—United States—German influences.
3. Nationalism in music.
I. Title.
ML3917.U6G54  2009
306.4'84209430973—dc22
                                                    2008029175

♾ The paper used in this publication meets the minimum requirements
of the American National Standard for Information Sciences—
Permanence of Paper for Printed Library Materials, ANSI Z39.48-1992.

*To my husband, Heiko Hecht,*

*with whom I am sharing*

*a turbulent household,*

*a crazy life,*

*and an abundance of laughter and joy.*

# Contents

# Illustrations

# Acknowledgments

Among all the musical compositions of the nineteenth century, Chopin's nocturnes are my favorite. Moving, haunting, and forever beautiful, to the layman's ear they may sound effortless. Yet, to create this illusion they demand a tremendous emotional investment, physical virtuosity, and hard work from the pianist. While writing this book, I often thought about the nocturnes, and about how much is required to accomplish a little. I was grateful for all the help I could get in the process.

Throughout my career as a scholar, I have been lucky to be able to return to a number of colleagues, friends, and mentors who consistently provide me with criticism, advice, and support. Exasperated by my insistence that German Kultur consisted of more than a stubborn obsession with the superiority of the Romantics, one night in Austin, Texas, in 1998, Richard Pells suggested that for once I should write rather than worry about this topic. Helping me develop my ideas in so many ways, he has become a lifelong friend, the kind that we all wish for. Likewise, my one-time teacher at the University of Virginia and later my friend, Joseph Kett, patiently listened to my confusing ideas, read drafts, and never lost an inch of interest in my project. Or at least I hope so.

My foremost gratitude goes to Hermann-Joseph Rupieper at the Martin-Luther-Universität Halle-Wittenberg; his enthusiasm for my work has been a constant source of motivation for me ever since I attended graduate school. Professor Rupieper died in August 2004; if I am glad to see this text go to press, I deeply regret that he could not. Reinhard Doerries was not only one of the people responsible for my decision to study American history in the United States, but also the first to grasp the viability of my project at a critical moment in my research and my life.

The scope of the project required the consultation of political, diplomatic, and artistic sources. Because of the unconventional nature of my archival research, I wish to express my profound thanks to the many archivists—or administrators in charge of archival material on top of their regular jobs—that I met between Berlin and Los Angeles. At the Geheimes Staatsarchiv Preussischer Kulturbesitz in Berlin, everybody from the receptionist to the team in the Forschungssaal and in the Aktenausgabe was not only nice and friendly but also incredibly efficient, cooperative, and helpful. Waltraut Elstner and Ute Dietsch helped me find my way through the collections and sped up the delivery process. At the Bundesarchiv Berlin, Herr Zarwell went out of his way to help me retrieve files from the Foreign Office.

I consider myself extremely fortunate to be the first historian to gain collective access to approximately one dozen recently opened archives established and maintained by symphony orchestras on the East Coast, in the Midwest, and in California, including those in Boston, New York City, Philadelphia, Pittsburgh, Cincinnati, Chicago, St. Louis, Minneapolis, San Francisco, and Los Angeles. Many of these orchestras recently celebrated or will be celebrating their centennial, which inspired their management to either create an institutional archive or consider donating their holdings to a public library (in one case I found myself literally rummaging through hundreds of boxes stuffed into a basement beneath the concert stage). Ironically, recent budget cuts have forced trustees to close or prune some of these celebrated collections, as has been the case in Philadelphia and Chicago; I appeal to them and all the others to continue making a crucial piece of cultural and international history accessible to scholars and laypeople alike. After all, the way we see and understand history depends on what we can actually examine in our research.

Among the archivists of the many U.S. performing-arts collections, I got to know some of the most original and inspiring people I have ever met. Often, they not only made the archival treasures of the oldest symphonies in the United States available to me but offered me their friendship—and, in many cases, the opportunity to sneak into performances by stellar soloists and orchestras. In Philadelphia, JoAnne Barry's enthusiasm for music encouraged my research from the beginning. At the Rosenthal Archives of the Chicago Symphony Orchestra, Andrea Cawelti surprised me with the extent of her help and friendship. In Los Angeles, Steve

Lacrosse, hidden behind zillions of boxes in the Department of Justice, spent much time advising me on the early history of the Los Angeles Symphony. Bridget Carr and Barbara Perkel at the archives of the Boston Symphony Orchestra, as well as Teri McKibben in Public Relations at the Cincinnati Symphony Orchestra, offered advice and support beyond the call of duty. Steve Wright, then director of the Cincinnati Historical Society, not only hauled out box after box of presumably "missing" material from the archives but also became a good friend. Martha Clevenger, Chuck Hill, and the staff at the Missouri Historical Society considerably facilitated my research on St. Louis music life. At the Carnegie Library in Pittsburgh, Kathryn Logan's questions and suggestions pointed my research interest in altogether new directions. At the San Francisco Performing Arts Library and Museum, Kirsten Tanaka and Lee Cox provided helpful guidance and support. At the Newberry Library in Chicago, Diane Haskell helped me to access several collections, as did Lesley Martin at the Chicago History Museum. Alan Lathrop at the University of Minnesota patiently pulled out record after record for my perusal, even though as Curator of the Archive for the Performing Arts he had many other things to do. At the archives of the New York Philharmonic, Richard Wandel coped with my exasperating calls for yet more boxes and information, as did Gino Francesconi at the Carnegie Hall Archives.

I am indebted to numerous colleagues for reading early outlines and essays written in preparation for this book. At Harvard University, Akira Iriye has been a friend and an inspiration for my research, even before we met face to face in 1999. Hans-Jürgen Grabbe, Axel Schäfer, Kevin Mactavish, Erica Benson, Daniel Levy, Charlie Maier, Karen Painter, Marianne Beetz, and Rebecca helped me to clarify my confusing ideas on music and the exportation of Kultur; most of them read early papers, which I also had the good opportunity to present in workshops at the Center for European Studies and the Charles Warren Center, both at Harvard University, and at the annual convention of the historians of the Deutsche Gesellschaft für Amerikastudien in Tutzing, Germany; the Graduate Workshop in Diplomatic History at Ohio State University; St. Joseph's University, Philadelphia; Oxford University; and a number of professional meetings since. Manfred Hettling, Mathias Tischer, Friedrich Kießling, Heiko Hecht, and Jon Rosenberg, among others, read the full text at various stages of its development, offering helpful advice at several turns. Guido Müller, Wolfram Kaiser, Frank Trommler, Toby Thacker, and William Weber likewise took time to comment on individual chapters while Joseph Horowitz checked the appendix. Joan Gaul never read anything I wrote, but pointed me in the right direction to the right archives when I did not have a clue where to start.

At the University of Chicago Press, my editor, Doug Mitchell, proved to be an early believer in my research project; and once the Press offered me an advance contract, he and his associate, Tim McGovern, did their best to cope with my concerns and my schedule. Thank you also to the anonymous outside reviewers from the fields of history and musicology, for their pressing questions and concerns; they encouraged me to reconceptualize and prune the manuscript. I am grateful to my copy editor, Sandy Hazel, whose ability to detect typos, errors, and inconsistencies is mind boggling; my book designer, Natalie Smith, for creating a handsome interior design and the book jacket; and my promotions manager, Rob Hunt, whose familiarity with things musical as well as cultural and historical is impressive. Thank you also to Martin White, for compiling the index.

Various foundations have supported me during my years of archival research and writing, and I wish to express my profound gratitude to them. The German Academic Exchange Service (DAAD) awarded me a John F. Kennedy stipend at Harvard's Center for European Studies in 1999–2000. A grant from the Gilder Lehrman Institute of American History allowed me to plow through New York archives in the summer of 2000. In 2000–2001, the Charles Warren Center in the Department of History at Harvard welcomed me as a fellow in the workshop "Global America." The German Research Association (DFG) awarded me a substantial research grant that enabled me to complete my habilitation in 2003, then appointed me as a Heisenberg Fellow at the Johann Wolfgang Universität-Frankfurt am Main, where I revised the manuscript for this book.

On a more personal note, I wish to thank my music teacher, Frau Karbaum, and my grandmother, Emi (Margarethe Gienow), both of whom introduced me to the beauty of instrumental performance and musical self-expression. Thank you also to Sally Smithwick, in whose house in Gloucester, Massachusetts, I wrote this book while gazing out at the very object of my research project: the Atlantic Ocean. Karen Michael Hofmann, Sylvia Bartz, Katie Sibley and Joe Horwitz, and Daniel Levy and Emily Miller welcomed me into their homes for weeks at a time while I was plodding through local archives. Many thanks to my parents, who have always supported me in my complicated ways and wishes. My husband, Heiko Hecht, deserves unlimited praise for all that he has done and is: we are sharing a turbulent household and a crazy life marked by organizational chaos, day-care schedules, erratic shopping sprees, heaps of laundry, children's diseases, years of sleep deprivation, and above all, an abundance of laughter and joy. He has continued to be the most ruthless critic of my ideas but also the most reliable comforter when never-ending archival trips, technological challenges, and countless revisions were bringing me down. *Tausend Dank* to my children, Imina, Sicco Theodor, Petronella, and Josephine, who were born while I was writing this book. They are the best things that ever happened to me. I know that I do not need to apologize for setting them up with an armada of nannies, day-care providers, and kindergarten teachers while I disappeared into my study, a library, or an archive. But if they ever wondered what Mama actually did in those places, here is the answer to their question.

Wiesbaden, April 2008

# Introduction

In Joel Oliansky's 1980 Hollywood drama, *The Competition*, Richard Dreyfuss (playing a character named Paul) and Amy Irving ("Heidi") enter a piano competition, pitting Beethoven's *Emperor* Concerto against Prokofiev's Third Symphony. Heidi's instructor, a woman named Greta, can trace her own instructors all the way back to Beethoven himself and is fanatic about her student winning the contest. Other contestants reveal all the stereotypes in the international music world of that era. The Russian participant is a sort of music robot whose mentor mysteriously disappears in the midst of the competition. The Italian has just one concerto in his repertory and is really trying to be Robert De Niro. The black pianist always practices in the nude. And so on. Paul himself is an odd character who at first is bent on winning (it is his final competition, as he's nearing thirty, that crucial cutoff age for participation in such recital programs): he's rough, tough, arrogant but also vulnerable; at one point he even cries. Halfway through the competition, Paul falls in love with Heidi and eventually abandons all his ambitions for the tournament.

*The Competition* neatly encapsulates all the myths that "classical music" has come to entail today: the towering preponderance of nineteenth-century European masters; the claim that classical music is a universal language of emotions transcending all borders; and the enduring beliefs that emotion triumphs over reason, that aestheticism matters more than competition, and that music will bring people together instead of driving them apart. Most important, set in a prominent West Coast symphony hall, the film portrays the United States as the center and chief exporter of classical music production.

Historians know this image of the United States as a cultural merchant all too well. Throughout much of the twentieth century, it has persistently been accused of exporting its culture, especially after World War II, when the U.S. government along with a host of private organizations, churches, and foundations became the key propagandist of American values and consumer goods.[1] But the United States' efforts were not unique; they followed a tradition set by other countries during the preceding centuries. Since the Renaissance, European governments and private associations, as well as individuals, have fostered a variety of cultural exchange programs, though they did not always hope to spread their empires simply by exporting their cultures. The British in India and the Middle East, the Germans in Africa, and the French in Indochina all implemented their own culture abroad as a powerful tool to strengthen trade, commerce, and political influence and to recruit intellectual elites for their own purposes in lands they wished to dominate. In the history of the rise and fall of cultural hegemonies, the United States represents the taillight and a nation whose first role was not an exporter but a target of other countries' cultural expansion during the nineteenth century.[2]

In the nineteenth century, the major European powers began to compete with one another for cultural preponderance in the United States by sending agents and artifacts that they perceived as representative of their respective national cultural scenes. Alongside and often quite different from this official effort, cultural transmission also was carried out by nongovernmental individuals. At the same time, Victorian Americans[3] embarked on an international quest for taste, fashion, history, and cultural artifacts, an interest that eventually led them to Europe. The resulting alliance of taste, fashion, and artistic preferences established a vital financial, commercial, political, and, eventually, cultural link between European and American elites, and they continue to define U.S.-European relations to this day.

Victorian Americans worried little about the consequences of these multicultural imports; indeed, many saw the American character as particularly apt for the assimilation and digestion of foreign cultural artifacts. "I think that to be an American is an excellent preparation for culture," Henry James contemplated in 1867, in a letter to Thomas Sergeant Perry. "We have exquisite qualities as a race, and it seems to me that we are ahead of the European races in the fact that more than either of them we can deal freely with forms of civilization not our own, can pick and choose and assimilate and in short (aesthetically etc.) claim our property wherever we find it."[4]

James was evidently proud of the eclecticism of American civilization, but he completely ignored the efforts on the part of European governments, artists, and private individuals to push their respective cultures upon the United States. Without the migration of European artists and lay musicians beginning after 1848, without the general climate of expansion prevailing in Europe after 1880, without the cunning sales initiatives of French government officials and vendors, without the interest of British elites in American cash, and without the German Reich's effort to boost Kultur in the United States, the American cultural scene would probably look very different today.[5]

This book reflects on formal and informal German and, to a much lesser extent, French and British efforts to influence American culture during the nineteenth and early twentieth centuries. It shows that due to cultural imports, "high culture" continued to play a vital role in the United States, despite the rise of mass culture in the twentieth century and Americans' ironic dismissal of such presumably elitist influences as part of their own identity. The diplomatic dimension, I believe, is key to an understanding of American artistic life. Foreign artists and administrators played a central role in the United States' quest for high culture, artists whose lives for the most part defied any notion of elitism. Their story thus addresses, first, the emergence of a "national" American culture and, second, current debates on international cultural relations.

———

Cultural, social, economic, and diplomatic historians have outlined various ways in which national history could be interwoven with supranational and global events. For the United States, David Thelen and Thomas Bender, along with the Organization of American Historians, have demanded that the study and teaching of U.S. history be (more) internationalized. Students of this history, they suggested, should be acquainted with the view of it from the perspective of scholars outside the United States; they should be stimulated in new ways by what they hear and learn—just as a cosmopolitan feels when confronted with a different culture.[6]

In the field of foreign relations, the last fifteen years have brought about a virtual palace revolution on the part of a new generation of historians who have begun to probe new analytical concepts such as gender, literary criticism, travel, environmentalism, race, and culture. They have written on nongovernmental organizations, tourism, religion, sports, bird migration, and the spread of diseases within the framework of international relations. Under the influence of cultural studies, scholars of international history have explored cultural perceptions, global culture systems, and cultural theory.[7] "Culture," writes Akira Iriye, "determines what the ends of a nation are; power provides the means for obtaining them."[8] Today, the history of foreign relations is characterized by an intense pluralism, and an increasing awareness that the state is only one of many principal actors in the international arena.[9]

The title of this book reflects this change, as the new international history has led to a reassessment of the term *diplomacy*. *Diplomacy* means to conduct relationships for gain while avoiding conflict. Aware of the crucial role played by nongovernmental actors such as missionaries, teachers, and other cultural envoys in international relations, scholars have recognized that these actors constitute ambassadors and diplomats in their own right.[10] Diplomacy thus refers not only to state-to-state relations conducted by officials on the payroll of their governments but, increasingly, to other forms of overt or covert negotiation by individuals acting—often unwittingly—in the name or the interest of the state. The following pages will introduce dozens of such informal ambassadors whose actions—even though they were not directly inspired by state policy—achieved a desired political effect.

Transnational history is fast becoming one of the central trends in the new diplomatic history, as it allows for the systematic exploration of nongovernmental actors in the context of international relations, notably in the nineteenth century. Their story adds tremendously to our understanding of intercultural and international relations prior to the "short century." Historians who have written about transnationalism and globalization, such as Anthony Hopkins, Christopher Bayly, and Akira Iriye, have dated the first phase of these developments from the mid-nineteenth century through the end of World War I.[11] Pointing to the flow of ideas and agents on the transatlantic highway, scholars such as James Campbell, David Armitage, Volker Berghahn, Richard Pells, and numerous others have contextualized U.S. history with international political, cultural, economic and social developments.[12] In *Schnitzler's Century*, Peter Gay evokes the concept of a transnational middle-class culture between Boston, London, and Paris, which shared similar values, paradoxes, and predicaments. *Victorian* is "all of Western civilization, and synonymous with 'nineteenth century,'" Gay observes.[13] In a similar vein, Daniel Rodgers has argued in his study on Atlantic crossings during the Progressive age that quite often the traffic of ideas and material goods flowed in reverse, notably when U.S. reformers went to Europe to examine social programs developed abroad.[14]

While Gay's and Rodgers's studies discuss the cultural, intellectual, and sociopolitical dimension of the European-American encounter, this book focuses on emotional crossings. Cultural and emotional relations, I believe, fashion their own form of power in the international arena, and their interactions should not be viewed solely through political lenses. In the case of European-American relations, cultural representatives sometimes cooperated with policy makers. More often, however, these agents operated on their own. Their intentions hence need to be considered apart from the policy-making process, even though the consequence of their actions occasionally produced an advantageous political result.

The story of these cultural envoys cuts across two different strands of scholarship. While diplomatic historians typically define political agents as the protagonists of their analyses, social and cultural historians emphasize the significance of social agents and their surrounding environment. The musicians portrayed in the following chapters, however, are cultural agents who operate within an international and even a diplomatic context.

By looking at American culture in the context of diplomatic and international history, my analysis builds upon the increasing public and academic interest in "internationalism." In its most basic form, internationalism refers to the idea of an international community dedicated to connections, topics, questions, and problems that cannot be addressed within a national framework. As Iriye has argued, the development of cultural internationalism paralleled the emergence of the nation-state in the nineteenth century, when supranational organizations, conferences, and exhibitions as well as religious leaders, artists, and scholars created international flows of communication.[15] While most historians interested in international contacts have concentrated on governmental documents, capital flows, and trade as well as the exchange of ideas, literature, and paintings, this study focuses on "nonmaterial" means of communication and people who dedicated their lives neither to words nor goods but to the power of music and emotions in international relations. Nonverbal cultural and artistic contacts, I argue, proved much more intense and enduring than political ties, surviving broken treaties, mutual alienation, and even several wars.

———

We know little about the foreign artists' story, because most of them acted on the informal, less visible level. They have escaped the attention of diplomatic historians, whose work in this era focuses primarily on the role of official political actors in the international arena.[16] Social historians, in turn, have been reluctant to study the international dimensions of American culture in terms other than migration and ethnic history. Indeed, for years the historiography of American culture has assigned the origins of and agency for domestic developments exclusively to domestic actors, thereby downplaying foreign activism.

More than two decades ago, Paul DiMaggio and Lawrence Levine coined what has become the overriding consensus on late nineteenth-century American culture. In a gesture toward Pierre Bourdieu's concept of cultural "distinction,"[17] they studied highbrow consumers' reception of art, music, and poetry, and argued that after the Civil War, American elites purposefully adopted trends of European high culture in search of taste, class, refinement, and philanthropy. DiMaggio, Levine, and countless others after them scolded late nineteenth-century Americans for their "submission" to European taste at the expense of indigenous artists, who struggled in vain to establish an American national culture. Portraying post–Civil War Americans as elitist, antimodernist, oppressive, confused, and, most important, helplessly dependent on foreign imports, scholars from the right wing to the left have been quick to write off this era in U.S. history as culturally deluded, strange, and unprogressive.[18] Victorians' interest in a supposedly "high culture," foreign artifacts, literature, sculpture, landscapes, paintings, and music, seemed to mark them as decadent and un-American. In that respect, this period does not "fit" into the otherwise progressive tale woven by historians for the last one hundred years.

Notwithstanding these authors' revisionist antagonism toward U.S. political patriotism, they criticized Victorians for their complete failure to develop a cultural patriotism that would have accelerated the emergence of a genuine American culture, popular or otherwise. Because Victorians, more than any society before them, capitalized on foreign ideas and expressions, this period "has long been maligned for its supposedly feeble culture as well as its stifling society," as the historian Mark Rennella has observed. "From Van Wyck Brooks in the 1940s to David Hollinger in the '70s, and more recently from T. J. Jackson Lears in the '80s to Robert Crunden and Ann Douglas in the '90s, the arts and letters of Boston between 1865 and 1915 have been used to draw a story of pathetic failure and pretension."[19]

This argument has recently come under attack, with some scholars pointing to the multiplicity of social and aesthetic motivations people experienced when creating a tradition, attending a theater performance, visiting a museum, or subscribing to a concert series.[20] What has remained in place, however, is a common dismissal of high culture as "elitist" and un-American, and hence unworthy of historical research altogether. Instead, for the last forty years scholars of cultural history and cultural studies have focused heavily on popular and mass culture, industrial art, and the artistic expressions of workers, women, and ethnic minorities.[21]

As a result, for decades the historiography of American culture has remained oblivious to the long-term legacy of foreign influences. Each year in the United States, an abundance of book titles beginning with phrases like "The Rise of" or "The Origins of" inundate publishers' catalogues and university bookshelves. Such titles anticipate a narrative that, although originating yesterday, explains to readers how Americans came to be the way they are today. Regardless of their political bent, many scholars regard U.S. history in rather "patriotic" terms, as a story of origins and progress that climaxes in the present and originates nowhere but in the United States proper.[22] And they often forget that not only did the United States—including its informal actors—create and expand proper cultural forms to contribute to the global reformulation of the world, but that others influenced the United States in the same fashion, with an equal amount of force and persistence.

This tendency is particularly explicit in the realm of social (notably immigration and ethnic) history and in the history of nineteenth-century American culture, where historians occasionally pay nodding attention to ethnic European art and artists before proceeding to uncover the richness of a seemingly independent mass culture. While mass culture counts as genuinely American, elitist aspirations are typically labeled "European" and have no room in the antielitist history of the United States. As a result, the story of Europe's cultural expansion in the United States remains untold by those historians who insist on American social elites as the principal agent for European cultural imports and social change. The ongoing search for a distinctively American culture, the absence of a dialogue between diplomatic and cultural historians, and the skepticism toward what has been misleadingly called high culture all have contributed to this silence. Bridled by language constraints and the resistance to books by non-English-speaking authors, many historians have been reluctant to recast the nation's history in a multinational context where the United States appears as just one among many actors.

This book merges the analysis of European cultural exporters and their American recipients. It shows that American concepts of culture were and continue to be deeply affected by European nineteenth-century political and cultural expansion. It tells the story of a group of men and women who purposely set out to educate American society by introducing people to the accomplishments of German Kultur, notably orchestral music, a culture that they believed was both unique and universalistic and, therefore, appealing to everyone. Their story outlines a Gramscian definition of the term *hegemony*, according to which subordinated groups tend to accept another group's values not because they have been ideologically brainwashed but because they have individual reasons to do so. In exercising what Joseph Nye labels "soft power,"[23] these pioneers blazed the trail for an emotional elective affinity, a relationship of the heart that created the foundation for a German-American accord and would survive two world wars and last through the cold war.

––––––

Much of this book focuses on symphony orchestras, their conductors, soloists, and musicians, as well as on orchestral music. In the nineteenth century, the symphony and the symphony orchestra were increasingly defined as both "German" and "universal," and symphonic works eventually became the most influential genre on the transatlantic music highway. In the 1800s, for a number of reasons the inhabitants of the German states began to perceive themselves as the "people of music," a vision that was eventually adopted by audiences around the world. David Gramit has argued that German critics, artists, and administrators perceived the "classical" genre as distinct from other music because it constituted a key part of human cultivation. Their belief originated in a highly specific set of circumstances within German-speaking countries, where music lobbyists attempted to legitimize music as a socially acceptable activity and thereby secure the income, status, and professionalism of contemporary musicians.[24]

Throughout the nineteenth century, music critics, writers, intellectuals, concert organizers, journalists, and music teachers, but also government officials and the public at large, increasingly conjured up the notion of a German musical heritage that was closely related to German national identity. What these men and women referred to when they pondered the power of music was what some observers call *Ernste Musik* (serious music), and it is precisely this genre that the present study investigates. German musicologists often favored (and still do favor) the term *Ernste Musik*—even though much of the music thus connoted is not serious at all—to distinguish classical or serious compositions from popular music, *Unterhaltungsmusik*.

In 1810, E. T. A. Hoffmann's review of Beethoven's Fifth Symphony coined the idea of *absolute music*, which would remain the dominant concept governing music-related writing for decades to come. Absolute music combined universalistic and nationalist traits, and it is here that we encounter the single most important characteristic of what made music both German and globally appealing. Absolute music was instrumental, romantic, and elevating, all values appreciated universally in Western society. Simultaneously, however, absolute music glorified the symphony, a musical form that became internationally associated with "German masters" (strictly speaking, *sinfonia* originated among seventeenth-century Italian composers such as Alessandro Scarlatti, but differed profoundly from the structure of the nineteenth-century symphony). Hoffmann's absolute music invoked the idea of a spiritual world community—provided the composition originated from a German hand. Conversely, to be German meant to be capable of an artistic creativity that transcended the fetters of human existence and worldly interest.[25]

Through much of the nineteenth century, German identity remained romantic, idealistic, and, most important, geographically vague. The diplomat and philosopher Wilhelm von Humboldt believed that serious music, universalism, and *German* were inextricably intertwined. Serious music had to be intellectually and emotionally challenging to express the human free will. The ability to search and suffer, to probe and demand was German and, therefore, universal: the two terms were not exclusive, since the term *German* was not more circumscribed than *universal*. To the contrary: Humboldt believed that to be German meant to be open-minded, free-spirited, and unconstrained by the fetters of any geographically or intellectually restrained way of life or thought.[26] Beethoven, to cite the most prominent example, counted as "German" precisely because there was no Germany.

For its ostensible contradiction and the burden of Germany's more recent history, the idea of a universal German identity continues to puzzle historians and musicologists alike. Attributes such as universality and timelessness may blur our understanding of the lurking risks of German chauvinism. How can nationalism—and German nationalism in particular—be understood as universalist, apolitical, and not precarious to its exponents and its followers? How long is it safe to label any music "German" before questions of an artist's social and political responsibility enter the discussion? Can we admire Brahms and concede that his music reveals fundamentally nationalist implications? In an era dedicated to the priority of the political, musicologists feel drawn to evaluate cultural motivations in politicized terms. The idea of a merely "cultural" German identity seems to belong to the realm of fiction, even and in particular when related to musical development and reception in nineteenth-century Germany.[27] By concentrating, for example, on the universal and absolute aspects of Brahms's art, writes Daniel Beller-McKenna, "we have done so at the expense of understanding Brahms as a German artist or acknowledging the great extent to which his identity as a German affected his music."[28]

The recent historiography on national identity has opened a way out of the dilemma between idealism and territorialism. Nineteenth-century German cultural identity exhibited a form of soft nationalism or, in the words of philosopher Kwame Anthony Appiah, "rooted cosmopolitanism," according to which people defined themselves by their cultural background, not merely their geographical birthplace. The cosmopolitan believes, according to Appiah, "that sometimes it is the differences we bring to the table that make it rewarding to interact at all," even though "what we share with others is not always ethnonational in character."[29] The transatlantic musicians introduced in this book saw no contradiction between their roots in a specific history while simultaneously acting as citizens of the world. Nor did they have trouble pledging political allegiance to one country while situating their work and their identity within a framework of universal values and identities.

Efforts to promote a German identity through music served to overcome the lack of cohesion among the German states' dialects, administrative structure, and cultural ways. The consolidation of the German Empire in 1871 spurred the attempt on the part of statesmen, demagogues, and musicologists to promote the unity of music and national identity. Memorials, publication series, musical biographies, national conventions, and the creation of shrines to music such as the Bayreuth Festspiele helped to solidify the marriage of music and the nation, all idiosyncrasies notwithstanding. From the first German emperor to the Federal Republic's recent chancellor, all have exploited the musical connection for political ends, be it to celebrate birthdays, victories, or, more recently, reunification.[30]

Enhancing the national and international image of the Germans as the people of music was the fact that at the end of the nineteenth century, scholars across all disciplines and international borders became increasingly convinced that music represented the ego ideal for the arts, the discipline of all disciplines. From Friedrich Schiller and Johann Wolfgang von Goethe to Oscar Wilde, and from Jack Butler Yeats to Hegel and Schopenhauer, artists and philosophers ascribed various metaphorical and supernatural powers to music. And throughout the Western world, scientists, art critics, administrators, and the general public began to discuss the meaning and influence of music in human society. Classical music, many believed, had the potential to represent a "language of emotions," and thus form a powerful counterweight to rationalism, industrialization, and international wars.

No one, it seems, troubled himself with the idiosyncrasy of the Habsburg connection or the international life many composers had chosen to live. Much of this presumably "German" music was not composed in the German states or by artists from the German states. Most of the composers invoked as "German masters" would have refuted the label or at least remained ambiguous about this geopolitical identity. Georg Friedrich Handel, for one, proclaimed himself an Englishman. That sacred icon, Beethoven, given his Flemish origins and his long affiliation with the court of Vienna, might have been proclaimed a stateless citizen to begin with. And even Richard Wagner, who did his utmost to define *What is German* in music, eventually concluded, somewhat disillusioned, "I have come up against this question with more and more confusion . . . it is impossible to answer."[31] While historians may find this discrepancy problematic, contemporaries left it, for the most part, unaddressed.

So did foreign observers. International critics from England, France, or the United States, writes Thomas S. Grey in an essay on *Die Meistersinger*, remained oblivious to the national image of German music. "They made no special efforts to deny or resist it, but tended simply to leave it alone," he observes. "Cultural nationalism was accepted as a self-evidently positive value even in artistic production, yet there seems to have been a tacit agreement that it could be checked at the border when such works were exported."[32]

Grey's assumption of a world community of joyous music lovers is as idealistic as Peter Gay's and Daniel Rodgers's visions of an open transatlantic culture. It is true that Germans were internationally acclaimed as the "people of music" thanks to their self-promotion. But it is implausible that foreign nations did not take issue with this notion in an age dominated by geopolitical imperialism and cultural expansion. German musicians and administrators supported the exportation of the German masters for political ends. At the same time, American critics, impresarios, educators, and journalists readily promoted the idea of music as the most German of the arts, and superior to all others—before dismissing it toward the end of the nineteenth century as part of Germany's *Weltpolitik*.

Authors writing about this period often refer to works underlining the quest for American national music, or dictionary entries that write off the story of German musicians in the United States as preliminary and out of place.[33] Cultural historians have minutely retraced the international influence of Anglo-American rock, pop, jazz, and hip-hop music abroad, notably in the context of twentieth-century youth culture, Americanization, and the cold war.[34] But they remain curiously reluctant to retrace foreign (as opposed to immigrant) "highbrow" influences on American culture, particularly music. Though the story seems familiar, few want to tell it.[35] To write about classical music is not the politically correct thing to do in an age skeptical of the influence of elites, notably the influence of white European males.[36]

Music historians who have studied foreign influences in the United States have typically paid more attention to English legacies than those of non-English-speaking countries, often in an effort to track a more "indigenous" element on American stages. Katherine Preston has alerted us to the lively music scene in the first half of the nineteenth century, when Americans of different social ranks enjoyed both English-language and Italian operas on a multitude of occasions, including band concerts, dances, and theater shows. This happy democratic period ended, Preston tells us, with the arrival of a musical elite that epitomized the serious music of the German Romantics. Culture became differentiated into various segments, with each part confined to a certain social strata. From then on, music was either "popular" or high art but never both.[37]

This story of how American music life went elitist (that is, sour) after the Civil War has been taken for granted in much of the historiography of American culture. Folk, ethnic, and popular music and, most important, that crucial date in time marking the emergence of a genuinely American music (Foster? Sousa? Joplin? Paine? Copland? Armstrong? Ives?) have preoccupied the research agenda of many music historians.

Yet the story of nineteenth-century classical music in the United States deserves more than the interest of a handful of music lovers, for its implications were vast, political, and universal, and extended far beyond the development of American musical life. The solidification of a "classical" canon in the United States (and elsewhere) coincided with the rise of the German Empire and its self-appointed role as a *Kulturnation* (a nation based on a cultural canon). Far removed from the diplomatic chess games that have characterized so much of our understanding of the late nineteenth-century international scene, German artists and administrators believed they had a mission to bring music, the language of emotions, to audiences around the world. By catering to images of the "internationalism" of music, these individuals sought to promote the message of the universalism of German musicianship.

*Sound Diplomacy* attempts to elucidate the cultural agency of representatives of German music (and what American audiences perceived as "German") and their art in the United States in the context of transatlantic relations since the mid-nineteenth century. It investigates international cultural initiatives in the United States before World War I. It retraces the lives and motivations of musicians as well as their immediate impact on audiences from Boston to San Francisco. It illuminates the growing antagonism of American audiences and critics toward the preponderance of German music in the decades before 1917. And it glances at the long-term legacy of German classical music in the United States. Of course, there were countless foreigners and Americans on the U.S. music scene. Yet in this eclectic musical landscape, classical music composed by a set of German masters advanced to a more prominent position than all other genres, and the reasons for this were by far not merely aesthetic.

––––––

Artists and music theorists agree that the creation, manipulation, and release of tension represent the basic technique for projecting an emotion into a given medium, including music composition and performance. According to the central thesis in psychological theory, emotion arises when our tendency to respond is interrupted. Typically, the connotations and feelings music arouses are based both on our knowledge of and experience with music, and on our knowledge of and experience in the world of images outside the world of music, such as a landscape, night, buildings, or joy. Some of those may even display specific sound effects that music can reproduce, such as a rainstorm, a cry, or a knock at the door. While we can never "know" such processes, we are aware of feelings that penetrate into our consciousness.[38]

In the past thirty years, much of the debate on emotions among psychologists and anthropologists has focused on whether emotions are universal or culturally conditioned.[39] Some psychologists believe that culturally derived meanings do not influence the development of emotional reactions. Cultural anthropologists, in contrast, argue that emotions are not merely part of the physiological system but attain their meaning through their expression and interpretation in social interactions.

In this context Kenneth Gergen proposes a fascinating psychological account of emotion as being constructed in social context. He argues that emotions are necessarily woven into the communicative relations between social groups and cultures. Emotions are not individual expressions but constructed and reconstructed by social interaction.[40] Historians interested in the exploration of emotions have adhered to this anthropological approach, because it allows for the study of expression as a pathway to historical meaning. Emotional history encompasses the study of how certain societies have either suppressed or promoted the expression of particular emotions, and how individual social groups were entitled to the expressions of emotions while others were not; it analyzes the interplay between emotions, emotional control, and the social environment.[41] Emotional history also traces emotional expressions and shifting distinctions between "the emotional" and "the rational" throughout different periods of history; it examines the tension between impulses and socially accepted emotional standards; and it analyzes the impact of feelings and emotional change in the history of nationalism, immigration, war, law, politics, or social and economic transformations.[42]

Diplomatic historians, in turn, have traditionally analyzed rational decision-making processes and logical thought, and they have paid considerably less attention to the role of emotions, which are often perceived as "irrational." When concerned with emotions, they focus on threat perception, fear, and, recently, women and gender perceptions as a force in international relations. Current research projects in political sciences and governmental affairs focus on the role of emotions in politics, notably the cognitive processes of decision makers.[43] While the work of these scholars concentrates on traditional paradigms of foreign policy, I seek to develop a framework that is less concerned with policy making than with informal relations.

In search of an alternative to the pallid term *relation*, I use the term *elective affinity* to designate political and cultural interaction between nations and cultures in a descriptive sense in the context of international history. According to the sociologist Max Weber, elective affinity signifies a noncausal process in which two sets of interests seek each other out and reinforce each other. "A mutual favoring, attraction, and even strengthening is involved whenever ideal types coalesce in a relationship of elective affinity."[44] The term was originally coined by the Swedish scientist Torbern Bergman, then popularized in Johann Wolfgang von Goethe's 1809 novel, *Die Wahlverwandtschaften* (The Elective Affinities).[45]

In *Die Wahlverwandtschaften*, two men and two women are torn by their mutual though socially unacceptable attractions to each other. The "election" in this elective affinity is embedded in the choice of a situation that allows these emotions to be set free. The choice, in turn, only seems conscious when judged from the outside; the actors involved find themselves within an action that they have not deliberately planned. Even though they could have done otherwise, at the same time they could not help it. In Goethe's novel, a couple—Charlotte and Eduard—mildly bored with married life, put themselves into a risky situation by inviting a young girl, Ottilie, and an unmarried man, "the Major," into their home. In time, both husband and wife develop an affinity for the least likely candidate.

The course and the premise of this novel inspire the argument and the structure of this manuscript: the *Wahlverwandtschaften* symbolize German-American cultural relations before World War I. Like the Major and Ottilie, the German artists came to offer their best: music and emotions from a magical land. Like Charlotte and Eduard, Americans invited and welcomed German artists to present their art without giving much thought to the possible effects. And just like the *Wahlverwandtschaften*'s couple in search of distraction, Americans may not have been aware of the consequences of their choice. But for the historian, as for the reader of the novel, the consequent plot unfolds irresistibly from the moment the new guests enter the house and make themselves feel at home. Americans' invitation to German musicians who were eager to come to the United States gave way to a broad and long-lived affection for musical culture, even though this attraction seemed—from a political point of view—increasingly inappropriate. Americans did not consciously develop an affinity for Germans, but covertly, they picked German music, associated it with the universal language of emotions, and then found themselves in a situation where they could not but develop an elective affinity for the "people of music." Thus, inasmuch as music grew into a cultural variable in the political context, its emotional effects become purposeful for the historical analysis, notwithstanding and sometimes accompanying deliberate cultural policy.

Focusing on the influence of "culture" in international relations, chapter 1 sketches out the historical premises of this research project. In the late nineteenth century, U.S.-based representatives of the Alliance Française, the French art elite, as well as the British government and aristocracy and the alumni of British universities zealously tried to lure the upper crust of American society into their cultural domain. Faced by numerous diplomatic crises, on the eve of the twentieth century the German imperial government, too, created art and academic exchange programs in order to export German Kultur to the United States and thus win political allies. Promoters of Kultur perceived their mission not only in terms of manifest destiny but also as a competition among European powers over whose culture would prevail in the United States. Most of the German efforts, however, were a disaster, yet there was one German export that seemed to attract an enormous amount of attention everywhere: the German symphony.

Chapter 2 discusses the various meanings experts at home and abroad attached to music in the late nineteenth century. Musicians, critics, politicians, psychologists, philosophers, and scientists at large believed that music entailed power, emotions, and an uplifting moral force, and they devised the most curious experiments to prove their theories. Music could improve humanity, prevent wars, and serve as an international language of communication. The marriage of these perspectives, the political significance of German music in the context of German nationalism and nation-building during the nineteenth century, paved the way for the German-American emotional elective affinity when thousands of Americans crossed the Atlantic Ocean in search of magic and "the grand emotion" at the shrines of German music, including Bayreuth, Leipzig, and Weimar.

The third chapter introduces the orchestral artists, composers, conductors, soloists, and musicians involved in this tale—the "houseguests," in Goethe's elective affinity. Spurred by the exodus of countless German "music missionaries" and without much governmental support, music composed in German-speaking countries, German conductors, German musicians, and German musicology and music pedagogy virtually monopolized the American music scene (including its symphonies) between 1850 and 1918. In the United States, music became synonymous with German. As the nineteenth century drew to an end, to be German meant to be musical. Conductors who were not German born saw their careers greatly enhanced if they had been trained in Germany or Austria, had a German-sounding name, and at least had a Continental accent.

The ambassadors of music quite literally ran through open doorways, as Victorian Americans were eager to welcome artistic imports from the Old World. In chapter 4 we meet the American hosts, wealthy sponsors and trustees involved in the scenario of transatlantic musical migration and the founding of American symphonies before World War I. And as we shall see, their collective biographies reflect an interest in cultural philanthropy far beyond progressive refinement, cosmopolitanism, or social adornment.

Chapter 5 discusses the development of the *Wahlverwandtschaft* proper, the appeal of German sounds and stars, notably symphony orchestras and soloists, along with the profiles and the responses of audiences and critics to the repertory of the leading orchestras in the country. This chapter highlights the psychological reasons for the unexpected success of German symphonic music and its performers in the United States. The German musicians and their product clearly tapped into a "market gap" there. Music seemed an "unmanly" occupation to many Victorian Americans, who interpreted the display of emotion, leisure, and a taste for culture as dangerous, decisively feminine, and unfit for admission to Theodore Roosevelt's vigorous concept of manliness and civilization. Music became a belief system and part of a broader discourse, positing feminine feelings and cultivation against Darwinist manhood. This perception of music as feminine and emotional automatically discredited the achievements of American male composers and performers, thus opening a professional gap that German musicians could fill.

Emotions, however, can move in unintended directions: the growing antagonism of American audiences and critics toward the preponderance of German music and musicians in the United States in the years leading up to World War I forms the focus of chapters 6 and 7. The American labor movement as well as nationalist journalists, politicians, and musicians formed a coalition calling for an independent American national music. Collectively, they highlight the interplay between cultural, social, and political tensions between 1850 and 1917. Ironically, at the very moment when people around the world began to fear the impact of "Americanization" on their respective local cultures, no one worried as much about cultural identity as Americans themselves.

Chapter 6 investigates the long-term origins of this Kultur resistance. At the end of the nineteenth century, American musicians and music critics were wringing their hands over the fact that the United States had no national music, no national culture. Meanwhile, local unions fought the temporary immigration of German artists, arguing that such practices violated the labor law. Such resistance to German music, as chapter 7 concludes, culminated shortly after the U.S. entry into World War I, when countless musicians found themselves scolded, investigated, expropriated, and, in some cases, interned and deported to Europe.

The twentieth century did not serve to liberate the high-cultural music scene in the United States. The epilogue reflects on the star cult and the global promotion of American symphonies, the continuous appeal of the old masters, and the emotional partnership between Germany and the United States throughout a century that saw two major wars and more than forty years of nuclear antagonism. The real long-term legacy of the musicians' proselytizing became evident during the cold war, when the U.S. government embarked on a concerted effort to convince its allies, notably the Germans, that Americans and Europeans cherished the same composers, the same music, and the same Kultur. The United States' dedication to classical music became a central theme in U.S. propagandists' efforts to create a transatlantic intellectual alliance, with the New York Symphony and American soloists touring dozens of metropolises between Moscow and Gibraltar.

———

*Sound Diplomacy* represents an investigation of ideas as much as facts. My project does not aim to present a comprehensive review of German classical music, musicians, singing clubs, home education, or musical pedagogy in the United States. German-American ethnic communities play a minor role in this tale.[46] Save for the works of Richard Wagner and selected concertized versions of opera excerpts, opera did not feature prominently in the debate on the social and political meaning of music at large. I do not attempt to judge the universalism (or nationalism) of music proper, or the "Germanness" of the same. Nor am I concerned with "proving" the existence of emotions in international relations or the "actual" emotional content of music.

Rather, this book analyzes the cosmopolitan identity and influence of an exemplary cast of actors; the changing definitions and interpretations of music in the larger context of international relations, including the discourse on emotions; and the clash between universalist and nationalist ambitions. By looking at state, private, and performing-arts sources collectively, I wish to show that these spheres do not simply coexist but are interlaced and must be understood in unison. The missionary impulses of artists such as Theodore Thomas or Carl Bergmann look at best pathetic unless viewed in the context of Germany's cosmopolitanism and successive expansionism. The appointments of men like Ernst Kunwald, Carl Pohlig, and Karl Muck derive their salience from their close connection, either political or spiritual, with their governments. Culture sometimes intersects with politics. That does not mean that culture necessarily follows the political context. Instead, sometimes culture paves the way for a political partnership. It may be analytically more complex to grasp this context, but that should not keep us from investigating it.

Finally, my ideas should not be misunderstood as an effort to whisk away the sociological questions that New Left historians have been posing. They do not dispute the elitist manipulation of highbrow culture or the cosmopolitanism exhibited by the upper classes. Nor do I wish to argue with what Joseph Horowitz has recently and controversially labeled "The Rise and Fall" of classical music: the idea that the history of art music in the United States is a performer's rather than a composer's history. But as much as the American elites participated in the construction of a cultural canon, they were not alone in the concert hall. Ultimately, symphonic concerts constituted an international affair brought about by agents of German Kultur. To recognize their influence means to grasp that in the past, Americans have been at least as much the agents as the recipients of international cultural expansionism; and the long-term consequences of this development are still visible and audible today, including in movies such as *The Competition*.

# ONE

# Transatlantic Cultural Relations before World War I

Reichskanzler Theobald von Bethmann-Hollweg was deeply worried about German cultural diplomacy. In a letter to the historian Karl Lamprecht in 1913, he conceded that French and British diplomacy profited to no small extent from their cultural propaganda. If the Reich wanted to outdo those nations' efforts, the German people, not the government, would have to assume a stronger role. "What France and England accomplish in this area, is not due to the accomplishment of their governments but to the national whole, the unity and closeness of their cultures, the unerring desire for prestige of the nation itself. We have not come quite as far yet. We are not yet as certain and as conscious of our culture, our inner self, and our national ideal."[1] Not policy makers but private individuals and organizations should guide Germany's cultural foreign relations.

During the latter part of the nineteenth century, several European nations were entrenched in a massive campaign to influence American culture in order to win the amity of Anglo-American elites. While the French capitalized on the arts and the British stressed literature and social ties, Germany's cultural ambassadors explored a variety of avenues to win U.S. sympathies, avenues that for the most part were very similar to the strategies chosen by their neighbors to the west. French, British, and German officials offered much leeway to nongovernmental cultural exports, and the Germans' efforts were not quite as futile as Bethmann-Hollweg would have us believe. Private individuals and nongovernmental organizations mutated into the principal carriers of nineteenth-century cultural diplomacy. Indeed, the less the state got conspicuously involved in cultural exports, the more effective they turned out to be.

These developments framed the exportation of German classical music to the United States and are the subject of this chapter. In a climate of nationalism, international cultural competition, accelerating territorial and cultural expansionism, and military armament, the efforts of artists, agents, and administrators to bring symphonic music to American stages assumed a decisively missionary political and diplomatic note. They served the interest of the state to expand German Kultur all over the globe.

All over Europe, the promotion and study of national culture flourished in newspapers, magazines, arts associations, research projects, and academic curricula in the second half of the nineteenth century. In Germany, for example, Kultur became not only a central feature in the public discourse but also one of the principal paradigms in the sciences—advanced by philosophers and sociologists such as Georg Simmel and Max Weber. Institutionalized cultural competition and propaganda did not constitute a novelty in European affairs. Since 1851, world exhibitions served as powerful department stores for national representation, technological superiority, academic innovation, and cultural grandeur. Young nations such as Canada and Germany or weakened powers such as France used these exhibitions to demonstrate national unity and strength. Postcolonial countries in Latin America struggled to convince the old world of their advanced industrialized development. The imperial officers of the German Reich worked hard to create a harmonious picture of German trade, craftsmanship, and art. By stressing cultural factors, officials intended to portray Germany in the international arena both as a new, yet important participant and as a country whose traditional culture was superior to that of any other nation. By 1900, cultural propaganda machines were firmly in place all across Europe.

Cultural competition was not confined to policy makers. Indeed, these leaders believed it was the duty of citizens to participate in and conduct the debates. As Wolfram Kaiser has shown, world exhibitions were heavily influenced by nongovernmental organizations and commercial entrepreneurs whose interests did not necessarily comport with those of their governments.[2] An intense—and often localized—nationalism marked the public discourse in all countries. Secret societies, churches, popular images, architecture, maps, souvenirs: all revealed a strong belief in the nation as a metaphor that encompassed local, regional, religious, gender, political, and cultural identities.[3] Patriotic associations such as the Action Française or the Verein für das Deutschtum im Ausland and private individuals such as Ernst Borsig, director of the Deutsche Bank in Germany, constituted some of the most outspoken individuals in foreign relations. While it is disputable how much influence these associations and persons held in public affairs, they often believed that they had a better grasp of their respective national interests than their weak governments. Whatever compromises officials were ready to sign, patriotic associations always threatened to turn issues of marginal diplomatic interest into disputes over the life and death of their countries, a mortal clash in which national honor was at stake.[4]

Particularly, France and Germany came to see the fin-de-siècle as an international competition for the exportation of national culture. More than anyone else, the French feared that German Kultur threatened their leading position in the arts and crafts.[5] French administrators and intellectuals dreaded the encroachment of Teutonic culture just as much as German observers loathed French civilization. "Clearly, French culture is entangled in a combat with German culture," the Paris journal *Le Temps* wrote in 1908, calling for a national association for the spread of the French language in Belgium. "This is the necessary counteraction against the progressing Germanization."[6] The influence of French literature and ideas among German intellectuals since the early nineteenth century raised suspicions notably among authorities, who regarded this "Parisian influence" as a fundamental threat. Likewise, thanks to commerce and trade, British culture percolated through northern cities such as Hamburg in the nineteenth century, much to the disdain of German nationalists.[7]

The inner-European quarrel over cultural superiority quickly escalated to areas outside Europe as well. In this scenario, the United States emerged as one of the foremost targets of the European competition for cultural preponderance. Despite its industrial and political power, to most Europeans the United States still seemed to represent both a cultural wasteland ready to be civilized and a battlefield of foreign cultures.

———

Take the example of France: after 1870, France's reputation was at an all-time low, while Germans enjoyed a high popularity in the United States.

Though a republic, France was seen as a corrupt, racist, and anti-Semitic country, ruled by an elite of opportunist republicans. From a social and economic point of view, France lacked innovation while its population stagnated. Even French observers lamented that French decadence could not compare favorably with neighboring Germany, a country that seemed infinitely more progressive, modern, and dynamic.

To counter these charges and win the minds of U.S. audiences, French propagandists zealously tried to lure the upper crust of American society into their cultural domain, and their strategies, though influenced by state policy, delegated the government to the backbench. French cultural diplomacy was closely linked to the Napoleonic expansionist ideology and the defeat of 1870/71, both of which led to a rejuvenation of France's "mission civilisatrice." Its most powerful institution was the Alliance Française, a nongovernmental association founded in 1883 to promote French language and culture abroad, which had no equal in Europe. The Alliance's vigor derived from a broad national consensus on the superiority of French civilization. By the turn of the twentieth century, it established so-called committees in San Francisco, Boston, Los Angeles, Texas, Chicago, Denver, Brooklyn, and New York City, while it also inspired French seminars in San Francisco, Kansas City, and Dallas. Until World War I, it established some 150 new local committees around the country. By 1904, the Alliance counted more than twenty-five thousand adherents in the United States.[8] It was a significant tool in the exportation of French culture because it functioned like an NGO and operated with a relatively small budget, yet expanded its presence abroad effectively.

Producers and merchants of French impressionism likewise exerted a strong influence on American art and architecture that lasted well into the twentieth century. In the famous salons of the nineteenth century, the Ministry of Fine Arts selected the range of exhibitioners, encouraged particular themes, and awarded individual artworks. And the winners of the awards bestowed by the state were the ones whose works were most likely to be selected for export.[9]

The central administration of the arts in France also created a full-fledged yet informal advertising campaign for national artwork abroad that catered to the lack of art in the United States. "Born yesterday, without history, without a past it is not astonishing that America does not yet possess a national art," observed Paul Lefort in the *Gazette des Beaux-Arts* in 1879. Despite the discouraging U.S. tariff on foreign art, professional Paris dealers such as Cadart, Gambart, Durand-Ruel, and Goupil, Vibert & Cie. exported whole collections and established renowned galleries along the U.S. East Coast to sell paintings chosen and promoted by the French government.[10]

Believing that at least some of the contemporary paintings they saw would go down in history as eternal masterpieces, American businessmen purchased French art in ever-increasing numbers. In 1883 alone, American buyers spent $1,754,000 at the Paris Salon.[11] According to a study produced by the German Generalkonsulat (which took a great interest in the matter), in New York in 1906, 57.2 percent of all paintings imported by the United States originated in France, followed by Great Britain (17.9 %), Italy (10.5 %), and Germany (5.1 %). By 1907, French art merchants exported close to one million dollars' worth of artworks to the United States while the German market stagnated somewhere around $100,000.[12]

The exportation of visual art, as Pierre Miquel observes in his biographical analysis of French art merchants, does not constitute a purely cultural phenomenon but has a double effect: the education of sensibility and the global colonization of taste and mind through the medium of the image or the painting. French art merchants, perhaps even more so than French painters, were keenly aware of their influence in the United States and worked hard to expand their enterprises.[13]

The French government also made an effort to attract American students, offering them a free and first-rate education. American painters such as Frank W. Benson, Cecilia Beaux, William Glackens, and countless others dutifully spent part of their formative years in France, notably Paris, to return with a knapsack full of impressionist techniques and visions. Broken French tinged with an American accent became a familiar sound in the streets of Paris, and many young French artists cynically observed that American students were becoming more French than they themselves, besides taking away their money and prestige.

Back in the United States, a rapidly expanding exhibition and construction market awaited those young American Francophiles. Between 1870 and 1900, Americans founded major museums and art schools, among those the Metropolitan Museum of Art in New York City (1870), the Boston Museum of Fine Arts (1870), the Art Institute of Chicago (1866–82), the San Francisco Art Institute (1871), and the Harvard program in the history of art (1874). The art boom inspired the construction of universities, department stores, railroad buildings, museums, and private homes. Artists such as Richard Morris Hunt from New York, Arthur Dexter and Francis Peabody from Boston, and H. H. Richardson from New Orleans thus became architectural ambassadors in the French-American service.[14]

At the end of the nineteenth century, France's prolific informal efforts to boost its culture in theUnited States had proved successful; by 1900, the French reputation in the United States was thriving. Paris, no longer a cave of Bonapartism and promiscuous sins, emerged as the art capital for most American intellectuals. French naturalist novels, French symbolist poetry, and, above all, French impressionist painting now commanded the attention of American artists as well as the public at large.[15] Equipped with the message that France was the cultural capital of the world, for the next four decades French propagandists would attempt to foster goodwill among U.S. leaders. Indeed, as Robert Young has argued, they consciously manipulated the United States' sense of cultural inferiority in the face of European history and tradition.[16]

————

Meanwhile, British leaders faced their own challenges in a rather rocky relationship with the United States. Many U.S. observers portrayed Great Britain as an undemocratic regime run by the landed aristocracy. Great Britain's ambivalent stance during the American Civil War, economic competition, disagreements over U.S. tariffs and fishery interests in the Bering Sea, and the British presence in Canada, as well as conflicting goals in the Far East and the Carribean, notably the United States' entry into Japan and the Venezuela crisis, put a continuous strain on what historians have benevolently portrayed as the "special relationship." British efforts to convince the United States of the advantages of a more liberal trade policy further irritated American political and business leaders.

Unlike German-American relations, these crises served to foster mutual rapprochement. Throughout the nineteenth century, the British government had attempted to contain U.S. continental expansionism. When these efforts failed, policy makers opted instead for an alignment with the United States in the 1890s. In journals and newspapers, British and American cartoonists increasingly replaced their reciprocally patronizing attitudes with images symbolizing Anglo-American equality, mutual understanding, family ties, shared economic interests, global leadership, and an almost paranationalist consciousness between the two countries.[17] During the Spanish-American War, public opinion in Great Britain sided with the United States, while the latter kept a neutral position during the highly controversial Boer War between 1899 and 1902. Both British and U.S. leaders made a supreme effort to compromise their positions in the negotiations over the border between Alaska and Canada and the building of the Panama Canal. Thanks to similar interests regarding colonial expansionism throughout the Western Hemisphere and the Far East, the United States emerged as an equal partner for the British Empire, in the eyes of both policy makers and the general public.[18]

After the Civil War, the Anglo-American cultural affinity intensified thanks to a rapid process of political rapprochement, during which the British Empire not only made as much of an effort to capture the attention of American elites as the French but also employed a similar, informal approach. Seeking to enlist U.S. support in the face of increasing European tensions, British officials strove to expand the "superpower" spirit among Anglo-American elites and to establish what Christopher Hitchens calls an "emotional diagram" between conservative Anglophile Americans and liberal radical Englishmen. Alfred Mahan's *The Influence of Sea Power on History* became the standard justification for late nineteenth-century expansionism by the United States, where Theodore Roosevelt gave the piece an approving review in the *Atlantic Monthly*. British readers likewise warmly and enthusiastically received Mahan's study: the Royal United Service Institution serialized the book while Mahan was showered with honors, toasts, and a banquet. Meanwhile, the British author Rudyard Kipling encouraged Americans to follow the British model—assume colonial leadership and civilize the world—in his acclaimed poem "Take up the White Man's Burden."[19]

British culture, too, enjoyed a special place in the imagination of American elites, fostering the Anglo-American special relationship. Anglo-American Victorianism encompassed a set of values such as Protestantism, morality, refinement, an orientation toward the future, and a separation of spheres along gender lines, also called "the cult of domesticity." It thrived on a rigorous behavioral code that included seriousness, self-righteousness, didacticism, and competition. And it embedded common taste, fashion, and customs. Most important, Victorianism was "middle class," transatlantic, and English speaking. Notwithstanding any political disagreements, when Americans bought furniture, picked styles and clothes, wondered about proper behavior and speech, or sought appropriate literature for their children to read, they consistently looked to Great Britain.[20] Victorian novels abounded with heroines and heroes dangling between London, Brighton, New York City, and Chicago, creating transatlantic liaisons and mutual appreciation. This world of ideas, literature, taste, and fashion was increasingly bound together by the arrival of the steamer, mass printing, and what one scholar has called "the Victorian Internet," the telegraph.[21]

The technological inventions made it possible for Anglo-American Victorians to travel back and forth across the Atlantic to an unprecedented extent. Since the early nineteenth century, British actors had engaged in theatrical tours up and down the East Coast and into the Midwest. American writers, including Mark Twain, were often hailed across the Atlantic before they were accepted in the United States. Most important, the British government made a tremendous effort to assist, protect, and advise travelers and migrants to the New World, much in contrast to officials in the German Reich who regarded emigrants with suspicion.

Though individual Americans were very receptive to British lineage, class, and nostalgia, it was the British who impressed ideas of imperial hegemony on their former colonies by means of publication, migration, and education.[22] Craving an ivy-covered education for their children, around the turn of the twentieth century upper-class Americans sent students increasingly to elite British schools rather than to Göttingen or Leipzig. The estate of the Oxford philosopher Cecil Rhodes founded a scholarship that enabled, from 1902–3 onward, more than one hundred American students to study at Oxford.[23]

Marriage and kinship likewise deepened the cultural relationship between both countries, as did the British aristocracy's increasing need of American cash.[24] Notwithstanding the warnings of Henry James's *Bostonians* and other novels depicting the United States' age of innocence in the face of decrepit European traditions, these ties proved remarkably promising and stable. Mary Endicott wed Joseph Chamberlain, Mary Leiter exchanged vows with Lord Curzon, Consuelo Vanderbilt said yes to the Duke of Marlborough (for whom the latter was rewarded with a block of shares in the New York Central Railway Company), and Jennie Jerome landed Lord Randolph Churchill. Hundreds of such weddings were celebrated during the years before World War I, the most famous of which produced Sir Winston Churchill, tireless advocate of the "special relationship" between the United States and Great Britain during World War II. These connections displayed the appreciation of American elites for "blood, class, and nostalgia," and they produced enduring political ties. At the same time, in an almost hypocritical effort to "play Greece to the American Rome," the British ancien régime sought to renew itself by spreading its culture along with its imperial politics in the United States.[25]

---

Monitoring French and British cultural activities in the United States, German politicians and private individuals increasingly feared that they would lose out in the European cultural courtship of American affection.[26]

Originally, after the reconstitution of the American Republic in the years following the Civil War and the unification of the German Empire in 1871, Germans enjoyed a special reputation in the United States. U.S. policy makers and legal experts, who had come to regard national unity as the cure-all for setbacks in progress and liberty as well as for internal and external disputes, perceived Germany as the future agent of U.S. constitutional ideals on the European continent.[27] German culture influenced American science, education, and administration. Since the early nineteenth century, American students came to study in Heidelberg, Leipzig, Göttingen, and Berlin, noted centers of German intellectual life, in search of an academic education they could not obtain in the United States. Some nine thousand American students studied in Germany between 1815 and 1914, with most of them arriving between 1870 and 1914. Recognizing the need for academic expansion, American colleges after the Civil War began studying the Humboldt university in order to reshape higher education in the United States, and German academics migrated to the United States to help university administrators to implement Wilhelm von Humboldt's model.[28]

But this mutual amicability deteriorated due to conflicting economic interests. Since the 1880s, the "pork war," a dispute over the taxation of imported meat, ruffled some feathers among representatives on both sides of the Atlantic. Competing imperialist goals in the Pacific and the Caribbean added tension to an already strained relationship. Between 1885 and 1899, Germany and the United States consistently clashed over economic and political interests in the Samoan islands, where the two nations, along with Great Britain, had established a tripartite protectorate in 1879.[29] Although the British and the French expansionist goals in the Pacific conflicted with U.S. interests in the region, their diplomatic envoys managed to appease irate U.S. policy makers, much in contrast to their German colleagues. In 1898, Germany and the United States clashed again when the third German emperor, Wilhelm II, sent several battleships to Manila to demonstrate his sympathy for the Spanish crown in its war against the United States.[30]

Mandated in 1823, the Monroe Doctrine interpreted any territorial expansion of other powers in the Americas as a direct threat to U.S. national interests, which further fueled German-American tensions. During the Venezuela crisis of 1902–3, British and German warships bombed Fort Puerto Cabello, because the local government refused to pay its long-standing debts to the European creditors that had helped build the Venezuelan railroad from Caracas to Valencia. In response, the U.S. government sent a fleet into the Caribbean and eventually declared Germany to be a potential aggressor in its hemisphere while continuing to negotiate with the British. In combination, all of these conundrums sealed the British-American friendship while increasingly estranging Germany, a constellation that affected the Reich's diplomatic position in both the United States and Europe. "Close relations with Germany," observed the future British foreign minister Edward Grey in 1903, "means for us worse relations with the rest of the world, especially with the United States, France and Russia."[31]

The interest of Wilhelm II in foreign affairs likewise strained transatlantic amity. Proud, traditionalist, and gifted with an inherent sense of German cultural superiority, Wilhelm was determined to strengthen his influence in the world.[32] Though he displayed a keen desire to maintain the German-American friendship, his inauguration of *Weltpolitik* in 1896 and the creation of a German naval fleet, coupled with the Reich's rapid ascent as an industrial competitor, appeared as a threat to U.S. leaders. Clinging to the notion of the Monroe Doctrine, U.S. policy makers increasingly viewed Germany as the prime challenger of U.S. national security. While one German ambassador to Washington after another attempted to win over American sympathies by discrediting or at least distancing himself from British and French envoys and goals, in the end they all misread or ignored growing signs of U.S. alienation. As a result, the post–Civil War period saw the rise of the Anglo-American rapprochement as well as a renewed friendship between the State Department and the Quay d'Orsay, both connections dreaded by the imperial German government.[33]

German cultural initiatives faced several obstacles not encountered by France and England. The language barrier seemed to block German poetry and literature from the broader American public, and German artists had never made a significant inroad in the United States that could compete with the influx of French paintings. And marrying a German was not considered a particularly good catch among American elites. Even though all major cities in Germany had their contingent of unmarried American women, few of these led to German-American Romantic alliances. Oberved one reporter in the early 1900s, "The German, no matter from what part of the empire he comes, is not the ideal husband according to the American standard."[34]

This is not to say that Germany had nothing to offer. American Progressives praised the German social welfare system in their search for a model for their own communities in the first half of the twentieth century. German pedagogy, philosophy, and social science left a profound imprint on American culture. Germany's technological innovations fascinated scientists, businessmen, and political leaders across the Atlantic Ocean.[35] German industrial and cultural contributions to the various world exhibitions, particularly in 1893 and 1904, aroused admiration throughout Europe and the transatlantic world, while British exhibits were repeatedly attacked as wimpy and amateurish.[36] But Germany's international political ambitions led commentators to conclude that the country had become a bulwark of militarism and imperialism, driven by vanity and the quest for power. Observers such as Henry Adams stated that German universities had become pedantic and sterile structures; that the political situation was ridiculously provincial; and that German food was downright disgusting.[37]

The United States' seeming preference for French and British culture irked German diplomats at home and abroad. When Andrew Carnegie called France the "true homeland of art," v. Waetzold, the German consul in New York City, steamed: "For the majority of Americans, we Germans still represent art barbarians [*Kunstbarbaren*]."[38] Precisely for this reason, the German imperial government took an increasing interest in cultural contacts with the United States. Johann Heinrich Graf von Bernstorff, German ambassador in Washington, reviewed this interest in January 1914: "Our cultural efforts do not aim at doing a favor to the Americans, instead we wish to elevate German Kultur to its due right—a right which it claims unconditionally as the first culture of the world. This, too, is a part of world policy."[39]

Von Bernstorff merely confirmed a development that had been under way since unification, if not before. Most of the governmental efforts dedicated to cultural propaganda in tandem with foreign policy were launched after the turn of the century, when the Reich realized that its power policy had ignored Germany's image in the world. Yet nongovernmental and semigovernmental efforts had concentrated on Germany's cultural expansion for years.[40] Innumerable private associations, interest groups, and individuals had labored in the vineyard of cultural export even before the inauguration of the Reich.

German culture instilled a sense of protectiveness and pride in its citizens, artists, administrators, and eventually soldiers, fueling its expansionism abroad. To most observers at the time, Kultur had distinctly identifiable historical and Germanic roots, representing predominantly high culture and a distinct part of the country's national heritage. Until the latter part of the twentieth century, lowbrow culture such as dime novels and folk music did not compete with Kultur. In celebrating cultural distinction, German writers did not differ much from other nineteenth-century Europeans who devoted much political, diplomatic, and intellectual energy to elaborating the criteria by which non-European societies might be judged sufficiently civilized (*kultiviert*) to be accepted as members of the European-dominated international system. What was different in the German states, as Georg Bollenbeck has shown, was that until the late nineteenth century the notion of Kultur was mostly associated with liberalism and strongly tied to the notion of *Bildung* (knowledge, education). In particular, members of the middle classes regarded Kultur as a means to liberate and uplift humankind.[41]

The cultural consensus is key to the perception of Germany as a "cultural nation," one that defined its coherence by a common artistic, musical, and literary heritage. Unlike the other great powers of the nineteenth and twentieth centuries, German unity began as an imagined cultural collective, not as a politically defined entity. As a result, many Germans complained that while German Kultur enjoyed international prestige, the empire remained politically weak.

Yet in the nineteenth century, there was no centralized bureaucracy, no organizations such as the Kulturabteilung or the Goethe Häuser that would have offered themselves as a tool for cultural diplomacy. Since cultural affairs belonged in the realm of the individual states, the Imperial Foreign Office remained lukewarm to the proposal of cultural involvement. Most politicians agreed that the presentation of German culture abroad should remain confined to individual interest groups and entrepreneurs.[42]

Whenever the state did get involved, its efforts were typically not met by success, as several samples suggest. As in the case of France and Great Britain, German-American formal cultural relations before 1914 were characterized by first, the selective nature of official ties; second, the centrality of symbols; and third, the emphasis on academia and the visual arts. Sporadic ventures focusing on exhibitions and mutual visits sprinkled the years before World War I.[43] At the symbolic level, pompous official visits and the exchange of luxurious gifts created a meager accord between the kaiser and the U.S. president. For example, in 1902, Wilhelm sent a bronze statue of Frederick the Great to President Theodore Roosevelt, which eventually wound up on the esplanade of the Army War College at the Washington Barracks military base.[44]

Academic exchange constituted the foremost official enterprise in German-American relations during these years. In 1900, German academic interest in the United States looked back on a tradition of several decades. Between 1870 and 1919, German institutions of higher education listed a total of eighty-nine courses in U.S. history, 25 percent of which had been taught before 1900.[45] Yet since 1900, American interest in the system of German higher education as well as the ideals of German scholarship began to dwindle, no doubt due to the fact that Americans had begun to built their own graduate schools and curricula. Consequently, not only Imperial Reich administrators but also private individuals, professors, artists, and businessmen began to look for alternative avenues of cultural influence.[46] In 1904–5, Germany and the United States initiated an exchange program between the University of Berlin and Harvard and Columbia universities (both alma maters of Theodore Roosevelt).[47] Due to the initiatives of German professors teaching in the United States, in 1903 the Reich also funded a "Germanistic Museum" in Cambridge, Massachusetts, to portray *Deutschtum* (Germanness) from the Stone Age to the sixteenth century.[48]

Official and nongovernmental efforts to promote German culture likewise coalesced in the realm of the arts, and with as little success. Following a rather miserable showing of German art at the World Exhibition in Philadelphia in 1876, officials made an effort to increase both the quantity and quality of German exhibits at subsequent World's Fairs, but their success remained moderate. At the Chicago World's Fair of 1893, American art lovers had the opportunity to admire more German paintings, but reactions remained lukewarm. Visitors were said to be attracted to the German pavilion for its cool indoor temperature rather than the high level of art on display. When the time came for the World's Fair in St. Louis in 1904, officials proposed a militarylike preparation, both for a new exhibition and to influence American art. In 1903, irked by the preponderance of French paintings on the U.S. art market, Cuno von Uechtritz, renowned sculptor and professor of art, recommended to the Foreign Office that German artists visit American studios. Always keeping grand strategy and foreign interest in mind, he propounded that "like Steuben organized the American army, Germans organize American art."[49] Still, the show at the St. Louis Louisiana Purchase Exposition was not a success for Germany, as the depressing sales records indicated. Women ruled the American art market, one secretary of the Washington embassy reported, and they did not appreciate anecdotal paintings (notably those involving drinking scenes) or drawings depicting obscure scenes from German history.[50]

Two things matter in all these initiatives in the context of German cultural diplomacy: first, in their motivation, content, and strategy, they did not differ much from French and British activities. But second, in both instances the German government kept a hand on the program, and it was precisely this level of involvement that made these enterprises fail in the end. If anything, these experiences taught political administrators

to confine their role to the sponsorship and observation of nongovernmental activities.

State officials monitoring the exportation of scholarship and the visual arts remained more diffident vis-à-vis "serious" music. Their reluctance coupled with the enormous prestige of the German symphony in
the United States explains why this particular export received such for-
midable press throughout the nineteenth century and beyond. Germans
attached more significance than any other country to music. Classical
music played an important role in the self-perception of the German
middle class as well as in the nation's prestige abroad. Its music probably
won the Reich more sympathizers in the United States than all its other
cultural programs and all its diplomatic gestures combined.

Traditionally, music has occupied a special place in German history.
While until about 1800 music was typically associated with either the
church or the world of entertainment, after the turn of the century it
became increasingly politicized. As Celia Applegate has shown, in the
eighteenth and early nineteenth centuries, music became instrumental
to the shaping of German national identity and loomed large as the cen-
terpiece of German Kultur, much larger than painting and sculpture ever
had.[51] During the Napoleonic occupation, when French civilization and
language seemed to threaten German cultural independence, the tunes
of Beethoven's symphonies, along with the spirit of Goethe's *Faust* and
the philosophy of Gottfried Herder and Georg Hegel, consoled millions
of Germans, convincing them of their cultural superiority in the face
of political and military defeat. Ushering Johann Sebastian Bach into
the league of German cultural heroes, Felix Mendelssohn's 1829 performance of the *St. Matthew Passion* in Berlin became, in Applegate's words,
"a paradigm of the German nation," a moment in time when the nation
was being performed. And throughout the nineteenth century, musicians, music critics, and musicologists argued that German music was vital to the development of a German national consciousness, long before
there was a German national state.[52]

Much of the cultural power attributed to music originated in the increasing preponderance of large orchestras dedicated to the performance
of serious music. In an age that had limited travel possibilities and pre-
dated the microphone, the loudspeaker, the radio, and the phonograph
record, symphonic music still constituted a sensation for most nineteenth-
century audiences.[53] Developed in the eighteenth century by composers
such as Johann Stamitz, Georg Matthias Monn, Christoph Wagenseil,
and Joseph Haydn, symphonic productions expanded during Ludwig
van Beethoven's lifetime but declined after his death. By the 1850s, the

symphonic poem appeared, and musicologists often talk about a "Second Age of the Symphony" beginning in the 1870s. Nineteenth-century composers such as Franz Schubert, Beethoven, Felix Mendelssohn, and Johannes Brahms developed ever-longer forms of symphonic music. While Joseph Haydn's symphonies spanned no more than twenty minutes and called for no more than 25 musicians, Gustav Mahler's Eighth Symphony, first performed in Munich in 1908, lasted close to one and a half hours and required 171 musicians and 858 singers.[54]

What struck audiences about the symphony was its complex form, the tension it created between emotionalism and control, its length, and the number of instruments needed for its performance. The sheer size of the symphony orchestra required a new type of leadership. In the smaller eighteenth-century orchestra, responsibility for marking time often fell to the first violinist (the baton was originally a violin bow), while Haydn directed his London symphonies (1791–95) from the cemballo. As orchestras grew and compositions became longer, this job could not be handled by one of the musicians anymore. As a result, the modern conductor emerged, a leader at the top of an ironclad and nearly premodern, feudal hierarchy, with the concertmaster (or first violinist) as his second-in-command, and the players arranged in the order of significance. And for one hundred years, the orchestra as a form of live cultural experience ruled the concert stage.[55]

In a sense, the symphony can be regarded as a symbol if not a literal reflection of the political situation in nineteenth-century Germany and Austria, when tensions between the traditional adherence to the monarchy and the promise of a more equal democratic state rocked societies. The symphony exemplified order, structure, and control, where each man found his place, and where out of cacophony, harmony was born. For all the social mobility within Germany thanks to the country's rapid industrialization, symphonic music and the symphony orchestra stood for political and social hierarchy, for German culture and nationhood, abroad perhaps even more so than it ever did in Germany proper.

The merger of nationhood and serious music climaxed in the late nineteenth century, after the German Empire's unification,[56] and it is perhaps not surprising that unlike any other country, German officials selected music from the realm of high culture as the national anthem. While the French picked "La Marseillaise" and the United States "The Star-Spangled Banner"—both decisively popular tunes—Haydn's patriotic song, later turned into the Quartet in D Major, op. 76, no. 3 (*Kaiser*), served as the antecedent for the *Deutschlandlied*.

No composer epitomized the political meaning of music more than Ludwig van Beethoven, whose symphonies, as Robert Schumann remarked, were literally synonymous with German cultural pride: "As Italy has its Naples, France its Revolution, England its Navy, etc., so the Germans have their Beethoven symphonies. The German forgets in his Beethoven that he has no school of painting; with Beethoven he imagines that he has reversed the fortunes of the battles that he lost to Napoleon; he even dares to place him on the same level with Shakespeare."[57] Especially after unification, Beethoven became not just an icon for national identity but a symbol for what, precisely, this national identity ought to be and look like.[58] The composer's birthdays became occasions of patriotic outpourings. His entire oeuvre, its dynamics, its greatness, and its emotional breadth, reflected German national pride in the fatherland. And his personal biography, his multifaceted if not confused political opinions (one may just think of his ambitious stand toward the aristocracy), and his physical suffering, a presumably "German" characteristic, appealed to generations of Germans after his death. Echoed by leaders from Bismarck to Friedrich Engels, Beethoven's music and personality grew into ubiquitous symbols of nationalist propaganda throughout the Second Reich.[59]

The new music form in Germany constituted the first serious challenge to the French and Italian musical leadership since the 1780s. Beethoven and his music symbolized the overthrow of an established genre, the pride of the suppressed everywhere. Germans alone seemed to have access to that celestial "spark of music" that flourished only on German soil and only when composed by a German hand. Throughout the nineteenth century, musicians, music critics, and musicologists argued that music was vital to the development of a German national consciousness.[60] And when they said "music" they meant "serious" music, most notably the German symphony.

The Germans' cultural nationalism did not need a political infusion; quite the contrary, it thrived due to its apolitical appeal. "For whatever reasons," Applegate writes, "we have long accepted the romantics' vision of music as a direct expression of humanity or of divinity, in either case universal, and thus unsullied by the political world." According to diplomat and philosopher Wilhelm von Humboldt, it was imperative that serious music pose an emotional and intellectual challenge. Such challenges, along with the capacity to suffer, to insist, and to investigate, constituted characteristics that were not only German but universal. Since *German* was not more defined than *universal* and since both circumscribed the same set of characteristics, to Humboldt the two were compatible if not synonymous. In other words, to be German meant to be universal—that is, free-spirited, open-minded, and unfettered by any intellectually or geographically restrained way of life or thought.[61]

After 1871, political and cultural leaders recognized the power of instrumental and vocal music in cultural diplomacy. The files of the German Foreign Office pertaining to music are less extensive than those regarding the visual arts, but they do offer us a glimpse into its manifold musical activities. In the years between 1889 and 1903, for example, the Foreign Office's activities ranged from the engagement of musicians and a conductor for the city orchestra of Shanghai to support for the Brooklyn Arion Society's trip to Germany, the mediation of the Wagner family's protest against the performance of *Parsifal* in New York City, and the writing of letters of recommendation for the Orient trip of the Berliner Liedertafel.[62] All of these efforts were designed to cement the image of Germany as the land of music.

Similar to their involvement in the fields of the arts and education, the activities of both the Prussian cultural ministry and the Foreign Office in the field of music assumed no spectacular dimensions. Instead, officials entrusted this branch of interstate affairs to nongovernmental agencies and individuals. Private societies, concert agencies, sponsors, and artists appealed to the government, all of whom were even more eager than their political leaders to expound Germany's greatness through music. Thus, the Deutsche Bank of Berlin expressed a desire to send several military bands to the World's Columbian Exhibition in Chicago in 1893; the bank even authorized Wolff's concert agency in Berlin to obtain the necessary permission from the emperor.[63]

In 1902, the cosmetics manufacturer Ludwig Leichner, who in his youth had risen to fame as an accomplished baritone, successfully submitted a plan to the Foreign Office to erect a Richard Wagner memorial in the downtown area and initiate a series of conventions for Wagner enthusiasts from all over the world. The congress was supposed to address "highly scientific questions" in the fields of instrumental innovation, music pedagogy, and musicology. It was to be the first international *Musik-Fest*, Leichner promised, and he guaranteed officials that it would enhance the cultural ties among civilized nations. The list of committee members involved in this endeavor looked impressive, comprising the most renowned conductors of the day, including Richard Strauss and Arthur Nikisch, along with leading personalities from the military, the aristocracy, the academe, the diplomatic corps, European nobility, and Berlin cultural life. Leichner's grandiose vision climaxed in a gigantic new music hall to invite "all musical nations" of the world, including "the oriental people from Asia."[64] The World's Famous First Regiment and Orchestra from Cincinnati offered to come all the way from Ohio to represent the United States with "plantation music" and "original negro melodies."[65] France, Russia, Italy, and Spain wrote that leading representatives of their national music life would attend the event. Leichner's prophecy proved correct: Prince Heinrich along with a corona of royal and international celebrities attended the unveiling of the memorial in September 1903, and foreign observers took away positive memories. One of the French representatives even went so far as to circulate enthusiastic pamphlets on Franco-German cultural relations in the salons of Paris.[66]

In 1904, Timotheus Fabri, noted propagandist for German colonial expansion, board member of the Deutsche Kolonialgesellschaft, and general secretary of the Deutsch-Ostafrikanische Gesellschaft, suggested to the Foreign Office that it take the two hundred members of the Berlin Lehrer-Gesang-Verein to the World's Fair in St. Louis and a tour along the East Coast. The German Volkslied, Fabri proposed, ideally harmonized male voices to an extent unheard of in England or France, and no two peoples cherished their male choruses to the degree that the Germans and the Americans did.[67]

As late as February 1918, the Dresden Philharmonic Orchestra, which regarded itself as a "wartime orchestra" (founded in 1915), proposed to the Foreign Office that it tour the Austrian-Hungarian and Turkish cities, including Vienna, Buda and Pest, Belgrad, Sofia, and Constantinople. In March of 1918, the orchestra of the Royal Bavarian Infantry Leibregiment likewise proposed to tour Hungary, Rumania, Bulgaria, and Turkey "for propaganda purposes and the strengthening of the Deutschtum outside of Germany."[68]

Embarking on tours around the world, including all of Europe, Asia, and the Americas, these groups and individuals sought to spread German national culture, and they hoped to solicit the moral and administrative support of local embassies and consulates and the foreign offices.[69] Government administrators, in turn, minutely screened applicants who applied for funds and political support in their effort to present German opera and serious music abroad.[70] Officials in the Foreign Office as well as its delegates worldwide welcomed these initiatives, because they served the state's interest without smacking of propaganda and incurring astronomical bills.

While careful to keep official engagement in check, diplomatic envoys eagerly reported the strides made by German orchestras and musical associations abroad while also underlining the informal nature of their efforts. In 1911, the German consul in Atlanta, Dr. E. Zöpfel-Quellenstein, reported that the New York Metropolitan Opera Company's rendition of Engelbert Humperdinck's *Die Königskinder* had met with an astounding success. The auditorium was packed with approximately 6,500 people, and the consul proudly related that he had been elected vice president of a new Philharmonic Society in Atlanta, hoping to promote German composers in the United States.[71] From South America, the German consul reported that "Deutsche Richard Wagner Festspiele in Süd-Amerika" were scheduled to begin in 1914.[72] In Japan, thanks to the Royal Prussian Music Director, August Junker, young musicians received a first-class music education in the German tradition, as did the naval orchestra. Meanwhile, the Japanese government resolved to employ exclusively German instructors at the music academy in Tokyo, "despite all intrigues on the part of the French, the Italians, and the Americans," as Junker shrewdly added in his report.[73] And in the midst of World War I, Arthur Nikisch and the Berlin Philharmonic gave a series of guest concerts in Scandinavia under the auspices of the Imperial Foreign Office. With three appearances each in Copenhagen and Stockholm, and another one Göteborg, the tour constituted an overwhelming PR success. Yet due to anti-German demonstrations in Norway, the Kristiania police chief had to cancel the event, while the Foreign Office commented dryly that in the near future, the government should no longer promote such events.[74]

———

Nineteenth-century cultural expansionism in France, Germany, and Great Britain involved both state officials and a vast array of civil societies. The German government's reluctance to engage a propaganda machine administered by the state was, therefore, neither peculiar nor unwise but a logical conclusion based on observations made of neighboring countries and at home; this was just how things were done. If the imperial government learned anything from its experience with international art exhibitions, it was that it did not want to mess with the efforts of private individuals and nongernmental organizations any further, as increasing state control seemed to guarantee decreasing success. Particularly when considering music programs, officials refused to repeat their mistakes committed in other fields. German diplomats and policy makers realized that the appeal of German music in American orchestra halls had some implications for the two nations' relations. But the German government realized that the explicit use of music as an instrument of foreign policy would have countered the claim of universalism that was so vital in sending music across the Atlantic, as we shall see.

This does not mean that nothing was accomplished. A climate of cultural competition reigned in Europe, but that competition, despite its political undertones, was not dominated by politicians. Instead, nongovernmental groups and civil societies, only irregularly funded by the state, remained in charge of cultural diplomacy during the decades between 1850 and World War I. And as the German Reichskanzler's words quoted at the beginning of this chapter show, their actions—though achieving a favorable political outcome—often went unnoticed by policy makers. How this was so in the case of music is the subject of the following chapters.

TWO

# Music, Magic, and Emotions

It was a miracle that Emanuele Favre had not died. The thirteen-year-old woodcutter's assistant, known in Savoy for his bright and intelligent nature, had suffered a serious head injury caused by the blow of an axe. The axe had cleaved the boy's skull bones, almost splitting his head in two. Yet Emanuele survived and his wound healed, leaving a gaping scar three inches long and his brain covered merely by a layer of skin. Thus mutilated, he was discovered in 1895 by a young Italian professor named Mariano Luigi Patrizi, who was conducting a series of experiments in the Laboratory of Physiology in Turin. Patrizi hoped to determine the influence of different kinds of classical music on the circulation of blood in the human brain. More specifically, the scientist was trying to find out where emotions, notably the more elevated emotions—aesthetics—reside. The medical condition of the teenager from Savoy seemed to offer an ideal instrument to answer this question: Patrici attached to Emanuele a provisional apparatus named the plethysmograph to measure the pulse in the boy's brain, then played music to him. His principal conclusion: that every melody accelerated the flow of blood through the brain and thus increased and improved an individual's interior vision. These findings quickly evoked international attention, because Patrici appeared to be among the first who literally put his finger on the link between music and emotions.[1]

Patrici's research constituted one of hundreds of aca-

1   Thirteen-year-old Emanuele Favre of Savoy, with a gaping, three-inch-long scar on his head.
    The blow of an axe had sliced through his skull. From "Music and the Cerebral Circulation of
    Man.—First Experiments," *Music* 11 (December 1896): 232.

demic projects dedicated to the answering same question: how does
music influence human feelings? In the nineteenth century, critics,
lay musicians, philosophers, writers, poets, administrators, journalists, and scientists all across the Western world became increasingly
convinced that music could serve as a cure for all sorts of social, political and physical problems. Music entailed power, emotions, and an
uplifting moral force. Properly studied and performed, music could improve humanity and serve as an international language. It could transcend oceans, language barriers, and animosity of all kinds. It could
be the essence of the internationalism proposed by Wilhelm von

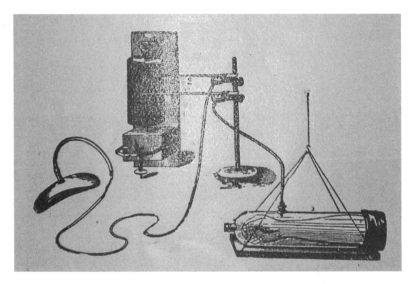

2 The plethysmograph attached to the boy's head measured his pulse rate. The instrument consisted of a closed glass cylinder for holding the arm in water, and a registering apparatus connected to the needle of a galvanometer. In order to register the pulse in the brain, Patrici had a cap of gutta-percha made, including an electrical connection that would indicate the slightest modification in pulse rate and blood volume. From "Music and the Cerebral Circulation of Man.—First Experiments," *Music* 11 (December 1896): 233.

Humboldt when he explained that serious music was both German and universal.

Participating in this debate, most Americans assured themselves that they would not be able to produce such musical medication; remedies were sought abroad. Wanting to learn the art of emotions, they began looking to Germany for a remedy: many believed that a musical atmosphere, filled with inspiration and enlightenment, could only be found in German-speaking lands. German administrators, in turn, held that music instruction would improve the relations between their nation and others. As a result, joining the wave of their compatriots already enchanted with German academic culture, an avalanche of American music disciples signed up with private instructors and state-run conservatories in the leading artistic centers of Europe. Two generations of critics, composers, and writers believed that a visit to the holy shrines of music would release their talent and help them penetrate music's deepest meanings. The discourse on the magical powers of music, along with Americans' search for this magic abroad, forms the core of this chapter.

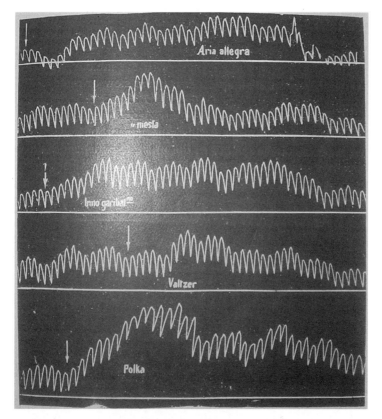

3    In the resulting tables produced by the plethysmograph, each beat of the pulse appears as a
line approximately 7 millimeters long; the table photographed shows the "elevation of the
cerebral pulse of Emanuele Favre through the incitation of music of different intonations and
different rhythms." From "Music and the Cerebral Circulation of Man,—First Experiments,"
*Music* 11 (December 1896): 237.

In the nineteenth century, European and American intellectuals and
scholars across all disciplines, as well as the general public, became increasingly convinced that music represented the most ideal of all the arts.
Middle-class citizens in Germany, England, France, the United States, and
elsewhere believed that music contained a special meaning unavailable
from the other arts, and they spent gallons of ink, mountains of paper,
untold amounts of dollars, and several decades of research investigating this idea. Music critics, philosophers, psychologists, and others led
a broad and intense debate on the meaning and the nature of music.
In countless meetings, conventions, papers, and essays, self-appointed
music experts discussed the link between music and daily life, music as a

force in education, and the power of music training, expressing their conviction that music was a science and an art, and as such its educational effect on the mind superseded that of any other subject. While this debate had been an integral part of musical culture for hundreds of years, it now contributed to the vision of an international community bound together by the power of German music, presumably the new international language of emotions. Book titles and headlines such as "What Is Classical Music?" "The Mission of Music," and "What Is the Meaning of Music?" found their way into specialized journals and the daily press. Entirely apart from the modernist discussion on whether music is simply form set in motion by sound, this was a highly public debate among people trying to understand the significance of classical music beyond mere aesthetics.

Many participants in this debate looked to music as the century's foremost therapeutic medicine for a self-appointed "nervous generation" struggling to cope with the stresses of the modern age, such as military escalation, diplomatic crises, and rapid industrialization, including streetcars, railroads, and telephones. In the United States, influential journals lamented the brutalizing effects of the strenuous and commercially oriented American way of life, which destroyed social connections, undermined friendships, and "[made] the human face immobile as marble and [turned] the warm heart's blood into cold, unfeeling fluid." Editors recommended orchestral music as a harmonic antidote to "the poison" of "unemotionalism."[2] Physicians told their clients that every day in the modern world added to their nervous discomfort while statistics repeatedly pointed to increasing rates of suicide and lunacy. Psychologists advocated music experiments and cures, in order to discern which personality reacted favorably to which kind of sound.[3]

Scholarly interest in music was not a novel enterprise; indeed, the Greeks and the Romans had already investigated the healing powers of tuneful sound.[4] But what was different now was the frenzy exhibited by scientists conducting an abundance of experiments to prove the medical value of music. One scholar discovered that music accelerated heart and breathing rates, while another stated that music acted as a stimulant on the human skin. In St. Petersburg, the Russian professor Iarchanoff claimed that music could revitalize fatigued fingers. A Viennese doctor hypnotized a patient, then played Wagner's "Ride of the Valkyries" to him during the trance, finding that his pulse and his breathing immediately increased while he grew agitated and began to perspire. Another patient remained passive to any music save the "Pilgrims' Chorus" from Wagner's *Tannhäuser*; he reportedly succumbed after the fourth bar.

Meanwhile, the London Guild of St. Cecilia sought to relieve pain and sleep disorders with the help of music; upon request, the society also offered this service via telephone. And in Chicago, musicians played works by Mendelssohn and other composers to the "mentally deranged" patients at a private sanitarium in order to cure them.[5]

Others studied physical signs in children, trying to detect whether they were driven by the mechanical, automatic activity of the nervous system or by the mystical power of emotions.[6] Instructors were advised to encourage their students to read poetry and play songs in order to study, internalize, and experience the great range of feelings that resulted, which they could then integrate into their lives.[7]

For all their eccentricity, the range of exotic research topics underlines the great interest and hopes in music held by people living in the nineteenth century. Phrenologists asserted that all of the recognized human faculties were represented by regions of the brain, and that some of these faculties are synonymous with emotion.[8] Psychologists and philosophers such as A. v. Oettingen (author of *Harmoniesystem in dualer Entwicklung*, 1866), Hermann Lotze (*Geschichte der Aesthetik in Deutschland*, 1868), Hugo Riemann, and others wondered what, exactly, defined harmony in music. After elaborating on the technical differences between dissonance and harmony, Hermann von Helmholtz conceded that in addition to mere physical sensations, music lived through a "stream of passion," "unimagined moods," and "everlasting beauty," which God had given only to a few "of his elect favorites."[9]

Most important, many of the participants in this passionate international debate believed that music would become a principal force inspiring global concord, and they all translated universalism into emotional internationalism. In the 1890s, Alfred Fouille, member of the Institute of France and president of the International Society of Sociology, expressed his conviction that music would become the herald of peace in the twentieth century. In spite of its national characteristics, "great music" anticipated the union of humankind and peace among nations.[10]

Both in Europe and in the United States, the debate participants agreed that as a universal language, music had the potential to create a global community transcending national borders. In 1852, the French scholar François Sudre proposed to turn music officially into the international language in order to prevent jealousy and rivalry among nations. Just as Latin functioned as the lingua franca of the Middle Ages, music was to become the international tool of communication of the nineteenth and twentieth centuries. In the future, Sudre held, people would learn only two languages: *la maternelle*, their native language, and *la générale*, a standardized form of music that he himself had invented. Sudre's neutral and universal language, titled Solresol, was based entirely on the seven syllables of music known around the world: do, re, mi, fa, sol, la, and ti, with no word comprising more than four sounds. The diction could be played by an instrument, or it could be sung; alternately, the speaker could indicate individual notes verbally or by his fingers. Sudre hailed his system's advantages as being at the disposal of blind, deaf, and mute people as well. To round things out, he also developed an abbreviated code for the army and the navy based on only three sounds that could be represented by any percussion instrument, a cannon, or even the telegraph.[11]

Similar to Sudre, many music experts sought to analyze music rationally as a language and a science, complete with rules of grammar and syntax. The idea to consider music as science, of course, dated to the major tradition of musical knowledge that preceded the advent of the Romantics at the end of the eighteenth century. What was new was the European Romantics' insistence that it was all about feeling,[12] and, successively, educators' insistence on "scientificizing" the language of emotions. As an organized and veritable language, agued the American professor R. P. Rider from a college in Missouri, music represented a full-fledged science with physical problems and principles that only the experts could understand. Facing the paradoxical task of establishing the language of emotions as a science, Rider postulated that American educators recognized music as one of the "legitimate sciences, the foundations of which should be well laid during the early years of the student's life." Music strengthened memory, reason, logic, imagination, perception, physical expression, emotional breadth, and mental comprehension, and cultivated the aesthetic principle.[13]

Rider is a good example of the eagerness by which American music critics, scientists, journalists, teachers, and even lay musicians and concertgoers participated in the discussion on music as an international language of emotions. A presentation at the 1896 convention of the Illinois Music Teacher's Association praised music as the fundamental power in education and retraced its influence to ancient Greece. The difference between ancient Greece and modern America, speaker Mrs. John Vance Cheney explained, equaled the one between life in beautiful Athens and life in a modern city. By abandoning moral sentiment and assigning supremacy to the intellect and to rational forces, Americans had come to ignore the soul of things—the belief in God, universal truth, and beauty.[14] This was bad news for a nation that traced its political principles to the ancient Greeks and the early Roman Empire.

For nineteenth-century Americans, the quintessential form of educational and uplifting music was the symphony. According to the *New York American*, the symphony constituted a much higher form of art than the opera, because it represented "pure music."[15] The symphony's union of many voices in order to create beauty appealed to observers of all ranks, as it seemed to represent the highest and most ideal type of musical art. No other music did as much to reach for the supreme and the ideal in musical arrangement. A symphony orchestra, observed a Minnesota critic, guaranteed progress, the depth of humanity, and human attainment. The symphony appealed to the masses by providing them with a variety of sound and a richness of sonority otherwise unthinkable. According to the *Boston Globe*, a symphony ought to be "primarily instructive," and its instruction ought to "be given in German, no Italian or French or mere common vernacular English being admitted except under protest and as a concession."[16]

The merger of a feeling for nature with a Germanic background in conjunction with the new emphasis on man's natural emotions and the fusion of God, man, nature, beauty, and art inspired many New England intellectuals, Romantics, and transcendentalists.[17] In 1859, *Dwight's Journal of Music* argued that different nations produced different kinds of harmonies depending on their national character. Next to traits such as tenderness, seriousness, and profundity, universality represented a German characteristic, as it sought to apprehend and encompass all. Universality aimed at discovering and assimilating "the good that exists in other nations and in other ages; which can comprehend and sympathize with anomalous circumstances." Because German composers used all forms of music applied by other nations, the journal claimed, they had achieved an emotional breadth of instrumental music and thematic treatment unparalleled by either French or Italian composers.[18]

What rendered German music so inspiring, critics repeated again and again, was its link to religion.[19] Borrowing from the idea of music as a *Kunstreligion* (art religion) that emerged in Germany around 1800, American critics agreed that music manifested the divine and constituted religion itself without denominational affiliation: "actual communion with the highest, rest in the ideal home. It is Eternity experienced in the passing moment," a message straight from heaven.[20] To the music critic John Sullivan Dwight, good music meant German music, and German music was a substitute faith.[21] "Music is the aspiration, the yearnings of the heart to the Infinite," he wrote when still in his twenties. "It is the prayer of faith, which has no fear, no weakness in it. It delivers us from our actual bondage; it buoys us up above our accidents, and wafts us on waves of melody to the heart's ideal home."[22] Another prolific music editor, John Freund, founder of the journal *Musical America*, originally titled his weekly column "The Book of Revelation"; in it he propounded his belief that music, if properly spread among the human race, would bring about unity, peace, and eternal happiness.[23]

Since many commentators during the Victorian era linked music to divinity, the most prevalent conviction among Americans regarding the meaning of music concerned its moral, educational, and uplifting force for the people and the nation. The critic Henry Finck, for example, declared that classical music could cure wife-beating and intoxication.[24] Others were convinced that music raised the ethos of American society.[25] And one even believed that music could appease social tensions, including household tensions, because the singing of quartettes or the playing of concert music exerted a soothing influence upon family conflicts. Children would become better citizens if they studied music; boys were kept from the streets if they stayed home and practiced scales.[26]

What remains peculiar about the debate in the United States was that for a long time, most critics agreed that Americans themselves would never be able to generate a homegrown brand of musical medicine. Their inability originated, presumably, in a variety of factors, including the insufficiency of the American diet and the optimistic bent of the American mind-set. In an essay titled "Music and Nutrition," the piano teacher Edward Baxter Perry scolded that the American "race" was "in imminent danger of becoming extinct," because American professional brainworkers (notably musicians) did not pay attention to their nourishment. Perry believed that an unhealthy diet consisting of white bread, starch, and an overdose of sugar contributed to the decline of American civilization. In contrast, German students lived on a diet of beef, dark bread, sausage, cheese, onions, and cabbage. As a result, German students thrived, while ever-increasing numbers of American music students fainted and collapsed at their pianos, violins, cellos, and flutes from want of adequate food. Each new generation displayed a nervous system weaker and worse than the last.[27]

But even if Americans watched their food intake, they were, as one midwestern critic put it, too happy to compose good music. In a nation reigned by a philosophy of cheerfulness that encouraged men and women to face the abyss of misery with a blissful smile and the will to succeed, "no confirmed optimist has ever written great music and it is quite unlikely, as our world is at present constituted, that any confirmed optimist ever will."[28] American culture left no room for the professional and the broad expression of feelings; indeed, Americans had never learned the art

4   John S. Dwight was a transcendentalist, a Unitarian minister, and the United States' pioneer
in music critic. To Dwight, good music meant German music, and German music was an er-
satz faith and a "universal language, tending to unite and blend and harmonize all who may
come within its sphere." From *Music* 2, no. 2 (June 1892), between pp. 230 and 231.

of celebrating melancholy. It was precisely the gloominess, the worries, the perception of melancholy coupled with productivity, the ability to be sad and blissful, to emotionalize, that American audiences identified with "German" and attracted them to musical artistry. Because Americans had repressed their emotions, observed the conductor Walter Damrosch, they had no national music save for a few folk songs.[29]

No one championed the power of music as a language more than did John Sullivan Dwight, perhaps the United States' most influential music critic in the nineteenth century. Dwight talked, lectured, and published incessantly on the power of music as a means of communication with the divine spirits. To him, music was "the art and language of the feelings, the sentiments, the spiritual instincts of the soul; and so becomes a universal language, tending to unite and blend and harmonize all who may come within its sphere."[30]

Dwight epitomized the period's thinking on the gradual conclusion of universalism, nationalism, and music. Music, he believed, was the principle of the universe and of all things, the expression of the pure spirit, and the most intimate of languages because, as he explained in 1862, it created instant harmony between two people as well as two cultures.[31] Like mathematics, music could penetrate the "walls of time and space," while composers like Bach, Handel, Mozart, Beethoven, Weber, Schubert, and Mendelssohn constituted common acquaintances among men and women around the globe. These artists had endowed the world with their feelings and thereby created an international language of unity for all human beings. Americans as a democratic, pluralist people needed classical music more than others, Dwight concluded in an 1870 lecture reprinted in the *Atlantic Monthly*. "We need some ever-present, ever-welcome influence that shall insensibly tone down our self-asserting and aggressive manners . . . and harmonize the free and ceaseless conflict of opinions." They needed to speak the "universal language," because "Music begins where Speech leaves off."[32]

———

Thanks to editors such as Dwight, nineteenth-century Americans remained keenly aware of the European music scene. Music journals featured regular firsthand reports from the concert scene in Leipzig, Berlin, and Vienna. Music critics perused the leading European newspapers and magazines, and often reprinted or cited articles, reviews, portrayals, and concert reports that only shortly before had been published in newspapers such as the *Kölnische Zeitung*. Many American music lovers subscribed directly to German music publications by mail.

While such reading contributed to readers' musical cosmopolitanism, it also aggravated their self-consciousness. What most readers got out of the occasional study of *Dwight's Journal of Music* or the *Neue Zeitschrift für Musik* was that Americans were behind, both in music performance and in music education. To escape the fetters of a mediocre teacher, to develop talent and, perhaps, become a star, American students had to say good-bye to their loved ones and cross the ocean, a verdict readily confirmed by European visitors. Yes, music training was available in the United States, the baritone Georg Henschel conceded during a visit to Cincinnati, "but in Europe one is in the very atmosphere of it."[33] Most Americans, the pedagogue Frank Damrosch lamented in New York City, lived in "almost total musical darkness . . . because the opportunities for hearing and doing the best music are not afforded them." In Europe,

Damrosch explained, citizens from all walks of life enjoyed a variety of artistic experiences without any or only a small expense, as galleries, libraries, and music halls were affordable and exerted a strong influence.[34] "We are not yet a singing nation," Damrosch told the General Federation of Women's Clubs. In the United States, people had grown up without habitual singing and "with the conception that music is a mere incident which may be cultivated if one has the means but without which one can enjoy life with the aid of a Ford car or the movies." Westward expansion had neglected "old institutions" such as singing schools, and produced instead a homogenous culture, "the great psycho-chemical process of the melting-pot." Damrosch was convinced that music constituted the only agency to unify Americans whose ethnic backgrounds, languages, customs, and traditions varied so tremendously.[35]

Damrosch's assessment was not totally fair. Americans enjoyed a vibrant musical culture before the Civil War era. Besides church music, recent historiography has drawn attention to indigenous American songs, theater and military music, and home music making. Early ballad-operas were heard, from the mid-eighteenth century onward, in larger cities such as Philadelphia, Savannah, Charleston, and Providence. Outside churches and stages, folk songs, black music, Creole music, and Spanish musical influences made a definite impression. The Revolutionary War brought a host of European war songs along with French and Italian operas. Men of letters such as Thomas Jefferson, to whom music was "the favorite passion of my soul," often studied one or more instruments throughout their lives. Jefferson himself favored the violin and harpsichord, and Monticello housed a large library of music scores.[36] What was genuinely American, however, were the folk songs of the pioneers, the melodies of American Indians, and the spirituals and gospel music of African Americans; and as is the case for most folk music, their original composers remain unknown. Prior to and immediately following the Civil War, songwriters and occasional composers such as Stephen Collins Foster, William Billings, Lowell Mason, and Louis Gottschalk were the only well-known American composers.[37]

In the early 1800s, American music was still primarily vocal, with a religious undercurrent. Clergymen and churchgoers worried whether music ought to be used exclusively for praising the Lord, or whether it could indeed be played for worldly audiences as well. The Protestant churches advocated the singing of hymns, which eventually led to the performance of the English-language oratorios of Handel, Haydn, and eventually Mendelssohn. These semireligious concerts in turn paved the way for totally secular musical performances. One of the first was the Peace

Jubilee in Boston's King's Chapel at the conclusion of the War of 1812, in which a choir sang Haydn's *Creation*, Handel's *Messiah*, and other works; from this the Handel and Haydn Society was formed in 1815.

The society was very ambitious; in 1823 its members wrote to Beethoven, offering him a commission to write an oratorio especially for the society's use. The plan never materialized, but we know from Beethoven's notebooks that he had toyed with the idea. In 1840–41, the Boston Academy of Music (founded in 1833) gave a series of Beethoven concerts for educational purposes. In 1866–67, the Harvard Musical Society was formed. And to further feed Americans' growing appetite for musical entertainment, a total of thirty new music journals were launched in the United States between 1818 and 1845, with the majority appearing in New York, Boston, and Philadelphia.[38] Individual composers, musicians, songwriters, and music publishers flourished in urban areas such as St. Louis as early as in the 1830s. They formed orchestral units, composed small pieces, and generally provided local dance halls, churches, and public gardens with music selections throughout the concert season.[39]

Still, the United States was far away from the European music scene; just how far is revealed by Margaret Fuller's journal entry in 1843, in which the poet expressed her admiration for Beethoven and addressed him as "my only friend"—a friend who by then had been dead for fifteen years.[40] Cosmopolitan travelers confirmed the belief of many Americans that Europe's music was superior to that of the United States. When traversing Europe, Abigail Adams (the wife of John Adams, second U.S. president, 1797–1801) enjoyed concerts in Paris and London. She loved Mozart's opera *The Marriage of Figaro* and wrote to Thomas Jefferson that the performance of the *Messiah* in Westminster Abbey was "sublime beyond description."[41] Abigail Adams's fascination symbolized the irony embedded in the artistic culture of the new nation: despite the emergence of the United States as an independent republic, American composers remained strangely indifferent to the development of New World themes. Indeed, while they were busy composing conservative church music, their European counterparts developed an early fascination with themes of the New World. Already in 1800, the Russian composer Yevstigney Fomin had produced an opera entitled *Amerikantsy* (The Americans). Johann Baptist Rupprecht's libretto, *Die Ankunft der Pennsylvanier in Amerika* (The Arrival of the Pennsylvanians), was under serious consideration by Beethoven in 1820.[42] By the mid-nineteenth century, the Italian conductor Luigi Arditi had performed *La Spia*, his version of James Fenimore Cooper's *The Spy*. Puccini's 1911 composition, *La fanciulla del West* (The Girl of the Golden West), captivated audiences in both Europe and the United States.[43]

Adding to the randomness of musical life, antebellum orchestras enjoyed little stability, and the quality of their performances varied tremendously. Still, in 1876, Jacques Offenbach noted in his reminiscences during his visit to the United States that New York directors and their companies were all "nomads." "So are the leading artists who, for the most part, are birds of passage coming from the old world and bent upon returning there."[44] Orchestras were habitually made up half of amateurs and half of professional musicians, and concerts often deteriorated into noisy, pompous, and rambunctious affairs. At a performance of Mendelssohn's *Midsummer Night's Dream* in Boston during the 1844–45 season, the conductor had never heard or seen the score and contented himself by rapping on his music stand to mark time—the result of which, as the orchestra's flutist, Thomas Ryan, remembered, was a sound "most distressingly out of tune."[45] When Offenbach came to the United States at the occasion of its Centennial to conduct his own composition, *La Jolie Parfumeuse*, he recorded that the oboist was a "capricious fellow who played from time to time whenever the fancy took him." The flutist performed whenever he could. The bassoonist slept through most of the performance, while the violoncello and the bass consistently skipped measures.[46] Several years earlier, in 1873, the Board of the New York Philharmonic reminded its members "to keep their seat during the rehearsals or Concerts whether they have a part or not, and not to tune their respective instrument immediately after playing."[47]

After the German Revolution of 1848, Americans were for the first time exposed to a massive influx of European musicians, most of whom came from the German states. While many artists fled Europe for political reasons, an even greater number felt that its concert stages did not look as promising or safe after 1848 as before. Consequently, touring the United States became the fashion, even though at that time its musical landscape more closely resembled a circus than any higher form of entertainment.[48] Ernest Frank Wagner, whose musical family had emigrated from Plauen to Chicago when he was still a child, began playing with brass bands in tents at the age of thirteen. He then joined a so-called fly-by-night company whose members shared all expenses if there were no receipts, and as a result often had to "fly by night" in order to avoid landing in jail the next morning. Orchestra members also quarreled over who should take in the tickets at the door, because that person typically disappeared into the night if the receipts were good.[49]

In U.S. cities, European soloists and singers from the West Indies, Cuba, Italy, and Germany competed for the attention and monies of the upper classes. Due to the scarcity of indigenous artistic efforts, American urbanites were eager for all forms of music and art. Traveling on the circuit of impresarios such as P. T. Barnum, virtuosos from all over the world hunted for wealth and opportunity. Prosperous southern planters and their wives entertained themselves during the winter months in New Orleans with operas and dances.[50] As a result, German agents had a firm grip on the American concert scene as early as 1865.

Yet for all the traveling virtuosos, singers, bands, and agencies in the United States, Frank Damrosch's criticism in regard to its "musical darkness" contained a grain of truth: Americans wishing to partake in the music circuit had to travel to Germany in order to study music in earnest. Until about 1860, musicians wishing to embark on a solo career had to receive "le baptême de Paris" to seal their success. The German poet and satirist Heinrich Heine reported in the *Allgemeine Zeitung* that each winter the French capital was afflicted by a veritable swarm of young pianists, less motivated to make money than to make themselves a name and a career outside France. A virtuoso who had been praised by the Paris press could be sure of a merciful reception elsewhere. After 1860, however, Berlin gradually replaced Paris as the center of musical approbation. Cities, audiences, and newspapers outside Berlin never completely yielded control and prestige to the capital to the extent that Paris had claimed a musical monopoly in France. Nonetheless, Heinrich Ehrlich observed in 1893 that "by and large Berlin represents the authority [on music]." Whoever succeeded in Germany would also succeed elsewhere.[51]

Thanks to the prestige and omnipresence of music in central Europe, Germany turned into an Eden of musical education and fulfillment for many aspiring U.S students. As the composer Frederick Root explained, in England music was a retainer; social prominence was the measuring stick of daily activities, and music "is made to walk humbly in the train of society." Hence, Americans who studied music in England typically returned with an empty bank account, because the "patronage of the mighty, [had] outweighed or suffocated their artistic endeavors." Italians, in contrast, considered music an "innamorata," a goddess to worship with the kind of passion and adoration that flamboyant lovers express toward each other. Therefore, American students studying in Italy returned with an inclination toward hyperbole as a rule. Their style emphasized tremolo and high notes, and their repertoire now contained the most famous operatic numbers, but nothing else. In France, music was "royalty." Musicians often found themselves honored in a most profound manner without displaying any talent. In Germany, Root concluded, "music is a Divinity." It lived a life apart from social distinction, ambition, and individual showmanship. Indeed, German musicians typically believed themselves to be superior to the aristocracy while the public worshipped music as a religion, an elixir of life. "From Germany, one is likely to return in pretty good order. They have worked toward as pure an art ideal as can be found anywhere upon the globe and they show the effects of few or no distractions from a course of earnest work."[52]

Thanks to the promotion of Root and others, German conservatories and private instructors became the gatekeepers to the shrine of musical culture in the American perception. Passenger lists of steamers heading to Europe during the summers were filled with the names of middle-class Americans searching for Kultur and inner soul cleansing, hoping to obtain tickets for concerts in Wiesbaden, Salzburg, and Bayreuth, or early-season admission to concerts in Munich, Berlin, Vienna, Leipzig, and elsewhere. "At the festival [in Salzburg] and, in fact, all over Europe," the conductor Fritz Scheel reported in the fall of 1906 in Philadephia, "there are more Americans than any other nationality of tourists."[53]

Since most travelers crossed the Atlantic during the summer months, often missing out on "the season," much attention was focused on summer festivals, spas, and vacation centers. In July 1901, Senator Henry Cabot Lodge embarked on a three-month European vacation trip on the steam liner *Commonwealth*. Interviewed by the *Boston Journal* on the dock, he stated that he had no plans except "that we are going to Bayreuth to be there during the opera season." He added sheepishly: "Then I shall be ready for politics again."[54]

"Going to Bayreuth" became the thing to do for music students as well as cosmopolitans like Lodge, and they all crowded into northern Bavaria right after the Festspielhaus had opened its doors, in 1876. Founded half a decade after German unification as a musical theater dedicated exclusively to the works of Richard Wagner, the organizers of the Festspiele encountered financial difficulties from the beginning. While the Reich government did not support the venture financially, thousands of American Wagner fans, recruited by leading conductors such as Theodore Thomas, did. In Bayreuth, Americans, notably women, were spotted following the aging master, ever hoping for a sign of attention and recognition. When attending the Bayreuth Festival in the 1880s, the composer and critic Louis Elson counted some fifty Americans among the audience.[55]

More than five thousand Americans studied music in Germany between 1850 and 1900, and nearly thirteen hundred of these attended the Leipzig Conservatory, founded by Felix Mendelssohn in 1843 and subsequently the leading conservatory in Germany if not the world. They also headed to music schools in Berlin, Munich, Frankfurt, Dresden, Stuttgart, Cologne, Sondershausen, Wiesbaden, Würzburg, and a host of smaller cities. They visited the master classes, studies, and even private homes of artists such as Franz Liszt in Weimar or Richard Wagner in Bayreuth. And they hoped to catch that magic spark of musical art and knowledge that would enable them to obtain a promising music education and, perhaps, rise to professional prominence back home.[56]

Their enthusiasm testifies to the persistence of aspiring students and fans. European audiences and instructors had no history of welcoming American music students and performers with open arms. When Louis Gottschalk of New Orleans came to Paris in 1842 to study with Pierre Zimmerman, the famous piano teacher in the Conservatoire, the *maitre* turned him down on the grounds that no good pianist lived in the United States, a land that had produced only savages and steam engines. In 1854, Henry Fry complained that the director of the Opera in Paris would not even look at his compositions, because people would question his sanity if he scheduled an opera by an American.[57] In 1871, Theodore Thomas's sister-in-law, Amy Fay, an accomplished pianist and writer, advised American students to invest at least several years of their music education in Germany, because "it takes fully a year to get started under a first class master. These great teachers won't take a pupil raw from America, still less trouble themselves with a scholar who cannot immediately comprehend." Theodor Kullak, one of Berlin's most famous piano instructors and founder of the Neue Akademie der Tonkunst, expressed his disapproval of American students regularly by stating, "Why, Fräulein, you play exactly as if you came from America." And Johannes Weidenbach, renowned teacher at the Leipzig Conservatory, held that Americans playing the piano reminded him of nothing so much as "big spiders going over the keys."[58] Berlin manager Wolff even refused to advertise Mary Harkness from Brooklyn as an American pianist. Reversing the letters of her name, he promoted her as "Arma Senkrah, from India" and successfully landed an engagement with the Berlin Philharmonic at the orchestra's opening concert on September 30, 1884. Harkness, alias Senkrah, later married a German and moved to Weimar, where she shot herself out of jealousy over her husband's infidelity.[59]

American students wishing to study "real music" to develop "real emotion" had to cross the Atlantic and absorb the musical atmosphere of the Continent. "Of all things don't make the mistake [with your children] which brought about our rootless & accidental childhood," Alice James wrote to her brother William, the famous Harvard psychologist, in 1888. "Leave Europe for them until they are old eno' to have the Grand Emotion, undiluted by vague memories."[60] The Grand Emotion was expensive, though: according to the *New York Times*, before World War I American families paid about $15 million annually to foreign countries, notably Germany and Austria, to train their children in the art of music.[61] Even after the onset of the war, in 1915, John C. Freund, editor of *Musical America*, still calculated that each year Americans spent $8 million to $10 million abroad on music education, foreign instructors, and foreign scores.[62]

An almost mythical belief in a "musical atmosphere" that Germany had and the United States lacked motivated both students and casual travelers. Part of it originated in the conviction that music and emotions were inherently German and simply could not be reproduced elsewhere.[63] In addition, unrestrained by the fetters of domestic, social, or professional requirements at home, American students abroad indulged in an intense culture of music learning. These students in Leipzig, Berlin, or Vienna, observed one music critic, "fall into the habit of coming together for companionship, and of talking over musical ideas and works, in a manner which is very rare in America. Indeed I doubt whether the students in Chicago come together at all." Students in the music centers of Europe, the author concluded, studied with a frenzy and dedication that was "rare in this country."[64]

No soloist could aspire to fame if he had not taken a pilgrimage to the shrine of serious music. Girls, advised the *Cosmopolitan*, "must have been given in charge of a music-teacher by the age of nine." After having been trained for five years, she "must have been 'finished' in Europe by the very greatest finisher, say a Leschetizki on the piano or a Lamperti for the voice. It is at the age of from eighteen to twenty-one that the greatest women-musicians have been ushered into fame."[65]

A successful debut in Berlin, Leipzig, or Vienna typically proved to be an open sesame in Germany as well as in all principal cities of Europe. Funded by two American philanthropists, the teenage violinist Leonora Jackson spent six years in Europe studying with Joseph Joachim, who eventually also conducted the orchestra in her Berlin debut. Her trip proved to be her ticket to fame among audiences in Europe and the United States. Jackson, the U.S. press reported, had become "the dearest pupil" of Joachim's in Berlin, mastered that "most difficult of all pieces," the Brahms concerto, and won the Mendelssohn state prize given by the Prussian government. She had played before the German empress, and charmed Queen Victoria at Windsor Castle, who gave her a "lovely cross of diamonds." In Paris she had played "the most brilliant concert of the spring" in honor of the king of Norway and Sweden. "All these laurels," concluded a Boston newspaper,

5   The Austrian-born pianist Fannie Bloomfield-Zeisler became one of the first famous woman pianists in the United States. Though she spent much of her life in Chicago, she went to Vienna to study with Theodor Leschetizky between 1878 and 1883. Upon her return to the United States, her performances were so successful that it motivated scores of American students to travel to Vienna to study with her instructor. From *Music* 1, no. 3 (January 1892), front matter.

"she comes to lay before the people in America, who can proudly hail her, as have the German and English public, as one if not the most gifted violinist of today." And the public did not fail her. Jackson's transformation was complete: not only had she acquired technique and a repertory, observed the journal *Musical Courier*, but she had mutated from "a sweet-faced, blue-eyed little girl, who last played at a few New England summer resorts," into "a tall, graceful young woman" whose "mystical gray-blue eyes" and "'Mozartian' brow" reflected "genius."[66]

Grateful for their successful transformation, American students never forgot their music instructors. Rumor had it that the piano teacher Theodor Leschetizky, orginally from St. Petersburg but who had migrated to Vienna, taught nearly one thousand American students. The first was Fannie Bloomfield-Zeisler (who was actually born in Austria). Upon her return to the United States, her performances were so successful that they motivated scores of American students to travel to Vienna to study with her instructor. When Leschetizky died, his European and American students raised funds to adorn his grave with a white marble niche that showed the pupils offering tributes to the master.[67]

Between 1850 and World War I, scores of American men and women journeyed to the shrines of Leipzig, Stuttgart, and Berlin to study the great masters and learn how to sing, compose, theorize, and play an instrument. Leipzig, according to many "the Jerusalem of American tradition," accommodated so many American music pupils that for decades "to study in Europe" was synonymous with "to study in Leipzig."[68] Often still in their teenage years, many of these students felt irresistibly drawn to the great master teachers who had trained some of the finest virtuosos and thus seemed to promise huge success on both sides of the ocean.

If they did not gain immortality as a soloist, the students successively chose a teaching career. St. Louis's William Pommer, grandson of an immigrant from Halberstadt, arrived in Leipzig in 1872. Immersing himself in music theory, conducting, piano, and composition at the Royal Conservatory, he graduated two years later, then moved to Vienna to study organ and counterpoint with Anton Bruckner at the Imperial Conservatory for one year. Pommer found Bruckner's personality arrogant, but he loved Vienna, "the land of music, beauty, and the joy of living" and the home of "the immortal Schubert." After a conversation with Franz Liszt at Weimar, he played for the composer and later noted that "very few of us can astonish him." In 1875, Pommer returned to St. Louis, where he continued to compose, eventually became Supervisor of Music for the St. Louis public school system, and later served on the faculties of Washington University, Christian College (Columbia, Missouri), and the University of Missouri.[69]

The German conservatories, such as the one attended by Pommer, were generally a product of the nineteenth century, when music instruction moved increasingly away from private lessons to state institutions.[70] Most of the great conservatories of Europe, save for Vienna (1817) and Leipzig (1843), were founded in the third quarter of the nineteenth century. Berlin's private Stern Conservatory opened its doors in 1850, while the state-run Hochschule für Musik was established on Königsplatz in 1869 to further "patriotic education."[71] Headed by the famous violinist Joseph Joachim, the Berlin conservatory was part of the Royal Academy of Arts. As such, it stood directly under the auspices of the Prussian kings, who, judging from the sheer amount of paperwork produced over the decades, took a sizable interest in the venture.[72] By 1914, the Prussian government had spent 619,855 marks (approximately $150,000) on musical matters, of which 271,014 marks went into the Hochschule für Musik.[73] By then, the school counted over fifty instructors and more than 320 students, most of whom studied the piano, the violin, or voice. More than a third of the student body consisted of women.

According to a statistical survey conducted by the journal *Die Gegen-wart* in 1893, there were 112 music schools, conservatories, and academies in Berlin, 60 in Vienna, and approximately 125 such institutions in the rest of Germany (without counting the major schools in Frankfurt, Cologne, Hamburg, and so forth, and without the royal institutes in Cologne, Dresden, Karlsruhe, Leipzig, Munich, Strassburg, Stuttgart, and Würzburg). Collectively they taught approximately 15,000 students each year. Between 1890 and 1897 alone, these schools produced a total of 18,000 professional musicians.[74]

Aspiring musicians living outside the German Empire played a significant role in the economic welfare of these schools. In 1871, foreigners at the influential Leipzig Conservatory (later the model for the Oberlin conservatory) accounted for 64 percent of all registered students, nearly half of whom came from the United States.[75] The annual reports of the Berlin Conservatory listed students from Russia, France, England, Poland, Romania, Hungary, the Baltics, Switzerland, Ireland, Japan, India, Scandinavia, Africa, Australia, Tasmania, Uruguay, Constantinople, Brazil, Borneo, Italy, Austria, Spain, Serbia, Galicia, and Chile. A sizable portion of the international students came from the United States. During the 1907–8 school year, some 20 out of more than 300 students were Americans, many of whom had won musical awards and royal decorations.[76]

Still on the eve of World War I, German conservatories were literally swamped with foreign students, who typically paid a fee at least 50 percent beyond that of German students. The *Berliner Neueste Nachrichten* reported in February 1914 that nearly a third of all students at Prussian music schools came from areas outside Germany (99 out of 329), while at other schools, the ratio of foreign students ranged from 8 percent to 16 percent.[77]

The conservatories now began to welcome foreign students with open arms. Advocates of international music education in Germany, such as the director of the Berlin Conservatory, Hermann Kretzschmar, argued that it contributed to favorable relations between Germany and other nations.[78] Not surprisingly, many teachers spoke and taught in English while administrators readily facilitated the admissions requirements for foreign students.[79]

American music students, in turn, made the best of their stint in Germany. Beginning with the Civil War era, reporters, musicians, music students, editors, and tourists went to Berlin, Leipzig, Dresden, and Vienna and published their accounts in one of the many music journals of their time.

Amy Fay's collection of letters, published under the unadorned title *Music-Study in Germany*, went through twenty-one printings in the United States while also being picked up by publishers in England, France, and eventually Germany, where Franz Liszt sponsored the German-language edition. According to one chronicler, Fay's recollections lured at least two thousand American music students to Leipzig, Weimar, and Berlin.[80]

American music students such as Fay would typically portray their first encounter with "a master," their immersion in "the atmosphere," their conversion to "real music" in the Gewandhaus concert hall or the opera, and their boundless enthusiasm with Germany's musical culture. They would try to visit Richard Wagner in Bayreuth and, after his death, his widow, Cosima, forever in mourning. They would call on Brahms in Vienna or Liszt in Weimar. They would also describe student life, their experiences in local "Kneipen," their confusion with German urban culture, and their dismay with the weather and the food.

And they would work untiringly to imitate the model of the great masters and develop their talents, as they testified in thousands of letters sent home.[81] In her youth, Amy Fay spent six years studying in Germany, between 1869 and 1875, in order to prepare for a music career in the United States. During her time in Berlin, Dresden, and Weimar, she studied with some of the most famous pianists of her time while also meeting Bismarck, the Bancrofts, and other celebrities. "I have been learning Beethoven's G major Concerto lately, and it is the most horribly difficult thing I've ever attempted," Fay reported home from Berlin on June 25, 1871. "I have practiced the first movement a whole month, and I can't play it any more than I can fly."[82]

What students like Fay were looking for was not mere music instruction; that they could have obtained at any of the new music colleges or the thousands of private music instructors in the United States. "Not manual skill," concluded Fay's collection of letters, but "wider and deeper musical insight and conception, and 'concert style' are what the young artist should now go to seek in that marvelous and only real home of music—GERMANY." The students who went to Germany sought something genuine that they felt no American environment could provide. They were looking for "the magic," that "effortless playing" that allowed performers to reach the soul of their audiences. Pianists such as Liszt, Ludwig Deppe in Berlin, Hans von Bülow, and others could, supposedly, make people feel things in ways that ordinary pianists could not. They could evoke emotions, make people laugh, cry, or grow melancholic by playing as little as a few measures. Fay, for one, was advised to study at the Berlin conservatory with Carl Tausig, "a young man who plays the piano like forty thousand devils." Tausig, a man still in his early thirties, had been a student of Liszt's. He hated teaching, but his skill as a performer and his reputation as one of Liszt's most unruly pupils attracted far more students than other instructors.

No event in Europe transformed Fay as did her encounter with Franz Liszt in Weimar, in the summer of 1873. Liszt stressed an understanding of the composer and the music, an emotional bond far more than technical training. Besides his very handsome looks (audiences still found Liszt's features magnificent when he was in his seventies) and hypnotic personality that mesmerized generations of adolescent students, Liszt had "that indescribably *something* that, when he plays a few chords, merely, makes the tears rush to our eyes. It is too heavenly for anything." Even though Europe's most famous pianist told the young American to stop moving her hands around as if she were making an omelet, Amy noted that "Liszt was so sweet," showed a distinctive interest in her personality—perhaps more so than in her musical talent—and continually encouraged her to play, so that she had "the most heavenly time in Weimar, studying with Liszt."

For pages and pages, Fay commented on Liszt's extraordinary emotional powers, his ability to mesmerize audiences with a single look, his skill at moving people to the brink of tears with his music. "His personal magnetism is immense, and I can scarcely bear it when he plays," she noted on June 19, 1873. "He can make me cry all he chooses. . . . Liszt knows well the influence he has on people, for he always fixes his eyes on some one of us when he plays, and I believe he tries to wring our hearts." The tone of her reports reflected her own self-consciousness, coupled with an almost religious adoration of a superhuman being. "All playing sounds barren by the side of Liszt, for his is the living, breathing impersonation of poetry, passion, grace, wit, coquetry, daring, tenderness and every other fascinating attribute that you can think of!" she noted on June 6, 1873. "I'm ready to hang myself half the time when I've been to him. . . . In short, he represents the whole scale of human emotion." To see Liszt was to have seen it all. In him, Fay concluded on June 19, 1873, "I can at last say that my ideal in *something* has been realized. He goes far beyond all that I expected."[83]

Key to an American student's future success at home was a concert opportunity before his or her return to the United States and, even better, a personal encounter with the European aristocracy. To win the favor of German royalty was to win the acceptance of all of Germany. Thus, artists would often try their luck at a smaller court or spa, and then, based on the reaction to the concert, decide whether to extend their sojourn in Europe as an artist, a student, or a tourist. The diaries of the soprano Emma Thursby, the "American Nightingale" who visited Europe and Asia in the second half of the nineteenth century, provide an insight into the heavy travel schedules of touring Americans abroad. At the age of seventeen, Emma visited Germany in June of 1862. Traveling from London and Paris, she went on to Baden-Baden, Koblenz, and Ems, where for the first time she lay eyes on European royalty when passing Emperor William, who "bows very low to us." In Cologne, she visited the cathedral and bought Eau de Cologne. In Berlin, she feasted on concerts and operas, then roamed three cemeteries in search of Felix Mendelssohn's grave. Eventually, she won an audition with a renowned professor of singing, Ferdinand Sieber, who encouraged her to stay in Berlin. In Potsdam, she visited "many palaces," then sailed down the river Elbe to Dresden, where she called on Marie Wieck and her father Friedrich, the teacher of Robert Schumann and von Bülow. From Dresden, she traveled to Prague and Vienna to visit the graves of Beethoven, Mozart, and Schubert before her trip to Italy. Thursby returned to Germany in 1881, now as a renowned singer. She sang before various royalties in Ems, Wiesbaden, Berlin, Leipzig, Cologne, and Vienna, who adored not only her singing but also her particular repertory. In Leipzig she became the first American singer ever to appear in the Gewandhaus.[84]

Along with the prodigies and soloists, swarms of mothers with their daughters in tow took a pilgrimage to the shrines of Berlin, Dresden, Leipzig, and Vienna to have their offspring breathe in music airs and sign up with one of the "masters." Sons typically came on their own. But whether boy or girl, man or woman, American journals minutely reported on their progress abroad, thus bringing a taste of European music education into Victorian American parlors. Essays titled "An American Student in Germany," "A Musical Editor in Europe," "Letter from Leipzig," and "Letter from Germany" became regular features reporting on the success (much less than on the failure) of American students at German conservatories. In Leipzig, "Kelly of Providence, and Wilson of Springfield are devoting themselves mainly to composition and the organ," stated a letter to *Dwight's Journal of Music* in 1855. "Pratt of Boston devotes himself to the cultivation of his fine barytone [*sic*] voice." In 1874, the journal portrayed by name over thirty-four American vocal soloists who were currently studying, making their debut, "making a reputation," causing "a rage," and "creating a sensation" in one or another music centers of Europe.[85]

And once American artists became recognized in Germany, commentators in the United States enthusiastically listed their achievements.

"Theodore H. Harrison, a Philadelphia baritone, has been accorded unqualified success as an opera singer and recitalist in Germany," announced the *Philadelphia Ledger* on 25 November 1911. Harrison had given his debut as Tonio in *Pagliacci* at the Munich Hof Theatre before singing in recitals and symphony concerts in Frankfurt, Godesberg, Leipzig, Cologne, Heidelberg, Amsterdam, and elsewhere. "It is gratifying," the *Ledger* concluded, "that Philadelphia can produce singers who rank with the artists of the world."[86]

The Grand Emotion and its dissemination among American believers comprised to no small degree a myth, a vision, and the will to obtain purification through distance, travel, and dedication. In reality, few of these continental tours met with unreserved success. Faced with financial problems, musical excursions often assumed catastrophic dimensions when the entire family went broke with no good teacher, let alone engagement, in sight. In 1874, an American church vocalist was told that if she went to Europe to study for only six months, she would return a superstar of the caliber of an Adelina Patti and never lack for engagements. The young woman then attempted a career as an opera singer in Italy, but instead of achieving success she suffered the hostility of local audiences, spent a fortune on room and board as well as music and language lessons, and was not even paid for her first engagement.[87]

Expectation and reality also differed when it came to the quality of European instructors. When Frank Damrosch visited Germany in 1903, he was deeply disappointed by the grand conservatories. German music teachers, he observed, were little motivated, and uncooperative, and once they retired, often living in poverty. In Leipzig, he found that Arthur Nikisch spent so much time on tour and with his orchestra that his conservatory students barely knew what he looked like. Moreover, those teachers who were present had never even made an effort to develop a curriculum. At Berlin's Hochschule für Musik, Damrosch met Joseph Joachim, a great musician but also a completely disorganized man. "We spread a rich table," Joachim remarked laconically. "Those who want to eat may do so." In Vienna, Damrosch visited the world-renowned conservatory, where he was likewise unimpressed by the complete lack of organization and cooperation. Nonetheless, when later looking for teachers for staffing a music school in New York City, Damrosch and his supporters went directly to Berlin, because, he reasoned, "it was at that time the center of musical life in Europe."[88]

Why did Americans convert wholeheartedly to nineteenth-century "German music"? What constituted the power of music? Americans, like people elsewhere, regarded German music as a universal heritage, on both the musical as well as the spiritual level, that could, however, be properly reproduced only by total immersion in the land of music and magic. This universalism consisted of several elements: first, German music embodied all art forms music had produced over the centuries, ranging from choral works to *Lieder*, operas, and chamber music to symphonies. Second, as Wilhelm von Humboldt explained, the canon embodied a set of humanist values: open-mindedness, a free spirit, and a way of life unconstrained by geographical or intellectual preconditions. Third and most important, while music meant different things to different people, all agreed that it constituted the language of emotions and could serve as a remedy for social and physical ills as well as a tool of international communication that would transcend language barriers.

This enthusiasm swept across all of Europe and the United States in the second half of the nineteenth century. Philosophical theories and scientific experiments such as the one involving the wounded boy from Savoy yielded perplexing and promising results. But what remained peculiar to the American perspective was a complete lack of self-confidence vis-à-vis the international music scene; music had to be imported from abroad, preferably from Germany. As a result, for decades the transatlantic music circuit flourished on both the educational as well as the creative level, bringing American students to Germany and, as we shall see, German artists to the United States.

# THREE

# The Houseguests: Rooted Cosmopolitans

Der feller vot schtands on the blatfrom dair
Unt fools der barber by vearing long hair
Unt shakes a schtick all round in der air
    Dot is der leader. . . .
Der feller pehind him mit der push and pule
Mit a pair of lungs yust like a mule
Unt tries to break it, dot awfull old fool
    Dot iss der brombone blayer.
Der feller vot sits, on his face a schmile
Unt tries to blay mit whole lots of schtyle
But gets a blue note in once a vile
    Dot iss der concertmeister. . . .
Der feller vot makes all the funny noise
Unt blays on der rattles und baby toys
Wot blease all der little girls and boys
    Dot iss der drummer. . . .
Unt ven all dose feller blays togedder
Dot sounds yust like a dunderwetter
Earmuffs zou need for such a cladder
Else giffs it a headache altogedder,
    Dot iss der Orchester.[1]

The archives of the St. Louis Philharmonic Society remain silent on the identity of the author of this poem, composed in the late nineteenth century. But there is little doubt as to our poet's intent: to mock the preponderance of German speakers among the members of the symphony orchestra, and their chronic resistance and even inability to speak English;

6    Theodore Thomas and the Chicago Orchestra (later renamed Chicago Symphony
     Orchestra) onstage at the Auditorium Theatre in November 1897. Courtesy of Rosenthal
     Archives, Chicago Symphony Orchestra.

the borderline between the serious and the elevated nature of orchestral
music ("Unt tries to blay mit whole lots of schtyle"); and, simultaneously,
the humorous aspect of the performance ("Earmuffs zou need for such a
cladder").

Clearly, the composers, conductors, and musicians who introduced
serious music to American audiences provided ample ground for humor.
But that was not the end of it. When our unknown poet rhymed, "Unt
ven all dose feller blays togedder / Dot sounds yust like a dunderwetter,"
he not only ridiculed loud music but invoked a political message as well:
exhibiting a form of soft nationalism or, in the words of the philosopher
Kwame Anthony Appiah, "rooted cosmopolitanism," the mission and
dedication to their work that these men shared were defined by their
cultural and national background, not their geographical birthplace. To
them, there was no contradiction between having roots in a specific history while at the same time declaring themselves citizens of the world.
They had no trouble pledging political allegiance to one country (often
the United States) while still perceiving themselves as within a framework of universal values and identities.[2]

And there is something more at play in this poem. Its mocking tone
and fake dialect reflect a theme that runs through the archived files of
orchestra trustees, the pages of music journals, and the program reviews
of the most renowned music critics: Americans expected their musicians
in general and their conductors in particular to be—or at least pretend

to be—both German and universal. *German* was the key word, but it had very little to do with the political borders of the Germans states or the German Empire. "German-ness" encompassed German-speaking areas and occasionally even those where German was not the primary language. It comprised a vague pan-German ethnic and cultural identity that transcended the lack of political unity as well as territorial distinctions such as Austrian and Bohemian. German-ness manifested itself in various and often competing elements, including eating habits, comportment, dress, birthplace, political views, and specific character traits such as sternness, repression, and domination. In short, the stereotypical German became a genuinely American invention.

The invented "German" musican was different from any other cultural and national group, because he combined two characteristics—masculinity and public emotions—that were otherwise incompatible in Victorian America: emotions were typically associated with femininity and childhood. The German symphony, however, reflected both feelings and military precision. National characteristics bypassed gender restrictions as the public expression of emotion, tied to German universalism and the music of the Romantics, became socially acceptable to Victorian men and women.

––––––

The expansion of the classical music life in the antebellum United States owed much to touring virtuosos, although most of their names have been forgotten. European artists began to visit as early as the 1820s, and their trips multiplied in the decades that followed, facilitated by new modes of transportation, new roads, and an increased audience interest in virtuosic performance. As Katherine Preston has shown, traveling opera companies, particularly those from England and Italy, counted among the most popular forms of entertainment into the 1860s.[3]

One of the first central European orchestras that toured the United States performing "serious" music and has left us significant documentary evidence was the Germania Musical Society. Founded in early 1848 in Berlin by a group of twenty-four men, it strove to establish an association outside the existing patronage system, and was designed to bring music to audiences outside Europe. The Germania was only one of several German-speaking orchestras that landed on the North American shore in the aftermath of the German Revolution, but it was the most successful group of its kind. In Boston alone, its subscription lists were supposedly twenty feet long; in the six years between 1848 and 1854, it gave over nine hundred concerts in the United States, many to audiences exceeding three thousand. The group's unique success provides us with a close-up view of the initial stage of German musical migration.[4]

The discernible motives behind the Germania's decision to leave the European continent vary. On the one hand, its organizers were very political: they clearly shared a Utopian vision of an independent communitarian musical association and were dedicated to the ideal of self-determination. Under the motto "all for one and one for all; equality in rights and duties," individual members were required to yield to the community's interest. Moreover, at least two, possibly three members—Carl Bergmann, Carl Zerrahn (both of whom assumed conducting posts), and Frédéric Ritter—had been involved in the German Revolution. On the other hand, they were driven by an almost missionary zeal to travel to the United States "in order to enflame and stimulate in the hearts of these politically free people, through numerous performances of our greatest instrumental composers . . . the love for the fine art of music."[5]

On May 4, 1848, the Germania played a farewell concert to Berliners. It left Europe via London and arrived in New York City on September 28. Mediocre incomes notwithstanding, the group enjoyed a warm welcome in most cities. Summers were often passed at seashore resorts, while the consert season was typically dedicated to urban music life, especially in Baltimore and Boston. In 1849, the orchestra experienced one of the highlights of its career by playing at the inauguration of President Zachary Taylor. For six years, the group toured the East Coast, with additional shows in the Midwest. Its repertory, often accompanied by famous touring artists such as Jenny Lind or Alfred Jaëll, consisted of European orchestral music, a potpourri that eventually included Wagner, Brahms, and Beethoven along with waltzes, lighter overtures, and pieces composed by orchestra members.[6]

The Germania Musical Society managed to remain together for over six years, a record at that time. But the very freedom of the market-oriented society that had attracted European musicians to the United States was also what typically tore them apart quickly. German singing societies, choruses, and orchestras had already established a favorable artistic reputation, but they were also notorious for speedy breakups and frequent infighting before the Germania arrived on the scene. It was the Germania's personification of political unity that impressed audiences between the Atlantic coast and the Mississippi River. As *Dwight's Journal of Music* informed its readers in July of 1853, "*Three and twenty Germans, who for five years now in this 'free' land have kept together faithful and united,—that is indeed a rarity, deserving to be held up as an example* to be imitated,—a phenomenon which shows us in a refreshing manner what Germans *could* accomplish here in every respect, *if* they would only remain faithful and united."[7]

In today's terms, then, the Germania was a boy band, replete with solidarity, friendship, and sex appeal. "There was a romantic flavor in the mutual devotion of the Germanians," John Sullivan Dwight later remembered. "They were young men, friends, who had been drawn together. . . . It was the fraternal spirit of their union, with their self-sacrificing zeal for art . . . it was this 'art religion,' so to speak that gave them an immense advantage over all the larger orchestras in every city."[8] The group disbanded in 1854 on friendly terms, and all of its members opted to remain in the United States, where they joined newly founded orchestras, music departments, and choral groups.

The story of the Germania Musical Society foreshadows the artistic, social, and political success of classical music and its performers in the United States. The political unity, the sense of mission, the clarity of voice, the fraternal spirit, and the solidarity of the mostly young, unmarried male musicians, along with their mastery of an art that in those days could not be reproduced outside the performance hall, all increased the tremendous appeal of German orchestras. Later conductors and musicians would build upon the Germania's reputation, thereby establishing orchestral music as an essentially German experience.

The Germania Musical Society was perhaps the first permanent, professional ensemble to realize the power of symphonic music in the United States as performed by trained musicians. Both as a musical entity as well as one composed entirely of men, the symphony orchestra personified taste, orchestral power, and the spirit of universalism. It represented an ideal microcosm of society, complete with a clear hierarchical structure that assigned a place, a function, and, quite literally, a voice to each member. It represented a democratic range of voices while similarly uplifting all of society. As the *New York American* conceded, "the symphony is a much higher form of art [than opera]. . . . The culture of the nation which loves symphony is surely deeper, though it may not be more lustrous, than that of the nation which swears first and last by opera."[9]

There is no doubt that the Germania's success had a profound impact on artists in Europe and audiences in the United States. The tremendous but short-lived success of this ensemble on the one hand, and the lack of unity and longevity coupled with the profit-oriented interests among self-organized orchestras on the other, triggered two developments: first, during the following decades, more and more Germans felt inspired to come to the United States and educate American audiences, as we shall see in this chapter. Second, more and more Americans wanted symphonic music, ideally presented by German male musicians; and as we shall find out in chapter 4, they began to form civil movements for subsidized concerts and symphony orchestras all across the United States.

———

Orchestral musicians are difficult subjects for historical investigation. They typically do not take to the pen to express their thoughts or feelings. Rather, they expose their inner selves in the music they perform. At the same time, their apparent remoteness, the inaccessibility of their world in words, and the presumably elevated aura of their profession have rendered their image strangely aloof.

Nowhere is this more obvious than in the image of the conductor. His position in the orchestra is a relatively recent one, at least in the way that we know it today, where he (or she) is expected to interpret and synthesize a composition. Until the early nineteenth century, the primary occupation of a conductor was to mark time and rhythm. Often the composer and the conductor were one and the same person, and an orchestra would typically number 15 to 20 men (Bach's Leipzig orchestra counted 18). By the end of Beethoven's life, however, this number had at least tripled, and had been subdivided into sections of instruments we typically ascribe to a modern symphony: strings, woodwinds, brass, percussion. And as orchestras grew in size and the music they performed increased in complexity, the modern conductor appeared. For it was his job, and his only job, to bring order to the chaos of sound.[10] When Boston's Wilhelm Gericke (1845–1925) was still a beginner, he recalled, "people [the audience] simply looked over or to one side of the conductor's head, and to call a conductor upon the stage was unheard of."[11] In contrast, at the height of his career Gericke had become the star of the orchestra.

Today, conductors are often glamorous personalities. In music circles, their celebrity is on a par with that of movie stars. Their dedication to the art of emotion and their prominent position in their musical organization make them obvious targets for international rumor and gossip columns. They seem to have access to the goblet of eternity and divinity; critics and musicians often invoke "this magic thing" when characterizing the conductor's power. Some of the best orchestras in the world have been rumored to be "unconductable," because the musicians' egos were too strong for an average conductor to bend—but enter a Leonard Bernstein, and they melt away. Then as now, without a word or even a gesture, men like Arturo Toscanini and Leopold Stokowski injected a chemistry into an orchestra and its work that inspired players and public alike. These conductors have become as famous as latter-day pop stars; indeed, they are the outgrowth of an age dedicated to the cult of idolization. As a result, to this day conductors enjoy a prestige and an invulnerability surpassing that of any other professional group. Their often irate and irrational behavior is duly accepted by critics and the public alike, and their errors and shortcomings deliberately overlooked until decades after their deaths.[12]

It is often hard to see the person behind the cliché, and the story becomes even more complex when we try to come to grips with the biographies and motivations of nineteenth-century musical leaders. First-generation musicians came to the United States for many complicated reasons. Some stayed permanently, whereas many others did not. Their position in the United States often remained tenuous, and their German heritage tempered by American assimilation. Nearly all of them maintained extensive cultural contact with Germany, the Austro-Hungarian Empire, and Switzerland, and many never even bothered to integrate themselves into the bilingual German-American ethnic enclaves. As a result, artists who stayed in the United States for long periods of their lives nurtured an identity that was much more divided, much more torn, and much more "Old World" than most of their fellow German Americans.

Unlike regular Americans of German ancestry, the musicians defined themselves, above all, through serious music, and they exhibited an almost missionary impulse to import it to their New World audiences. German music as an art form, Celia Applegate has recently argued, had developed into a direct expression of German national character in the early nineteenth century. To perform music onstage, then, was to perform the nation. This does not mean that musical artists drew their legitimacy from German unification or that their original mission was to build and expand abroad the political influence of the German states or the Reich. To the contrary, the German artists' national self-perception was principally cultural, politically vague, and highly heterogeneous, and it primarily served as a "cognitive model," an instrument to situate themselves in a pluralistic environment and seek international recognition. When they expressed their desire to bring serious music and German Kultur to the United States, they aimed for universality, not exclusion.[13]

Take the cases of Anton Seidl and Theodore Thomas. Both men reflect the rooted cosmopolitanism exhibited by so many foreign artists in the United States. Nonetheless, to this day American critics and music historians in search of transformed cultural heroes have labeled them "Americanized" or "deracinated." Born in Budapest in 1850, Seidl studied piano and composition at the Leipzig Conservatory before moving in with the Wagner family in Bayreuth. Richard Wagner, who originally needed just an assistant, became a father figure for the twenty-year-old man.[14] Seidl's interest in the United States was most likely inspired by Wagner, who toward the end of his life contemplated packing up the Bayreuth Festspiele lock, stock, and barrel and migrating to Minnesota. Like Wagner, Seidl dreamed about going to the United States and was certain that his work would find fertile ground there. The Seidls were in luck when Mrs. Seidl, an accomplished singer who toured with her husband's company, received an offer from Leopold Damrosch at the New York Metropolitan Opera. She accepted it on the premise that it would enable her husband to take a good look at his dreamland. When Damrosch died unexpectedly, Seidl succeeded him at the age of thirty-five.[15]

Seidl became a confirmed admirer of the American landscape, as well as the politics and freedom enjoyed there. He eventually assumed U.S. citizenship, bought a summer home in the Catskills, and tried to learn some English. On the musical level, he developed an interest in American composers and frequently played the music of George Chadwick, Arthur Foote, and George Templeton Strong. Inspired by American Indian mythology and Wagnerian music theory, he also began to compose an opera.

And yet throughout his life, Seidl sought to uphold his Germanness to such an extent that the *Staats-Zeitung* called him a quintessential example of *"Ur-Germanisch* liveliness and outwardness." He spoke German with his wife, his friends, and his orchestra. He never quite mastered English and retained a heavy trademark accent, similar to so many German artists in the United States. For example, Seidl pronounced *crime* like "cream," making some of his players believe that he was complimenting them on their performance—"This is a cream"—when actually he was fuming. He loved German food along with German *Gemütlichkeit,* and frequented German *Gasthäuser* such as New York City's Fleischmann's, at Broadway and Tenth. Even his manner reflected his background. Exceedingly handsome with wavy hair and deep black eyes, it took him longer than others to make friends. He never became an American-style businessman, never liked small talk. His home on East Sixty-second Street was filled with portraits and pictures of Wagner, Bach, Beethoven, and Bismarck. A lover of dogs, Seidl owned several dachshunds and one St. Bernard with names drawn from Wagnerian operas: Wotan, Mime, Freia, and Erda.[16] Seidl insisted on his German cultural ways despite his enthusiasm for the United States.

Theodore Thomas is another example of the rooted cosmopolitanism characterizing many German artists in the United States. Of all the conductors on the American scene, Thomas is the one contemporaries and musicologists most readily declare to be a product of the United States. "Thomas came to this country from Germany when he was ten years old," explains one music historian, "thus his adult musical career can be classed as American."[17] He "married an American and eventually turned his back on his German American [*sic*] beginnings," writes the eminent music critic and historian Joseph Horowitz. Theodore Thomas, concludes Harold Schonberg, "can thus legitimately be called an American product."[18]

Yet Thomas's biography is more complex: undoubtedly, he remains the most important influence in symphonic development in the nineteenth-century United States. Son of an East Frisian *Stadtpfeifer* (town musician), he had emigrated to the United States in the 1830s, then made him-

7  Theodore Thomas from Esens, East Frisia, became the first and foremost transatlantic pioneer of classical music and was a cosmopolitan conductor par excellence. Ever in touch with the European music scene, he corresponded—typically in German—with the leading music artists of his time, including Richard Strauss, Max Bendix, Jean Sibelius, Joseph Joachim, Edvard Grieg, Ferruccio Busoni, Camille Saint-Saëns, Alberto Franchetti, Antonin Dvorak, and Ignaz Paderewski. From *Music* 1, no. 3 (January 1892), front matter.

**8** Before picking up the conductor's baton, as a young man Thomas toured with the Mason and Thomas Quartette. Thomas, already sporting his trademark moustache, is the second from the right. Note the writing: "Ein Märchen aus alten Zeiten"—"a fairy tale of old times." Photograph taken in 1856. From *Music* 2, no. 1 (May 1892), between pp. 50 and 51.

self a name as a first-class violinist before picking up the conductor's baton in the 1860s. From then on, Thomas and his self-supporting orchestra toured the American landscape constantly, playing to audiences along what came to be known as the Thomas Highway throughout the Midwest, the plains, and the Rockies. "This is precisely how Theodore Thomas performed his greatest service to America in general," writes one music historian. "He created a desire for symphonic music" and thus became "the Father of the American Symphony Orchestra."[19] In 1891, he founded and then directed what became the Chicago Symphony Orchestra. While there, he became convinced that the music world was at the threshold of something new and great, and he sought to prepare both the city and his orchestra for this development.[20]

Very little is known about Thomas's political inclinations. He loved Germany and the German people "of the days gone by," but he also hated the Prussians, derided officers as "Prussian bullies," and ridiculed the military as walking in "that abominable goose-step." When learning that a German civil court had acquitted an officer who had killed a private for a minor reason, Thomas exclaimed: "Mere brutes! It almost makes me sorry that I am a German."[21]

Culturally speaking, however, Thomas remained a German at heart, and critics have readily belabored this fact, though not always in a benevolent manner. Thomas, Ezra Schabas complained in the 1980s, presented himself as "the standard-bearer of the German connection, a symbol of the artificiality and hypocrisy of the times."[22] Thomas was fond of German poetry and romanticism, and he dedicated his life to the promotion of central European music. He was one of the first to open up the German-American orchestra circuit when he went to Europe in 1883 to hire new soloists. He hated popular music, and his condescending opinions on ragtime have been cited over and over again. "Felsengarten" (rock garden) was the name of his summer refuge in New Hampshire, where he rested, gardened, and biked around the countryside, while "Nudeln und Strudeln" (pasta and cake) counted among his favorite culinary dishes. Most important, Thomas was keenly interested in William Vocke, a candidate for Congress from Illinois' Fourth District who hailed the German element in the United States, the German fatherland, and the significance of German *Lieder* as an expression of German *Heimat* (homeland).[23]

Thomas also continued to communicate in German with friends and associates who spoke the language. Ever in touch with the European music scene, he corresponded—typically in German—with the leading artists of his time, including Richard Strauss, Max Bendix, Jean Sibelius, Joseph Joachim, Edvard Grieg, Ferruccio Busoni, Camille Saint-Saëns, Alberto Franchetti, Antonin Dvorak, and Ignaz Paderewski, to request compositions from them or to invite them to music festivals in the United States. Indeed, the list of his correspondents reads like a *Who's Who* of late nineteenth-century composers: Franz Liszt thanked him for bringing his works to the United States, alerting him to specific music instructions for the performance of each piece. Peter Tchaikovsky politely declined an invitation to the 1876 World Exhibition in Philadelphia. Richard Wagner acknowledged the receipt of a donation of $1,000 raised by Thomas for the first operas at Bayreuth. Hans von Bülow and Thomas shared a profound disdain for the "gymnastics of taming a diva."[24] Like Seidl, Thomas retained a cosmopolitan rootedness that allowed him to merge cultural affinities and political preferences.

Artists who appeared to be undoubtedly German could afford to support the "American way of life." Frederick Stock, born in Jülich in 1872, shed his political loyalty in favor of his adopted country. While a student at the Cologne Conservatory, Stock was a profoundly political man and a member of the liberal Deutsch-Freisinnigen Party. When Theodore Thomas offered him an engagement as a member of the viola section of the Chicago Orchestra, Stock boarded the *Patria* and sailed for the United States in 1895. With his huge, clear-blue eyes and blond hair, the twenty-two-year-old did not go unnoticed by the other passengers. During the voyage, he fell in love with a girl from the German town of Fulda, and the two got engaged before the ship anchored at the Port of New York. When Thomas died, Stock succeeded him, in early 1905. He conducted the orchestra (renamed Chicago Symphony Orchestra in 1913) for nearly forty years and became a fixture of the institution.

Even though Stock became one of the most patriotic conductors, he remained culturally a German at heart and never pretended otherwise. He reportedly read the Psalms in German every morning before breakfast. The Stocks regularly visited Europe during the summers for leisure, recuperation, and professional reasons, and Frederick Stock occasionally conducted European orchestras. In 1912, he conducted the Berlin Philharmonic in an all-Stock program. The letters he composed to his daughter, Vera, during these trips were written bilingually, and he always signed them "Father—Vater." Stock's humorous misuse of words became legendary, he never lost his German accent, and, when rushed, would pronounce "th" as "t."[25]

Three motivations drew foreign conductors, composers, soloists, and ordinary musicians to the United States: there were, of course, the enthusiasm of most American audiences and the lucrative fees offered by American managers. Yet the foremost reason driving these men and women, notably the conductors, was the opportunity to carry out a mission to spread culture (notably music) from the German states around the world. Nikolaus Lenau's 1833 observation, that the United States was a land without nightingales suffering from a poetic curse, only told half the story. While Lenau opted to return to Germany after less than a year, two generations later many German artists came to the United States with the express intention of lifting that curse. "Rest assured that we are only writing this letter because we wish to help your enterprise with all our might and to lend that brilliance to German art in America which it deserves," Emil Scaria, a Vienna bass-baritone, wrote to Theodore Thomas before an American tour.[26]

Thomas himself was the foremost champion of the musical gospel, so it is hard to overestimate the influence this man has had on American symphonic culture. To his contemporaries, he was not only a great

# Chicago Symphony

9 "Chicago Symphony—Dr. Frederick Stock," cartoon, *Chicago Herald-American*, October 21, 1942; PR conductors, F. Stock, Rosenthal Archives, Chicago Symphony Orchestra. Courtesy of the Rosenthal Archives, Chicago Symphony Orchestra.

conductor, a director of musicians, but a "born leader among men," a Moses who led Americans through the unmusical Red Sea, "a man to whom it had been given to deliver a great message."[27] According to Thomas's vision, once common people had learned to respect and listen to good music, the world would be a better place. In his opinion, the United States was a country lacking beautiful and elevating recreation, which was prerequisite to the foundation of a morally superior society. "We are not through with Germany yet, politically or musically," he stated in an interview with the *New York Press* in March of 1898. Music thrived in Germany due to the country's peculiar history, traditions, power, and even geographical conditions, all of which the United States lacked. The surest way to implement musical culture in the United States, Thomas concluded, was by imposing German culture on Americans. This mission, he felt, "is of such importance to me that if we had <u>statesmen</u> in the country I should plead to them + try to make them understand it."[28]

Thomas's own sacrifices made him look like a prophet. "I have gone without food longer than I should. I have walked when I could not afford to ride. I have even played when my hands were cold. But I shall succeed, for I shall never give up my belief that at last the people will come to me and my concerts will be crowded." Worn out, tired, and depressed, he contemplated suicide at the age of fifty-three, his dream of a permanent orchestra still unrealized. When in 1889 the Chicago businessman Charles Fay asked Thomas, over lunch at New York's Delmonico's, whether he would consider coming to Chicago if the city gave him a permanent orchestra, Thomas's rapid-fire response was, "I would go to hell if they gave me a permanent orchestra."[29] His concerts were "sermons in tones," and he held himself responsible for deciding what was best and what was not, declaring, "I have been compelled by truth, without which the whole world would have been worthless." His death in 1905 was regarded as a national calamity, and cables from overseas bore witness to his international reputation. "It is hard to assess the debt that this country owes to Theodore Thomas," wrote the *New York Times*. "It is the debt of a people led out of a wilderness to the prophet who has shown them a sight of the promised land."[30]

Musical artists but also intellectuals of all fields, both in and outside the United States, shared the evangelism propagated by Thomas. Karl Muck's goal in Boston, recorded the *Berliner Börsen-Courier*, was to create traditions in the New World, and to defend German music against the encroachment of the French school.[31] In Cincinnati, Ernst Kunwald announced upon his arrival in 1912 that the United States needed one thousand orchestras in order to appreciate good music. "For that alone is it, that attracts me to come there, namely to bring our rich treasures of our great masters there to the world of the future and help them conquer the world," exclaimed the thirty-two-year-old Felix (alias Fritz) Volbach, who had been born in the Rhineland, trained in Cologne, and was serving as director of the Mainz Liedertafel when in 1894 he applied for conductorship of the Cincinnati Symphony Orchestra.[32] Anton Seidl continually declared his duty to "popularize good music in the big heart of the American people," and appealed to sponsors of his summer concerts on Brighton Beach that "our missionary work" was worthy of their support. When Seidl died, a speaker at his funeral declared in front of thousands of New Yorkers that "he was a leader perpetual in the everlasting war against evil, selfishness, and lust, his only thought to uplift and ennoble men."[33]

The conductors, soloists, and players were not merely traveling artists but leaders who could appreciate as well as interpret the composers of the new school. Uncompromising in their approach, these men cared little whether American audiences immediately appreciated the sounds of Bach, Beethoven, Brahms, and Wagner. Instead, they understood themselves to be missionaries preaching the gospel among ignorant heathens. "But, Mr. Bergmann," the conductor of the New York Philharmonic was told when selecting a heavy Wagner program for a new concert season, "the people don't like Wagner."—"Den dey must hear him till dey do," Carl Bergmann fired back.[34] When an audience in New York City's Steinway Hall hissed and booed a transcription of one of Liszt's *Mephisto* Waltzes by the Theodore Thomas Orchestra during the 1866–67 season, Conductor Thomas warned listeners: "I will give you five minutes to leave the hall. Then we shall play the waltz from beginning to end. Whoever wishes to listen without making a noise may do so. I ask all others to go out."[35]

American critics often repeated the conductors' evangelical terminology; indeed, they wanted their musical artists to convey a divine message, a mission, and the vision of a better world. According to numerous critics, Gustav Mahler was "a giant soul" transmitting "his own personal message through the medium of Beethoven's inspiration." The *New York Staats-Zeitung* declared in March of 1891 that the German seasons at the New York Metropolitan Opera fulfilled a great "educational mission." When the conductor Leopold Damrosch passed away, a London newspaper observed that he had just been "recognized a prophet in his adopted land."[36]

Damrosch's premature death points to a common characteristic among all conductors: an intense workaholism fueled by a sense of mission to bring the best of music to the United States. Head of the influential Damrosch clan that left its indelible mark in American music history, Leopold Damrosch was obsessed with musical evangelism. When he arrived in New York in 1875, he had already passed the zenith of his life and met the most famous musicians of his time. At the Damrosch residence in Breslau, German books, politics, and music had formed the center of family life. Leading artists such as Hans von Bülow, Clara Schumann, Carl Tausig, Anton Rubinstein, Joseph Joachim, Carl Reinbeck, and Richard Wagner came to dinner, and the Damrosches were proud to be a well-educated German family.[37] In Manhattan, Damrosch formed his own orchestra, the New York Symphony, in 1878, focusing on American premieres. He beat Thomas by six days in premiering Brahms's First Symphony in the United States, then packed his ensemble on a train and toured cities through the Midwest. Completely absorbed by his admiration of Bayreuth, Damrosch devoted much of his orchestra's repertory to Richard Wagner, despite the fact that he had very little experience in conducting opera music.[38] Having conducted fifty-two performances in just twelve weeks, in February 1885 Damrosch collapsed and died from pneumonia. Family members noticed that during his last delirious moments he still conducted his orchestra, calling players by name.[39]

Theodore Thomas likewise pushed himself into the grave. From whistle-stops on tour to grand metropolitan orchestras, he gave several thousand concerts in his lifetime. Well into his sixties, Thomas kept an almost inhuman conducting schedule, leading a permanent orchestra while also going on tour and honoring guest engagements in New York, Milwaukee, Cincinnati, and elsewhere at the expense of his health and his private life. When he learned that his first wife had died, he continued to conduct. When his son Franz was buried, Thomas did not visit the grave but instead conducted Chopin's *Marche Funèbre*, with tears running down his face. Obsessed with his goal of transferring his orchestra to Chicago's brand-new Orchestra Hall, in December of 1904 he was stricken with the influenza that developed into pneumonia. Still, he continued to conduct at fever pitch, instructing the choir, rearranging seating orders, and tirelessly rehearsing his orchestra. After a torturous illness, Thomas died in January 1905.[40]

As servant to his own musical mission, Anton Seidl, too, drove himself to his grave. While the successful conductor of the Met and the New York Philharmonic, offers from Hamburg, Berlin, Munich, Bremen, London, Warsaw, St. Petersburg, Moscow, and Pest piled up on his desk. Resisting the acceptance of any one of these, Seidl increased his concert activities in New York in his hopes of creating a permanently funded orchestra in that city. In the spring of 1898, over one hundred New York socialites pledged more than fifty thousand dollars to jump-start a Seidl Permanent Orchestra. The famous agent Maurice Gray offered a seasonal contract, and Eugene Ysaÿe was enrolled as concertmaster. Seidl would be free to travel to London and Bayreuth while also keeping his engagement at the New York Philharmonic. Yet in the midst of all this excitement, Seidl died from sheer exhaustion at the age of forty-seven; the autopsy report listed gallstone and liver ailments.[41]

Of course, other motivations for migration abounded. European musicians were often flabbergasted by the prestige enjoyed by conductors in the United States. "I am far more a big shot here than in Russia," Peter Tchaikovsky exclaimed shortly after his arrival in New York in April 1891. "Is it not curious!!!" When Brahms heard about Georg Henschel's position in Boston—a conductorship involving no supervision by a committee—he declared, "There's not a *Kapellmeister* on the whole of our continent who would not envy you [for] that!" Despite the presence of humbug, Brahms, like many others, believed European musicians would find musical autonomy in the United States.[42]

Lilli Lehmann, one of the foremost Wagner interpreters, excelled to an extent in the United States that she never had in Berlin, where she had long been relegated to minor operatic roles. Even in Bayreuth in 1876, she had to content herself with portraying a Rhinemaiden, a Valkyrie, and a Forest Bird. Her triumph in Wagnerian roles came in 1885, when she sang the role of Brünnhilde from Wagner's *Der Ring des Nibelungen* in New York, mesmerizing audiences as the incarnation of divine womanhood. Lehmann subsequently bought herself out of her Berlin contract, calculating that her income as a soloist in the United States would well make up for her lost pension. She continued to appear well into her sixties, and at the end of her life she had performed 170 roles in well over 100 operas.[43]

No one exemplified European hopes for American appreciation more than Gustav Mahler. During the ten years of his directorship at the Vienna Opera, he transformed the institution from a dull arena for nineteenth-century performances into a major stage of musical controversy. Nonetheless, appalled by the conservative reviews of his work, some of which contained clearly anti-Semitic elements, Mahler left Vienna in 1907 to join the New York Metropolitan Opera for two seasons before conducting the New York Philharmonic from 1909 to 1911. He hoped that the New World's vision of modernity as well as its heterogeneous makeup would prove to be more receptive to his compositions. "Everything now depends on the New Yorkers' attitude to my work," he wrote in the spring of 1908, filled with hopes for a proper Mahler orchestra. "Since they are completely unprejudiced I hope I shall here find fertile ground for my works and thus a spiritual home, something that, for all the sensationalism, I should never be able to achieve in Europe." Mahler, of course, had deceived himself; audiences wanted to see him conduct Wagner, not his own works. Besides, he felt that administrators were bossing him around.[44]

Money mattered too, of course. As we shall see in the next chapter, in the decades before World War I, Americans began to spend huge amounts on their orchestras. In 1913, the journal *Musical Leader* reported that the fifteen permanent or quasi-permanent symphony orchestras in the United States along with the three opera house orchestras carried annual payrolls exceeding $1 million. At the New York Philharmonic, salaries ranged between $45 and $80 a week, but a particularly successful musician could make up to $3,000 a season. The combined income of the 138 players of the Metropolitan Opera House exceeded $168,000 a season.[45]

Not surprisingly, then, many artists hoped to use the United States as a springboard to an advanced position in their home country. Royal superintendent Count von Hülsen in Berlin called the attraction of the American concert scene—notably the attraction of the American dollar for European artists—a "siren's song."[46]

Yet financial lures and fame were not the principal driving forces behind a musician's decision to come to the United States. Salaries for musical artists varied considerably, depending on the quality and location of the orchestra and the reputation of the candidate. In 1898, the New York Philharmonic offered Emil Paur, then conductor of the Boston Symphony Orchestra, the directorship for its fifty-seventh season, along with a guaranteed annual income of $3,000. In Pittsburgh, Frederic Archer would make $4,000 annually as director of Carnegie Hall and $2,000 as symphony director. By 1910, Frederick Stock in Chicago earned $10,000 per year, Max Fiedler in Boston $18,000, and Gustav Mahler in New York $25,000.[47] Soloists were typically paid by performance. In 1898, the New York Philharmonic offered $500 to the soprano Mme. Johanna Gadski and $400 to the pianist Emil Sauer. Salaries could increase quickly: between 1898 and 1912, the Wagnerian contralto Mme. Ernestine Schumann-Heink's fee rose from $425 to $1,500 per performance.[48] The salary of ordinary orchestral musicians was defined by season or by week, and the frequency of concerts likewise differed from orchestra to orchestra.[49] In the early 1880s, salaries at the Boston Symphony Orchestra ranged from $18 to $100 per week during the concert season. Ten years later, Boston's lead musicians could earn between $2,000 (oboe, bassoon, flute, clarinet) and $7,000 (concertmaster) a year.[50]

Such salaries compared favorably with the pay of musicians in Berlin,[51] who received rather scant remuneration: in the 1890s, a royal chamber musician would make between 2,500 and 2,800 marks per year, while an assistant musician—*Hilfsmusiker*—would earn 1,000 marks (by then, the German mark was valued at 4.20 to the dollar). But American salaries did not entail yearlong engagements, long-term security, pensions, and other benefits along the lines of many German contracts. Nor did musicians, soloists, and conductors in the United States count among the financial elite; and for all the advantages a musician might enjoy, there were also pitfalls. The American public was capricious, and donors' purse strings periodically tight. The uncertainties of a few seasons did not constitute a financially attractive challenge to the certainty of a conductor's prestige and tenure in the Old World. When Karl Muck was music director in Boston, he resided on the Fenway, at the time not the city's most glamorous district, and a bit out of the way for those who cared to mingle with the fashionable circle. Likewise, Frederick Stock lived on Chicago's East End Avenue, not the city's most elegant area. Furthermore, most symphonies continually faced the possibility of dismissal during the following season. "I wish I would get a decent offer from a permanent orchestra which would enable me to work artistically and continuously for the next three years or more," sighed the New York Philharmonic conductor Walter Damrosch, one of the leaders of the American symphony scene, in 1903. "Ours is a restless profession in this american [*sic*] land."[52]

Orchestras with less stable finances could not guarantee their players even a weekly income. Often, they had to perform with an incomplete roster of musicians due to financial problems. During an early performance of the Overture to Wagner's opera *Tannhäuser*, the Minneapolis audience waited in vain for the great clash of cymbals characterizing the section. Having run out of funds, the management had been unable to spare an additional $6 per performance for a percussionist. Frequently, there was not even enough money to subsidize an adequate number of rehearsals; as a result, musicians were often untrained, their performance lacking.[53]

In short, it was not just money and it was not just fame that lured European musicians to the United States and even made them pose as German. It was their common belief in the universalism of music, its national appeal to audiences everywhere, and their self-appointed mission to export this universal language of emotions.

Artists and critics in the German states intended the national tinge of music as a means to expand its appeal to both German and American audiences. We have seen above how the perspectives and aspirations of German musicians like Seidl and Stock reflected the marriage of cultural nationalism and universalism in the nineteenth century. And the strategy worked, not only among audiences in Europe but in the United States, where European musicians were expected to be or at least pretend to be vaguely German.

Since the late nineteenth century, the hiring process for conductors has been one of the great sensations of the international symphony scene. Once men like Hans von Bülow and Arthur Nikisch appeared on the stage, it was not the soloists anymore who made the difference in the sale of seats; it was the conductor.[54] A good orchestra wants to find the best (that is, least expensive yet most famous) conductor, who in turn is permanently on the lookout for the best (that is, best-paying and most prestigious) orchestra. Search committees juggle names, achievements, and recommendations while behind the scenes, agents secretly trade benefits and salaries, make offers and promises.

The most important qualification a conductor had to produce to please prospective American sponsors and audiences was his German pedigree. Of course, there were many non-German conductors in the nineteenth-century United States, such as the sensational Frenchman Louis Antoine Jullien, who brought a European orchestra to the United States in 1853–54 to perform monster concerts reportedly featuring more than fifteen hundred instrumentalists.[55] But as a rule, conductors and guest soloists had to be distinguished, foreign, and expensive.[56] And precisely because of these expectations, most of these artists remained (or became) German at heart in their habits and their speech. Throughout his stint with the Boston Symphony, Austrian-born Wilhelm Gericke read Viennese news-papers at his Brookline home and kept signed photographs of Brahms, Ferruccio Busoni, and Johann Strauss along with a lock of Beethoven's hair among his German memorabilia. Corresponding with the leading artists of his time, including Anton Bruckner, he scheduled predomi-nantly German music from the early nineteenth century for the sym-phony's concerts, plus some works from more recent composers, such as Wagner, Brahms, Liszt, Anton Rubinstein, and his own.[57] In Pittsburgh, Austrian-born Emil Paur talked to all of his musicians in German.[58] Even his looks held the promise of foreignness: reminding some of his con-temporaries of Wagner's Lohengrin, the dreamy-eyed conductor sported a rather long and wavy blond hairdo, a full beard, a long nose, and eyes that promised a twinkle to his conversation partners. He liked to wear a loose and flowing frock coat, and surrounded himself with what some observers called a Teutonic aura.[59]

The American press frequently "Germanized" musical artists to the ex-tent that territorial and political identity simply did not matter anymore.

**10** Born in Schwanberg, Austria, Wilhelm Gericke conducted the Boston Symphony Orchestra between 1884 and 1889 as well as between 1898 and 1906. Henry Higginson selected Gericke as a successor for Georg Henschel while traveling with his wife in Europe, where he attended a performance of *Aida* in Vienna that was led by the conductor. Photographer: Carl Pietzner, ca. 1900. Pres 86.2 f.1, Boston Symphony Orchestra Archives. Courtesy of the Boston Symphony Archives.

*Dwight's Journal of Music* occasionally called Vienna a German city, the Strausses German composers, and Austrians "South Germans." The Riga-born tenor Karl Jorn was presented as "Jorn, the German tenor," whereas the pianist Harold Bauer, who was born in London, was likewise portrayed as "the German." The press consistently referred to the Hungarian pianist and composer Josef Weiss as "Herr Weiss." Carl Halir, a student of Joseph Joachim's in Berlin, found himself labeled "the great German violinist," though one newspaper conceded that he had been born in Bohemia. And the Russian-born pianist Alfred Reisenauer was hailed as "a man of weight, or Teutonic heaviness, and also a player of Beethoven's music."[60]

These profiles allow us a glimpse into what Americans expected from their musical leaders. According to the cliché held by many critics, concert organizers, and the public at large, conductors had to present a German pedigree, and to be German meant to be a rigid taskmaster who drilled both musicians and audiences. They were free to embrace the

United States politically, though this was not a requirement. Preferably, their knowledge of English was scant or nonexistent (a heavy accent was mandatory), and they were expected to possess the aura of a suppressed lover who strangely happened to be leading an orchestra. Sex appeal was key and occasionally enhanced by cold, unsociable behavior. The conductors' sensuality seemed obvious both in their music and in their ravenous appetite for Teutonic food. This combination of characteristics guaranteed a foreignness conveying Old World status and civilization.

Artists who were not German were well advised to pepper their curricula vitae with some German references. Pittsburgh's Irish conductor, Victor Herbert, was constantly on trial as to whether or not he was sufficiently foreign and, therefore, talented. Herbert had moved from Dublin to Stuttgart as a child, then accepted Walter Damrosch's offer of an

11  The Austrian conductor Emil Paur led the Boston Symphony Orchestra from 1893 to 1898. The dreamy-eyed conductor reminded some of his contemporaries of Wagner's Lohengrin, sporting a rather long and wavy blond hairdo, a full beard, and a long nose, and surrounding himself with a "Teutonic" aura. Photographer: Georg Brokesch, Leipzig, ca. 1893. Pres 84.4 f.1, Boston Symphony Orchestra Archives. Courtesy of the Boston Symphony Orchestra Archives.

engagement with the New York Metropolitan Opera in 1886. Still, Herbert always emphasized his Continental education, notably his music study in Germany and his engagement as a violoncellist in the Court Orchestra at Stuttgart, at the expense of his Irish heritage: "I am quite a German in my musical methods, and have a great admiration for their leaders and their great bands."[61] Herbert corresponded in German with other conductors, conducted bilingually, and loved to sprinkle his speech with exclamations like "Viel zu laut" and even entire sentences in German.[62]

Next to heritage, one of the most important items on an artist's résumé was his close liaison with the leading European artists of the time. Not surprisingly, the two most sought-after referees were Franz Liszt and Richard Wagner, followed closely by Johannes Brahms. Nearly every successful musician, pianist, and conductor in the second half of the nineteenth century claimed to have some sort of connection with at least one member of the trio, either by pedigree, training, personal relationship, or just because they had wandered to Weimar, Bayreuth, or Vienna to meet with one of the masters. Anton Seidl was not only Wagner's prodigy but, as rumor had it, also Liszt's illegitimate son.[63] Philadelphia's Carl Pohlig, born at Teplitz, Bohemia, in 1864, the son of a bookseller, had been cordially received by Liszt in Weimar, then accompanied the composer on his journeys to Rome, Budapest, and other cities.[64] The reputation of Boston's first conductor, Georg Henschel, rested primarily on the fact that while in Jena he had befriended Liszt, who then invited him to his famous Sunday matinees in Weimar along with Anton Rubinstein, Hans von Bülow, Carl Tausig, and others.[65] Frank Damrosch, who later became a pioneer in the field of music instruction in American schools, prided himself on being Liszt's godson and sitting on Wagner's knee when he was a boy.[66]

A close acquaintance with European royals further accredited European artists in the United States, and American newspapers loved to report in detail about the decorations, favors, and invitations musicians had received from Europe's crowned heads. Vienna-born Ernst Kunwald had embarked on an international career that took him from Rostock via Essen, Halle, and Madrid's Teatro Real (where he mounted a sensational production of Wagner's four-opera *Ring* cycle) to the Philharmonic Orchestra in Berlin in 1906. The king of Spain conferred on Kunwald the Order of Isabella the Catholic. He was a special favorite of the Prussian crown princess and one of the most popular conductors with the public. Then the conductor Arthur Nikisch urged Cincinnatians to make him an offer, which Kunwald eventually accepted.[67]

These artists clearly responded to the public's need for celebrities, and they cultivated a variety of eccentricities—Teutonic, Austrian-German,

12 The conductor Fritz Scheel from Lübeck, Germany, specialized in military and string concerts. His trademark was pseudomilitary attire that replaced the customary tailcoat with a uniform complete with a short and stiff jacket, shining brass buttons, a tight belt, a helmet, and a pair of light gloves. Courtesy of the Museum of Performance & Design archives, San Francisco.

or simply exotic—that would set them apart from stars of other genres. The conductor Fritz Scheel, for one, specialized in military and string concerts. His trademark was pseudomilitary attire, which replaced the common tails with a uniform complete with a short and stiff jacket, shining brass buttons, a tight belt, and a helmet as well as a pair of light gloves.[68] In 1892, Scheel accepted an assignment to give historic concerts at the Mid-Winter's Fair in Chicago, then took his orchestra to San Francisco. Advertising the ensemble as "Vienna Life! Vienna Dance! Vienna Music!" and himself as "court director," he consistently employed a dramatic backdrop—a large watercolor depiction of the recently completed Vienna Prater—at concerts.[69]

Besides heritage and association, the most important assets of a

13 Fritz Scheel's Orchestra, 1894. Scheel often advertised the ensemble as "Vienna Life! Vienna Dance! Vienna Music!" and himself as "court director." He consistently employed a large watercolor depiction of the recently completed Vienna Prater as a dramatic backdrop for his orchestra. Courtesy of the Museum of Performance & Design archives, San Francisco.

conductor were his physical looks, his elegant style, and his sex appeal, and it is here that Victorian America exposed its starkest ironies. For the expression of emotion remained, officially, the domain of femininity. But with the professionalization of music, the symphony became an almost exclusively all-male institution. Indeed, the symphony orchestra seemed to project collective emotion, organized in a military fashion: draped into uniforms, endowed with military attributes such as "discipline," "drill," and "war," "generals" (conductors) at the top trained a hundred players according to their will. The public expression of emotion, forbidden to American men, had to be paired with what the public perceived as "Teutonic sternness" to be socially acceptable to all of nineteenth-century society. When Max Fiedler from Hamburg accepted the conductorship of the Boston Symphony Orchestra in 1908, newspapers devoted pages and pages to his appearance, notably his power and his charm: "The new leader is a veritable volcano in action, once the concert is on."[70] His high forehead topped by a brush of iron-gray hair, Fiedler's face featured bright bespectacled eyes, a "bristling gray mustache," and a "vigorous chin."[71] Virtually every single one of his movements and gestures was dutifully

## DIRECTOR FIEDLER AT WORK

Air: "Rings on Her Fingers"

Chorus:—

Sing go the cymbals and bang goes the drum—
Scherzo in skirtso, nocturne in Te Deum.
And you'll get a thriller that thrills you through and through—
When Fiedler's fiddlers fiddle a tune that's new to you.

14  The conductor Max Fiedler from Hamburg mesmerized audiences, and reporters called him "a veritable volcano in action, once the concert is on." The *Boston Herald*, 2 April 1910; BSO scrapbooks, MF Pres/13, Boston Symphony Orchestra Archives. Courtesy of the Boston Symphony Orchestra Archives.

recorded by the local press: "He is vigor, he is action, he is inspiration, he is a stimulant and a dominant force."[72]

Temperament represented a primary prerequisite for musicians, because it included the magical ability to live a life dedicated to a world where feelings reigned. Temperament also included the ability to transmit inspiration and feeling to the audience.[73] Here is how the *Philadelphia North American* sketched impressions from a performance featuring Beethoven, Mozart, Schubert, and Wagner by the city's orchestra under Carl Pohlig:

Full and resonant, surging like leaping ocean billows, the wave melodies of a majestic overture swept through the great building. Enthralled the 3000 listened. Like demons possessed of some melodious fury the ninety musicians played. Seemingly lifted above the earth, the creations of the varying melodies filling his vision, the conductor swayed back and forth, his hands moving, his fingers playing invisible keys, his eyes alight, his face varying with changing expression. Upon him the members looked, gripped by the spell, while the audience, too, was caught up with him as in a chariot of lyric ecstasy.[74]

The performance of presumably German artists established German music as the language of emotions, reigning over the hearts of listeners between Boston, Pittsburgh, and San Francisco. It conveyed an emotion, filling audiences with awe for the superiority of not just German art but Germany in general. And it was simply thrilling, because most other emotional expressions in public were taboo for middle-class Americans.

Consequently, individual artists were often ranked not so much in terms of their technical skills or breadth of repertory but their ability to speak the emotional language. The pianist Mark Hambourg was called "the chief exponent of emotionalism in piano playing." Gustav Mahler supposedly rested in the "Elysian fields," gracefully assured of his fame as a composer. But the two greatest champions of emotion, critics agreed, were Richard Wagner and Ludwig van Beethoven. "In Wagner it is the passion, the love, the sorrow of the individual, that fills the heart and mind," exclaimed A. E. Brand in the journal *Music* in 1894. In Beethoven, in contrast, "it is the cry of the pain and longing of the world that seeks an answering note in us."[75]

Conductors in particular were often judged as emotional leaders. The *Boston Advertiser*, for example, observed in March of 1917 that Karl Muck of the Boston Symphony read Haydn in a "masculine fashion." Newspaper editors perpetually commented on Fritz Scheel's emotional power over his players and his audiences, his "personal magnetism," and his "mental influence."[76] The musical blood of Emil Paur, observed Warren Davenport in 1901 in the *Boston Herald*, "was hot to an extreme degree,

15 The Hungarian-born Arthur Nikisch became the poetic conductor of the Boston Symphony Orchestra between 1889 and 1893. Thirty-three years old when he arrived in Boston, Nikisch was a rising star from the Leipzig Opera and strongly influenced by Richard Wagner. As the first modern virtuoso conductor, he possessed a remarkable personal magnetism and created a stir among Boston ladies with his graceful hand poses. Artist, place, date unknown. Pres. 86.3 f4, Boston Symphony Orchestra Archives. Courtesy of the Boston Symphony Orchestra Archives.

and the pendulum of his emotions at times swung to the utmost limit."[77] Arthur Nikisch, the critic Henry Krehbiel noted in 1889, "directs his men, controls and sways them; they are his agents of expression, the vehicles of his emotional proclamation."[78] Such terminology was by no means peculiar to Boston. "The Chicago Orchestra program for this week is not food for babes, nor even for nerveless dilettanti," wrote the *Chicago Journal and Press* in 1895. "It is throughout characterized by virile strength and vigor that is almost war like." On the program was Beethoven's *Eroica* piano concerto, clearly music "to fire a soldier's heart."[79] A New York City newspaper even established a column dedicated to reviews of music, signed by "The Emotionalist."[80]

Critics wanted to see emotion in action, and if they did not get it they were furious. *Dwight's Journal* dismissed a piano recital by Hans von Bülow, because he failed to "convey to us or light in us the flame which warms us up." And if an artist still did not grasp it, critics could even be more direct. "The emotional story of the Beethoven overture was not told," complained Henry Krehbiel in the *New York Tribune* when Max Fiedler and the Boston Symphony Orchestra visited the city. "We wanted more."[81]

Such high expectations required hard work from the conductors, both on their own appearance and on their style, but even more so on their orchestras, and quite a few went down in history as quasi-military drillmasters. Notwithstanding Theodore Thomas's profound disdain of German militarism, the *San Francisco Chronicle* called him a "Prussian General" whose "word is law" when the conductor visited the city during his "Ocean to Ocean Tour" with the New York Philharmonic in 1883.[82] Whether professional or cunning, young or old, renowned or little known, most conductors exhibited an almost dictatorial roughness vis-à-vis their players that corresponded to the image of the conductor as an absolute leader. "Mr. Gericke stands at his music desk like a stern dispenser of allegros, adagios and scherzos," wrote the *Boston Home Journal.* "There is an austere grace about him which bespeaks the natural ruler."[83] San Francisco's Alfred Hertz became famous for his exquisitely "athletic" way of conducting that included flapping his elbow, and thrusting his arm out like a knife while waving his arms around his head.[84] St. Louis's Max Zach typically broke several batons during a single rehearsal.[85]

People like their conductors to fall from the sky, Minneapolis's conductor, Emil Oberhoffer, once observed, so the notion of a "star" seems therefore all the more appropriate. Their Germanness—sometimes real, but more often simply assumed or perceived by American critics and audiences—mattered, it seems, more than anything else. When, in 1893, Hans Richter accepted (and later rejected) an offer from the Boston Symphony, the press rejoiced that "our orchestra again falls into German hands," because "a Frenchman, no matter what his musical abilities, could not have been in full sympathy with the men." The ultimate curiosity of this observation was borne out by the fact that the renowned critic who wrote these words, Louis Elson, labeled Richter "a German," adding only in passing that Richter was by birth a Hungarian: "But his long service in Austria and Germany has so Reutilized him that he may readily be classed with the army of the great German musicians of the present."[86]

When an accomplished artist (notably a concertmaster or string musician) was not German, newspapers pointed this out as a curiosity, hurrying to find evidence for the artist's "German" qualification by either education or affiliation. Next to the German states, Austria (including

Hungary) and occasionally even Switzerland were regular reference points. Critics and typesetters were so uneasy with the term *Austrian* that when mentioning it at all they frequently misspelled it as "Australian" or replaced it with "South German."[87]

In other words, the word *German* reflected not a territorial entity but a universal idea; while the German language counted as geographical fixation, German music did not. The image of the German musician as a gifted and attractive man who knew how to express his feelings became a symbol for Germany's ubiquitous and attractive Kultur. Johann Strauss the elder, wrote Ludwig August Frankl in 1849, was the most popular musician in the world. His waltzes delighted American, Chinese, and African alike. And when his son, Johann, traveled to the United States in 1872, one journalist declared that "the waltz king, personally, is evidently a good fellow. He talks only German, but he smiles in all languages."[88]

Orchestra boards of trustees scrambled to find German conductors for their ensembles, though their craving for foreign talent often blinkered their evaluation of a prospective candidate; indeed, often new conductors had no orchestral conducting experience at all. As soon as Pittsburgh had hired Frederic Archer, there arose doubts as to his conducting skills. Archer, it was said, had engaged soloists who did not display any talent. Those who were good, in turn, had to advise him on conducting. During a concert with the singer Mme. Carrion, the diva had to interrupt her performance several times and give him specific instructions on harmony.[89] At the St. Louis Symphony Orchestra, one of the early conductors was charged with frequently losing his place in the score while his musicians were reading magazines and newspapers during the performance, or wandering around.[90] Similarly, the musical gifts of the Boston Symphony conductor Georg Henschel lay in areas outside conducting. Born in Breslau and trained in Berlin and Leipzig, Henschel excelled in singing, particularly in tandem with his wife. But the critics were unyielding about his poor conducting: he was "rapping too much upon his stand to command silence in the audience and orchestra."[91] As late as 1921, when Swiss-born Rudolph Ganz introduced himself to the St. Louis Symphony Orchestra, he lifted his baton with these words: "Gentlemen, this is an instrument I know nothing about."[92]

These men and women constituted part of that group of international travelers commonly called the in-crowd today. Boston's Arthur Nikisch traveled extensively in Europe as well as in North and South America; he split his time between several orchestras in Germany and annually played with the London Symphony Orchestra.[93] Emil Paur came to the United States in 1893 to conduct the Boston Symphony Orchestra and subsequently

16 Born in Breslau and trained in Berlin and Leipzig, Georg Henschel excelled in singing, particularly in tandem with his American wife, Lillian Bailey, a distinguished concert soprano and formerly Henschel's pupil. Henschel became the first conductor of the Boston Symphony Orchestra (1881–84), based on a single performance he gave for the Harvard Musical Association in March 1881: an overture of his own. Pres. 86.1. f3, Boston Symphony Orchestra Archives. Courtesy of the Boston Symphony Orchestra Archives.

the New York Philharmonic. After the death of his wife, Marie, in New York in 1902, Paur returned to Europe, where he guest conducted larger orchestras in Germany and England. In 1904 he returned to accept a position with the Pittsburgh Orchestra, but again returned to Germany in 1910.[94]

Yet everyone agreed that the center of musical Kultur resided in Europe. In the summer, when the symphony season was over, the movement was eastward. East Coast and midwestern artists boarded Europe-bound steamers while West Coast artists boarded trains headed toward the eastern metropolises. Most conductors and many of the regular orchestral musicians would spend their summers in Europe visiting, seeking inspiration in various music centers, and listening to novel compositions. Henry Hadley, conductor of the San Francisco Symphony Orchestra between 1911 and 1915, went east each summer, even if that meant just New York City or New England. Walter Damrosch would travel to Germany in the summer to work with celebrities like Hans von Bülow, with whom he studied Beethoven's symphonies at the Raff Conservatorium in Frankfurt in 1887. Damrosch also got in touch with Brahms and Liszt in Weimar, and the latter took him to Bayreuth to meet Wagner.[95] Even if they did not wish to go to Europe, there seems to have been an implicit obligation for artists to do so. After having permanently settled in the United States with her eight children, Ernestine Schumann-Heink went to Europe for an entire year to be "cleaned up again" and to refresh her image as a first-class foreign artist.[96]

When conductors, soloists, and musicians returned to the United States in September after a summer in Germany, newspapers would hail their appearance as if they were the most recent contingent of exotic birds arriving at the zoo. Where had they gone, and what had they seen? Who had come back, and what did they bring?[97] Eager reporters awaited the artists at the dock, ready to announce their return from Europe accompanied by trunks and boxes filled with novel scores by European composers: Kultur had returned to the United States.

European composers, too, traveled to the United States, but their role as agents of musical transfer paled in comparison to the conductors. American orchestras tried to invite all of the leading European composers of the day, including Felix Mendelssohn, Richard Wagner, and Franz Liszt,

17 Georg Henschel and the Boston Symphony Orchestra in Boston Music Hall, 1882. This is the first photograph of the orchestra; note the artistic reproduction of the statue of Beethoven and the organ of the Music Hall in the background. Photographer: Notman. Pres 86.1 f3, Boston Symphony Orchestra Archives. Courtesy of the Boston Symphony Orchestra Archives.

but few of them chose to cross the Atlantic Ocean.[98] Efforts to induce Johannes Brahms to travel overseas foundered; Brahms abhorred traveling. Wagner likewise feared the voyage across the ocean.[99] Those who came nevertheless, such as Johann Strauss Jr., or Peter Tchaikovsky, were typically lured by financial offers far beyond anything they had ever earned in Europe.[100] Richard Strauss, *Kapellmeister* of the Royal Opera in Berlin, visited on several occasions, each time to great acclaim.[101] But the composers mattered less to the American music scene than did the performing artists. Most refrained from visiting the United States, and those who did voyage across the Atlantic typically limited their stints to just a few weeks.[102]

Next to the conductors, the soloists were the most important evangelists of serious music, although their motivations often differed sharply from the conductors. Some of the most famous ones were not German and did not pretend to be. The Polish pianist Ignaz Jan Paderewski rose to fame as the biggest piano star in American music history, earning half a million dollars during three tours in 1896 (over $7,000 at a single concert in Chicago, unthinkable in those days).[103]

But if they were not German, musicians had to come with an adventurous story originating in a dark, presumably uncivilized place that eventually climaxed with their arrival in Leipzig or Vienna. Of the young Russian, Mark Hambourg, it was told that his father was "languishing in a Siberian prison for his political opinions." The father was, in fact, an eminent piano teacher, with no political views reported whatsoever. Mark's career took off like a meteor when, at age eleven, he performed pieces by Bach, Chopin, Schumann, and Beethoven in London. Subsequently, he went to Vienna, where he changed his name to Mark Hamburg and studied with Leschetitzky, one of the famous music teachers. Then he began to tour Europe, Australia, Africa, and the United States.[104]

Learning, language, looks—if an artist had at least one, preferably two, or ideally all three of these keys in his hand, he could open the door to fame and wealth in the United States. Anton Rubinstein, for example, was Russian-born, but besides being a German-oriented conservative artist and a frequent visitor to Weimar, his physical features resembled Beethoven's to such an extent that Franz Liszt referred to him as "Van II." Rumor had it that he was the composer's illegitimate child.[105]

Male soloists as a rule had to remain at least unmarried and dashing in order to attract "the fair sex." Few exploited the rhetoric of sexual attraction as did Emil Sauer, born in Hamburg in 1862. Sauer had studied with Nicholas Rubinstein at the Moscow Conservatory for two years, then went on to Liszt. A suave virtuoso, in 1899 Sauer arrived in the United

States, where his unruly hairdo, his elegant attire, and countless love affairs became a central feature in gossip columns. Women sat spellbound
through his concerts, and the critics compared him to a "hypnotist."
Overnight, Sauer became a serious challenge to the seemingly unsur-
passable Ignaz Paderewski. To fire up the press, Sauer furnished reporters
with a wealth of fabulous (and probably fictional) stories relating to his
popularity among the European nobility, including one where "a lady
belonging to the highest aristocratic [circles] was forgetting herself so
far as to fall down on the platform on her knees and to scream out for
a kiss." In another tale, an eccentric Hungarian countess had purchased
all the seats for his concert in Vienna in order to enjoy his performance
by herself.[106]

Coupling the universalism of German music with emotional finesse
and sex appeal, these men (far more than the women) were the nineteenth century's major music stars, similar to Bono and U2 today. There
are, of course, the immortal stories about Franz Liszt, whose concerts
ended typically with shrieking women tossing their jewelry and garments on the stage; but Liszt was no exception. What added to foreign
artists' attraction in the United States was their fleeting promise, their
Europeanness, the briefness of their stay, indeed, the possibility that they
might never return at all. At Anton Rubinstein's last recital in Boston during his tour across the United States in 1872–73, "his very clothes were
rent by enthusiastic admirers in search of souvenirs. Women rushed on
the platform and embraced him, and the entire audience yelled 'Come
back again! Come back again!' "[107] When Mark Hambourg performed with
the Boston Symphony Orchestra at Carnegie Hall in November 1899, he
received nine curtain calls; finally, the stage workers had to remove the
piano from the stage in order to stop the applause. When performing in
the same city at the age of eighteen in 1893, Henri Marteau was reportedly called back to the stage twelve times, and, recorded one local newspaper, "some of the girls threw their corsage postes of violets at the feet
of the violinist."[108]

Female artists, in contrast, were supposed to be pretty, innocent, and
almost asexual. Whereas critics spent more time describing the physical
attributes of male performers, female artists were scrutinized for their
dress. Even the eminent critic Philip Hale, no fan of superficial judg-
ments, dedicated a lengthy paragraph to Ernestine Schumann-Heink's
various outfits during her Boston rehearsal concerts ("a Vienna costume
of pale green, embroidered, muslin, much of the skirt and bodice done
with insertions and runnings of narrow black velvet"), quite at the expense of reviewing her performance.[109]

**18** When Hans von Bülow, one of the most famous German conductors of the nineteenth century, led a rehearsal in Baltimore, he tore down a sign praising Chickering, the piano firm that was sponsoring his visit, tossed it on the floor as if it were a poisonous snake, and called the manufacturer's representative a "jackass." From *Music* 5, no. 6 (April 1894), before p. 633.

In line with the pop cult surrounding artists, concert-hall managers and agents made sure to plaster the market with promising posters and ads to get the most out of a performance. Classical repertories and biographical information on world-class artists were frequently framed by ads ranging from "Friends' Oats" by the Muscatine Oat Meal Company to L. Manasse Optician, "Importer and Manufacturer of Spectacles and Eyeglasses, Telescopes, Magic Lanterns, Thermometers, and Artificial Human Eyes."[110] When Hans von Bülow played at a rehearsal in Baltimore, he tore down a sign praising Chickering, the piano firm that sponsored his visit, tossed it on the floor as if it were a poisonous snake, and called the manufacturer's representative a "jackass." "Good God, the method they have here of turning people into celebrities makes one's heart sink into one's boots," wrote Ferruccio Busoni in 1910 while on tour in the United States.[111] What upset artists like von Bülow, Busoni, and others so tremendously was their profound discomfort at being in a situation that featured them not as cultural ambassadors but as consumer goods.

To their understanding, an artist was "not the slave but the leader of a people."[112]

———

Even though the composition of American orchestras revealed a highly international makeup, until the eve of World War I audiences perceived them as an essentially German institution, filled with German musicians who conversed in German during rehearsals and performed German music. As stated earlier, such perceptions were not entirely correct: the Minneapolis Symphony Orchestra was composed of at least thirteen nationalities, though the orchestra's historian notes that "the musicians were a homogeneous group, being mostly Germanic or German-trained." Under Wilhelm Gericke, the Boston Symphony Orchestra counted twelve nationalities, among those Germans, by far the largest group, but also French, Austrian, Hungarian, Polish, English, Dutch, Italian, Russian, Bohemian, Belgian, and American. Nonetheless, the American pianist Louis Gottschalk insisted in 1863 that "all the musicians in the United States are German."[113]

The fact remains, however, that the majority of players were Germans who had decided to perform in the United States for monetary but also idealistic reasons, as we shall see later.[114] The database of the Chicago Symphony Orchestra lists at least sixty players before World War I whose papers (citizenship records, birth certificates, newspaper clippings) prove that they were first-generation Germans. Many were directly hired for the CSO in Germany, while others had come over to play initially with a different orchestra. Most never mastered the English language, never acquired U.S. citizenship, and eventually went back to Europe.[115] The roster listing the original musicians in the traveling ensemble of the Theodore Thomas Orchestra reveals that most had been trained by famous European teachers and performed in great orchestras. Ludwig Corelli had received his music education in Munich. The cellist Bruno Steindel from Zwickau had played for the Berlin Philharmonic under Hans von Bülow, as well as under Brahms, Strauss, and Rubinstein. Carl Meyer, clarinet and bass clarinet, had played in the Berlin Bilse Orchestra and at the Prussian Royal Opera House. Theodor Seydel had studied with Friedrich Ehrman at the Leizpig Conservatory and played with the Gewandhaus Orchestra. Walter Unger had been cellist at the Royal Opera House in Dresden. Joseph Zettelmann, timpanist, had played at the court opera house in Mannheim, under Emil Paur.[116]

In a manner similar to the conductors and the soloists, orchestral musicians became the nineteenth century's boy bands in their own right. Elegantly dressed in evening fashion, their attire often competed with that worn by the men in the audience. The description of their physical attributes could take up entire paragraphs of concert reviews. Cellist Friedrich Voelker from Mainz, observed a Pittsburgh newspaper, "is of rather striking appearance. He is of medium height, with long, waving brown hair brushed carelessly back from the temples, and with a very intellectual face."[117] In 1898, one observer suggested that members of the Pittsburgh Orchestra dress up in military garments in order to avoid confusion with the dress circle.

Newspaper accounts of the eccentric behavior, love affairs, adultery, tragedy, and suicide attempts of the men who gave their hearts to the public each week endeared them to readers all across the United States, including those who never went to the symphony. The Boston violinist Willy Hess's wife had died of cerebral paralysis while sojourning at Wiesbaden. The flutist Maquarre of Boston had eloped with the wife of one of the oboists to San Francisco, where the renegades opened a millinery establishment. Pittsburgh's first cellist, Henri Merck, attempted to commit suicide in 1904, because a soprano soloist "had ignored the 'cellist's advances and he was depressed by her inattention to his overtures." And Copenhagen-born and Leipzig-trained Henry Bramsen, first cellist of the Pittsburgh Orchestra in 1906, found himself besieged by reporters from New York City and Chicago bent on finding out why his wife had appeared "with her carefully-cared-for feet encased in primitive sandals and devoid of hosiery."[118]

The star cult amplified the evangelism of German conductors and musicians, as did the thousands of tours orchestras undertook to the most remote corners of the nation with no financial profit in sight in the decades prior to World War I. "Going on tour" represented an important part of an orchestra's annual range of activities, and it reflected the obstacles musicians had to confront when bringing classical music to the hinterland. Touring ensembles had been the earliest form of symphonic performance before the establishment of permanent orchestras that were tied to one city. By the end of the nineteenth century, entertainment had become a gigantic industry; in 1905 there were more than 400 touring companies working out of New York from locations near Times Square. As early as 1865, when smaller midwestern communities showed an intensified interest in concert music, orchestras took to the road on a regular basis. The odds were in favor of such enterprises. There was little competition, and the new Pullman cars promised a relatively comfortable train trip

19 "Going on tour" represented an important part of an orchestra's annual range of activities. Among the highlights of the Swiss-German conductor Karl Muck's second tenure in Boston was the Boston Symphony Orchestra's first transcontinental tour, in 1915, to play a series of twelve concerts at the Panama-Pacific Exposition in San Francisco. En route the orchestra left its special train just long enough to pose for this photograph in Lucin, Utah, on May 12, 1915. Photographer unknown. Pres. 86.5 f3, Boston Symphony Orchestra Archives. Courtesy of the Boston Symphony Orchestra Archives.

overnight. In 1883, Theodore Thomas initiated his "Highway Tour" by train, also subtitled "The March to the West," which included 75 concerts in 30 cities along with 12 festivals, in less than three months.[119]

With a relatively limited repertory, orchestras could cruise from town to town, playing virtually the same concert over and over again. Orchestral tours served as effective advertisements for a city's commerce and culture, and particularly in the Midwest, business communities often supported individual tours. In 1916, the St. Louis Business Men's League raised money to send the city's orchestra on a tour across the local trade territory in order to bring goodwill to its economy.[120] The Minneapolis Real Estate Board regularly sent out personal letters, adorned with pictures of the city's high-rises and smoking chimneys, to other urban communities to announce the imminent arrival of the symphony, "One of our most highly prized Minneapolis institutions," to their town, and to promote Minneapolis as a seat of culture and successful business.[121]

But we really need to wonder why artists went on tour if not out of sheer evangelical zeal. The circumstances of these often extensive tours were invariably horrendous, and they allow an additional glimpse into just how driven these men were. Communities struggled to find a venue for the visiting orchestras, choosing corn palaces, creaky opera houses, tents, churches, high schools, lodge halls, armories, shrine temples, and cattle barns—anywhere there was space enough for fifty to ninety musicians on a stage, and an audience somewhere else. On its extensive tours through the West, the Minneapolis Symphony Orchestra played in a fruit warehouse in Oregon (with the listeners sitting on apple crates); in a state penitentiary for an audience of convicts; in drafty sheds in village outskirts adjoining cow pastures; in firetraps; and, at least once, in a circus tent. In Aberdeen, South Dakota, in May 1910, a local chorus assembled for their role in a performance of Haydn's *Creation* on a terraced platform onstage, with the orchestra below on the main floor. During the overture the rear platform supports buckled and crashed, dumping a number of surprised basses onto the floor below. The conductor, Emil Oberhoffer, inspected the wreckage and, noting that there were no corpses, quickly resumed the performance.

The worst adversaries of orchestras on tour were unfavorable weather conditions. Since tours tended to take place in the winter and early spring, orchestras were often trapped in blizzards, floods, and rainstorms. Midwestern orchestras occasionally began their tour amid howling gales and heavy snowfall. In Mitchell, South Dakota, the Minneapolis Symphony Orchestra performed in an old corn palace as a torrential rain swept through the city, causing the roof of the building to leak. Someone distributed umbrellas and the concert continued, with Oberhoffer conducting with one hand while balancing an umbrella in the other. Yet as it began to rain harder, he lost track of his players, who were constantly moving their stands and chairs in order to avoid the leaks. "Finally," observes the orchestra's historian, "the sections were so thoroughly scrambled that the conductor was cueing the violins for oboe passages."[122]

Examples such as these abound. When Walter Damrosch toured the Midwest with the Metropolitan Opera Orchestra in the early spring of 1885, the train was delayed by a blizzard on the Westshore road and arrived late for the orchestra's performance in Chicago, whereupon musicians and singers were immediately taken to the Columbia Theater. Because all valises had been accidentally delivered to the main entrance instead of the stage door, a stunned audience looked on as the troupe, including the eminent and stoutly built Bayreuth soprano, Anna Materna, marched across the auditorium hauling along an avalanche of baggage. Behind the stage, chaos reigned. Suitcases, boxes, and trunks were piled twenty feet high, sections of the scenery for Wagner's *Tannhäuser* were lying around, and some fifty people were desperately trying to find their costumes. Though Damrosch and his orchestra played the overture once over in order to win time before the curtain was raised, the opening caught the singers by surprise. Anton Schott, performing as Tannhäuser, had been unable to find his trunk containing the appropriate costume, so he appeared onstage dressed as Max in *Der Freischütz*. Another singer could not find his stage shoes and came out in Congress gaiters. "But they all sang like angels," stated the chronicler, "and no one took umbrage at such minor shortcomings."[123]

Aspiring to perform serious music, even for people whose towns did not house a symphony, all orchestras toured at one point or another, though these engagements differed widely. While the New York Philharmonic confined itself to brief trips to cities such as Baltimore, Ann Arbor, Toronto, Detroit, Cleveland, and Kent, typically during the early spring, its tours were not nearly as extensive—and exhausting—as the orchestras of Cincinnati, Pittsburgh, and Minneapolis. Between 1903 and 1917, the Minneapolis Symphony Orchestra gave 564 concerts in 215 different towns and cities. In its first decade of travel, the orchestra brought music to 170 communities, and established an identity not only as the city's orchestra but also as "our orchestra" in scores of towns and cities where the men returned year after year. In 1912, the orchestra's eighty-five members set a prewar record when in addition to the regular concert season at home, they gave seventy concerts in twenty-three weeks in locations as far as Birmingham, Alabama, in the South and New York City in the East. Indeed, the orchestra was out of town so frequently that the *Minneapolis Morning Tribune* sent its music editor on tour with the players to write a series of articles titled "5,000 Miles of Music."[124]

From a financial point of view, out-of-town engagements were even less lucrative than performances at home. It required that local notables guarantee a number of concerts, which proved to be a risky endeavor. When the Philadelphia Orchestra went on tour across Pennsylvania in early 1909, one guarantor asked for a release from the contract "on account of depressed business conditions in Trenton" while the guarantor in Reading reported that the local situation was not encouraging either: "City has had scourge of typhoid fever." In Wilkes-Barre and Scranton, managers could not even raise the necessary guarantee funds, and in Hazleton, the YMCA had to jump in and arrange a series.[125]

Rural audiences were often grateful for the rare entertainment, and their fidelity made up for the many hardships and frustrations the orchestras endured on tour. In 1910, in Deadwood, South Dakota, the impending visit of the Minneapolis Symphony was hailed as the "biggest event of the kind in the history of the Black Hills as well as the biggest drawing card in the history of Deadwood." At Devils Lake, North Dakota, in 1913, the audience was so moved after the performance of Tchaikovsky's *Pathé-tique* Symphony that instead of applauding, all rose quietly to their feet in a spontaneous expression of praise. This kind of homage, one observer wrote, measured "the extraordinary progress within the memory of men now living of a section overrun by buffalo and the same tribe of Indians found there by Lewis and Clark."[126]

Occasionally, however, road audiences exasperated the artists, and Pittsburgh's Frederic Archer even compared them to "one-night stands throughout the country." Often, orchestras outnumbered their audiences, and revenues were poor. When the Pittsburgh Orchestra came to a thriving city of central New York in 1888, locals eagerly asked the assistant manager, Fred Comee: "When do you parade?" — "Parade?" — "Sure. Don't your troupe always parade before the show? You won't do no business without it." When Ferruccio Busoni traversed the American hinterland, he once found himself playing next to a screen indicating the different sections of the sonata he was playing: "First Subject," "Bridge," "Second Subject." In Texas, local authorities felt compelled to put up a sign reading: "Don't shoot the pianist; he's doing the best he can." "[A] good many of us honestly don't care for him," stated a Reading, Pennsylvania, newspaper in 1900 when the Philadelphia Orchestra came to town. "We'd rather seen Eliza on ice, or Peck's Bad Boy and the grocer, or the Bards Brother act on a flying trapeze. Mr. Scheel isn't in their class. There's not enough excitement about his show to please many of us." At the height of her international career, the contralto Ernestine Schumann-Heink was greeted by a tobacco-chewing old man in a rural town with the words "Say, ma'am, ain't you that big, fat, famous female singer whose face we're a seein' all the time in the newspapers?"[127]

To cope with the hardships of touring, orchestras often led drinking orgies off- and occasionally onstage, a habit common among the German players. Musicians frequently grew bored during the long train rides, and drinking was a form of entertainment. On a visit to Wichita in February 1911, the Cincinnati Symphony Orchestra brought along a "private oasis" of 1,200 bottles of beer for its seventy members because it had heard that the city was dry.[128] The Pittsburgh Orchestra developed an unfavorable reputation in Akron, Ohio, in 1899, because "several of the orchestra were somewhat under the influence of liquor, when they played here." Pittsburgh's cellist Henry Bramsen was eventually fired because he was supposedly "slightly intoxicated at times," as was the new concertmaster, who had apparently given a foretaste of his addiction at the Fort Pitt

Hotel. Second violinist Louis Human was likewise labeled "very undesirable" by the management, as he was known to be "addicted to drink and to gambling."[129]

———

The story of these artists can only be understood in terms of international history. Apart from personal hopes for money and fame, artists like Thomas, Seidl, Damrosch, and others were clearly driven by an artistic zeal to share the German masters with foreign audiences. Their mission was not mandated by the state but represented an unofficial, implicit endeavor. It was precisely the fact that these men did not operate under the auspices of the Reich—that, indeed, they did not even feel politically close to Germany—that rendered their venture so successful. They were, to borrow from Goethe's *Wahlverwandtschaften*, the visitors offering their best and making themselves feel at home, in both metropolitan and rural areas. Their nonchalance and independence made their quest a matter of choice and thus turned them into the perfect agents for the creation of an emotional elective affinity.

The emerging symphony scene in the United States, in turn, owed much to the influx of foreign conductors and musicians, but all agreed that that scene had to be German. Critics and audiences consistently perceived the orchestral scene as a genuinely German genre, even though most orchestras counted several nationalities among their players and did not restrict their repertory to German music. Often, the portrayals of conductors, soloists, and musicians read more like sketches of supermen or, alternately, cartoon characters than musical artists. At the same time, many German-speaking artists deliberately nurtured characteristics that were associated with their cultural background, while non-German artists eagerly strove to point out a spiritual, moral, or educational pedigree linking them to Germany and the mission to spread the eighteenth- and nineteenth-century music around the world. Consequently, *German* did not refer to a territorial entity but represented an idea that encompassed universalism in a most radical sense: it included different cultures and dialects under the umbrella of a set of artistic ideals.

What distinguished these presumed Germans from Americans—indeed, from any other cultural and national group—was that they seemed to unite two characteristics, masculinity and emotions, that according to the gender standards of the time were diametrically opposed. Private relations and correspondences aside, in Victorian America emotions and their expression remained officially a characteristic attributed to women and children. At the same time, the professionalization of music turned the performance of symphonies into an almost exclusively male endeavor. The symphony orchestra and its programs reflected organized collective emotion but also military precision, appearance, and hierarchy. National characteristics overrode gender considerations as the public expression of emotion, tied to "Teutonic sternness," became socially acceptable to all of nineteenth-century society.

# FOUR

# American Hosts

For a long time, Americans used the word *symphony* in a de-
rogatory fashion; "dull as a symphony concert" was a figure
of speech circulating in Boston before the Civil War.[1] But
by 1900, symphonies had sprung up in Chicago, Pittsburgh,
Rochester, Toronto, Cincinnati, St. Louis, Minneapolis, St.
Paul, Kansas City, Denver, Seattle, and San Francisco. "Every
up-to-date town must have its local 'Symphony Orchestra'
as it has its 'Grand Opera House,' " scoffed Charles Norman
Fay, one of the orchestra trustees in Chicago, when he resigned from his office in 1913.[2]

Between 1860 and 1920, the United States had not only
become a military and industrial power but also developed
a vibrant musical life complete with leading opera houses,
symphony halls, conservatories, academic music departments, music magazines, critical reviewers, and a multitude
of instrument manufacturers. Crediting German artists with
the growth of musical life in the United States, the critic
Henry Krehbiel observed in 1880 that "under the influences
of a Puritan ancestry the people of our country would have
been very tardy in developing an appreciation of the art of
music."[3]

Unlike in Europe, most American orchestras began like
stock companies or business ventures, organized by professional managers, a board of trustees, and an often shaky
subscribers' fund. As a result, criticism abounded that symphonies were prone to rank profit above quality. Likewise,
historians in search of the origins of American consumer
culture have made much of the Barnum-like marketing approach to performance music in the mid-nineteenth century.

It is true that individual stars like Jenny Lind, Ole Bull, and others made great profits. Yet the reality was different. Most orchestras never got out of the red. Sponsors had their own, often very personal reasons for expending their funds in a venture that yielded European prestige but not American wealth, and professional critics did their best to support these enterprises.

The significance of these philanthropists, editors, and bureaucrats emerges in the context of the historiographical debate on cultural transfer. In recent years, major critics of U.S. colonialism and cultural imperialism, such as Armand Mattelart, have stressed that cultural influence or expansionism can only be effected by a combination of international and native (elite) forces, such as in Chile.[4] In the context of the present story, we may reapply these arguments to the United States. The collective biographies and actions of music sponsors in the United States confirm the model outlined by Mattelart: they emphasize the support of indigenous elites as prerequisite to the intended or coincidental transfer of musical culture.

We have seen in the previous chapter how early German ensembles, notably the Germania Musical Society, affected the transatlantic music circuit. After the Germania's success, the symphony began to occupy a special place in the eclectic American musical landscape. To many music lovers in urban areas, the challenge was not just to have an orchestra: indeed, throughout the nineteenth century, bands of different sizes and instrumental combinations existed in many cities and played for all kinds of occasions, such as banquets, outdoor parades, university balls, operatic and choral programs, and cotillions.[5] Instead, the challenge was to create and maintain a symphony based on secure and long-term financial support. And it is precisely at this junction that foreign artists endowed with a sense of mission encountered indigenous cash and philantrophy.

———

Between 1850 and World War I, Americans began to build music halls in order to accommodate the increased number of orchestras and concerts. Philadelphia laid the cornerstone of its Academy of Music in 1850, Milwaukee in 1864. Cincinnati erected its Music Hall in 1878.[6] New York City built Carnegie Hall in 1891, which to this day is arguably the most prestigious concert hall in the world. In 1900, Boston erected Symphony Hall with the support of Henry Cabot Lodge, Charles W. Eliot, Mrs. Louis Agassiz, and Miss Alice Longfellow, among others.[7] In Pittsburgh, the enlarged and renovated Carnegie Institute complex opened to the public in 1907, featuring a music hall next to a hall of architecture, an art gallery, and a museum.[8]

German-born artists and their American sponsors conspired to create an unprecedented symphony boom. Until 1920, at least a dozen metropolises, including New York (1842), St. Louis (1879), Boston (1881), Chicago (1891), Cincinnati (1895), Pittsburgh (1896), Philadelphia (1900), Minneapolis (1903), and San Francisco (1911), established permanent Philharmonics, with Baltimore, Cleveland, and Detroit following suit during or shortly after World War I. Population growth had an enormous impact on musical development. In 1800, for example, the city of Pittsburgh counted 1,565 inhabitants; in 1890, shortly before the foundation of the Pittsburgh Orchestra, almost a quarter of a million people lived there, most of whom having migrated into the area between 1870 and 1890.[9] The symphony craze reached its climax in the 1890s with the simultaneous establishment of five orchestras within roughly a dozen years. Most of these were sponsored by local elites and organized under the tutelage of a German-born conductor, such as Anton Seidl and the Damrosches in New York, Theodore Thomas in Chicago, and Emil Oberhoffer in Minneapolis. By the turn of the century, New York alone had two regular symphony orchestras, the New York Philharmonic and the New York Symphony Orchestra, both of which performed regular concerts each year in the city as well as on tour.

In their collective quest for public and accessible agents of taste, pleasure, and refinement, these cities did not lag very far behind their European counterparts.[10] The New York Philharmonic, for one, was founded just eleven days after its counterpart in Vienna, in 1842. Designed as a stock company and membership organization with a constitution governed by a board of directors, the Philharmonic invited its members to purchase a certain number of shares, while its conductors would occasionally be paid in share dividends. By 1857, its membership had risen to ninety.[11]

The New York Philharmonic's governing body was a board of directors, and the conductor was a member of the board "ex-officio." His duty was to hold an immediate interview with every artist who was to be engaged to perform, but also to report his opinions, and all other matters requiring attention, to the board of directors "for their consideration and supervision."[12] The Philharmonic's records show that most of the early board members were Germans or of German descent: R. Ogden Doremus, President; U. C. Hill, Vice President (American-born); David Schaad, Secretary; J. G. Beisheim, Treasurer; J. Leis, Librarian; and Carl

20  The businessman Henry Higginson created the Boston Symphony Orchestra on the basis of
the German musical traditions he had experienced when he was a student in Europe. All six
conductors appointed between 1881 and 1918 were central European and hailed for their
"Germanness." Note the combat scar on Higginson's cheek, dating from his service during
the Civil War. Photographer Notman, ca. 1882, Boston Symphony Orchestra Archives. Courtesy of the Boston Symphony Orchestra Archives.

Bergmann, F. Rietzel, F. Bergner, E. Boehm, G. Matzka, H. Schmitz, Directors. Meetings were frequently held in prominent locations known
among the German-American community: the Germania Club, the
Aschenbrödel Club, and Steinway Hall.

Two hundred miles to the north, the situation looked very different. In
Boston, a single benefactor organized and financed the local symphony
orchestra: Henry Higginson, a man who some claimed "would undertake
to run the universe on twenty minutes' notice."[13] In 1881, Higginson
wrote up a detailed proposal, including the number of musicians per instrument section, their annual salaries, and the kind of music that they
were to play. Based on his extensive musical knowledge, he hired a young
Bohemian conductor, a manager, and a group of local musicians, form-
ing an enterprise called the Boston Symphony Orchestra. He insisted that
no entertaining or sentimental (that is, opera) music would be performed
(Higginson abhorred Wagner),[14] then left the choice of musicians, rep-

ertory, and direction to the conductor. Anticipating a yearly deficit of $50,000, he established a $1-million fund for the symphony. When other cities sought Higginson's guidance for the foundation of their own symphonies, he consistently advised that organizers should never ever "look at the bills."[15]

Chicago's orchestra, in contrast, originated in the collective engagement of a group of businessmen. In 1891 a board of trustees consisting of five men, among them Charles N. Fay, founded the Orchestra Association, designed to finance the Chicago Orchestra (later renamed Chicago Symphony Orchestra).[16] Each trustee paid annually into a fund to cover the orchestra's expenses as well as all debts, and to establish a guarantee against loss of $50,000 per annum for three years. Such arrangements, the trustees believed, would also prevent the orchestra from being forced into entering financial deals with piano houses, music colleges, or newspapers.[17]

Most orchestras arose from a mixture of motivations, combining the aspirations of musicians and conductors with income from often unsteady subscribers' funds. In Minneapolis, a Philharmonic Club under the tutelage of the German conductor Emil Oberhoffer had been in existence for years, but the decision for permanent backing came only in 1903. The club gathered leading citizens, who thrashed out a program guaranteeing the conductor a three-year contract and full freedom of decision over appointments and repertory. A twenty-five-member board of directors took upon itself the responsibility for booking artists. It administered season ticket sales and raised an annual guarantee fund of $10,000 for three years.[18] In San Francisco in 1881, a local Philharmonic Society gave a series of concerts, but it was thirty years before a regular orchestra was founded. The earthquake and fire of 1906 erased half the city, and only in 1911 did a permanent symphony come about under the leadership of Henry Hadley.[19]

In St. Louis, a twenty-eight-year-old German organist named Joseph Otten founded the St. Louis Choral Society in September 1880 after gathering the support of a group of wealthy citizens, including prominent Jewish merchants such as the Epstein brothers, and wealthy brewers such as Adolphus Busch and Hugo Koehler. In tandem, they funded what would be the forerunner of the St. Louis Symphony Society, with thirty-five instrumentalists and some ninety singers.[20]

Religion played no role at all in the setup of boards, guarantors' lists, and subscribers. A variety of faiths freely intermingled in all these groups, and in many cities Protestant, Catholic, and Jewish merchants contributed heavily to the symphony scene. In Cincinnati, most of the money had come from Anglo-Saxon and, to a lesser degree, Teutonic Protestants; but here also the Jewish community contributed.[21]

Orchestral societies were not simply business ventures, for they also revealed strong socialist ideals that looked out for the welfare and future of their staffs. They created funds designed to support the families of orchestra members in case of illness or sudden death. The Orchestral Association of the Chicago Symphony Orchestra occasionally supported individual members in bringing their families from Europe.[22] Nearly all the orchestral societies created minimal pension funds that enabled members to retire once they had served for a specified number of years. Boston started a pension fund in 1903, with a concert to raise funds for it on March 1.[23] By 1917, the pension fund of the Chicago Symphony Orchestra had securities amounting to more than $375,000.[24]

Even though both orchestras and their management boards were predominantly staffed by men, women played leading roles in the promotion of symphony orchestras throughout the nation. In St. Louis, a group of over thirty women convened to organize a permanent orchestra in 1897. They wrote hundreds of letters soliciting subscriptions, developed individual concert programs, and finally appointed Alfred Ernst to a three-year term as conductor, with a salary of $3,500 per annum.[25] This orchestra's Executive Committee consisted almost equally of women and men by 1916.[26] Similarly in Philadelphia, a women's committee directed the early organization of the city's orchestra, raising funds and soliciting subscriptions.[27] In Pittsburgh, under the auspices of a local Art Society, a group of women organized a membership committee securing subscriptions for an orchestra fund of approximately $50,000.[28] The Philharmonic Society of New York admitted women as associate members as early as 1847.[29] And in Cincinnati in 1894–95, a group of women founded the "Ladies' Musical Club," headed by Mrs. William Howard Taft, wife of the future president, with the specific stipulation that "the Club shall be exclusively a Woman's Association."[30] They formed a corporate body under the name of the Orchestra Association Company, passed the hat, and within a week had secured seventy-eight subscriptions to the capital stocks, 10 percent of their goal.[31]

Yet no matter how they were structured, no matter how incessantly their organizers worked, wrote, lobbied, and raised funds, orchestras never did well financially, and none of the Philharmonics ever really made money. Instead, they staggered from one financial crisis to the next. During a typical season, disbursements would exceed the receipts by over 100 percent, and old deficits frequently had to be carried over into the next season.[32] To the end of his life, Higginson in Boston never made a penny of profit with his enterprise; in a thirty-three-year period, the annual deficit of the Chicago Symphony Orchestra climbed to $900,000.00.[33] The deficit of the city's Orchestral Association amounted to more than $287,000 during its first seven years, almost 50 percent of the gross receipts.[34] By 1913, the orchestra had accumulated such a deficit that it paid $8,000 in interest on the debt incurred.[35] The St. Louis Symphony Society named the 1911–12 season a "satisfactory" year, as the orchestra had a deficit of nearly $30,000, to be met by a guarantee fund yet to be paid. And in Pittsburgh and Cincinnati, symphonies had to be temporarily disbanded because they could no longer meet their financial demands.[36]

Who were these men and women who invested their money, time, and interest in the creation and administration of urban orchestras? In Cincinnati, most of the supporters were lawyers (17 percent), with "old money" and old names, while only a few were Teutonic entrepreneurs who came into prominence after the Civil War. George Ward Nichols, principal organizer of the Cincinnati Symphony Orchestra Company, was art editor of the *New York Evening Post* and married to the daughter of Joseph Longworth, a wealthy real estate owner and president of the Harmonic Society from 1873 to 1878.[37] Trustees and organizers typically lived in "respectable" neighborhoods. Their backgrounds were predominantly Anglo-Saxon, Protestant, and Republican, and two-thirds of them were unmarried. All of the initial founders belonged to the local wealthy elite, including Helen Taft, Edith Forchheimer, Louise Anderson, Virginia Wright, Helen Chatfield, Henrietta Billing, and Emma Roedter. Many had been engaged in the instruction or performance of music.[38]

Likewise, Chicago trustees were often men engaged in creating fortunes, up-and-comers, businessmen: typically lawyers, real estate investors, bankers, and manufacturers from the community who had some tie to Europe, an interest in the arts, and time. They lived in fancy, palatial homes in prime neighborhoods developed after the Chicago Fire, and above all on Prairie Avenue, that landmark stretch immortalized in Arthur Meeker's turn-of-the-century novel.[39] They were members of the same university, literary, and commercial clubs, and most of them were involved in the preparations for the Chicago World's Fair of 1893, the World's Columbian Exposition. Bryan Lathrop, first a trustee and later president of the Orchestral Association, had gone into the real estate business and joined a variety of boards. Harold Fowler McCormick, son of Cyrus Hall McCormick, inventor of the reaping machine, had gone to Princeton, then married John D. Rockefeller's daughter, Edith, and went into the family business. Philo Adams Otis, a real estate tycoon, was one of the founders and board members of the Apollo Musical Club in 1872 before joining the board of trustees of the Chicago Orchestra in 1894.[40] Daniel Burnham, world-renowned architect and planner of the Columbian Exposition, served as trustee and vice president of the Orchestral Association from 1894 until his death in 1912. Burnham was a member of every civic club, ranging from the Union League to the Cliff Dwellers, and rubbed shoulders with important businessmen all over the United States.[41] John Jacob Glessner, son of an Ohio newspaper publisher of German extraction, had joined the firm of Warder and Cholds, a manufacturer of harvesting machinery, and bought the firm in the late 1860s.[42] The Glessners were close friends of the Chicago Symphony Orchestra conductor Theodore Thomas and his wife as well as other music celebrities of the city, including Fanny Bloomfield-Zeisler and the great Ignaz Paderewski (Frances Glessner even had a little crush on Thomas, judging from her diary entries).[43]

Several factors drove the individuals who became involved in the foundation of orchestras. The most important motivation was personal background: many of the sponsors had personal ties to the European cultural scene and an interest in the spread of symphonic music not unlike that exhibited by the musicians from Europe. Quite a few of the trustees and friends of the Chicago Orchestra had visited Europe in their youth. Many had studied music, and some even composed. Bryan Lathrop, for example, constantly emphasized that Chicago needed music as a counterforce to sheer materialism. Born 1844 in Alexandria, Virginia, Lathrop went abroad for study under private tutors in Germany and France. His will bequeathed $700,000 to the Orchestral Association to found in Chicago a School of Music along the lines of the Conservatoire in Paris, "in which an education can be obtained in the higher branches of music and musical composition not inferior to that found in the cities of Europe." Philo Otis had spent some time in Europe in his midtwenties, then composed an essay, "Impressions of Europe." In later life, he also wrote a book on hymnody and composed music that was performed by the Chicago Symphony.[44]

Memories of a European youth also motivated the key organizer of the Pittsburgh Orchestra, Charles Woodruf Scovel. Born in Springfield, Ohio, in 1862, he came to the city at the age of three and attended local high schools. After attending Columbia Law School, in the winter of 1884–85 Scovel took special law courses at the University of Berlin. Though he spent most of his career in the life insurance business, Scovel was intensely interested in music and literature: he was an amateur organist and from 1885 onward served as music editor of the *Pittsburg Dispatch*. He personally solicited the original three-year guarantee fund, and persuaded Frederic Archer to come to Pittsburgh as conductor of the orchestra and director of music at its Carnegie Hall.[45]

By far the most driven Europhile was Boston's benefactor, Henry Higginson. In his twenties, Higginson had traveled through Belgium, Germany, and Switzerland. During his Alpine trip, he decided to pursue his studies in Germany, an experience that would change his life forever. In Munich young Henry discovered his love for concert and operatic music. Almost daily he went to hear the operas of Verdi, Beethoven, Mozart, Flotow, Bellini, and Lortzing. In Dresden, where he spent the summer of 1852–53, Higginson first heard the Wagnerian opera *Tannhäuser*. He began taking music lessons, and when faced with leaving Germany, asked his father for an extension. "There is one thing," he wrote to his father in the spring of 1853, "that makes me very, very sorry to leave Europe: the loss of music. . . . I do not believe there is anything more refining than music, no greater or stronger preservative against evil, and at least for me it has done much."[46]

Higginson returned to Europe in 1856 to travel and study in Germany and Austria, primarily Vienna, where he grew increasingly infatuated with the Romantics and their music while abandoning any ambitions for a career in the business world: "Germany seems to me best of all lands for music, Vienna to combine most of all German cities. . . . I have no desire to return to America and earn money." He studied music eight hours a day, concentrating on harmony, composition, learning German, singing, and playing the piano. In fact, he practiced the piano so intensively that his arm was crippled and had to be treated in a Styrian bath, never to fully recover. And he sang so hard that his throat troubled him from irritation. When realizing that his musical dreams would never become reality, he wrote to his father: "What I had wished for years was at hand . . . [but] now it is over forever. I can *never* play freely again."[47]

Higginson was spared the fate of Somerset Maugham's "Alien Corn," the young gentleman who shoots himself after discovering that he is not cut out to be a pianist. In 1860, Higginson quietly returned to the United States, infused with an appreciation for German music. He served in the Civil War as a major in the cavalry, then speculated—unsuccessfully—in oil and cotton before entering the stock-brokerage firm Lee, Higginson, and Co. in 1868, where he remained for the rest of his career, accumulating a significant personal fortune.

The Boston Symphony Orchestra, Higginson once stated, was his yacht, his racing stable, his library, and his art gallery, but his correspondence reveals a more familial relationship with the organization. He had an intimate knowledge of his orchestra, a close relationship with his men, an in-depth knowledge of music and the European music scene, and a generous heart. He knew his players, their characters, weaknesses, and strengths, and he would discuss the qualities of each new candidate in great detail with his manager and conductor: was a horn player fit to play first horn or third? Would the present cellists live up to the standards of the incoming conductor? Yet for all his generosity, Higginson did not hesitate to fire a musician who didn't please: "Sautet must go, and we want a man to take his place as extra oboe. We want also somebody to take Elmar's place as second clarinet, for I think he is rather dull," he wrote to his conductor, Karl Muck, in March of 1912. He devised detailed lists each year indicating which players should be kept and which should be dropped in the next season. "All to be reengaged," he concluded when reviewing the trumpet players' reengagement for the 1912–13 season, "except Merril, who is a drunkard."[48]

And while Higginson claimed that he did not interfere much with his conductors, his correspondence proves otherwise. "I wish to be allowed to speak to the conductor in decided terms about his fashion of interpreting," he stated in 1906, when instructing his manager to go to Europe and hire a new music director. "And I don't wish him to be annoyed that I do not like so much noise or so much accelerated tempi, or this or that. Naturally he may say 'You don't know anything about it,' but then, I do, and (what is more) after listening to the best music for fifty years under the best men, I am entitled to know something about it and to have an opinion."[49] An abundance of letters from the players to the benefactor of the Boston Symphony Orchestra, collected by the Baker Library at Harvard University, testify to his intimate relationship with the orchestra members. They wrote in English but also in German. They asked him for help, for a renewal of their position, for a loan, or for a good word. They told their life stories and apologized for taking up his time. And sometimes they just wrote to say thank you. To Henry Higginson, the members of the orchestra were almost like his children—the children he and his wife had never had.

Of course, motivations behind creating and sponsoring a symphony were complex, and other reasons played into the decision. To be on the board of a philanthropic or charitable organization was considered a form of noblesse oblige by leading American families. Indeed, the lives of these trustees closely resembled that of a textbook philanthropist. Bryan Lathrop, for example, was trustee of the Orchestral Association, director of the Chicago Relief and Aid Society, trustee of the Art Institute and the Newberry Library, member of the Lincoln Park board, and member of the

Literary Society, the University Club, and others. Lathrop gave frequently to charity, more than most people, and up to $25,000 at one time.[50]

Boosterism likewise played a role in the formation of symphonies. Many sponsors were compelled by their fear of living in a city that was not quite as attractive as other American metropolises. An "unattractive" city held a reputation for discouraging the growth of business and culture. In the latter part of the nineteenth century, urbanites all across the nation felt an urge to equip their cities with zoos, art museums, railroad stations, theaters, orchestras, and colleges in an effort to compete with and outdo one another. Ironically, the historian Jeffrey Hyson has argued, the effort was seen as the triumph of one locality (city) over another, while none of these institutions reflected any localism at all (since all the artifacts were imported).[51] Sponsors in eastern cities such as Philadelphia and Boston placed a high priority on civic adornment and social recreation. West of the Appalachians, in contrast, the argument that culture attracted business (and not vice versa) carried more weight.[52] To have an orchestra meant to have local pride, to strive, to progress. Whether it was Boston, Chicago, New York City, Philadelphia, Cincinnati, or any other city—everywhere citizens believed that they had the leading orchestra of the nation, if not the world, and the degree of their self-confidence is remarkable. "The cities which maintain their own permanent orchestras are the true musical centers of America," the journal *Musical America* proclaimed in 1914. "A city which possesses its own symphony organization, even though it is not equal to the Boston orchestra, is better off than the one which has its occasional feasts of music."[53] Consequently, Boston competed with New York, New York with Philadelphia, Minneapolis with Pittsburgh, Pittsburgh with Cincinnati, Cincinnati with Chicago, Chicago with every orchestra on the East Coast, and San Francisco with every city in the nation. Their strivings resonated with a terminology that unmasked the missionary impulse of the venture: wrote the *Musical Courier* in 1887, "Mr. Wilhelm Gericke and his Boston Symphony Orchestra carried the war into Africa, the great conductor from the hub and his admirable forces simply came, played and conquered."[54]

Two things are striking about the profiles of these sponsors. First, those who might be commercially interested in an orchestra rarely provided financial support on a regular basis. Instrument manufacturers, publishers, and concert agencies played no role on the boards of symphony orchestras. Second, save for New York, in many other cities the German immigrant community played a disproportionately small role in the administration or regular sponsorship of these orchestras. Among the board of trustees and the forty members of the Orchestral Association of the

Chicago Orchestra, none even had a German-sounding name, the roster featuring instead McCord, Lowden, Burnham, and Bards, among others.[55] Even the lists of sponsors who only occasionally attended fund-raising dinners and supported the orchestra reveal few or no names from the German-American community.[56] The city's Orchestral Organization did not bother to send out complimentary tickets to the multitude of German-language newspapers.[57] In Cincinnati and St. Louis, strongholds of German immigrant life, the trustees, the subscribers, and the occasional donors were for the most part not German. Among the presidents of the St. Louis Symphony Society, there was not a single German between 1899 and 1927, even though Germans had until recently constituted nearly a quarter of the city's population.[58] While they may have represented a portion of the audience, German immigrants typically remained reluctant to subsidize cultural events.

Several reasons account for this reluctance. Well-to-do first-generation Germans rarely counted among a city's elite but remained confined to their ethnic enclave. Second- and third-generation immigrant families, who had already undergone a process of Americanization, may simply have felt less compelled to sponsor the culture of their parents and grandparents. More important, the German American's political heritage strongly opposed private donations. Originating from a culture where the state sponsored the arts and people paid taxes to this end, German Americans were chronically unenthusiastic about giving money to non-profit and community organizations.[59] "Although we have a large number of citizens of German birth or descent," the St. Louis composer Ernst Kroeger observed, somewhat disillusioned, "they have supported but meagerly musical enterprises appealing to the community at large." The many *Sängerbünde* and *Bundeschöre*, important in their own right, were little known among the population of St. Louis at large. When traveling musical ensembles such as the Theodore Thomas Orchestra came to town, they often played to half-empty auditoriums, while Theodore Spiering and his quartet seldom counted more than one hundred people at their concerts. "This is difficult to account for in a city containing so many German-Americans," noted Kroeger, "to whom the expense of the subscription would have meant little or nothing." The ones who did attend were a small portion, perhaps 20 percent, of the Anglo-Saxon elites, merchants, businessmen, bankers, and lawyers, who had purchased subscriptions for themselves or their wives and daughters.[60]

Of course, there were exceptions. Various breweries of German origin in St. Louis regularly supported the Saint Louis Symphony Orchestra, with Anheuser-Busch taking the lead in this effort.[61] In New York, local Germans were willing to contribute to the Seidl Orchestra shortly before the conductor's death.[62] Fred C. M. Lautz, founder of the Buffalo Symphony Orchestra, had migrated from Germany before 1856, then became a very successful businessman in the soap-making industry.[63] Joseph W. Drexel was the son of a Tyrolean immigrant who had escaped Napoleon Bonaparte's conscription laws and founded a banking firm in Philadelphia. Next he founded, in 1871, the firm of Drexel, Morgan & Co. in New York, and accumulated a fortune of at least $20 million. President of the New York Philharmonic Society, Drexel was a philanthropist and a well-known benefactor of New York's cultural life.[64] Yet these exceptions merely confirm the rule: German Americans may have attended concerts, but they entertained little interest in backing classical music in the United States. Instead, Anglo-American leaders dominated the ranks of sponsors and patrons.

Philanthropists who supported symphonies maintained close ties to the European music scene. They knew the reputations of leading musicians. They were in touch with a variety of insiders and experts. They understood the market. And they comfortably juggled bidding prices. When Henry Higginson picked a conductor in 1906 to replace Wilhelm Gericke, he compiled a list of some twenty-five candidates, which read like a *Who's Who* of Europe's symphony scene: Arthur Nikisch, Gustav Mahler, Hans Richter, Richard Strauss, Bruno Walter, Felix Weingartner, Karl Muck, and Felix Mottl, among others. Then he appointed two delegates in Europe who were to investigate the scene and conduct negotiations: his manager, Charles Ellis, and the composer George Chadwick. For inside knowledge, he listened to European acquaintances, including a close friend from his student days, the pianist and professor of music Julius Epstein, and the soprano Milka Ternina.[65]

The trustees and organizers of symphony orchestras nurtured very definite ideas regarding the prospective candidates for the job they advertised, and they consistently looked to Germany, their own past, and their youth when hiring a new conductor. Higginson, for one, wanted his future *Kapellmeister* to know that "I don't want crazy work, and perhaps you had better tell them that I hate noise." Some of the leading artists of Europe he declared "distinctly second-rate" and "not a genius." "I should like Mottl, if he would come and do the work well," he mused on March 18, 1906. "Weingartner is a composer and wishes to compose and not to conduct much . . . he seems to me difficult, and <u>mannered</u>,—Do you call it gekünstelt?" Arthur Nikisch, he observed, was an inveterate gambler, a chain-smoker, and "an unreliable man, with real genius, and with a pleasant nature if he isn't cross." In short, Higginson clearly knew the central European music scene like the back of his hand: "Mottl means to stay in Munich; Mahler is a fixture in Vienna; Steinbach doesn't want to leave Cologne—and so it goes. The person I wish we could have is Ternina, but she is a woman and wouldn't like the work, and we haven't got as far as that yet."[66] When Higginson decided to hire Karl Muck, general music director of the Royal Opera in Berlin, he went all the way up to the kaiser to obtain his permission.[67]

The seven initial founders of the Orchestra Association Company in Cincinnati likewise carefully tested the transatlantic waters before hiring a conductor. In 1894, when the orchestra was founded, they believed that "a young man having his future to make might possibly be better suited to the conditions which prevail here," as they informed Franz Wullner, *Kapellmeister* in Cologne at the time.[68] To Otto Floersheim in Berlin they explained, "We need a young man of ability, a well instructed musician who could rally these forces and by bringing in some new material would give some real good concerts." That person should be "a well educated young man full of the divine fire who would be content to work and create something."[69] The founders solicited names and references from Europe's leading conductors, among them Hans von Bülow, and even initially flirted with the idea of making an offer to Siegfried Wagner (who was then dismissed for lack of experience).[70]

Two things matter about these administrators, trustees, and managers. First, they were in close touch with Europe's music scene. They knew the prominent conductors, the influential concert agencies, and the famous soloists. Accordingly, orchestra trustees and sponsors were keenly interested in maintaining a close relationship with their conductors, and they were often quite opinionated. Certainly the German music scene in the United States had closer ties to the community of music and high culture in Germany than to the German-American community in the United States.[71] Second, they shared a collective urge to uplift and improve society, not simply because they wanted to set the parameters of social control (as Paul DiMaggio and others have claimed), but because they seriously wished to share their musical enthusiasm with their city at large. In this missionary endeavor, they did not differ much from that of the imported music artists such as Theodor Thomas and others.

———

Besides the sponsors and trustees, music critics likewise belonged to the loyal elite celebrating the universalism of German music in the United States. Professional music criticism did not come into being until at least the 1830s. In the eighteenth century, nothing of the kind existed, save for a few pieces in scattered journals. By the time it came of age in the late nineteenth century, music criticism represented a new form of authority: "experts" who were entitled to "tell" audiences whether a performance they had actually heard themselves lived up to the standards of performing and composing at the time.[72] And from the 1880s onward, an abundance of music journals with titles such as *Music, Musical America*, and *The Musician* jammed the magazine market in response to the growing interest in classical music.[73] Early journals such as *Dwight's* appealed to their readers' cosmopolitanism with regular columns such as "Music in Berlin" or "Music in Vienna." For the years 1858–59, the index to *Dwight's Journal of Music* listed a total of 117 reports from music centers abroad, ranging from Baden-Baden to Bordeaux, Cologne, Gota, Lisbon, London, Paris, Prague, Rio de Janeiro, St. Petersburg, and Zurich. Dwight clearly sought to emulate the model of German music journals who cultivated freelance editors all over the world.[74]

Most critics favored German composers, conductors, soloists, and musicians. When George Templeton Strong attended Carl Bergmann's rendition of *Tannhäuser* in New York's Stadttheater on April 4, 1859 (the first complete performance of that opera in the United States), with Anton Schott singing the lead, he commented that the chorus "did Deutschland credit."[75] By the end of the nineteenth century, American fans and promoters of Wagner, observes Joseph Horowitz, "championed German culture." In light of the surging wave of Italian immigrants, they dismissed Italian music as "hurdy gurdy," while German singers, according to the critic Henry Finck in 1890, "are, as a rule, superior to Italians, not only in the more sonorous and richer timbre of their voice, but in their use of them."[76]

Much of this new appreciation had to do with the coming of age of a new generation of critics after the Civil War that differed markedly from its predecessors. While antebellum reporters and editors often had no more than a layman's education in music, these new critics had strong ties to the music profession and the European continent. Similar to the makeup of a typical orchestra's board of trustees, many critics had a German-related background.

The critic Henry Krehbiel, dean of American music criticism, was born in Ann Arbor in 1854 to German-born parents. Fluent in English and German, Krehbiel traveled extensively, including to Europe to hear music, meet international artists, and climb in the Alps. Though he lacked formal music training, he worked as a lecturer and program annotator and wrote a dozen books, including *How to Listen to Music* (1897) and *Music and Manners in the Classical Period* (1898), as well as a study of Wagner operas, a history of opera in New York City, and studies on African and popular music. More than anything else, Krehbiel made an immense effort to introduce German music and German artists. His heroes were Wagner, Mozart, Brahms, and above all Beethoven (who to him ranked next to God), and he also edited and revised Alexander Wheelock Thayer's biography of the composer. For forty-three years, Krehbiel observed and analyzed the music scene for the *New York Tribune*, and from the beginning to the end, he did his job as if his life depended on the quality of a review. He welcomed new music, including American music, though he professed to be confused by most of it; he abhorred jazz but composed, in 1914, a collection titled *Afro-American Folksongs: A Study in Racial and National Music*; he saw Richard Strauss's genius in *Salome* but missed the beauty. "Ugliness not only revolted but puzzled him," commented Royal Cortissoz from the *Tribune*. "He couldn't see how it persisted."[77]

Many critics originally aspired to become artists themselves. They studied composing, singing, or a particular instrument with a renowned teacher in one of the famous music centers of Europe. Born in 1863, the New York critic Richard Aldrich had learned music theory and appreciation under John Knowles Paine at Harvard University and also studied piano. As a young man, he went to Germany to study music for two years, then continued working as a reporter. Eventually, Aldrich joined the *New York Tribune*, where he often helped Krehbiel with music reviews. In 1902, he succeeded W. J. Henderson at the *New York Times*, where he remained until 1923.[78]

Similarly, Felix Borowski, born in England in 1872 and the son of a Russian-Polish émigré, learned music theory and composition and, in 1887, recommended by the famed German violinist Joseph Joachim, went to the Cologne Conservatory, where he met Frederick Stock. Stock later became conductor in Chicago, while Borowski solicited an appointment as instructor at the Chicago Musical College in 1897. He composed numerous works for orchestra and ballet, chamber music, sonatas, songs, and choral works. He taught and eventually became, from 1915 to 1925, president of the college, but also made himself a name as a prolific writer and journalist. He annotated the programs for the Chicago Symphony Orchestra and served, from 1905 onward, as music reviewer for the *Musical Courier*, and later for various Chicago newspapers and the *Christian Science Monitor*. In 1926, Borowski became superintendent of the Chicago Civic Music Association; from 1937 to 1942 he served as professor of musicology at Northwestern University in Evanston, just north of the city; in 1942 he was appointed music editor for the *Chicago Sun*.[79]

Boston-born Louis Elson studied music with American and German teachers, among them August Kreissmann, the renowned singer of German *Lieder*, as well as composition with Carl Gloggner-Castelli of Leipzig. He composed songs, operettas, and piano works and taught for many years at the New England Conservatory, where he was head of the department of music theory since 1882. Elson served as editor for the *Musical Herald, Musical Courier,* and *Boston Advertiser,* among others, and also as Boston correspondent for the Berlin journal *Die Musik* and the *Paris Revue Musicale.*[80]

Likewise, Philip Hale, born in 1854 in Vermont, had attended Yale University, where he studied law before he delved into music studies and spent five years in Europe. As had so many New England musicians (including Horatio Parker, Paine and Chadwick), Hale studied organ, piano, and composition in Germany. In 1903 he joined the *Boston Herald,* where he embarked on his reign as "Philip the Great"—or "Philip the Terrible," depending on contemporaries' point of view. In 1901, he began writing the program annotations for the Boston Symphony.[81]

To supplement their artistic aspirations, many critics wrote learned books on music and took to the lecture circuit to explain the meaning of music to thousands of concert audiences. During its 1902–3 season, for example, the Philadelphia Orchestra hired a number of renowned critics as lecturers in the Young People's Educational Course. W. J. Henderson lectured on "The Orchestra and Its Instruments" and Louis C. Elson elucidated "Wagner's Theories and Music," while Henry Krehbiel limited his remarks to sweeping topics such as "Beethoven."[82]

Music critics such as Philip Hale, Felix Borowski, and Henry Krehbiel often served as annotators for orchestral programs, and thus became gatekeepers of the new musical canon. At the Chicago Orchestra concerts, for example, annotations from the fourth season onward often spanned several pages and quoted extensively from music dictionaries and biographical recollections. A new section, called "Entr'Acte," introduced audiences to interesting background details, quotations, and aphorisms from composers and philosophers. Since concertgoers typically left their seats during intermission, programs now gave them something to read in the hallway and talk about in an educated manner. At the Boston Symphony Orchestra, Entr'Actes included essays written by music connoisseurs on topics such as a particular composer or music piece, or even theoretical essays with titles such as "Beethoven and Goethe," "Music by Principle," and "Wagner and America."[83]

These men constituted the first generation of music critics who, as near-artists themselves, eventually opted for observation rather than creativity.

All of them saw their calling not merely in writing about music but also in other forms of education. Some taught music, while others lectured widely. Music was gospel to these men, just as it was to the conductors. To both, there was no greater sin than to play or talk about a performance without a serious professional knowledge.

Also like the conductors, many critics believed they had a quasi-religious mission to spread knowledge about music. John Sullivan Dwight, son of a Boston physician and a student at Harvard University, was committed to preaching the gospel of music as a divine art.[84] He wrote music reviews, translated German poetry, and eventually joined Brooks Farm near Boston, the most famous Utopian community on the continent at the time. There Dwight fully developed his belief in transcendentalism and the spiritual power of music. Upon the collapse of the experiment at Brooks Farm, Dwight established the *Journal of Music* under his name, starting publication in April 1852. The journal existed until September 1881, and it became the most influential music journal in the nineteenth-century United States, despite the fact that its weekly circulation never exceeded fifteen hundred copies.[85] It featured contributions from various writers, but most articles, it seems, came from Dwight himself, among them a collection of letters he composed during a sojourn in Germany. At a time when systematic musicology was just emerging in Europe, he made a pioneering effort to introduce Americans to this new field. According to Dwight, Americans had no choice but to fall in love with Beethoven, Mozart, Handel, and Bach, not because they were supposed to or out of reverence for the classics, but "because our souls thrill to the perennial life of genius in their strains." Yet because Americans were still children in the art of music, "we should first lay for ourselves those same foundations of culture which the musical world in Germany, and in Europe, has to build upon in laying out this 'Future.' "[86]

Of course, in an age of the penny press, not all critics were professionals. Daily newspapers often decided to abandon expensive music critics in favor of freelancers, many of whom had no musical experience at all. When Richard Strauss landed in New York in February 1904, one such reporter promptly asked him at the dock if he was the "Waltz King."[87] Often, reporters simply made up stories based on ignorance and misinformation without even bothering to attend a performance. According to a midwestern newspaper, "The Minneapolis Symphony orchestra was engaged in the final rehearsals today of Stravinsky's *Fireworks* and Glazounov's Sixth Symphony, and outside the Auditorium all the fire hose of the building was laid out in preparedness for these and other pyrotechnical explosives of the Russian symphony program of tomorrow night's concert."[88] No doubt this reporter had confused the com-poser's work, *Firebird*, with pyrotechnic displays. At the *New York Herald*, the music editorship was relegated to the city editor, who juxtaposed cultural essays to police reports and horrid portrayals of murders and hangings. The music critic of the *New York Times*, Frederick Schwab, was persistently charged with venality and at least once engaged in a legal battle with a famous soprano. Others, such as the New York–based *Sun*, *Commercial Advertiser*, and the *World*, delivered a mixed quality of musi-cal notices with little regard to the subject or composition reported.[89]

Exceptions confirm the rule, and even though some people who wrote about music were not authorities on the subject, the generation of pro-fessional music critics around the turn of the twentieth century had a profound impact on American musical culture. These men represented and internalized the whole of nineteenth-century music, took their cues from Germany at large, and supported the German-American emotional elective affinity to no small extent.[90] Based on their biographical profiles and their intellectual ambitions, these men regarded themselves more as academics than reporters. Like some of the trustees of orchestras, many critics had passed their formative years in Germany, spent their summers in Europe, and had an in-depth knowledge of the European music scene. Some had mastered one or more instruments, while others regularly trav-eled on the lecture circuit or taught at American universities. And they all believed they had a mission to educate the American public in the art of understanding the music of the Romantics.

––––––

Sponsored out of love of music but not out of economic interest, Ameri-can symphony orchestras went their own way in the second half of the nineteenth century. Run by trustees and professional managers and cheered on by a new generation of music critics, they reflected cultural universalism, cosmopolitan perspective, and philanthropic aspiration coupled with the business acumen of the men and women backing the venture. As to the gatekeepers of the new canon, from Dwight to Henderson, most music critics contributed significantly to the fostering of the canon and the promotion of German musical supremacy. Having lived and studied in the great music centers of Europe and perhaps once aspired to become composers themselves, they readily supported the Ger-man music missionaries in their quest to spread Romantic culture. In tandem, these American organizers and writers along with the European musicians formed a seamless alliance, paving the way for the expansion of the symphony as part of the cultural canon in the United States. In terms of Goethe's *Wahlverwandtschaften*, they represented the other side of the emotional elective affinity, the hosts inviting German artists and artistry to the United States to make themselves feel at home.

The degree to which the European and the American cultural scene interlaced was remarkable. Men such as Henry Krehbiel, Charles Fay, and the music manager Arthur Judson knew the European concert scene inside and out. The transatlantic flow of letters, cables, and people who crossed the ocean in the name of art far outdid diplomatic communications, both in frequency and in volume. Artists and organizers visited Europe every year to personally secure soloists for the next orchestra season.[91] Driven by collective zeal, the sponsors, managers, editors, conductors, soloists, concertmasters, and hundreds of orchestral musicians responded to an enormous need for foreign imports and cultivation. They also made a powerful argument, unique in both the pre– and post–Civil War United States, that money did not matter in the face of a fleeting muse, that it was worth spending tens of thousands of dollars on an art form that lasted no longer than a single moment.

# FIVE

# Love Affairs: Audiences and Programs

Those who went said later on that the event had been beyond belief. As evening fell, hundreds of women besieged
the New Exposition Building in Pittsburgh. A solid mob—
"a sardine box jam of fussy women and girls" hemmed in
by the tape line forty feet wide and eighty feet deep—had
planted itself against two doors. These women, of all ages
and from all walks of life, pressed their umbrellas, handbags,
skirts, and shoes toward the front, willing to incur any risk
to get into the building. Those in the rear pushed forward
for fear of not getting in; those in the front, afraid of being
crushed in the onslaught, in turn pressed against the doors.
With each moment the tension, the nervousness, and the
noise within the crowd rose. Panicking, the officials eventually decided to throw the two doors open and let the mob
in. And then, observed one chronicler, "were enacted scenes
that put woman, sensible ordinarily, yet frightfully sense-
less at times, in her worst possible light."

Squeezing, screaming, shouting, fuming, fretting, and hit-
ting, more than thirty women tried to rush through the
doors at once, with many getting stuck and some falling to
the ground. Those pressing through the left door headed
right to obtain seats in the front of the hall; those pouring in
through the right door stumbled to the left. Midway, like two
armies in a deadly battle, the two parties clashed, and numerous frontliners immediately collapsed on the floor. Their aggressive followers mercilessly trampled them, jumping across
bodies, bags, and hats as they surged onward to obtain a

seat. Shoes, heels, hats, hairpins, gloves, bags, coats, and at least four sets of false teeth flew to the ground. One lady saw her gown torn into two when she got stuck on a rail, but never mind, she stormed ahead to conquer a chair. "A football rush," observed one reporter in comparison, "with its accompaniments of charcoal eyes, tattered clothes and battered limbs, is merely circumstantial." It was the night of Saturday, October 24, 1903, and the Damrosch Orchestra was giving its final concerts in town.[1]

In the previous chapters, we have seen how foreign artists and indigenous elites conspired to import classical music, above all the symphony, from central Europe to the United States. As the examination of repertory and audiences in this section shows, their efforts met with an enormous success among social leaders and also the public at large. Between 1865 and 1914, the consumption of classical music became an important feature in the U.S. economy as well as the cultural scene at large. Published calculations vary, all but point to exorbitant numbers. In 1907, the Berlin newspaper *Der Tag* reported that Americans spent $3 million annually on foreign soloists, conductors, and royalties alone. According to the *Cincinnati Times Star*, in 1913 the American public expended $600 million for music, including production, admittance, and natural expenses, amounting to $6.25 for every man, woman, and child in the nation.[2]

The profiles and the responses of audiences and critics to the leading orchestras in the country reveal who in the late nineteenth- and early twentieth-century United States attended performances, who felt attracted to classical music, and how this attraction translated into an affinity for a different culture. Post–Civil War audiences were not homogeneously elitist, nor was the repertory uniformly German and highbrow. But for all the variety encountered onstage, audiences shared the sponsors' and artists' credo in the juxtaposition of music to "German," however vaguely defined.

---

"Going to the symphony" became a dictum, a favorite pastime, and a standard expression in the late nineteenth-century United States. It meant that one went to listen to music, but also that a listener frequented a specific building designed to celebrate the canon. Opened in 1900, Symphony Hall in Boston was among the first buildings in the nation that was exclusively dedicated to "a consonance or harmony of sounds agreeable to the ear, and not at intervals to be relegated to the dogs or the cats, or to politics or pugilism."[3] For the most part, these new institutions were a success. In Philadelphia, the audience more than tripled from the first season (1900–1901), with six performances and 14,176 people attending, to the fifth (1904–5), with thirty performances and 50,869 attending. During the twenty-sixth season (1916–17), the Chicago Symphony Orchestra played to a total of 453,000 listeners, including concerts given on tour and summer park concerts.[4]

We still know very little about audience makeup, namely who went to the symphony and why, and who merely pretended to go. Few researchers have taken the pains to look into this part of the story in greater depth, and for good reason. There are no statistics and few pictures, and the sources that we have (such as programs, reviews, and diaries) are extremely partial to the fashionable dress circle. We know and have heard ad nauseam that symphony halls offered plenty of space for the crème-de-la-crème of local society.

And that is partly true. The subscriber lists reprinted in programs and newspapers provide an insight into those patrons who frequented the symphony without necessarily donating funds to the organization. Many of them resemble the upper-middle-class crowd so astutely and mercilessly portrayed in the novels of Henry James and Edith Wharton.[5] Among the 732 subscribers of the New York Philharmonic in 1892, we find Mrs. Andrew Carnegie, Elihu Chauncy, Mrs. S. Richard Ely, Mrs. W. Rothschild, and Mrs. A. Steinway. Among the patrons of the Chicago Symphony Orchestra were the leading figures of the time: the Fairbankses, the Glessners, the Adamses, the McCormicks, the Pullmans, the Spragues, and the Websters. Like the orchestra trustees, these men and women lived in the city's fashionable districts Chestnut Street, Dearborn Avenue, Jackson Boulevard, Prairie Avenue, Goethe Street, Astor Street, and Indiana Avenue.[6]

Newspapers extensively described and commented on elegant ladies who exhibited expensive robes, conspicuous hairdos, and precious jewelry in boxes and other premium seats around the country. "Mrs. John Evans, blonde and statuesque [*sic*], 'listens well'—she seemed absorbed in the music, although I never heard that she has talent in that art," observed the reporter Peggy Perkins during a concert of the Minneapolis Symphony Orchestra in Denver, in April 1910. "Mrs. Thomas Daly was chaperoning her pretty daughter, the fair Imogene, who wore a long trailing gown of peacock blue satin and looked a grown-up lady. There were scores of others, and they make Mr. Shakespeare's 'Dream of Fair Women' look like a school picnic." How strange, Perkins concluded, to see all this in Denver, "where only a few short years ago no musician dared venture into the city unless equipped with an Arctic outfit, so chilling was the frost."[7]

There is no doubt that classical music smacked of snobbery. "Not to be an attendant upon one of these entertainments," one observer felt, "is to argue oneself outside the pale of 'society.'" To many a concert visit represented a bulwark against less-educated members of urban populations. Ritzy boxes and parquet seats could cost as much as $2 per evening. Some orchestras even auctioned off season subscriptions to individual seats for several hundred dollars, as was the case in Boston, where Isabella Stewart Gardner paid $560 for her balcony seat during the 1900–1901 season.[8]

On the other hand, "going to the symphony" did not require riches, as conductors, managers, and symphonies, systematically and successfully, drew listeners from all walks of life. Concert halls offered plenty of inexpensive seating, and we need to wonder about who sat there before running to conclude that symphony culture was elitist. In Chicago, St. Louis, and Pittsburgh, individual tickets ranged between 25 cents and $1.50 to $2.50.[9] The inexpensive entrance fees for the gallery and the rear seats often accounted for as much as 40 percent of all tickets sold in a hall; and though they cost more than tickets to the nickelodeon, they were less expensive than a those to a theater performance (already priced at 25 cents in the antebellum period).[10] Even vaudeville theaters ranged in price from ten cents to one dollar in the 1890s, and they attracted thousands of working-class visitors each year.

Next to upper-class ladies and gentlemen who spent their fortunes on the dress circle and the boxes, lower-income audiences—workers, office girls, "toilers," single women living in city boarding houses, and other middle-class Americans—likewise filled the ranks of every auditorium in the United States. When Emil Oberhoffer resigned from conducting in Minneapolis, he received numerous notes from "average citizens," ranging from housewives to nurses to ministers, often people who had attended the concerts since childhood. The Saint Louis Symphony Society reported in its annual report of 1911–12 that among the most enthusiastic supporters of the society were men and women who had only lately developed a taste for classical music.[11] Observed the *Boston Daily Globe* in 1892, "Verily, verily democratic was the audience traversing the scale from the seat-owners, who covered them with gold eagles, to the 'rushers,' the people who pay a quarter and face murder, sudden death and annihilation to get the upper balcony unreserved seats."[12]

The heterogeneous makeup of the audience is significant, because it defies the notion of concerts as an elitist affair designed to help patrons distinguish themselves from the lower classes and exhibit taste and refinement. Ticket sellers confirmed over and over again that social standing was a poor indicator of a patron's preference. Some wealthy listeners insisted that the second balcony seats were the most desirable in the entire auditorium. Others might spend a week's pay on a seat in the orchestra circle, because that's where they wanted to be. The Minneapolis Symphony Orchestra even established a policy by which patrons could pay for their tickets in installments, an opportunity seized by many of more modest means. Likewise, a number of wealthy patrons in the city purchased season tickets and had them passed on to people who could not afford to attend a symphony concert. During World War I, a Minneapolis philanthropist issued the orchestra's manager a carte blanche, instructing him to distribute tickets among those he knew would enjoy the concerts, while she covered the expenses.[13]

More than anything else, people expressed their appreciation of classical music through their ticket purchases, their subscriptions, their contributions, and their letters. When Chicago music lovers were asked to contribute to an endowment fund for a new concert hall, 8,000 people—wealthy merchants but also scrubwomen, janitors, doormen, and clerks—gave more than $750,000 to the fund in less than a year, with donations ranging from 24 cents to $25,000.[14] Many listeners stressed that symphony concerts were not simply a fashionable event. "The concerts and rehearsals are attended largely by people of moderate, and even scanty means," wrote a Dedham pastor to Boston's Henry Higginson, in March 1882. "I see them there. The low price enables many parents to take, or send, children who are just beginning musical studies." Workers wrote to apologize for their late arrivals at afternoon rehearsals because they had to work until 2:00 p.m.[15]

Similarly, organizers made a consistent effort to draw listeners into symphony halls "without distinction of sex and color," occupation, or age. There were afternoon concerts to attract single and "unchaperoned" female listeners, who until the advent of the movies hardly participated in the world of public entertainment.[16] Chicago's Theodore Thomas Orchestra designed special workers' concerts and children's concerts to reach wider audiences, a concept that appealed to orchestras in Pittsburgh, Minneapolis, and other cities as well.[17] In New York City in 1910, a number of wealthy citizens subscribed to a fund specifically designed for a series of free music concerts.[18] The Philadelphia Orchestra offered special package deals for students, while the city's Germania Orchestra in 1895 placed the price of admission for its symphonic concerts "so low that no student or lover of music can be prevented from enjoying these performances because of the expense."[19]

It is difficult to tell to what extent African Americans attended symphony concerts. Observers did not comment on this group any more than they commented on other ethnic minorities in the makeup of audiences. Photographs and reports of queues lining up before tickets went on sale in Boston, for example, indicate the presence of well-dressed African Americans. In 1911, Rudolph Ganz observed that his piano concert in Dallas included more than twenty African Americans in the audience.[20] We also know that Henry Higginson took a great deal of interest in bringing African Americans to symphony concerts and, moreover, worried about segregation in the audience. In 1914, when the New York Philharmonic performed in Washington, DC, its president, Oswald Garrison Villard, a civil rights activist and owner of several newspapers, reported on "a great many colored people" who had protested that their seats had been moved to a specific corner of the auditorium in order to enforce segregated seating.[21]

In some cities, the demand for concerts exceeded the organizers' wildest expectations. The annual report of the New York Philharmonic for the season of 1855–56 apologized for the insufficient accommodation for associate members and subscribers at concerts and rehearsals. Overwhelmed by the increasing demand for orchestral music, the society had to cram people into small concert halls and stop the sale of extra tickets.[22] Often, crowds in front of ticket offices became so aggressive that people feared for their lives. In Pittsburgh in October 1898, eager listeners waited in line for over forty hours in order to purchase tickets. Well-to-do music lovers sent envoys to hold their place until the box office opened, and several policemen kept order around the clock. The Postal Telegraph company, the Holmes electric company, and the Western Union sent an army of boys to hold places in line. Three years later, the average wait had grown to sixty-two hours, but by then the lines had become a much more structured affair. Envoy boys were organized into relief corps, with two occupying one spot alternately for twelve hours.[23]

In Boston in 1889, ticket scalpers hired tramps, vagabonds, and homeless people to stand in line for over a week, in order to be first when the ticket office for symphony concerts opened. The line of more than 120 men meandered from Winter Street to Music Hall. Some speculators had several dozen men in line, a motley crowd aged anywhere between child and senior, who typically came from the other side of the tracks and belonged to one of Boston's gangs. The deal they had agreed on was always the same: for four to five dollars, rain or shine, the men would never leave an assigned spot unless permitted to do so by the agent of the speculator. When the ticket office opened, each man could purchase four tickets, the maximum allowance per buyer. After one week of waiting in line, the crowd was on the brink of a riot. Boredom and fatigue had led to argu-

THE FRIENDLY FENCE

WITHOUT DISTINCTION OF SEX OR COLOR

FIRST OF THE BOOK AND LAST OF THE LINE

BOSTON DAILY ADVERTISER, SATURDAY MORNING, MARCH 13, 1909

21 In some cities, the demand for concerts exceeded the organizers' wildest expectations. Lines often meandered through the street and around the corners, increasing to hundreds of people so that the police had to be called. "The Friendly Fence," "Without Distinction of Sex or Color," and "First of the Book and Last of the Line," photo spread, *Boston Daily Advertiser*, 13 March 1909; BSO scrapbooks, MF Pres/13, Boston Symphony Orchestra Archives. Courtesy of the Boston Symphony Orchestra Archives.

ments, fistfights, and "disorderly conduct." The manager of the Boston Symphony Orchestra asked city police to dispatch a number of officers to preserve order and protect the sleeping men on the opposite side of the court. The city even contemplated declaring camping in front of the concert hall a felony, but to no avail. Motley passersby began to block the street, staring at the crowd in awe. A group of old missionary ladies visited the men, concerned they might catch cold and die. Aspiring writers stopped by to gather material for essays and novels. Street vendors made their regular rounds to sell apples, drinks, and Washington pie.[24]

The diversity of the audience may account for the fact that behavior in concert halls was not quite as reverent as we have previously believed, both before and after the Civil War. In the antebellum period, programs reminded Philharmonic audiences in Philadelphia that "no gentleman will be permitted to wear his hat in the room during the evening, or dance in his boots," and that "standing on the seats is strictly prohibited."[25] Music lovers frequently threw objects at singers to express their disapproval. A news notice posted in Philadelphia promised a "Pistole Reward—To whoever can discover the person who was so very rude as to throw Eggs from the Gallery upon the Stage, last Monday, by which the Cloathes of some Ladies and Gentlemen were spoiled and the performance in some measure interrupted."[26]

Well into the 1880s, stamping feet during the flaring of trombones and trumpets was a popular pastime, while those who did not enjoy a particular piece would often continue to converse, whistle, or even get up and leave the hall. Boston's conductor, Georg Henschel, initiated a rule of closing the doors to the hall before the first piece was performed, thus leaving latecomers out in the lobby until the first movement was over.[27] At a concert in 1882, two patrons of the Boston Symphony Orchestra— George F. Hall, a commission merchant, and Charles Eustis Hubbard, a lawyer—engaged in a bloody fistfight, during which the lawyer lost a good part of his frontal dentures. The Hubbards and the Halls had season seats next to each other, and Hall's wife claimed that Mr. Hubbard's conduct during the concert had been insulting.[28] "I am playing very well, but it seems that the people did not understand the 'Rhapsody,'" the pianist Rudolph Ganz reported in 1904, from a tour that took him to San Francisco, Los Angeles, Portland, and Seattle. "According to the accompanying notes I must expect to be among the fatalities or dog shows at the next concert."[29] Indeed, in Ann Arbor, Michigan, a patron brought along a large dog, whose barking annoyed the conductor Victor Herbert "very much."[30] The habit of conversing—especially in the fashionable boxes—caused numerous subscribers to send complaints to their orchestras. "Would it not be possible," asked one in Chicago, "to make this interruption of the music a social offense which would not be tolerated any more than it is in Baireuth [*sic*]?"[31]

Well into the twentieth century, music critics sought to counter rude behavior by instructing audiences on how best to prepare themselves for the challenge of a German-style symphony. Women were advised to be dressed in time and men to smoke a pipe or a cigar before the mad rush for seats began. Wives were urged to treat their husbands with utmost tact; husbands were asked to commend their wives on their attire. Both were to consume easily digestible food and light wine before a concert. "Strong waters should be studiously avoided, but much coffee may be recommended in case of a symphony by Brahms," advised one critic in 1906. "The conversation at table should be cheerful, modeled on that of Sir Thomas More before he went to the scaffold."[32]

The author of this recommendation pointed to one of the key characteristics of the symphony scene: women clearly led the armada of subscribers and fans. Kara Gardner has shown the ways in which aspects of nineteenth- and early twentieth-century American culture were perceived as feminized. As patrons, cultivators, producers, and consumers, women reigned in the field of culture. Ideals of masculinity that emphasized physical strength and character building rendered entry for into the cultural scene increasingly difficult for American men.[33]

In the audience, women were the mainstay of enthusiasm. "The symphony girl," the "Boston girl," or "the rehearsal girl" was one of the most commented-on audience members in the press, and over the decades she became a regular feature at rehearsals across the nation. For unmarried women, the symphony clearly was a respectable place to attend without an escort. Furthermore, active amateur performing groups were a crucial aspect of public life, as was the growing profession of female music teachers.[34]

In October 1907, fifteen hundred people waited in line for hours in front of Boston's Symphony Hall to secure rush balcony seats to afternoon rehearsals. Traffic on Huntington Avenue, including the trolley cars, had to stop, then inch their way through the crowd. Less than 10 percent of those in line were men (mostly music students), and were scrutinized curiously by the surrounding women. Eventually, two-thirds of the queue had to be turned away, many with tears in their eyes. "I have been in theaters when 'Fire!' was cried, I have been on the water when it was reported that the steamer had a hot shaft, but I never saw anything cause such a violent panic as the mere opening of Music Hall doors causes before a Symphony rehearsal," commented Louis Madison from the *Boston Gazette*.[35]

The symphony girl had no name or a particular occupation. She could be a working-class or office girl who took the afternoon off in order to enjoy classical music. She could be a conservatory student who denied herself any luxury in order to attend symphony concerts. She could be an educated middle-class girl who went to the symphony because her mother told her so, and also because it provided her with an opportunity to do something alone with a female companion. Or, she could be a picturesque socialite who loved to be part of the fashionable throng, even though she herself had to sit on the steps. They all were part of the mad rush for seats on Friday afternoons where elbows were used at liberty to secure the best seats available and women stepped on each others' toes, evoking comparisons with "greedy animals" and "escaped lunatics."[36] A young female member of the Milwaukee Musikverein, founded in 1850, experienced such a strong level of musical fanaticism that she did not speak for an entire year once rehearsals had begun but only sang while consistently tapping her feet and clapping her hands to keep time.[37] "And yet, I give you my word of honor," stated one reporter, that the symphony girls "looked as pretty, and as artless, and as quiet as if they had not two thoughts in their two heads."[38]

The fan cult of adult women and teenage girls for individual artists continued to fascinate music critics across the nation. The poet Fanny R. Ritter compared Liszt, Wagner, and Berlioz to "strange, rich, foreign, fine, bewildering perfume," while a Boston reporter attributed a "decidedly effeminate air" to Georg Henschel. "Girls, listen!" exclaimed the *Cincinnati Post* upon a new conductor's arrival. "Stokovski [*sic*] is handsome; he is tall; he is blond; he is 29, and they say he has a great future. And he is single."[39]

An air of loneliness—and hence availability—added considerably to a male artist's attraction among the symphony girls. "No wonder Sauer pleases the women!" observed a Boston newspaper in November 1898. "He is tall, handsome and athletic-looking, and has about him a dreamy, poetic look, as if he were dwelling amid things ethereal."[40] "Soloist Likes American Girls: So, Girls, There's a Chance" is how the *Cincinnati Post* advertised the arrival of the forty-one-year-old pianist Alfred Reisenauer in 1904, when he performed a concerto by Franz Liszt. Reisenauer capitalized on this adulation by commenting publicly on American girls in his broken English. "Ah-a woman-a ah lady—ah kee-esed me in New York," he related in one interview. No, he wasn't married, he informed a young lady seeking an autograph. "You can have me at any time." Though Reisenauer's looks did not strike observers as being exactly handsome—he was rather obese or, as Liszt said, "malheureusement trop

"OH, YOUNG LOOHINVAR OAME OUT OF THE WEST!"
JOURNAL.
March 12. 1912.

22  Minnesota girls were so infatuated with their German conductor, Emil Oberhoffer, that
newspapers likened him to Sir Walter Scott's poetic hero, knight Lochinvar, who took away
the bride of Netherby. "Oh, Young Lochinvar Came Out of the West!" Cartoon, *Minneapolis
Journal*, 12 March 1912; MSO scrapbooks, vol. 10, Home Season 1911–12, Performing Arts
Archives, University of Minnesota. Courtesy of the Performing Arts Archives, University of
Minnesota.

sujet à l'embonpoint"—he was a recognized genius, big on the piano, witty, jovial, and, according to the *Cincinnati Post*, "would make a first-class Santa Claus."[41] Rudolph Ganz observed in 1907 that "so many girls have been falling in love with me, for 6, 12, or even 24 hours, regular concert-first-sight-affairs. . . . I have accepted dinners, receptions, automobile rides and have been a real star."[42] At Anton Seidl's funeral in Metropolitan Hall, female mourners reportedly outnumbered men twenty to one; fifteen thousand music lovers had applied for tickets, but only four thousand had been admitted.[43]

Still, we need to be careful with the suspected effeminate quality seen in musical activity. After all, the men ran most of the orchestral associations, they sat in the audiences, and they paid the performers. Even the great conductor Arthur Nikisch conceded that fashion and female sociability did not account for Bostonians' attention to serious music. Music "is the last material in the world which anybody would chose pour passer le temps," he said. "You can't get people to sit it through merely that they may elbow some local leader of fashion and be counted 'in the swim.' "[44]

And even if people could not attend a concert for lack of funds or because their residence happened to be too far away from one of the music centers, they still strove to participate in the post–Civil War music craze. Music lovers across the nation familiarized themselves with the canon as music making and performance became integral parts of the Victorian American home. Amateurism flourished, and that in itself reveals the appeal of serious music among those who did not print and publish what they thought. In Boston and New York, the composer Lowell Mason taught public schoolchildren rhythm, melody, expression, and how to sing and sightread. Facilitated by readily available sheet music, the international publishing industry as well as instrument manufacturers catered to an increasing clientele in urban and rural areas who grew accustomed to singing or playing an instrument at home not only for recreation and family entertainment but also for education.[45] As a result, many Americans had more performing experience than we do today. Home music-making was the only way to listen to music around the house before the advent of the gramophone as a consumer product in the early 1900s.

The piano became a standard piece of furniture in middle- and upper-class homes nationwide. By 1850, the piano, manufactured by German, French, and, increasingly, American companies, dominated parlors. Generations of sons and, even more so, daughters were put through years of practice, often at great financial sacrifice for the rest of the family, in order to finish their cosmopolitan education. Piano manufacturers targeted parents of young girls, urging them to prepare their daughters for marriage with the purchase of a piano, because "Music hath charms to sooth the savage beast [sic]." The harsh lessons of the German "Klavierschule," the standard teaching repertoire for pre–World War I piano students, occupied generations of American girls, who spent long hours at their instrument, thus depicting the conspicuous consumption of Victorian life so vividly dissected by Thorstein Veblen.[46]

Still, in 1910 139,000 teachers taught Americans how to play on parlor pianos, uprights, baby grands, and grands. Six years later, William Geppert's *Official Guide to Piano Quality* counted over forty American piano companies with a capital stock between $100,000 and $2 million or more who produced more than 300,000 pianos per year.[47] In New York City alone, there were 9,000 music instructors (2,000 violinists alone and 54 triangle experts) who collectively earned approximately $750,000. New Yorkers bought pianos adding up to $750,000 per year.[48]

At the same time, indigenous music publications, music dictionaries, and music history collections began to appear in the United States, such as John W. Moore's *Complete Encyclopaedia of Music*. In 1891, John Knowles Paine edited a four-volume work titled *Famous Composers and Their Works*. The series was designed to provide American music lovers with biographies of seventy famous composers, descriptions of individual compositions, and a compilation of of essays on the development of music in Italy, Germany, France, England, the United States, and other countries. Most important, *Famous Composers* also included a selection of music scores arranged for the pianoforte in order to provide amateur players with accessible samples of music.[49]

Such widespread activity did not mean that everybody *could* play or sing. Along with critical music teachers and chorus directors, family members exposed to households full of piano scales, voice practice, and chamber concertos voiced their dismay. "I am blessed with a wife, and afflicted with four daughters," wrote a reader in a letter to the editor of the *New York Music Trade Review*. His tranquil days, this father related, were disturbed by his daughters' hours of Czerny's exercises and scale practices, as well as Wagner transcriptions and vocal exercises. "The former is death on music, and the latter will be the destruction of their parent's reason unless you intervene." Why, this agitated father asked, were all girls supposedly musical if women in general had never displayed any genius for music? "Why must Chopin be murdered and Beethoven be massacred to make a domestic holiday?"[50]

But the experts insisted that domestic holidays had to be sacrificed on the United States' road to music education. John Van Cleve, editor of the journal *Music*, believed that "the element of newness in our civilization must be constantly taken as a silent but potent factor" in the United States' musical development. Rushing through "chemical changes" and "still in the early ferment," Americans had nonetheless learned to appreciate music to the extent that it now loomed large in the nation's social and educational life. The interplay between music and character, Van Cleve held, strengthened nerves and muscles.[51]

———

Music historians investigating the history of repertories in the nineteenth-century United States have suggested that concert programs at the time were highly eclectic. One could find parts of a symphony and an overture of German or Austrian origin along with Italian opera selections, quadrilles, and virtuoso items of Franco-Italian origin on one and the same program. Indeed, conductors and soloists frequently mingled "serious" music with lighter fare, including folk songs and arias from French and Italian operas. Thanks to the abundance of antebellum touring opera companies, elite and ordinary Americans alike knew the operatic canon almost as well as did their European counterparts.[52]

Nonetheless, they all believed in the juxtaposition of music to *German*, however vaguely defined. This is all the more curious since, all claims notwithstanding, neither the performers nor the musical repertory in nineteenth-century United States was entirely German. For one thing, directors like Louis Jullien, pianists like Louis Gottschalk, and composers like Amy Beach, George W. Chadwick, Edward MacDowell, Horatio Parker, John Knowles Paine, and Arthur Foote—in short, the Boston classicists— all sought to carve a niche for their music; many of them were inspired by European training, but others were not. Their music was heard, and particularly in the fifteen years before World War I, directors strove to include American compositions in their programs. Musicians, whether German, American, or any other nationality, bonded with one another and often formed an international community.

There was also a vast amount of music besides symphonic music, Lutheran hymnody, and Wagnerian opera, and much of the music played and performed did not originate with German composers. Until 1900, Americans attributed much significance to vocal music, especially in the form of sacred music and opera. We have seen how Italian, British, French, and German vocal artists and opera companies contributed to the shaping of the United States' general music scene. Apart from Wagner and Weber, Italian composers still dominated the opera. Moreover, turn-of-the-century music journals reveal quite a few articles on French music, especially regarding pedagogy, the tours of Saint-Saëns and D'Indy, the reception of Debussy, and the like. Likewise, there were countless popular folk ballads, Tin Pan Alley songs, drinking songs, church hymns, choral music, and later on ragtime, jazz, blues, opera, piano music, band music, guitar and fiddle music, and many others.[53]

At the same time, there is no doubt that the German-Austrian repertory outweighed everything else on orchestral concert programs throughout the nation. Between 1890 and 1915, more than 60 percent of all music performed by American symphonies stemmed from Austro-German composers, followed by approximately 12 percent each of French and Russian music. Less than 4 percent of the music played was composed by Italian composers, while American music occupied less than 1 percent of the program selections.[54]

This may not be a surprise, since German and Austrian composers dominated the canon of symphonic music. Still, it is important to understand the difference between the repertory and the canon. While a repertory merely comprises actual performances, the canon manifests an ideology. To play and perform a certain kind of music does not integrate it into the canon of accredited masterpieces. Critics, pedagogues, performers, connoisseurs, and the public needed to accept and establish a regular place for a specific kind of music (in this case symphonic) in the surrounding musical culture; their consensus and the longevity of a composer or a piece then made that composer or piece part of the canon. As William Weber argues, in the past, composers from different regions had always competed for control of styles on an international scope, with the result that one region typically became hegemonic for one or several genres. The nineteenth-century canon defined music as a spiritual, moral, uplifting, and purifying force. It drew its strengths from the assumption that some composers and their music could withstand the threat of commercialization. These composers would rescue musical life and help their audiences reach a "higher plane" untarnished by the concerns of a capitalist society. By the second half of the nineteenth century, the preponderance of classical music was, thus, at once German, universal, and cosmopolitan, less a "living repertory" than a new canonic repertory, which spread to all areas of the Western world and even to Asia.[55]

In other words, not the repertory but the ideology attached to classical music set German compositions apart from all other genres. For all their popularity and tradition, opera music and virtuoso music, which featured prominently on concert programs throughout the Western world, never found themselves explicitly associated with humanist values, cosmopolitanism, or the national soul. Consequently, the preponderance of German music was mostly visible in a set of social ideals rather than in concert programs or in what people preferred to play on their home pianos.

The recognition of music as a higher art developed gradually, and conductors worked hard to lure their audiences to concerts celebrating the masters while also offering music for the heart. To reach this goal, they often employed a "carrot-and-stick" strategy, offering a combination of musical fares that appealed to all tastes. The idea was not altogether new; lightening up heavy symphonic music with solos and arias, so-called divertissimos, had been common in Europe in the early nineteenth century, because concert organizers felt that it was unreasonable to make audiences sit through four movements in a row. When Felix Mendelssohn took over the Leipzig Gewandhaus in 1835, he nearly caused a scandal by abandoning all variety programs and divertissimos and instead bombarding audiences with full-length symphonies. Even the Berlin concerts of Benjamin Bilse's band in the 1860s and '70s, which in 1882 formed the core of the Berlin Philharmonic, often presented a mélange of symphonic, "modern," dance, choir, and entertainment music in a restaurantlike setting, where audiences enjoyed light libations while listening to the performance.[56]

After the Civil War, interplays and surprises remained distinctive features of American concert stages. In the late 1860s, when cruising with his orchestra across the American landscape, Theodore Thomas attracted audiences with lighter fare and did not even shy away from dance music and popular songs before he beat them over the head with entire symphonies. His early concerts in Central Park (starting 1868) were frequently complemented with beer and refreshments, and often featured a lot more light music than serious compositions. Thomas even inserted little stage surprises into his performances, including piccolo players hiding in nearby trees or a tuba player concealed by shrubbery.[57] As late as 1908, Chicago socialites posed and dressed up to entertain the public during a concert of the Chicago Orchestra (known as the Theodore Thomas Orchestra between 1905 and 1913) that included compositions by Wagner, Grieg, Handel, Bizet, Chopin, Liszt, Mendelssohn, and others. "Mrs. George Rublee took the part of a moth," the *Chicago Herald-Record* reported that January, "and received much applause, executing a dainty dance with much finish and grace."[58]

What exactly did orchestras play? Concert programs focused on, first, the canon and the music that was considered German (and Austrian); second, modern European and American music; and, finally, popular music designed to attract larger audiences.

By 1890, Beethoven was the most performed composer on American orchestral programs, followed by Wagner. The sponsor of the Boston

Symphony Orchestra, Henry Higginson, specifically requested that all nine Beethoven symphonies be performed and repeated during the second and third seasons, along with nine other works by the composer. In 1903, the Philadelphia Orchestra gave consecutive performances of all the Beethoven symphonies within the span of seven days. Wagner dropped to number three in 1900 (after Tchaikovsky), and number four in 1915 (behind Brahms).[59]

Out of 92 pieces performed during the first season of the Boston Symphony Orchestra, in 1881–82, 74 were German, 10 French, 4 Italian (Cherubini, Boccherini, Rossi), 2 Scandinavian (Grieg, Gade), 1 Czech (Dvorak), and 1 American (Paine). While French music received some attention and remained a point of interest throughout the following years, British and Russian music entered the orchestra's repertoire during its second year; Russian music became very prominent on the orchestra's programs around the turn of the twentieth century. The local composer John Knowles Paine just made it into the final program of the first season with his Prelude to *Oedipus Tyrannus*.

Given their cultural mission and their audiences' preference, it is not surprising that Austrian and German composers dominated most orchestral programs. When Wilhelm Gericke joined the Boston Symphony Orchestra in 1884, American music immediately vanished from the program, as the conductor had not yet met Paine or Chadwick; later, he invited the two to lecture on Beethoven symphonies and German music at large. Only during his fifth season did Gericke repeat a work by an American composer, Paine's symphonic poem *The Tempest*.

Blockbuster concert programs also included performances of Wagner operas. Though this study is not principally concerned with opera, it's important to note that Wagner achieved the impossible: utterly novel and exclusively operatic, his works entered the canon to an extent no Italian opera composer ever had. For about a dozen years at the end of the nineteenth century, Wagner ruled the American stage, and conductors such as Walter Damrosch, Theodore Thomas, and Anton Seidl took great strides to promote his music. During the Met's season of 1885–86 (late November to mid-April), it gave 95 performances of Wagner compositions, nearly half of which took place outside New York City in Cincinnati, Cleveland, Philadelphia, Chicago, and St. Louis. Due to Wagner's enormous popularity, conductors in Boston gave Wagner programs more than one hundred times.[60]

Again, German music constituted part of the canon, the ideology. In reality, all orchestras presented an increasing amount of contemporary and non-German works. The Russian-French repertory, for example, grew steadily. In Boston, arguably the bastion of musical conservativism in the United States, Arthur Nikisch scheduled 48 standard works (written before 1866) but also 39 contemporary ones (written in or after 1866 or by a living composer) during the season of 1891–92. During the 1894–95 season, when Emil Paur was conductor, the Boston Symphony Orchestra gave three concerts without any German music while playing plenty of contemporary pieces from American, Russian, Czech, Hungarian, and Scandinavian composers (even so, 76 out of the 114 works presented were German-Austrian). Gericke, during his second term in 1899–1900, gave a hearing to compositions by Parker, Goldmark, Chadwick, Paine, and Beach. In 1904, Paur even conducted Tchaikovsky's Sixth Symphony, written in 1903 and premiering in St. Petersburg that same year (he repeated the performance four times). Karl Muck gave an all-Russian program and presented more American works during one season than had any other conductor up to that time. During the 1910–11 season (under Max Fiedler), only 51 out of 100 works performed by the Boston Symphony Orchestra were of German or Austrian origin, while 4 stemmed from American, 17 from French, and 12 from Russian composers.[61]

That pattern did not seem to have varied much elsewhere. At the Minneapolis Symphony Orchestra during its first couple of seasons, Beethoven, Mozart, Liszt, Saint-Saëns, and Wagner led its repertory, while Brahms, Tchaikovsky, and Debussy, still regarded as daring novelties, were missing. Among the repeated favorites were Dvorak's symphony *From the New World*, Goldmark's *Rustic Wedding*, Schubert's *Unfinished* Symphony, Liszt's *Les Preludes*, Wagner's Prelude to *Die Meistersinger*, and the Overture to Weber's *Oberon*.[62]

These programs reveal both the viability of the "German canon" and the reality of the international repertory. Compositions by Beethoven, Bach, and Mozart continuously dominated the seasonal programs. But there was always an abundance of music that, while popular at the time, is forgotten today, including works by Karl Loewe and Niels Gade. Moreover, musical leaders wanted to experiment with European modern music that had never been played in the United States, including works by Bedrich Smetana, Nikolai Rimsky-Korsakoff, Peter Tchaikovsky, César Franck, Henry Vieuxtemps, and Jean Sibelius.[63] Richard Strauss's *Festival Prelude* premiered in Vienna just a few days earlier than it had in its U.S. debut, in Minneapolis in October 1913.[64] His compositions counted among the most sought-after pieces orchestras tried to give "first." Often several orchestras premiered his works within the span of a few days, among those the controversial *Till Eulenspiegel*. Nearly every orchestra in the United States eventually played the piece, and many more than

23 "Open: The Pop Concert Season Opened at Symphony Hall Last Evening." Cartoon, *Boston Globe*, 3 May 1910; BSO scrapbooks, MF Pres/13, Boston Symphony Archives. Courtesy of the Boston Symphony Orchestra Archives.

once.[65] In Philadelphia, Leopold Stokowski crammed over one hundred world or U.S. premieres into twenty-nine seasons, among them Gustav Mahler's Eighth Symphony in E-flat ("Symphony of a Thousand").[66] Hailed as gatekeepers of the canon, these conductors nonetheless proved more courageous than the many professional critics, committees, and connoisseurs exasperated with modern music.[67]

Finally, many orchestras introduced popular programs to attract even larger audiences. Often called "pops," these programs began with Musard and Jullien in Paris in the 1820s, from which place they spread to London and the rest of Europe and, finally, to the United States.[68] Popular concerts became one of the most persistent features of the American symphony scene. In Minneapolis, audiences could even leisurely walk around enjoying ice cream and strawberries. At the 1904 World Exhibition in St. Louis, the local orchestra played a mélange of popular music that included Strauss waltzes; customers accompanied the "Anvil Chorus" from Verdi's *Il Trovatore* by clanking their spoons against beer steins.[69]

American popular concerts meant what the term connoted: they included music that was particularly favored by audiences and "easy to digest." Such concerts typically contained a larger number of short pieces that could range from light overtures, such as Weber's *Oberon*, to ballet music, opera music, arias, songs, and solos for flute, piano, or violin to waltzes, polkas, polonaises, and other dance music, though the audience was not supposed to dance. Symphonic poems, suites by known composers, and marches featured prominently on popular concert programs. Among the most performed composers were Johann Strauss, Richard Wagner, Fréderic Chopin, Carl Maria von Weber, Anton Dvorak, and Mozart. Excerpts from Wagnerian operas, too, became favorites at popular concerts at the turn of the twentieth century.[70] Although the conductors typically disdained the pop concerts (for fear that such concerts might compromise their artistic standards and erode the orchestra's reputation),[71] many orchestras introduced so-called request concerts, where subscribers could vote on a selection from a variety of pieces circulated in advance.[72] The artists' effort to meet the audience halfway is evidence for the fact that their message was not meant to be elitist and confined but, rather, all-embracing and universal: the more people from all walks of life listened to symphonic music, the better.

––––––

The symphony canon favored German classical compositions, notably those nineteenth-century masters who American critics and audiences perceived as "German." The canon constituted the core of the emotional elective affinity and the heart of the German artists' mission. The musicians worked hard to familiarize audiences from all walks of life with the master composers—and were successful in enthusing them, as the numbers outlined show. American audiences came to embrace serious music—and identify it as fundamentally German.

But in reality, the orchestral repertory was more diverse. New U.S., French, Russian, Slavic, and Scandinavian composers found their way into American concert programs, as did modern German composers whose works were often performed in the United States shortly after their world premieres in Europe. The canon facilitated the entrance for these latter composers, including Ferruccio Busoni, Kurt Weill, and Paul Hindemith (because they were German), but it also disappointed many listeners, who felt that the neoclassicists betrayed the cultural heritage of Germany. Peter Gay has written that much of this reaction was part of a transatlantic phenomenon. Audiences in Boston and Berlin once responded with the same degree of dismay (if not fear) to the compositions of Johannes Brahms. Indeed, that notorious exit sign, "This Way Out in Case of Brahms," is said to have been put up in Boston's Symphony Hall as well as in the concert hall of Vienna's Gesellschaft der Musikfreunde.[73]

Women played a key role in the reception of music and the formation of an emotional elective affinity. As organizers, as fans, and even as occasional stars, their impact on the American music scene is indisputable. Most important, many of the values attributed to music were borrowed from the feminine sphere, including its emotional power as an uplifting moral force. Still, it would be misleading to reduce American reactions to the symphony to a mere class-and-gender analysis. Soloists cruising the American "symphonyscape" represented a particularly heterogeneous mélange, whose countries of origin ranged from Australia to Venezuela. Likewise, going to the symphony was by no means a highbrow form of entertainment: many listeners were from the middle and lower-middle classes. And many leading artists, organizers, sponsors, and audience members were men.

Curiously, the celebration of German high culture, and German music in particular, never connected with the actual German community in the United States, but remained firmly grounded in central European culture. The universalism of German music depended on its spiritual closeness to Europe, however geographically vague. As mentioned in chapter 4, German Americans, in contrast, remained loyal to their ethnic enclaves and reluctant to donate privately; they refrained from mingling extensively with the crowd frequenting the temples of Anglo-American entertainment—even though the canon celebrated favored German music.[74] This explains why symphony managers did next to nothing to attract German audiences. Their ads targeted Germans in Germany, but not German Americans. In February 1872, the New York Philharmonic's Board of Directors prepared a list of periodicals and societies in Germany to which it would send programs and begin correspondence. One year later, it resolved to advertise concerts in the German *Musik Zeitung*. But the Philharmonic never targeted the German-American press, and some critics from German-language newspapers were turned down when applying for free tickets. In 1899, the Philharmonic resolved to discontinue the advertising of its performances in the *New Yorker Staats-Zeitung*, one of the most important German-language newspapers in the United States.[75] In other words, the emotional elective affinity formed a direct link between U.S. elites and Germany without a detour via the German-American community.

# SIX

# Musical Patriotism and the Fear of Europe

Oh, Henschel, cease thy higher flight!
And give the public something light;
Let no more Wagner themes thy bill enhance
And give the native workers just one chance.
Don't give the Dvorak symphony again;
If you would give us joy, oh, give us Paine![1]

If all the symphonic composers in the United States congregated for a rally, the critic Louis Elson contemplated in 1886, they would probably fit into one double room in any country hotel. Nonetheless, Elson believed, those few lodgers ought to be heard more frequently, so he urged Boston's conductor, Georg Henschel, to spruce up his programs accordingly. The critic's frustration mirrored a growing dilemma in American music circles, between a continuing admiration for Europe as the center of Western culture and an intensifying cultural nationalism.[2] For all his love for the European masters, Elson feared that indigenous composers were being deliberately shunned by the public. In 1900, the renowned publishing house MacMillan and Co. proposed the publication of a history of American music. Yet the editors could barely find an author, since everyone they approached backed off, indicating that there was no American music (meaning art music) to write about.[3]

Such an explanation, of course, was sheer hyperbole. From 1760 to 1820, the first New England school had featured musical luminaries such as William Billings, Andrew

**151**

Law, Daniel Read, Justin Moran, and Jeremiah Ingalls. The second New England school, coming of age in the 1880s and '90s, encompassed composers such as George Chadwick, Horatio Parker, Amy Beach, Frank Van der Stucken, and others who strove to establish a genuine American school of composing. During the Gilded Age these men and women formed, in the words of the Ohio composer Wilson G. Smith, a "a tidal wave of encouragement" for American Composers' Concerts, that is, concerts featuring selections by composers whose work differed but who shared an American background.[4]

A new generation of genuinely "American" musicians, men like Charles Ives, Arthur Farwell, Daniel Gregory Mason, Edward Burlingame Hill, John Alden Carpenter, and David Stanley Smith (all born between 1872 and 1877), was just coming of age. "Genuinely 'American,'" in this context, refers not simply to their music but to the fact that their families had lived in the United States for many generations. Teaching from avant-garde positions at elite schools such as Harvard, Yale, and Columbia, these men held very definite ideas about a new American music based on radical conceptions of both formalism and imaginative naturalism, all of which would serve to express the American spirit.[5]

Equally important, in the second half of the nineteenth century, Americans founded their own music schools, such as the New England Conservatory, the Chicago Musical College, and the Cincinnati Conservatory of Music, established in 1867. The National Conservatory of Music in New York City was founded in 1885 as the American School of Opera and renamed the National Conservatory in 1886.[6] In the Greater New York area, Frank Damrosch emerged as a pioneer in the field of music instruction for children. By the early 1900s, he had trained thirty-five assistants, whom he would send into more than three hundred public high schools to instruct teachers in music education.[7]

Advocates of American music exhibited two distinct types of nationalism. First, there were those who complained that it was no longer necessary to go to Europe to hear good music, that the United States had enough conductors and musicians to perform symphonic classics without the benefit of imported Europeans. Second, there was a different group of critics who wanted to hear American music, not European music, performed by Americans.

It is impossible to grasp the growing resistance to German music both in and outside the United States without understanding the role of the nationalism that swept across Europe and the United States in the late nineteenth century, and historians have used gallons of ink analyzing the rise and fatal consequences of this phenomenon.[8] As a direct consequence of various political developments and the Second Industrial Revolution, throughout the West the standard of living and self-governance improved dramatically. While more people migrated from the countryside to cities for economic reasons, politics, inspired by notions of autonomy and liberalism, began to focus increasingly on the duties and rights of the individual citizen and, eventually, on his or her contribution to the country as a whole. At the same time, Charles Darwin's and Herbert Spencer's theories of the "survival of the fittest" captivated the European and the American public, who nurtured the view that only the strongest states would thrive. This is where nationalism came in, so to say, as a fitness requirement. In order to grip the public's imagination, nationalism demanded an unusually intense commitment beyond local and regional ties to the state. To improve public life, governments appealed to citizens to be loyal to their nation in order to protect both their individual rights and the greater good of everyone. They promoted hygiene, invested in health and the sciences, cleaned up cities, and built better housing to provide for the long-lasting vigor of the nation.[9]

In the race for national fitness, cultural endeavors played an increasingly prominent role. Major European nations such as France and Germany made a tremendous effort to promote the arts both at home and abroad. Smaller and politically less potent nations in eastern Europe and Scandinavia, in turn, increasingly developed a sense of cultural deprivation fostered by the state (as in the Austro-Hungarian Empire) or by a stateless but dominant culture (as in Norway or Belgium). Collective frustration eventually inspired a powerful cultural nationalism that affected debates about language, religion, and cultural expression.

Nationalism was not a state-imposed program. We have seen how nongovernmental groups pushed their own and often diverging national agendas, long before governments were able and willing to do so. As Jörg Echternkamp has argued, the nation emerged as a product of the social need for nationalism, not vice versa. Recent studies in Germany have highlighted the quasi-political opportunities for and even nonverbal forms of nationalist expression developed by social groups such as religious leaders, business lobbyists, sports associations (*Turner*), and Masonic organizations.[10]

The United States formed a peculiar case in this scenario. On the one hand, the country was rapidly becoming a major industrial and political player in the international arena; in this, it moved closer to the major European powers. On the other hand, like many minor European nations, Americans' sense of indigenous culture remained extremely fragile. Cultural openness and import thus served to compensate for a profound inferiority complex. The resulting debate focused increasingly on the irony of being a "body politick" without a soul.

Music became a powerful ingredient in the nationalization movement throughout the Western world,[11] particularly in the United States. Beginning in the 1890s, an avalanche of articles exploring the nature and significance of national music crowded journals and even the daily press. Headlines such as "Nationality in Music," "The Origin and Growth of National Music," "The National Element in Musical Art," and "The Future of Music" fascinated readers in both Europe and the United States. "Map music," music originating in certain territorial areas, was counterpoised with universal music, music that belonged to everyone; and authors discussed whether the two could coexist, how they could be distinguished, and how they could be heard, understood, and studied.

Many Americans believed that their country had arrived at the industrial, political, and military pinnacle of its fame. The United States had become the fastest-growing economy in the world. Its democratic ways were unique in modern society. Leaders throughout Europe sought the sympathies of the U.S. government. And finally, the Spanish-American War, albeit fought for altogether unclear goals and in territories that most Americans would have been unable to locate on a map, assured people that the nation's military could rival any in Europe.

Yet when Americans looked at themselves, their cultural achievements did not match their international leadership in other areas. In fact, some speculated, the United States' success as a great nation explained its inferiority in the realm of the arts. The government did not spend tax dollars on lavish paintings or erudite theater plays. A democratically inclined citizenry favored popular forms of entertainment over higher forms of art. And perhaps the proverbial speed and restlessness of the American character literally left no time to sit down to write the great novel, create the timeless painting, or compose the immortal symphony. The growing antagonism toward the preponderance of German music and musicians in the United States, the unionization of American musicians, and the aggressive demands for an independent American national music all highlighted the interplay among cultural, social, and political tensions between 1890 and 1914. Ironically, just as people around the globe started to fear the influence of U.S. culture on their own local cultures, no one fretted as much about cultural authenticity as the Americans themselves. And it was precisely this fear that challenged their previous affinity with their houseguests, the "people of music."

It is difficult to overestimate the influence of nationalism on the composition, production, and reception of music throughout the Western world at the turn of the twentieth century. Musical nationalism continued to expand in practically every European country outside Germany and Austria. English critics and artists had worried for decades whether British composers could still produce anything worthwhile in the face of German musical preponderance, whereas French musical critics bluntly called for a ban on German music from French concert stages. Although all over the world music presumably spoke in one universal language, its phraseology was influenced by national characteristics, observed Maud Matras in the *British Monthly Musical Record*: "National idioms can be most clearly discerned in the music of those countries that are the least civilized; for civilization always produces a somewhat neutralizing effect."[12]

In the sciences, research projects concerned with the relationship between music and the nation began to replace those dedicated to music as a tool of international communication. Scholars investigated the national in composition and harmony. Some employed modern polling techniques in an attempt to detect the national element in music, to investigate whether composers borrowed from folk music, songs, and dances, and to find out how they had come to compose national music. In 1911, a team of Polish and German musicians aimed to find out whether individual works revealed conscious or unconscious traces of a composer's national identity; they distributed questionnaires among known and unknown artists all over Europe, inquiring about their work, their citizenship, and their race.[13]

Such international research projects underlined the enormous political and scientific interest in the interplay of music and the nation. Physiologists investigated connections between music, poetry, muscle use, and body attitudes. A lawyer in Munich, Ottmar Rutz, proclaimed in 1911 that certain nations assumed a specific body posture while singing. Based on the research of his father, Josef, a voice teacher, Rutz divided singers rigorously into three types: Italian, French, and German. The Italian, Rutz believed, pushed his lower body forward, which enabled him to express heat and suavity. The German type moved the muscles beneath his hips backward and the chest forward, which enabled him to sing in a high and liberated voice. The French type was subdivided into two parts, both of which sounded, Rutz explained, as if a singer were about to cripple himself.[14]

According to widespread belief, certain nations produced particular harmonies and excelled on specific instruments. In both Europe and the United States, conductors often recommended particular nationalities for individual instrument sections. In Karl Muck's orchestra in Boston, the French dominated the woodwind instruments and Germans ruled in the brass section, while Austrians and some Americans played the strings.[15]

In the United States, music critics dedicated a wealth of essays to the significance of national music in the context of a country's emotional well-being.[16] Among the most prolific American writers on the genre of American music was Jean Moos, in the journal *Music*. In a multitude of articles, Moos tried to explain which criteria countries had to fulfill if they were to become the breeding ground for an indigenous school of composers. Going all the way back to the ancient Egyptians, Greeks, and Romans, Moos argued that material prosperity and a cultivated receptivity to music were key to a national music. A nation's art, he explained in April 1892, depended in general on its mental disposition and particularly on its imagination. Consequently, Moos believed that the northern countries produced an emotionally deep and beautiful music.[17]

As a result of the increasingly nationalized perception of music, critics began to evaluate concert programs accordingly. They would let readers know that there was no composer of German birth represented on a program, or that "Nationalism [was a] Feature of Music Played by [the] Symphony."[18] They periodically reviewed an orchestra's repertory for the year, minutely counted the nations represented, and compiled statistical summaries. At the end of the 1896–97 season on May 2, for example, the *Boston Journal* calculated that among the modern works presented by the Boston Symphony, 2 were American, 5 French, and 12 German, "reckoning Handel and the Bohemians as German." The journal then presented its annual countdown of composers: 25 were Germans (including, curiously, Dvorak, Smetana, and Liszt), 8 Frenchmen, 3 Russians, 2 Italians, 2 Americans, 1 Pole, 1 Scandinavian, and 1 Englishman. Promoting hospitality toward cosmopolitanism but also patriotic pride, the *Chicago Tribune* reviewed the Chicago Orchestra's 1911–12 season by tallying 59 Germans, 17 Slavs, 13 Frenchmen, 8 Hungarians (this time Liszt counted as Hungarian), 7 Americans, 5 Italians, 5 Scandinavians, 3 Englishmen, 1 Romanian, and 1 Dutchman.[19]

Modern composers still were considered controversial, even when coming straight from Germany. The music of Johannes Brahms became so controversial in late nineteenth-century Boston that during the first performance of the Third Symphony, hundreds of listeners left the hall. According to rumors, the management considered installing red emergency lights in the corridors of Symphony Hall, reading, "This Way Out in Case of Brahms." John Sullivan Dwight candidly confessed in his valedictory that modern music "fails to stir us to the same depths of soul and feeling that the old masters did." True, the new European radicals were brilliant and original, but "they do not bring us nearer heaven."[20]

Modern German music confused American audiences because it questioned their emotional preference for Germany: first, it defied audiences' belief in German composers as superior artists. "The Germany of the twentieth century," observed the *Boston Transcript* sarcastically, "is in music, as in all the fine arts, painting, sculpture or architecture, at a lower level than it has been for centuries."[21] Modern composers were bent on confusing and crushing the listener.[22] In doing so, they seemed to exhibit an increasingly anachronistic and undemocratic bent while refusing to appeal to a broader public. When Bruckner's Seventh Symphony was performed in Boston, listeners began to leave after the second movement, and continued their exodus after the third. The *Saturday Evening Gazette* defined the composition as "a prolonged moan and groan, varied now and then with a gloomy and soul-depressing bellow;—Wagner in a prolonged attack of sea-sickness; a huge barnacle-covered whale of a symphony but without any lubricating blubber."[23]

Moreover, modern German music turned the cultural promise of its nation into a demonic ogre. Antimodernist sentiments, as T. Jackson Lears has shown, were widespread among Victorians, and concerned virtually every aspect of life, including religion, family relations, literature, and business. What was peculiar in the context of music was the antimodernists' identification of a clear-cut German culprit. They charged that the young German composers coming of age after Wagner never managed to step out of his shadow. Instead of exhibiting spontaneity, creativity, and inspiration, they turned into manufacturers of monotonous sounds, producing orchestral monsters that might "destroy . . . the Frankensteins who are creating it."[24]

Efforts to "Americanize" music in the United States can be traced to the eighteenth century, even though their influence remained marginal until 1900. Since the Revolution, American publishers such as Andrew Law did much to promote national composers, notably the works of psalmists. But in a manner typical of the short-lived cultural nationalism springing up after 1776, Law ultimately deemed European compositions superior to American ones. And once Law had experienced his musical conversion, he not only ceased to publish American compositions but also demanded that others do the same. Like Law, many New Englanders, in churches and in secular spaces, moved to reform the musical taste and impose a "musical correctness" that limited itself to European imports.[25]

In the 1830s, Ralph Waldo Emerson had urged Americans to develop and express a national mind in their literature and in the arts. Yet there was no unanimity among the participants of the national-music debate. As Betty Chmaj has shown, one camp believed that Americans should develop an artistic independence, a genuinely American form of expression in the arts, and a new American identity unconstrained by "the courtly muses of Europe." The other camp remained wary of efforts to arrive at an American national identity through innate self-discovery. Fearing American artists' parochialism, they instead advocated that American art and American identity be universal and cosmopolitan, bridging the borders that confined the nation-state and its culture.[26] Nativists (such as Emerson) were typically homegrown talents nurturing a profound suspicion of Europe's decaying ways. Universalists (such as Henry Adams), in contrast, were typically well traveled and often regarded themselves as semi-expatriates who sought to unite the values and artistic standards of the old world and the new.[27]

As early as 1852, *Dwight's Journal of Music* detected signs of what it called "Germano-Phobia," mostly brought on by defenders of Italian music and artists. "I can hardly read your journal now, growing worse and worse as it is every day," a subscriber wrote to Dwight in September of that year. "From page 1 to page 192, what is there besides about 50 pages of advertisement? German music, German composers, German artists." Dwight's response to this was plain and simple: Americans were not a musical people; they did not introduce early musical training, they failed to create a musical atmosphere and a broad appreciation for music.[28] Therefore, Americans had to import music and musicians from Germany.

Dwight's foremost opponent before the Civil War was Henry Fry. Born into a well-established Philadelphia family around 1813, Fry was educated in literature, took up journalism, and began to develop an interest in music early on. He composed while working as a journalist and his opera, *Leonora*, became in 1845 the first American opera publicly performed. He composed a few more operas and several symphonies along with some choral and chamber works, none of which won him immortality. In 1852, Fry became editor of the *New York Tribune*, where he began his crusade for the American composer. Untiringly, he wrote and lectured on the necessity of creating a genuinely American opera, a national lyric stage, and a national American music. He widely toured the East, spreading his ideas of an American national music scene while scolding critics and public alike for their musical ignorance. "It is time we had a Declaration of Independence in Art, and laid the foundation of an American School of Painting, Sculpture and Music," Fry postulated in one of his lectures. "The American composer should not allow the name of Beethoven or

Handel or Mozart to prove an eternal bugbear to him, nor should he pay them reverence; he should only reverence his Art, and strike out manfully and independently into untrodden realms."[29]

Much of Fry's argument focused on his own work, notably the *Santa Claus* Symphony, which the composer had reportedly written in four days. When the piece received negative reviews, Fry interpreted the critics' position less as a professional review of his own work than a sneering attitude toward American composers at large. There was no fault with his works, he implied, other than his own national identity.[30] European composers like Beethoven, Mendelssohn, Spohr, and Weber, he held, had "committed blunders" and required written explanations that the musical community accepted, while his, Fry's, own errors and explanations were supposedly inexcusable.[31] Fry did not live to see his arguments take hold; he died from tuberculosis in 1864. But the latent debate on a national if not a nativist music resurfaced in the 1890s and climaxed in the years prior to World War I.

In other words, long before Copland, Gershwin, and others reached the concert halls, American national music, and the study thereof, became entangled in the sometimes militantly nationalistic Americanization movement that swept across U.S. cities around the turn of the twentieth century. This is a curious development, because it contrasted with the previous cultural openness displayed by many Americans in the late nineteenth century. Urban elites who felt threatened by the increasing influx of immigrants from southern and eastern Europe developed an almost hysterical patriotism, exposing a variety of conspiracy theories and demanding the cultural naturalization of each and every new arrival. Many American composers felt equally threatened if not bypassed by the preponderance of German music, and they devised conspiracy theories according to which foreign musicians, bolstered by the financial support of indigenous "cultured elites," sought to control the land and suffocate the native composer.[32]

As Americans experienced a version of the cultural nationalism sweeping European nations, they found themselves in a thicket of internal controversies when they tried to define musical patriotism. The controversy in the United States was especially intense, or perhaps just confusing. Patriotism could urge the playing of music with a distinctly American sound, but what was that sound? What was American music? American music critics believed that the American genius would express itself in American musical composition, written by a composer who was clearly American and, thus, could give a voice to the American experience. Eventually, the debate in the United States shifted to personnel, because this was much easier to define. Supported by American unions, musical patriotism between 1880 and 1920 primarily took the form of focusing on the makeup of the orchestra. The question of art thus became a question of agency: who and what defined an American composer?

Some music historians have foregone birthplace as a basis for national musical identity, emphasizing instead the career path of an artist. If a composer wrote his immortal works in his native land, he was accorded the status of being a national composer of that country: Rachmaninoff remained Russian, Schoenberg Austrian, and Bartok Hungarian, despite their successive relocation. But those who passed their formative years and the pinnacle of their career in another country were identified with their country of residence: Chopin was French (rather than Polish), Handel English (not German), and Rudolph Ganz American (instead of Swiss).

According to this classification, many nineteenth-century American composers could not pass as American, though some nationalists occasionally strove to turn them into musical patriots. Most influential American composers had received their training in Germany. Edward MacDowell had been educated there, then became the secretary of Joseph Raff, a much-played composer, from whom he learned many of his musical ideas. Victor Herbert was Irish but had received all of his training in Germany, as he liked to point out. In the surge of turn-of-the-century cultural nationalism, Herbert's multicultural background led one reporter to conclude that despite Herbert's "accident of foreign birth," and despite his cosmopolitan training, "there is no escaping the one thought—he is a typical American." Frankfurt-born Friedrich Voelker, wrote the *Pittsburgh Post* of the new concertmaster in 1897, was an American because he spoke fluent English and had resided in the United States for nine years.[33] Newspapers classified George Chadwick as "the most American of our composers," not only because he was born in Lowell, Massachusetts, but because the "mood and spirit" of his music sounded "distinctively American," notably in his *Symphonic Sketches*.[34]

Those composers who could have made the final cut on all accounts (birth, heritage, territoriality, novelty, preference) were the ones who were often shunned by the musical inner circle in the first place—due either to their racial profile or their compositions' not meeting the audiences' or the critics' approval. The *Boston Transcript* declared that it was not sufficient to be born in the United States, pointing to the compositions of Templeton Strong, Arthur Bird, and "sundry other Teutonized Americans." Nor did MacDowell compose American music, because "he would have dreamed his dreams of Arthur's court, Celtic queens and

Norse warriors anywhere, and shaped his 'Woodland Sketches' or his sea pieces as readily in Wiesbaden as in Boston."[35]

If it was difficult to determine the Americanness of the composer, the question of identity for the American conductor exacerbated the confusion: who should conduct American music, and who should be privileged to sing, play, and perform it in an appropriately American fashion? Beginning in the late 1890s, critics freely charged that individual conductors were not American enough or that they had not made enough of an effort to become American. Boston's Wilhelm Gericke, said one, had remained as German as he had been on the day of his arrival in the United States, and there was no indication that his extensive stint in the United States had led him to a more accurate grasp of American culture and taste.[36] The majority of German conductors, observed the *New York Morning Telegraph*, had impaired their usefulness to the American music scene because they had remained indifferent to the American way of life, including the English idiom. The problem of foreign artists, then, was not their lack of skills but their sheer foreignness—precisely what had originally attracted American audiences. "Our concert public has been Germanized to death, nearly, for years," wrote Warren Davenport in a review of Schubert *Lieder* accompanied by Arthur Nikisch. "It is time we had a change in this direction."[37]

The foremost hurdle to the success of American music, American critics and artists agreed, was not German conductors and orchestras; nor was it foreign soloists. The foremost hurdle was the American public. Again and again, when conductors such as the Chicago Orchestra's Frederick Stock scheduled all-American programs, the people protested or voted with their feet—and stayed away. The "taste publics" for a genuinely American music, to use an expression coined by Herbert Gans, had not yet found their proper niche.[38] Instead, American music seemed to represent only popular or folk music and was unsuitable for performance in a forum devoted to high culture, at least before Aaron Copland and George Gershwin came on the scene. American musicians would not perform indigenous music because they risked falling out of favor with their audiences, and audiences remained ignorant about American music because they never had a chance to hear it. In Philadelphia, the young conductor Leopold Stokowski proposed an all-American concert once a year outside the regular season, but the orchestra management rejected the idea outright.[39]

The advocates of American music focused on four points: a general antipathy for the preponderance of German musicians; the lack of opportunities for American artists; the search for "the" American composer along with designs for a national school of music; and an almost evangelical belief that the center of the music world would gradually shift westward, from Europe to the United States.

In regard to the first point, newspaper critics increasingly took offense at the importation of foreign artists. American audiences often preferred inferior European imports to American talent, and critics charged that musicians whose talents did not amount to much often tried their luck in the United States after having failed in Europe. "America is to-day over-run by incompetent foreign artists" who felt "that they have but to land and . . . some one will gallop up and hand them a check," observed John Sears in the *Evening Telegraph* in 1904.[40] In 1897, critics reprimanded the Pittsburgh Orchestra conductor Frederic Archer for his preference for European talent and composers, and his alleged anti-American bias—at the same time that subscriptions for season tickets soared to an all-time high: 1,800 out of 2,000 seats were reserved before individual tickets went on sale.[41]

Much criticism focused on the sparse representation of American names in the orchestras of Chicago, Boston, Pittsburgh, and elsewhere. In 1903, a subscriber to the *Musical Courier* expressed bafflement that Henry Lee Higginson, well known for his political patriotism, allowed his orchestra to be managed in an "unpatriotic manner" by passing over local talent for imported musicians whose performance often failed to live up to their advance billing.[42] Conductors and managers retorted that American talent was untrained, because many American orchestra musicians lacked the proper conservatory education typical of European players.[43]

Next to the concern over the importation of musicians, critics worried about the importation of music at the expense of indigenous compositions. Their essays as well as their letters to newspaper editors encouraged the performance of more American music. After the turn of the century, concert reviews intensified their complaints about the American love affair with foreign cultural artifacts. "We always import—especially in music," observed the *Musical Courier* in 1909. "It sounds so much better when it is imported, just as imported Frankfurter tastes so much better because it is imported than our healthy, succulent American sausage. . . . We yell and hurrah for America and then we rehearse our orchestras in German because we import them, instead of educating our own bright and dashing and joyous American boys to play in them."[44]

The third concern driving American criticism of German music was an almost religious belief in the quality of a future native school of composition. Indeed, in the imagination of progressive critics, the future American composer gradually assumed messianic dimensions. American critics and the public waited for the "American composer" as if he were a supreme being, and the terminology employed echoed evangelistic themes. One day, the American composer would arrive. He (and there was never any question that this individual would have to be male) would be able to play American masterpieces around the country. One day, Frederick Root envisioned in 1892, Americans would be able to hear "the tone epic of the birth of our nation," complete with the "sound of the primeval forests," "the undertone of the oceans dashing upon 'a stern and rockbound coast,'" and "the rugged faith bequeathed by the Pilgrim Fathers." There would be no shortage of topics for a talented composer, Root maintained, ranging from the Yankee Doodle and the battle of Lexington to the depiction of brotherhood and peaceful prairie homes to the conflict between slavery and freedom. To that purpose, Root concluded, American art germs needed protection, adding: "Possibly, [the U.S. president] Mr. McKinley could help us!"[45]

The critic Herbert Krum cited Theodore Roosevelt's credo that Americanism was a question of spirit, conviction, and purpose, not of creed or birthplace. "The day is at hand," Krum exclaimed, for American music to appear on the scene.[46] The Boston-born bass singer and voice instructor Karleton Hackett even prophesied that the United States (like the people of Israel) would soon be freed from bondage. What did it matter if America's musical messiah had not yet appeared? As far as this author was concerned, that person could already be one of thousands of American public school students, or perhaps his grandfather was not even born. But Hackett was certain: one day, the deliverer was bound to come.[47]

Finally, even the staunchest supporters of German music in the United States believed that the center of musical art was about to shift from Europe to the United States. During a visit to Germany in 1886, the critic Henry Krehbiel became convinced that Cincinnati would eventually evolve into an American Weimar, a center for culture and music. "We are the salt of the earth," he remarked. "The English know it and the wise men among the Germans confess it. We need some seriousness but it will come in time."[48] The center of music was shifting, the age of German universalism as once envisioned by Wilhelm von Humboldt almost over.

No journal epitomized the quest for musical nationalism better than *Musical America*. Founded in 1898 by the Oxford-trained music critic John Freund and Milton Weil, *Musical America* was a staunch advocate of American musical independence. Like *Dwight's Journal of Music*, it appealed to the broad public as well as professional musicians with a sense of mission, even though its mission questioned a number of John Sullivan

**24** Karleton Hackett, bass singer, voice instructor, and music critic, became one of the staunchest opponents of German music. In 1896, he prophesied that the United States (like the people of Israel) would soon be freed from bondage. From *Music* 6, no. 1 (May 1894): 81.

Dwight's preferences. Freund knew that Europeans preferred to see the United States as the land of money grabbers, inventors, big crops, crazy drinks, political corruption, and women who twanged an unspeakable dialect. But "Things have changed!" he announced in the premiere issue. "Today the world realizes that there is an Artistic America, a Musical America, an America that teems with aspiration for all that is beautiful and true, that sends forth her children year by year."[49]

Comparisons of the American and the German music scenes abounded, with Germany increasingly rated as second choice. In 1911, the Philadelphia Orchestra's manager, H. M. Watts, declared that "America Outranks Europe in Music." Returning from a two-month trip to Europe, Watts concluded that Americans did not need to travel to Europe anymore to listen to first-rate or even third-rate concerts. Former European music centers were becoming increasingly anachronistic, unable to revive the once "great atmosphere."[50] And by 1914, the *Chicago Inter Ocean* had reduced the failure of the American musical genius to a conspiracy by Italians, Germans, French, and other nations.[51]

To bring forth the American genius, a number of artists began to look to folk music as a possible source of inspiration. Following eastern European composers' search for indigenous music, in the spring and summer of 1916 the singer Loraine Wyman and the composer and pianist Howard Brockway, two self-designated "patriotic Americans," traveled along the Appalachian Mountains between Kentucky and Georgia to collect a "flora of folk-song" from the hinterlanders, who had been living there relatively untouched by modern progress for centuries.[52] After six weeks of research, Wyman and Brockway returned to New York City with a knapsack full of songs and immediately presented their findings in concerts. Critics lavished praise on the two, and for a number of years Wyman and Brockway performed their melodies and songs and even compiled a summary of their experience, "The Quest of the Lonesome Tunes."[53]

It does not matter what became of any of these efforts in the long run. What matters is that they took place at this moment in time. For at the core of the national-music debate lay a revolutionary understanding of the nation as a fully functional organism complete with a heart, limbs, and a soul that could flourish and perish like any human being. In "The Origin and Growth of National Music," Jean Moos concluded that music represented a character trait that distinguished nations from each other. Echoing the theories of Charles Darwin, Moos explained that music had passed through a number of states and presently reached its ultimate maturity. The art of a nation, the author believed, formed a window that allowed contemporary and future generations to look into its very heart, "disclosing the innermost folds of its character."[54]

One of the foremost proponents of a new American music, Homer Moore, a contributor to the journal *Music*, believed that the United States' dependence on German music would "ultimately result in its own musical suicide." In his "13 propositions to encourage American Music," Moore admonished Americans for their deferential admiration of European cultural imports.

We cannot claim to be their equal until we can produce works that are equal to theirs, not only in average merit, but on *originality*. We can never claim to be the equal of Germany musically while we copy Beethoven and Wagner. There are more reasons than one for this. One is that Beethoven and Wagner are German in their natures and in their music; we are not German *in our natures*. Our music must find its source in our natures, and as we cannot bring out of them that which they do not contain, we cannot produce a musical expression of German nature. . . . *We must develop a music which will express our own American natures fully and completely.*[55]

The key term in this debate remained *emotion*. A nation without music was a nation without soul. Few observations struck American pride harder than Jacques Offenbach's judgment in 1876 that "America today is like a giant a hundred cubits tall, who has attained physical perfection, but in whom something is lacking: a soul. The soul of a people is art, the expression of thought in its most elevated aspects."[56] That was a troubling scenario in an age obsessed with the image of the nation-state as an organic body. A soulless nation did not simply lack culture—it was no nation to begin with, let alone one that could compete with other hegemonic powers.

The expostulations by Moore and Moos along with others such as the composer Arthur Farwell exemplify a discussion about the national spirit in music that, for two decades before World War I, aroused the scorn and passion of critics and composers, notably those who criticized the preponderance of nineteenth-century German music in the United States. As time went by, Anglo-American critics incorporated these arguments into a general antipathy for foreign influences of all kinds, including consumer goods, ethnic culture, and southeast European immigrants. The Spanish-American War of 1898 formed the climax of this debate, when the U.S. government jump-started an Americanization program that essentially required immigrants to replace their own cultural and ethnic identity with American superpatriotism, complete with waving flags and nationalistic songs.

Yet for all their assurance something was wrong and missing in the national music scene, the propagandists of a new American music remained hesitant to realize their most radical dreams. In 1885, a group of wealthy socialites founded the National Conservatory of Music in New York (originally under the name American School of Opera, it was renamed in 1886). The conservatory was designed to "unify American musical interests," create a generically American music, and train young Americans in the art of performance and composition.[57] Among its directors were such luminaries as Henry Higginson from Boston and the businessman Howard Hinkle from Cincinnati, though by far most members came from New York City. The principal driving force behind the venture was a woman named Jeannette Thurber. Thurber had been privately educated in New York and Paris, and it was in France that she had been profoundly impressed by the system of government-sponsored music education. She married Francis B. Thurber, a wholesale grocer and lawyer, and then became deeply involved in music education in the United States. At first, she donated funds for American music students attending European conservatories, then supported the free young peoples' concerts produced by the conductor Theodore Thomas, and in 1884 also provided funds for Thomas's Richard Wagner Festival. Due to her untiring lobbying, the National Conservatory of Music was incorporated by an act of Congress in 1891; the following year, Thurber invited Antonin Dvorak to sign a three-year contract as director of the new school.[58]

This ironic choice reflected a theme that ran through the entire debate on national music: Americans had been requesting foreigners to tell them what was American. On the one hand, Antonin Dvorak, a famous composer from Prague who by the time of his appointment had become a virtual pop star in Europe, exuded both a character and an identity appealing to the American public, and thus seemed a natural choice. On the other hand, he belonged to the generation of musical nationalists in Europe who borrowed heavily from local folk music. So, of course, Dvorak was a national composer, just not an American one. He had been imported. Dvorak was flattered by Thurber's offer but also overwhelmed by the irony of his task: "The Americans expect great things from me," he wrote home shortly after his arrival in Manhattan, "and the main thing is, so they say, to show them to the promised land and kingdom of a new and independent art, in short, to create a national music. If the small Czech nation can have such musicians, they say, why could not they, too, when their country and people are so immense."[59]

Still, Dvorak was pleasantly surprised by the wealth of talent he found in the United States. Encouraged by his work with several African-American students at the conservatory, at the end of his three-year visit he recommended that in their quest for "indigenous music," Americans should not seek the help of foreign composers. Rather, they should listen to the two most powerful non-European musical sources their culture had to offer: African-American gospel and American-Indian folk songs, a recommendation that at first raised eyebrows around the country. These melodies, Dvorak asserted, "are the folk songs of America, and your composers must turn to them."[60] Many of Dvorak's students went on to compose according to the ideas (and encouragement) of their foreign-born instructor. Henry Walley, Henry Rowe Shelley, William Marion Cook, William Arms Fisher, Harvey Worthington Loomis, and Rubin Goldmark continued to incorporate elements of African-American music into their compositions, as did many others whom Dvorak never met. The integration of black, Indian, and ethnic elements became acceptable once Dvorak had conferred his stamp of approval on such musical syntheses.

Some, such as Henry Gilbert and Arthur Farwell, ardently uncovered and transcribed songs transmitted by Native Americans and former slaves.[61]

Dvorak's influence on American music remains an issue, and by his own testimony, he deliberately failed to initiate an American school of music. His Symphony no. 9 in E Minor, *From the New World*, celebrated by American critics as an homage to the American landscape, constituted, in his own words, a greeting to the composer's friends in Prague. What was important about Dvorak's visit to New York City was not so much what he told Americans but what they made of him. His new symphony captivated the hearts of listeners between Boston and San Francisco. Numerous critics rushed to conclude that, with *From the New World*, Dvorak was showing the way to a genuine American music. The *Chicago Times* called Dvorak's sojourn in the United States a "historic event" and the "epoch of the foundation of American music."[62] When Henry Krehbiel heard the Symphony no. 9 in New York, he exclaimed that at last, Americans had found their own great national symphony.

From a purely technical point of view, Krehbiel, like most others, had difficulties legitimizing his verdict. The work was "American" because it had a rhythmic construction "characteristic of the music which has a popular charm in this country." It was American because the American musical phrase "is built on the pentatonic, or five-note, scale, which omits the fourth and seventh tones of our ordinary diatonic series." It was American because the "Oriental tinge" of the subsidiary melody resonated with Americans. It was American because the larghetto movement focused on the legend of an Indian girl, and Indians were Americans. It was American because the finale contained a paraphrase of the tune "Yankee Doodle" (itself actually an English composition).[63]

Controversies soon arose. In Chicago, Theodore Thomas felt that *From the New World* was neither white nor American but Bohemian. The *Boston Transcript* declared that Dvorak's experimentation with "aboriginal music" was geographically American but did not reflect the vivid American mind, its jolly humor, and its "loud" and vigorous voice. The New York critic James Huneker specifically labeled the symphony "not American" but of "Celtic character," and postulated that "the American symphony, like the American novel, has yet to be written. And when it is, it will have been composed by an American." The work was "strongly American, though not exclusively such," wrote the *Pittsburg Dispatch* in March 1895. "Distinctively the spirit of it is Antonin Dvorak and none other. As pure music it is absolutely delightful. That is better than being American."[64]

A thorough cosmopolitan and now at the height of the career, Dvorak himself sensed American critics' quest for cultural independence in the face of the German canon. He exploited Americans' confusion to pro-mote his own ambitions, but remained adamant about his identity and that of his work. "So I am an American composer, am I?" he marveled at the end of his three-year stint as conservatory director. "I was, I am, and I remain a Czech composer. I have only showed them the path they might take—how they should work. But I'm through with that! From this day forward I will write the way I wrote before!" Dvorak's irate statement did not answer the American music question at all. For decades, critics would passionately debate the extent to which the symphony *From the New World* may be called American.[65]

If to the promoters of the National Conservatory Dvorak turned out to be an ideologically unruly director, they received firm support from a completely unexpected and much more pragmatically oriented group of men and women: the American Federation of Musicians (AFM). Based in Cincinnati with local chapters all over the United States, the AFM had imposed a stern residency rule on immigrating musicians, to protect local players from foreign competition. Since most conductors and orches-tras preferred European players to indigenous talent, and even paid the former more attractive fees than the latter, the AFM constantly battled against orchestra leaders, who either did not give union members access to their orchestras or at least sought to limit their influence.

Musicians had formed musical aid associations and unions as early as the 1860s. For example, in 1864 the St. Louis Musiker Unterstützungs-Verein was founded to prevent competing German bands from working for lower fees. The foremost purpose of all of these formations was to protect individual artists in their relationship with permanent or tem-porary employers, regardless of whether they played in pit orchestras or restaurant bands. These organizations served various constituencies, but they soon began to compete with one another for prestige, mem-bership, and dues. In 1896, delegates from all organizations convened at the invitation of the American Federation of Labor President Samuel Gompers to create a comprehensive musicians' trade union. The majority voted to form the AFM, with Owen Miller at its head and initial member-ship of 3,000 musicians nationwide. They resolved that "any musician who receives pay for his musical services, shall be considered a profes-sional musician." Within ten years, the AFM expanded to Canada; it now counted 424 locals, and represented 45,000 musicians throughout North America.[66]

According to the Cincinnati Musicians' Protective Association no. 1, musicians engaged from foreign countries were not permitted to join any AFM local without the explicit approval of the federation. Likewise,

## IS IT COMING TO THIS?

25   Musical unions took an intense interest in the debate on American vs. foreign music and mu-
sicians. "Is It Coming to This?" Cartoon, *Boston Transcript*, n.d. (approx. 13 December 1903);
BSO scrapbooks, M125.5/7, Boston Symphony Orchestra Archives. Courtesy of the Boston
Symphony Orchestra Archives.

musicians from elsewhere in the United States could not become members of the Cincinnati Local if their engagement threatened the unionized musicians in that city. In other words, the unions protected city
players from competition with musicians imported from Europe as well
as with players from other cities.[67] By 1917, eleven symphony orchestras
in the United States (as well as opera-house orchestras) were members of
the AFM. Every union member had to be an American citizen or at least
have applied for U.S. citizenship.

The AFM quickly converted practical concerns over employment opportunities for indigenous musicians to ideological and patriotic arguments. To them, the key question was whether artists ranked beyond (or
below) the position of a unionized worker. The unions contended that
they had to defend native talent to create both decent working conditions
and a new national art scene. Conductors, in contrast, insisted on picking their players at will, as they did not work for commerce but for art.

It would be unfair to characterize conductors' preference for foreign musicians as a mere fad. Men such as Thomas, Max Zach, and Wilhelm Gericke sincerely believed that their orchestras sounded better when staffed with musicians from abroad, and they did not care to compromise their point of view. After his first season with the Boston Symphony Orchestra, Gericke went back to Vienna to engage Franz Kneisel as concertmaster, along with a large number of musicians who then performed with players already engaged in Boston and New York City. And even in his second year, he still cancelled a concert in New York at the last minute, arguing that "the Orchestra is not playing sufficiently well for me to appear before that public."[68]

Because of the conductors' appeal to aesthetic arguments, union leaders were careful to tie their usual language of labor struggle to the musicians' self-perception as artists. At the annual meeting of the AFM in 1907, the union leader Joe Webber emphasized his conviction that only if Americans gave their musicians a chance would American music flourish. "We, in America, have high protection, so high that many things cannot be exported and must depend upon the home market," stated a correspondent. "If there are Beef Trusts, Steel Trusts, Sugar Trusts, Coffee Trusts, Rubber Trusts, Book Trusts, Paper Trusts, then there certainly must be Musicians' Federations."[69]

The activities of the AFM comported with a larger movement in the arts sector. Thanks to a variety of exhibitions orchestrated by prestigious French art dealers, after the Civil War American artists became increasingly fearful of European competition and advocated the continuation of protective tariffs. Already in the late eighteenth century, the U.S. government had raised a levy on imported works of art; now the artists asked for higher rates, particularly on contemporary artworks. In 1866, American artists petitioned Congress to tax each painting $100 plus 10 percent of the value exceeding $1,000.[70] These artists feared that in their struggle to create a national art, the imported works would hurt their income as well as their quest to create American art. Why should global art not be created by America, asked William Page, president of the Academy of Design at its annual meeting in New York City in 1873, if all the other important jobs of and in the world were inevitably destined to be performed by the United States in the future?[71] In 1885, Congress enacted the Alien Contract Labor Bill, aimed at preventing the importation of skilled labor to the United States.

The bill was never explicitly intended to include musicians, but already in the 1880s, newspapers complained about the economic effects of the influx of European musicians.[72] At the Chicago World's Fair of

1893, the Musical Mutual Protective Union vehemently protested the importation of "cheap" European bands who, masquerading as artists, flooded the Chicago music scene and deprived American musicians of their livelihood. Recently, the union had written to the U.S. Department of the Treasury, "a band of Hungarian Gypsy musicians were permitted to land here, 12 in number, of whom but three could read a note of music." Who could define the criteria of admission for musicians when the only people present at customs were the collector and the commissioner of immigration?[73] It was precisely this unresolved problem that the unions hoped to solve in favor of indigenous players.

After the turn of the twentieth century, both the political influence and the membership lists protecting musical nationalism increased dramatically. The National Federation of Musicians opened its headquarters in New York City, along with branch offices in larger U.S. cities. The federation hoped to keep on its rolls the best orchestral musicians, who would become members only after a severe examination. It permitted foreign players to join, but asked that they reside in the United States for several months without employment. A foreign player might also appear as a concert soloist or teach, but he could not be permanently employed or be admitted to the federation before that time.[74]

Even though the National Federation of Musicians could not force nonunionized orchestras to observe its rules, its political effectiveness was remarkable. As early as 1902, the Philadelphia Orchestra faced disbandment when its director, Fritz Scheel, had imported some fifty German musicians without paying attention to the alien contract labor law. At the end of the first season, Scheel fired a good number of the men he had previously selected, many of whom had sold their homes and household goods and brought their wives and families to the United States. Outraged, more than fifty of the eighty musicians reportedly threatened to withdraw and return to Germany.[75]

When Carl Pohlig joined the Philadelphia Orchestra in 1907, newspapers rumored that the manager had not even informed the new conductor about the union rules prevailing in the United States, for fear that he might pack his bags and leave. Without Pohlig's knowledge, all the players he examined had obtained union "traveling cards" from their respective cities, then registered with the Philadelphia Musical Association before the audition.[76]

In 1896, members of the Pittsburgh Orchestra threatened to go on strike, claiming that their salary for an individual concert ranged below the one set by a union. In 1904, Emil Paur, then conducting the Pittsburgh Orchestra, imported four artists (two from Europe, two from

New York), but the office of AFM Local no. 60 announced that the foreigners would be barred under union law in order to promote native talent. Paur's only chance was to either maintain the imported men for a sufficient amount of time in Pittsburgh until they could join the union, or build up a new orchestra of foreigners, which might not meet with the approval of the subscribers. All these quarrels had a devastating effect on the public image of the orchestra, and subscriptions plummeted to such an extent that in 1910 the orchestra was disbanded.[77]

Similarly, in Cincinnati, quarrels over the international makeup of the orchestra destroyed the organization. The Cincinnati Symphony Orchestra had been a union organization from its beginnings. No union member was supposed to play with a nonunion member,[78] and no foreign musicians were allowed in the city as long as a player of the same instrument was available in Cincinnati. Once the orchestra moved to its new Music Hall and its size accordingly increased for the 1896–97 season, only 39 players had been retained from the previous season, but 24 were playing in the orchestra for the first time, primarily in the string and brass sections. The new principal players were signed to multiyear contracts at fixed weekly salaries for the five-month duration of the regular symphony season. Their salaries were more remunerative than those of the resident Cincinnati musicians, who received a flat fee per rehearsal and concert. The union then tried to strengthen the interests of member musicians by imposing a series of demands and scale raises, and continued to discourage the employment of out-of-town musicians. The conflicting interests of the orchestral board and the union eventually led to a profound struggle between the two. The union demanded that the conductor not be the sole judge of a musician's talent—he could discipline but not discharge. The management, in turn, felt that the Cincinnati union was asking for much more than its counterparts in other cities. Eventually, the situation escalated, and in 1907 the orchestra was dissolved.[79]

Orchestra leaders, managers, and sponsors reacted in very different ways to the unions' resistance against foreign players. Theodore Thomas, for one, unionized his entire orchestra for purely utilitarian purposes. When traveling across the South and West, he often needed local musicians to fill in for a player who had fallen sick or had an accident. Thomas himself joined a union, but made it clear that he and his orchestra would quit should the unions ever dare to interfere with his wages, his personnel appointments, or his discipline. When Thomas came to Chicago to conduct the Chicago Orchestra, he felt it was appropriate in this case also to unionize his orchestra and maintain good relations with the union in case one or more of his musicians should fall ill. Thus, in a polite gesture, he would post a search notice for a particular instrumentalist at the union's headquarters, then import a player from New York, Europe, or elsewhere, all in order to keep the peace with the musicians and the union.[80]

In contrast, the Boston Symphony Orchestra did not admit unionized musicians, because Henry Higginson loathed the unions' interference with his organization. Moreover, the symphony's benefactor feared public reprisal. When Arthur Nikisch accepted the leadership of the Boston Symphony Orchestra, he barely made it into the country because the Musicians' Union said he violated the Control Labor Law. Nikisch was scheduled to land in New York City, where a grandiose reception had been planned, followed by a triumphal entry into Boston with beating drums and flying flags. But the orchestra management advised Nikisch to travel into Boston, where he sidestepped customs and then was transported by a closed carriage to Higginson's residence in the suburbs.[81] When Emil Paur succeeded Nikisch, Higginson pulled all strings to avoid a similarly embarrassing situation, and even inquired at the Treasury Department about legal ways to import a foreign conductor.[82]

Importation of international musicians thus became an increasingly difficult endeavor in more than one way. In addition to barring foreign players from the United States, in 1892 the federal government passed a law stating that reimported dutiable merchandise was liable to customs duty on every importation to the United States. Since musicians frequently traveled to Europe for summer engagements and leisure, they were thus required to pay an importation tax on their instruments every time they reentered the United States. This struck the owners of precious instruments particularly hard; at the Boston Symphony Orchestra, one player owned a Stradivarius, another one a Cremona, and both were unable to come up with the necessary import duty.[83]

---

The most striking aspect of the debate on "the national" in music is the extent to which audiences and critics merged local politics and international art. Although the nineteenth-century American musical landscape was remarkably variegated, German musicians and German music became the focus of the national-music debate long before World War I. Notwithstanding the important role of Italian opera, novel French compositions, and folklore songs, throughout the nineteenth century critics and audiences had revered the symphony as quintessentially German and the highest form of music. And when searching for a generic brand of American music, activists across the board—critics, journalists, musicians, unions, manufacturers, artists, audiences, and even people who never bothered much about music to begin with—targeted German, not French or Italian, music as American artists' foremost adversary, long before political tensions between the United States and Germany began. This resistance uncovered the downside of musical universalism as Wilhelm von Humboldt had proclaimed it earlier in the century: once universal values and artifacts met with resistance, the values themselves were not universally acceptable anymore.

Unlike European nations, the United States lacked a scapegoat or an enemy image, and, one might say, a sense of cultural direction. In Europe, a Hungarian could enjoy Magyar folk tunes over German or Bohemian compositions. But Americans had no historical enemy except Great Britain, which was, however, not a significant musical power. Nor was speaking English controversial in the United States. Thus, many Americans felt the need to be American, but they were also continually looking for someone to tell them what it was to be American. In a nation that defined itself by an allegiance to a set of political principles rather than by ethnicity, blood, or history, this was perhaps inevitable and explains why, in the end, critics could only agree on one point: foreigners could not join American musicians' unions.

Again, the most perplexing aspect remains that right when Europeans started to fret about "Americanization," Americans themselves began to worry deeply about the essence of their cultural identity. While American cultural critics expounded on their apprehension toward "Teutonization" and deplored the American people's incapacity to create their own brand of artistic expression, European conservatives began to rail against what they perceived as the menace of American culture. European critics of American culture, such as William Stead, D. H. Lawrence, and Adolf Halfeld, counted among the first to voice all those fears that have since become so commonplace around the world: fears that American standards, culture, and way of life would overrun everyone else's; fears that American consumer products would wipe out other countries' economic and, eventually, cultural independence; fears that American culture would smother local identities. In the eyes of many European critics, American civilization was not merely strange and dissimilar; instead, it directly threatened the cultural integrity of the Old World.[84]

Like the Europeans, who began to dread the influx of American cultural artifacts and its presumably subversive impact on their national cultures,

Americans felt jeopardized by the predominance of foreign sounds. Their hospitality toward Kultur ended when the accepted canon of classical music conflicted with a growing desire for national culture. Such resistance did not originate in the anti-German craze of 1917/18, but went back to a struggle for cultural identity several decades old. As we shall see, World War I contributed to this rupture. But it did not cause it.

# SEVEN

# Facing the Music in World War I

It was swelteringly hot in Bayreuth that summer of 1914, but as usual the heat had not kept away the avalanche of Richard Wagner fans from all over the world. From the United States, the music director Karl Muck had traveled across the ocean to conduct his operatic showpiece, Wagner's *Parsifal*. A handsome, dashing man in the prime of his life, the former *Kapellmeister* of the Royal Opera in Berlin was known for his reserved manner and conducting style. Nonetheless, that day he led the Bayreuth Orchestra with a rarely displayed fervor that came to a sudden halt as cries of "War" sounded from the audience. People began running in all directions. Women fainted as men flung aside their instruments, champagne glasses, and evening wear to report for army duty at once. Muck managed to finish the opera that day with only a few musicians remaining, then fled Bayreuth. It must have been one of the most difficult moments in the conductor's life, feeling both grounded and trapped in his adopted *Heimat*, Germany. *Parsifal* was the last performance that year at Bayreuth. The Festspiele had to be prematurely terminated: all the stagehands and half the orchestral musicians were either soldiers or eligible for military duty.[1]

The outbreak of the war had a profound impact on the transatlantic music highway. In the United States the clash between political tensions and cultural expectations resulted in a widespread campaign to rid all American orchestras of German personnel and repertory. Historians have shown how, in 1916–17, many Americans associated Kultur with German cultural imperialism, Prussian militarism and espionage, designed to subjugate American art, democracy, and patriotism.[2] But such suspicions paled in comparison to the cultural anxieties Americans had nurtured for decades. The U.S. entry into the war ruffled some feathers among German cultural representatives in the United States, but from a cultural perspective it did not mark the inspiration for anti-Germanism. The war served first as a catalyst and then as a culmination, but never as the cause of a long-standing inferiority complex among American elites, intellectuals, artists, and the public at large.

———

European artists brought the war into American homes long before the United States' entry into the conflict. In August and September of 1914, soloists, orchestral musicians, and conductors were either stranded in Europe or had barely managed to sneak out. At the outbreak of the war, 24 of the musicians from the Boston Symphony Orchestra were traveling through Europe for their summer break and engagements, including 7 first violinists, 2 second violinists, 4 violists, 4 cellists, 2 oboists, 2 clarinetists, 1 bassoonist, at least 1 bassist, and a harpist. The manager, Charles Ellis, rushed to Europe personally to retrieve the players and the star conductor, Karl Muck, who was eager to march off to Belgium but then agreed to return.[3]

Numerous other musicians dear to American audiences joined the war effort on either side, which led to flashy news stories of fragile artists freezing in the trenches of Verdun and Argonne. To American musical observers, the war remained an exotic anomaly where musicians, painters, and literati now aimed their guns at each other for altogether obscure reasons. Featuring headlines such as "How Great War Hits Famous Violinist," reporters' stories covered the experiences of men on both sides of the trenches, Belgian, German, French, and Austrian alike, complete with pictures, interviews, and human-interest stories.[4] The pianist Ferrucio Busoni, a favorite with American audiences, had to cancel a $50,000 tour. The Polish pianist Leopold Godowski, for six years a resident of Chicago, had fled his Brussels home without a cent. Josef Weiss, a prominent pianist, was now playing at a third-class café.[5] The violinist Jacques Thibaud spent nineteen months in French trenches, where he became temporarily half-blind and "as deaf as Beethoven" due to the explosion of the new French mortars.[6] Meanwhile, the soprano Johanna Gadski hurried to assure reporters that "musical harmonies have no effect on bursting shells"; therefore, the war would not affect music, and music would not affect the war.[7]

The reaction of American music critics to the war, in turn, reflected both concern and hope. On the one hand, as *Musical America* pointed out in August 1914, it was impossible to foretell how American orchestras would be able to maintain the quality of their performances in the future. On the other, the journal stressed that the war offered a unique opportunity to American artists in their homeland: "The path is clear for the first true *practical* demonstration of our latent powers in the country's artistic annals. Competition of the sort that stifled and paralyzed is ruthlessly shattered and crushed." The American concert stage suddenly seemed within reach of an armada of American musicians and composers. No longer could young artists travel abroad in order to finish their music education; no longer could orchestras look for players abroad; no longer could conductors peruse European novelties. All talent had to be found at home. "And once a *fair* trial has been accorded American instruction the evil spell under which it has labored will doubtless be forever exorcised," the author concluded, adding, "there is truly something millennial about them."[8]

Critics and the public alike immersed themselves in visions of an all-American music scene, free of foreign competition. Since many of the Boston Symphony Orchestra's musicians were bound up in Europe, a patron from Brooklyn suggested to Henry Higginson, the orchestra's sponsor, "Form a new orchestra—composed of Americans, led by an American and re-name the orchestra, calling it the '*American* Symphony Orchestra.'" When hearing that the symphony had hired a member of the Paris conservatory instead of an American flutist, another patron fumed: "Why call it the Boston Symphony Orchestra? Why not rather the Franco-German-European Trust Co. for the Sole Benefit of foreign musicians?" European musicians, he grumbled, did not even belong to the crowd of hyphenated Americans; instead they were carpetbaggers with little interest in the local public or the national music scene: "They make me tired, and they ought to be thrown out bodily."[9] The patron's criticism summarized the frustration of many music critics: in the eyes of most Americans, American orchestras presented as an essentially German institution, run by German conductors and staffed by German musicians who played predominantly German music.

As political tensions escalated, musical competition formed the most crucial agent in the "purification" of orchestral repertories and personnel. Competition dictated that the German musicians could not avoid interrogation and internment during the war. The community of German musicians, in turn, worsened their fate by reproducing the mistakes and arrogance displayed by most middle-class German Americans: they invoked the universalism of music and then pointed to the superiority of German compositions, hoping to dismiss charges of conspiracy and militarism.

The military conflict immediately forced musicians, benefactors, trustees, administrators, and all others involved in the reproduction of nineteenth-century music to take a stand. In centers of German immigration such as New York City and Chicago, the German-American community displayed an outpouring of pride in the fatherland, complete with marches, singing festivals, flag-waving, and speeches that surpassed anything that Anglo Americans had ever seen or heard from their immigrant neighbors. What rendered their enthusiasm even more strange, observes Jörg Nagler, was the fact that in the past, German Americans had not displayed much political interest in their country of origin.[10]

That point can be applied to the field of music as well. Although for decades the German Americans' financial support of symphony concerts had been weak at best, with the onset of the war they rallied to praise the German influence on the American stages. German-language newspapers such as the *New York Staats-Zeitung* frequently pointed to the merits of German compositions and their superiority in comparison to French and American musical works. What was more, German Americans at first wholeheartedly embraced the kaiser's cause. They organized meetings, charity bazaars for the relief of widows, orphans, and wounded in Germany and Austria-Hungary, and unequivocally declared their intention to side with the Central Powers.[11]

To avoid the dilemma between American nationalism and cultural universalism, Anglo-American music benefactors drew an increasingly idiosyncratic line between Germany's political and cultural identities. Boston's Henry Higginson, for one, distinguished sharply between the German people and their leaders.[12] Politically, Higginson's heart was on the side of the Allies; culturally, he was in love with Germany. In 1915, Higginson suggested in his correspondence with President Woodrow Wilson that the German ambassador be chased away, German trade cut off, "all intercourse" stopped, and all Germans leave the country.[13] He tirelessly lobbied various senators and the president to defend England and fight Prussian rule. He even became chairman of the committee that arranged a Preparedness Parade in Boston in May of 1916, and despite his age (Higginson was almost eighty-two by then), he marched the entire distance on foot.[14]

All this, however, did not affect Higginson's infatuation with German Kultur, his engagement with classical music, and his utter faith in the members of his orchestra and its conductor, the kaiser's favorite, Karl Muck. In anticipation of the war, Higginson tried to "nationalize" the individual sections of his orchestra as early as 1912. "To mix the nations would not be advisable, all the more on account of their nature," he contemplated when hiring a new second clarinetist.[15] Notwithstanding all his spite for "the German system," Higginson could not let go of its Kultur. And as we shall see, it was precisely this predicament that brought the Boston Symphony Orchestra to the brink of disaster.

Higginson's dilemma epitomizes the heated debate surrounding the meaning of German Kultur. Even before World War I began, American intellectuals had started to perceive German culture as a tool of imperial control, anti-individualism, elitism, and military power. Their perception that Germans gave Kultur to their own state abruptly terminated the American fascination with the "culture of kaiserdom." After 1900, American observers perceived German Kultur and German cultural representatives increasingly as the spearhead of an effort to launch a military conflict over the preponderance of civilization or Kultur. As early as 1903, Secretary of State John Hay received notice that a number of Germans in the United States were on the payroll of the Information Bureau of the Foreign Office. Reportedly, German professors working at American institutions of higher education such as Harvard, Columbia, Yale, the University of Chicago, and the University of California had been ordered to undermine Americans' belief in their political institutions, their ideals, and, above all, the Monroe Doctrine.[16]

Among the many anti-German writings that emerged after 1914, Kultur clearly featured as the most prominent target. John Cowper Powys's and James Gerard's analyses alerted the Anglo-American public to the dangers posed by kaiser and Kultur. Writers such as Gustavus Ohlinger and James Middleton hastened to expose the triad of *Kultur*, *Kaiser* and *Krieg* (culture, emperor, and war) as German propaganda designed to undermine American neutrality and society. Their concerns were not unfounded. As Reinhard Doerries has shown, quite a number of the intellectuals involved in the academic exchange programs, such as Eugen Kühnemann or Hugo Münsterberg, later became active in the German Information Service, a press office opened in New York by Johann Heinrich Graf von Bernstorff (the German ambassador to the United States from 1908 to 1917), to improve the German image in the United States after the outbreak of World War I.[17]

Now Kultur became synonymous with the apocalypse, which was certain to arrive unless Americans banded together and fought it. Kultur meant that man would become the natural prey of his stronger-armed neighbor. Kultur meant that women's sole function was to breed, that labor was punishment, that man remained eternally unhappy and in bondage. Kultur meant assassination, robbery, barbarity, rapine, and mutilation. Certain professions such as brewing were increasingly seen as German and unpatriotic, despite the fact that by 1918 most brewers in the United States were American-born.[18]

Most observers agreed that Germans were particularly apt at using the most unlikely tools to manipulate foreign minds and indoctrinate them with the superiority of German political, commercial, artistic, and social Kultur. Indeed, by 1917 the daily press used Kultur as a collective term denoting German efforts to dominate the world. One scolded, "German cloth, cookery or cutlery, laws and logic, science and art, war or peace, all were pictured as being superior to all other, and no college was supposed to be complete unless it had one or more German professors among its teachers." These teachers, scientists, and artists, the charge went, were supposed to powerfully influence the men and women they encountered in America and to convince them of German superiority, "to the belittlement even of their own country and themselves, so that before 1914, almost without exception, the conductors of the orchestras in our cities also were Germans." Suspected aliens now included Hans Tauscher, husband of the soloist Johanna Gadski, who had presumably served as a spy transferring messages between Berlin and various agents in the United States. Tauscher had reportedly assembled one hundred thousand rifles in a warehouse in New York City and intended to blow up the Welland Canal. Despite his acquittal, his wife was forced to resign from the Metropolitan Opera only a few days after the U.S. entry into the war, because her house had supposedly been "the scene of a jubilant party after the sinking of the Lusitania."[19]

Led by George Creel, the Committee on Public Information initiated a bombardment of propaganda designed to destroy the image of the civilized German. It grappled with the challenge to explain to Americans why they should loathe the Germans when German scholarship and culture constituted such a central position in the United States. Prussian militarism had manipulated, raped, and extinguished German Kultur, Creel's committee expounded. To the Germans war represented "the god to whom they have offered up their reason and their humanity, behind them the misshapen image they have made of the German people, leering with bloodstained visage over the ruins of civilization."[20] German secret agents were everywhere, eager to provide Berlin with information about U.S. troops, ships, and munitions.

In a comprehensive study, Jörg Nagler estimates that during World War I, from 8,500 to 10,000 German Americans were arrested, with many eventually interned. By the end of the war, approximately 8 percent of all male "enemy alien Germans" had spent some time in federal prisons due to their national identity and resulting suspicions of espionage and sabotage.[21] The pursuit and apprehension of enemy aliens within the United States provided citizens with an *ersatzkrieg*, a substitute war, in their backyard and the satisfaction that they were taking an active part in the war effort. Many cities and towns began organizing "Americanization" festivals in early 1918, designed to either convert or ban citizens who remained skeptical of the war cause.[22] Anti-German hysteria in Boston escalated to the point that even pretzels, a longtime feature at the Boston Pops' summer concerts, disappeared because they were considered "enemy aliens."[23]

Much of the public ire focused on classical music, notably the presumed military subtext of the German masters' compositions: did the tunes of Beethoven and Schubert carry German propaganda into American concert halls? Some of the best American music critics rushed to expose Germany's plot: "The Teutonization of our music in American began with the establishment of the symphony orchestra," raged Karleton Hackett in the *Chicago Post*. "The orchestra has always been the chosen form for the expression of Germanic ideals in music." Hackett criticized German musical training, because it produced primarily orchestral players, particularly in the string sections, where many musicians had to play the same notes, like soldiers marching into battle. And because the Germans had been doing poorly in the realm of opera (despite the works of Wagner, Weber, and Gluck), they had wrongly convinced the world that opera was an inferior form of music.[24]

To counter charges of anti-Americanism, orchestras struggled to maintain their existence both as patriotic institutions and as harbingers of high culture. Many began to speak English during rehearsals, take public oaths of allegiance, and purchase Liberty Loan Bonds regularly. Quite a few took to the road to perform at U.S. military camps and add a bit of glamour to the troops' daily routine before they departed for the front lines.[25] The singer Nellie Melba charmed the soldiers at Camps Lewis, Fremont, and Kearny, as well as in Balboa Park at a Sunday service. The violinist Mischa Elman entertained camps sometimes twice a day.[26] The New York Philharmonic, the Philadelphia Orchestra, and the Chicago Symphony Orchestra likewise featured a variety of charity and camp concerts.[27] In December 1917, Walter Damrosch, along with 75 members of the New York Symphony Orchestra, gave a concert at Camp Upton on Long Island with more than 3,500 officers and enlisted men in attendance. As a finale, Damrosch chose Strauss's *Blue Danube* Waltz, explaining, "This piece is written about a river which is now far from the seat of war, but which you men may be crossing victoriously within a year."[28]

Orchestras weathered the storm in very different ways and with varying degrees of success and failure. A number of symphonies dropped parts of their German repertories during the war. The New York Philharmonic banned the music of all living German composers, while the Metropolitan Opera dismissed nineteen "tainted" singers and forbade performances in the German language. In San Francisco, the orchestra director Alfred Hertz dropped the music of living German composers and of Richard Wagner.[29] The Minneapolis Symphony Orchestra banned all German soloists and resorted to those of French, Russian, Brazilian, and other friendly nationalities. As part of their contracts, orchestra members were required to sign an affirmation pledging "unswerving loyalty" as well as their complete support of the United States against Germany."[30]

In Philadelphia, English-born Leopold Stokowski, who had labored hard to develop his trademark central European accent, now struggled to rid himself of anti-Americanist charges, and his wartime concert programs reflected his anxiety over maintaining a positive public image. For the twenty-five concerts of the 1917–18 season, Stokowski favored national themes portraying the United States and her allies: Russian, English, French, and Scandinavian.[31] In late fall of 1917, the Philadelphia Orchestra dismissed eight German and Austrian string and wind instrument players whose citizenship papers were incomplete and thus kept the orchestra from fulfilling its out-of-town engagements. According to an order issued by President Wilson, enemy aliens could not travel without permission and could not approach politically and militarily precarious locations. This would have precluded the orchestra from traveling to a record company in Camden, New Jersey, because the guard placed at Front Street prevented all enemy aliens from reaching the waterfront. Playing in Washington, DC, was likewise out of the question, because aliens were prohibited from entering the District of Columbia. Finally, the orchestra collectively purchased Liberty Loan Bonds worth $189,000 to underscore the fact that the city called The Cradle of Liberty had an orchestra "led by a conductor who is an American citizen and whose members are either Americans or citizens of friendly countries."[32]

In Pittsburgh, citizens displayed a particularly patriotic zeal to censor symphonic programs, notwithstanding the fact that the local orchestra had gone bankrupt seven years earlier. City authorities announced in early November 1917 that all works by German composers as well as those by composers holding citizenships in nations allied with Germany were to be banned from its programs. They blocked the appearance of

Fritz Kreisler just hours before the violinist was scheduled to appear on the evening of November 9, arguing that he had sent money to Austria (which was true, though it was not for military purposes).[33] The Philadelphia Orchestra returned to the city in March of 1918, no doubt hopeful that Pittsburghers had come to their senses and were ready to enjoy German music at its best. The scheduled concert in the city's monumental Syria Mosque featured Wagner's *Tristan and Isolde* among others on the program of March 12, 1918. Upon entering the hall, however, Leopold Stokowski was informed that the local police had banned the performance of German compositions. Without the chance of a rehearsal or even an announcement, that night the orchestra played compositions by Finnish and Russian composers. The next day, at an afternoon concert in the Nixon Theater, Schubert's *Unfinished* Symphony was likewise dropped, and tunes that were more "pro-Allied" were substituted.[34]

To prove their utter patriotism, orchestras and soloists were frequently asked to perform "The Star-Spangled Banner" as part of their programs. At that time, the song was not yet officially the anthem of the United States but typically passed as such. Orchestras had performed it regularly for years. Only in 1931 did an act of Congress make "The Star-Spangled Banner" the official national anthem. Composed by the 35-year-old poet-lawyer Francis Scott Key during the defense of Fort McHenry by American forces during the British attack on September 13, 1814, the lyrics were written to match the meter of the English song "To Anacreon in Heaven."[35]

During World War I, performing the anthem became a must for every orchestra and soloist. At the Minneapolis Orchestra, its wartime activities encompassed playing "The Star-Spangled Banner" at the start of every program and "America" at its close. The orchestra prominently displayed its service flag of five stars (one of them gold), and it refrained from discussing war issues at home or on the road.[36] To clear her record, the opera singer Ernestine Schumann-Heink began to sing "The Star-Spangled Banner" in army camps, hotels, hospitals, and in the streets between California and New York.[37]

———

Much public concern revolved around the fact that many musicians had been negligent in becoming U.S. citizens. In 1913, eight out of 105 million Americans had either been born in Germany or had at least one German parent. Across the United States in 1914, twenty million out of a total one hundred million claimed German ancestry.[38] Immigration laws stipulated that a person could apply for citizenship by "taking out papers" twice. An applicant filled out a form and took it, along with two witnesses who had to be U.S. citizens, to the clerk of either the circuit or the superior court, who issued "first papers." Originally, the law imposed no deadline on the filing of "second papers," but a revised version stipulated that applicants for citizenship had to take out these papers after two and before seven years had elapsed from the issuance of the "first papers." In World War I, thousands of hyphenated Americans got caught up in this change of legal procedure, as many had taken out their first but not their second papers and therefore remained imperial subjects. They thus qualified as "enemy aliens."[39] In legal terms, an enemy alien was someone who had published, printed, written, or uttered statements containing "disloyal, profane, scurrilous, or abusive language" regarding the U.S. government, constitution, flag, or armed forces and intended to evoke slander, scorn, or contempt.[40] Because of their ancestry and their occupation, and because they often failed to take out their papers, musicians belonged to the most conspicuous group of enemy aliens, next to brewers.

All the patriotic songs, all the Liberty Loan Bonds purchased, and all the camp concerts could not do away with the fact that American symphony orchestras were, in the eyes of most Americans, essentially German institutions, run by German conductors and staffed by German musicians who played a lot of German music. Not surprisingly, then, during the war a number of artists found themselves scrutinized, investigated, and threatened. Many lost their jobs, such as the conductor Frederick (alias Friedrich) Stock in Chicago, while others suffered the loss of their property and were deported to one of the enemy alien camps, among those Karl Muck in Boston. Collectively, their fate demonstrates the cultural and political dilemma faced by many musicians in 1917–18.

When Frederick Stock landed in the United States in October 1895, he appeared before the authorities at Chicago's City Hall the morning after his arrival to renounce his allegiance to the German emperor and become a U.S. citizen. As conductor of the Chicago Symphony Orchestra, he had led concerts in military camps, composed public-spirited songs, taught children's choirs patriotic songs, and orchestrated a rendition of "America" so successfully that bandleaders across the nation included the piece in their own repertory.[41] Once the United States entered World War I, Stock urged his men to be loyal to the United States, arguing that "our heads and our brains must out-rule sentiments founded on cherished memories and sweet illusions of our boyhood-days, of days long gone by, never to return."[42]

And still, he got into trouble. First protests arose outside Chicago, while the Chicago Symphony Orchestra was on tour. In February 1918, following its Milwaukee performance, the Milwaukee Orchestral Association received a number of complaints from angry subscribers who opposed the programming of German music. While the Milwaukee association pointed out that the United States was fighting German autocracy, not German music, it still asked the Chicago Symphony Orchestra to eliminate German songs and possibly a number of German composers from its local repertory.[43] Then in April 1918, a Chicago clubwoman inquired at the local bureau of investigation whether Frederick Stock had registered as an enemy alien. Investigators subsequently interviewed Stock regarding his opinion on the war, and the resulting transcript reveals the extent of his patriotism as well as his ignorance of political traps.

—What is your opinion of the war?

—A commercial war—pure and simple.

—Do you believe the powers of the world could have got[ten] together and stopped the war?

—Yes.

—Do you know of any effort to do so?

—No.

—Do you think the allies, England, France, Italy and Russia made any attempt to prevent the war?

—No.

—Why?

—They thought they had the situation in hand and could handle it. They were, indeed, unprepared, in a military way, but they thought they had the man power, the men, to do it.[44]

Stock's papers are filled with correspondence, personal statements, memoranda, and newspaper clippings testifying to his efforts to convince the public of his loyalty. He corresponded with the orchestra's board. He made public statements. He hired a lawyer. And in his typically German scarped handwriting, he composed pages and pages of personal testimony that he was as loyal as any American could be.[45]

Stock had good reason to worry. While he had enthusiastically taken out his first papers shortly after his arrival, he had forgotten to complete the naturalization process. When he took out his second papers in February 1917, the circuit court informed him that his first filing was no longer valid. He could not reapply before 1919 and was classified as an enemy alien. Meanwhile, the Chicago Federation of Musicians suspended all enemy aliens from its membership list, thereby effectively squeezing all Germans out of the orchestra, including the conductor. This, in conjunction with his statement that the war was "a commercial war," deeply hurt Stock's standing within the Chicago community, and on Friday, August 16, the *Chicago Journal* announced: "Stock Forced to Quit."[46]

Soon the entire Chicago Symphony Orchestra became an object of public suspicion and governmental surveillance, despite the fact that eighty-eight of its ninety-one members were U.S. citizens. In a gesture foreshadowing the activities of Senator Joseph McCarthy some thirty years later, in August 1918, federal officials announced that they would soon present a list of names comprising those members of the orchestra whose dedication to the United States remained doubtful. Within a few days, more than ten musicians had to report to the office of the district attorney to answer charges of disloyalty. One had reportedly stated that he would commit suicide if Germany were defeated. Another was said to have refused to honor Marshal Joseph Joffre, head of the French military mission to the United States, during the latter's visit to Chicago, because the orchestra was a German organization. Richard Kuss, who played the bass trombone, had allegedly declared that he would rather kill his son than have him learn the English language. Trumpet player Wilhelm Hebs had uttered disloyal statements and then supposedly struck cellist Walter Ferner in the street for the latter's sympathetic attitude toward the United States. Flutist Curt Baumbach had asked, "How is America going to get a million men to France? Have them swim across?" Fellow flutist Alfred Quensel, from Thuringia, had likewise questioned the quality of the U.S. Army. The charges went on and on, and the defendants typically met them with emphatic denial.[47]

Much of the public's scorn focused on the Chicago Symphony Orchestra's first cellist, forty-nine-year-old Bruno Steindel, and his wife. A Saxonian from Zwickau and a senior member of the orchestra, Steindel had played for years with the Philharmonic Society of Berlin before coming to the United States. While a member of the Theodore Thomas Orchestra, Steindel had built up a reputation as a fabulous cellist but also as something of a ruffian. In 1909, he had physically assaulted Glenn Dillard Gunn, because the renowned Chicago critic had stated that Steindel's playing was "dull and spiritless."[48] Worse, according to a former pupil, Steindel had stated that President Wilson worked for England and that all Americans could "go to hell except for their dollars." When the orchestra had performed "La Marseillaise" during an out-of-town concert, Steindel had given another player "hell" for standing up. Mrs. Steindel, apparently, had a quick tongue. She had told a phonograph record clerk that she was not interested in "such stuff" as recordings of "Somewhere in France Is a Lily," because she was an upstanding German. Some ninety unionized musicians in Chicago testified against Bruno Steindel. The orchestra's board of directors encouraged him to resign, then accepted his withdrawal immediately, thereby implicitly naming him the scapegoat of the orchestra's difficulties. On the basis of the charges raised, the assistant district attorney, Francis Borelli, announced that he had gathered a sufficient amount of evidence to warrant denaturalization and to intern Steindel as an enemy alien. Borelli, incidentally, had ties to the Musicians' Union and was very close to one of the leading unionists in the country, James Petrillo, a staunch opponent of foreign performers.[49]

To quell the uproar, the orchestral board decided on a unique solution. On August 17, 1918, the day after the press had announced Stock's forced resignation, the members of the Chicago Symphony Orchestra gathered for a solemn service at Ravinia Park. In the sweltering Chicago heat and closely monitored by the local press, the men publicly renounced the fatherland and the kaiser. Personnel manager Albert Ulrich, who had been repeatedly under scrutiny by the district attorney, then lectured his colleagues on the dos and don'ts of living in a nation at war: don't speak German in public places; don't forget it's every man's duty to be loyal to the United States; and certainly don't forget that the trustees of the orchestra will report anyone showing signs of disloyalty. "If I hear the faintest whispering of disloyalty or of pro-Germanism among you, I will do more than report your names to the association," thundered Ulrich, eager to distinguish himself as an upright patriot. "I will report you myself to the Department of Justice and let the guilty ones suffer the consequences of their folly." The meeting then developed into what one newspaper called "a patriotic session with all players competing for the privilege of being reckoned as true American citizens." Under the critical eyes of Chicago's newspaper corps, they responded with a hearty rendition of "The Star Spangled Banner," collectively subscribed more than $16,000 to the third Liberty Loan, and announced that their wives would serve in the Red Cross. Then everybody went home, hoping that the worst was over.[50] On that same day, Stock turned in his resignation to the Orchestral Association, acknowledging that the public might judge him to be an enemy alien whose failure to take out his second papers in due time reflected his disloyalty.[51]

Still, a few critics remained dissatisfied with such demonstrations of allegiance, and their worries reflected the real issue at stake. It was a deplorable circumstance, lamented the critic Henry Krehbiel in the *New York Tribune* in June 1918, that American orchestras remained dependent on foreign conductors, and their sudden expressions of pro-American sympathy and devotion could never exculpate their past behavior. Pseudo-Americans like Stock, Emil Oberhoffer, Alfred Hertz, and others, Krehbiel exclaimed, "have lived through a period in which Germany conducted an insidious campaign to establish *imperium in imperio* here; by the federation of German societies, sending royal messages, medals and flags to German military veterans, exchanging professorships with our universities, founding Germanistic societies, establishing a museum at Harvard by direct imperial gift, and finally by sending the Kaiser's brother as an imperial ambassador to weld together all the agencies designed to disintegrate American nationalism."[52]

Other conductors did not get off as lightly as Frederick Stock in Chicago. Boston's Karl Muck suffered by far the most tragic consequences. Born in 1859 in Darmstadt to Bavarian parents, Muck had acquired Swiss citizenship in 1867, when his father had become a Swiss himself. Serving as Generalmusikdirektor at the Royal Opera in Berlin, Muck was spotted by Henry Higginson when conducting the operas *The White Lady* by François Adrien Boieldieu and *Lohengrin* by Wagner. The organizer of the Boston Symphony Orchestra immediately set his mind on hiring the young conductor, and embarked on lengthy negotiations to obtain permission to invite the kaiser's favorite conductor to a temporary conductorship. The kaiser agreed, on the condition that Muck would not ask for an extension of his term. In 1906, Muck left Germany to spend one year with the Boston Symphony Orchestra. Bostonians were so infatuated with the man that well before the year had passed, Higginson was pulling every string to obtain a one-year extension of Muck's term from the kaiser.[53]

Muck had never been very happy in Berlin, where he constantly clashed with the Royal Superintendent, Reichsgraf Bolko von Hochberg. He also felt suppressed by the presence of Richard Strauss, his famous colleague, who held a similar position but had obtained a much better contract. Consequently, Muck had developed a habit of taking every opportunity to conduct orchestras outside Berlin and not return from his vacations on time. Royals in Moscow, Copenhagen, Madrid, St. Petersburg, London, Prague, and elsewhere bestowed a multitude of honorary decorations upon the dashing young conductor, while his superiors carped that Muck was either absent or sick during most of the year.[54] Since his position at the Royal Opera worsened after his return from the United States, in 1912 the conductor accepted Higginson's offer of a permanent position at the helm of the Boston Symphony Orchestra.

The Boston audience was overjoyed to welcome the elegant conductor back to the stage. Muck's attire and demeanor evoked conservativism,

26  As *Kapellmeister* at the Royal Opera in Berlin, Karl Muck was chosen as one of twenty-five candidates, including Gustav Mahler, Hans Richter, and Willem Mengelberg, to succeed Wilhelm
Gericke as conductor of the Boston Symphony Orchestra. Muck reportedly smoked several
packs of cigarettes per day. Photographer Herm, Leiser, Berlin, 1894. Pres. 86.5 f.1, Boston
Symphony Orchestra Archives. Courtesy of the Boston Symphony Orchestra Archives.

nobility, and the memory of the nineteenth century, where the *Kapellmeister* felt more at home than in the present. He typically sported a high,
stiff collar with a black tie and a matching precious stick pin (a gift from
Wilhelm II), white cuffs, and a long black coat. To calm his irate temper,
he chain-smoked up to five packs of cigarettes a day. Poring anxiously
over his scores and programs for hours, Muck conducted practically everything, including the works of moderns such as Sibelius and Debussy,
and even composers he disliked, such as Tchaikovsky.[55]

When Muck returned from his annual summer trip to Europe in the fall
of 1914, Higginson hurried to assure him that the United States opposed

the German kaiser but not the German people. Worrying that Muck might encounter difficulties, Higginson made a Herculean effort to keep his men, representing many different nationalities, together, urging them to disregard national backgrounds and maintain political and musical harmony.[56] Even at the beginning of the 1917–18 season, when the United States had been in a state of war against Germany for six months, the Boston Symphony Orchestra was a multinational corpus: according to the orchestra's files, it had 44 German-born players (some of whom had obtained or applied for U.S. citizenship), as well as 12 Austrian, 3 Bohemian, 14 American, 4 Belgian, 5 French, 7 Dutch, 3 Italian, 1 Romanian, 3 Russian, 1 Hungarian, 1 Polish, and 2 English players.[57] Things seemed to work out at first. In May of 1915, the Boston Symphony Orchestra traversed the entire country from east to west to give fifteen performances at the Panama Pacific Exposition in San Francisco, no doubt filling in for many European bands whose participation had been frustrated by the onset of the war. Throughout 1915, Boston newspapers hailed the symphony as living proof that art united men whose countries were at war. After the sinking of the *Lusitania* in May of 1915, neither Muck's citizenship nor the nationality of some of his musicians nor his concert programs incurred any criticism.[58] Shortly after the U.S. entry into World War I, Muck gave a concert in Sanders Theater at Harvard University, where the Glee Club as well as the Choral Society of Radcliffe bestowed a wreath on the conductor while the audience gave him an ovation the likes of which was rarely heard at Harvard.[59]

But Henry Higginson found himself in a quandary. Having urged Wilson to declare war and having supported the president's naval policy for defense against German submarines, he worried increasingly what would become of the Boston Symphony Orchestra. Should he keep Muck and the orchestra, or not? Was it possible that some of the German members conspired against their French colleagues and perhaps even operated as spies? Muck, after all, had even wished to enlist in Germany but was refused for lack of strength. At the same time, he seemed uniquely gifted to conduct the Boston Symphony Orchestra, and was enormously popular among local audiences.[60] In his anguish, Higginson deliberated the matter with his most intimate friends, but mostly he tried to come to terms with a predicament: "If Dr. Muck should be sent away, plenty of the men should be sent away on the same ground."[61] In other words: the orchestra would have to be disbanded.

As for Muck himself, information remains scant. For all we know, he ended the season of 1916–17 to much acclaim, then retired for the seasonal break, most likely to his summer home near Seal Harbor, Maine, and returned for a splendid beginning to the 1917–18 season. At his first afternoon concert, on October 13, he was greeted enthusiastically by an audience eager to experience a broad range of masterpieces and some novelties. The conductor opened with a program filled with Wagner (Prelude to *Parsifal*), Liszt (*Prometheus*), Berlioz (*King Lear*), and Beethoven (Symphony no. 5).

Then trouble arose. A few days later, on Tuesday, October 30, Muck took the Boston Symphony Orchestra to Providence, Rhode Island, where the orchestra had given almost regular annual programs since its inception. The concert program was to include excerpts from works by the same composers featured in the October 13 concert (Wagner's *Tannhäuse*, Liszt's symphonic poem *Prometheus*, Beethoven's Overture to *Egmont*) plus Tchaikovsky's Symphony no. 4. Muck knew his orchestra, he knew the score, and the trip was going to be routine. What Muck did not know was that all routine had been abandoned in Rhode Island. That very morning, the *Providence Journal* had launched an attack on the orchestra, notably its conductor, for its "pro-German" inclinations. Muck had not yet played any patriotic American air at his local concerts, the *Journal* fumed. Now it was time to test his loyalty: "The Boston Symphony Orchestra should play 'The Star Spangled Banner' tonight." Both Higginson and orchestra manager Charles Ellis were informed of the challenge as nine women's clubs of Rhode Island telegraphed this request to the symphony. But the two men decided to withhold the message from Muck, since no one was permitted to interfere with his concert programming.

Their resolution proved short-sighted. To angry Rhode Islanders, Muck's subsequent "failure" to perform the anthem in Infantry Hall came close to treason. For months, the *Providence Journal* had rallied patriotic forces in the state by printing lead articles alerting unsuspecting Americans to spies, aliens, and traitors living in their midst. "Every German or Austrian in the United States, whether naturalized or not, unless known by years of association to be absolutely loyal, should be treated as a potential spy," the *Journal* had declared weeks earlier, on October 1. "Keep your eyes and ears open. Whenever any suspicious act or disloyal word comes to your notice, communicate at once with the Bureau of Investigation."[62] Though there was no notable protest at the concert that night, the next day the newspaper continued its bashing of German musicians. The foremost enemy, the paper's editor, John Revelstoke Rathom, decided, was Karl Muck. With an intricate feel for the drama and sensibility of the time, the *Journal* then counterpoised Karl Muck, the promoter of

# Fourth Programme

FRIDAY AFTERNOON, NOVEMBER 2, at 2.30 o'clock

SATURDAY EVENING, NOVEMBER 3, at 8 o'clock

Sibelius . . . . . . Symphony No. 4, A minor, Op. 63
    I.  Tempo molto moderato quasi adagio.
    II.  Allegro molto vivace.
    III.  Il Tempo Largo.
    IV.  Allegro.

Saint-Saëns . . . Concerto in G minor for Pianoforte, Op. 22
    I.  Andante sostenuto.
    II.  Allegretto Scherzando.
    III.  Presto.

Beethoven . . . . Overture to "Leonore" No. 3, Op. 72

SOLOIST
Miss FRANCES NASH

STEINWAY PIANO USED

There will be an intermission of ten minutes after the symphony

*The ladies of the audience are earnestly requested not to put on hats before the end of a number.*

*The doors of the hall will be closed during the performance of each number on the programme. Those who wish to leave before the end of the concert are requested to do so in an interval between the numbers.*

City of Boston, Revised Regulation of August 5, 1898,—Chapter 3, relating to the covering of
the head in places of public amusement

Every licensee shall not, in his place of amusement, allow any person to wear upon the head a covering which obstructs the view of the exhibition or performance in such place of any person seated in any seat therein provided for spectators, it being understood that a low head covering without projection, which does not obstruct such view, may be worn.
Attest: J. M. GALVIN, City Clerk

197

**27a,b** The Boston Symphony Orchestra's fourth program during the 1917–18 season, on Friday afternoon, 2 November 1917, and Saturday evening, 3 November 1917. This was the first program in which the management inserted a slip announcing the addition of the national anthem to the regular program, three days after the Rhode Island incident. Pres. 86.5 f3, Boston Symphony Orchestra Archives. Courtesy of the Boston Symphony Orchestra Archives.

# Fourth Programme

FRIDAY AFTERNOON, NOVEMBER 2, at 2.30 o'clock

SATURDAY EVENING, NOVEMBER 3, at 8 o'clock

Sibelius . . . . . . Symphony No. 4, A minor, Op. 63
    I.  Tempo molto moderato quasi adagio.
    II.  Allegro molto vivace.
    III.  Il Tempo Largo.

## The National Anthem will be played as the closing number of the programme

STEINWAY PIANO USED

There will be an intermission of ten minutes after the symphony

*The ladies of the audience are earnestly requested not to put on hats before the end of a number.*

*The doors of the hall will be closed during the performance of each number on the programme. Those who wish to leave before the end of the concert are requested to do so in an interval between the numbers.*

City of Boston, Revised Regulation of August 5, 1898,—Chapter 3, relating to the covering of the head in places of public amusement

Every licensee shall not, in his place of amusement, allow any person to wear upon the head a covering which obstructs the view of the exhibition or performance in such place of any person seated in any seat therein provided for spectators, it being understood that a low head covering without projection, which does not obstruct such view, may be worn.

                                    Attest: J. M. GALVIN, City Clerk

militarism and a friend of the German kaiser's, to peace-loving mothers, wives, and daughters who hailed the spirit of America by requesting in vain that he play "The Star-Spangled Banner."

During the next few weeks a wave of emotion swept across music circles inside and outside Boston. Higginson and his manager swiftly inserted a slip of paper in the upcoming Boston concert program, on November 2: "The National Anthem will be played as the closing number of the program."[63] Most of Muck's colleagues in the music world, such as Felix Leifels, manager of the Philharmonic Society of New York, still supported the conductor. In New York City, Walter Damrosch declared that Muck should not be expected to conduct "The Star-Spangled Banner," because "he is a loyal citizen of Prussia and is in this country not by his own desire, but at the request of Major Higginson, patron of the Boston Symphony Orchestra." A few days later, however, Damrosch revoked his statement and issued a new one in which he attacked Muck as "cowardly." Now he suggested that the conductor had no right to play the anthem, which should be conducted only by an upstanding American assistant conductor.[64]

Much has been made of the "case of Dr. Muck" in subsequent decades, mostly as an extreme example of the anti-German hysteria raging across the United States in 1917–18. The story seems to fit in neatly with the overly zealous campaign by George Creel's Committee on Public Information, as well as by local and private organizations dedicated to the task of ridding the United States of enemy aliens in their midst. The case of Muck also illustrates the correlation between the Department of Justice and citizens' organizations officially sanctioned by the government. Having opened the Pandora's box of public action, the department worried about the extent to which patriotic groups disregarded principles of freedom of speech in the face of disloyal, unpatriotic utterances. As the department conceded, often these groups would engage in violence and illegal acts in their efforts to keep the country clean.

Muck's defense of the orchestra's action did little to alleviate the situation. Upon his return from Rhode Island (whose governor meanwhile had approved a resolution prohibiting the conductor from ever playing in the state again), Muck explained to reporters that he had never been consulted regarding the decision not to play the national anthem. That might have tamed reporters' spirits, had it not been for his subsequent statement, which whisked away all doubt about his apostasy. "It would be a gross mistake, a violation of artistic taste and principles, for such an organization as ours to play patriotic airs." Art, Muck emphatically stated, was greater than any national considerations, and his duty was to give the public "the most exquisite artistic compositions." "The Star-Spangled Banner," unfortunately, did not count among the most exquisite artistic compositions; nor was a symphony a military band. "To ask us to play The Star Spangled Banner is embarrassing," Muck concluded. "It is almost an insult. Such an attempt would be destructive of the very thing the Symphony stands for—musical art."[65]

With these words, Muck literally sealed his own fate. His opposition to the merger of patriotism and art, his insistence on classical music as a superior value, and superior to the national anthem, did not go over well with a press and a public bent on destroying all signs of German Kultur. To refuse to play "The Star-Spangled Banner" now meant to spit on American music, American identity, American pride, and American patriotism. "Art is not a thing by itself. It is an expression of human ideals," fumed the journal *Outlook*. "Wherever there are national ideals there is national art, if there is ever any art at all."[66]

Within days, the public outcry reached fanatic dimensions. At a mass rally in Baltimore, the cradle of the national anthem, angry citizens led by the former governor Edwin Warfield engaged in battle cry, shouting "Kill Muck!" "Kill such a man!" "Hang the Kaiser!" and "Kill the Hun!" Warfield himself announced, "The day is coming when that anthem will be sung by every nation on the globe!"[67] Muck received angry letters threatening death. In Chicago, audiences tore up a large photograph of him that decorated a wall in Orchestra Hall. Theodore Roosevelt publicly declared his disapproval of the conductor and called for his speedy deportation. "I am shocked, simply shocked that anyone should apologize for him on the ground that it [the national anthem] is not an artistic, but a patriotic work."[68]

The interesting aspect of all of this is not Muck's personal fate, tragic as it was, but how fast Muck's critics associated his condescending statements on "The Star-Spangled Banner" with a general disdain for the United States at large. Muck had played American composers in the past, particularly during the war years. As regards the national anthem, many people at the time felt ambivalent about its harmony and its aptness as a national song, because it seemed difficult to sing.[69] Muck's statement, however, played on the insecurities, fears, and profound cultural inferiority complex that Americans had lived through for decades. The war seemed to deliver an opportunity to end the universalism of German music on American concert stages.

German music represented the kaiser and Prussian militarism. Indeed, the preponderance of German musicians on concert stages around the

**28** Like his father, the New York conductor Walter Damrosch did much to promote the music of the Romantics in the United States. His family had emigrated from Breslau. During World War I, he first defended Karl Muck, then declared a few days later that Muck was "cowardly" and did not even have the right to lead the national anthem. *Music* 9 (December 1895): 214.

country seemed to point to a gigantic military, cultural, and political plot to undermine American purity and innocence. Only an Allied victory could extinguish the Reich's political and cultural influence for good. "Even art must stand aside so that every possible influence can be brought to bear to terminate the war with an allied victor," wrote Mrs. William Jay, former member of the board of the New York Philharmonic Society, in her effort to ban Muck along with all German music from American concert stages. "There seems no swifter means of emphasizing the wholeheartedness of the United States than by terminating the German influence in musical efforts." For months Mrs. Jay kept up her one-woman crusade against Muck in leading New York newspapers, tirelessly repeating her charges of espionage and corruption. "Are we to pour forth our blood . . . and brain and treasure and still hold to German musical domination? Rather a thousand times that the orchestra's traditions fade from our lives than one hour be added to the war's duration by clinging to this last tentacle of the German Octopus."[70]

On December 10, 1917, the Department of Justice informed Henry Higginson that Karl Muck had been classified as an enemy alien under Section 4067 of the U.S. Revised Code. His Swiss citizenship had been declared irrelevant due to his longtime residence in Germany; consequently, the ruling barred the conductor from approaching the District of Columbia and required him to obtain permission from the Justice Department for all travel outside Boston. Likewise, all alien members of the Boston Symphony Orchestra had to register with the department and

Hungerford, in Pittsburgh Sun.

## IT LOOKS LIKE A HARD WINTER FOR STUBBORN GERMAN PUPILS

29  "It Looks Like a Hard Winter for Stubborn German Pupils," *Pittsburgh Sun*, n.d. (November 1917); BSO scrapbooks, MF Pres/17, Boston Symphony Orchestra Archives. Courtesy of the Boston Symphony Orchestra Archives.

ask for special permission when going on tour. The management of the symphony, in other words, became a nightmare.

Then, on the evening of March 25, 1918, Boston's district attorney arrested Muck as the latter was entering his home on the Fenway, and interned him in an East Cambridge jail for several days. The timing could have not been more infuriating to the conductor, as it directly followed a rehearsal of Bach's *St. Matthew Passion*, to be mounted the following day—the very symbolization of German nationalism since its recovery by Mendelssohn in 1829. For years, Muck had labored to solicit and restore the original score, and he was eager to present the piece for the first time in Boston.[71]

To justify Muck's arrest, agents of the Department of Justice cited an array of documents proving Muck's disloyalty to the United States, punishable by the Espionage Act. Those documents, it turned out, consisted of a number of love letters the conductor had composed between 1914 and 1917 to a young woman named Rosamond Young, heiress and teenage music student from Milton, Massachusetts. The letters had been found in her room as well as in a safe-deposit box in Boston.[72]

As the press later reported, in these writings Muck had poured out his heart, his antipathy for the American public and its artistic ignorance, his hatred of the U.S. government, and his love for the German kaiser. In January 1916, for example, Muck had explained his feelings about a performance in Pittsburgh, the center of the ammunition industry in the United States: "When I came upon the stage yesterday . . . and saw thousands sitting before me who have earned and are still earning millions through the murder of my people everything was red before my eyes and it took my whole strength not to yell out loud." In this remarkably frank correspondence, Muck referred repeatedly to his loyalty to Germany and his disdain for American patriotism. "I can't keep up this horrible life much longer in a country full of fanatical enemies far from my country which is struggling for its existence," he wrote on one occasion. The conductor also elaborated on his friendship with leading German officials, including the diplomatic corps and Johann von Bernstorff, the German ambassador, who had been asked to leave the country in 1917, due to charges of espionage. To protect himself from the onslaught of "American dumbness," Muck repeatedly stressed the significance of surrounding himself with Kultur, the very Kultur that raised a red flag with citizen patriots and district attorneys throughout the nation.[73]

Even though the letters became public only after the Mucks had left the United States in November 1919, the press sensed that the justice authorities held "sensational" material pertaining to the wartime activities of Karl Muck, and stories about his enemy alien activities escalated. Some charged that there had been coded messages between the lines of scores Muck had ordered from Germany. At Seal Harbor, residents wondered about bizarre incidents at the Mucks' vacation residence, which typically occurred at night. Neighbors reported hearing strange hammering sounds, while others were convinced they had spotted flashes of light from the windows, perhaps designed to signal German submarines off the Atlantic coast. When Justice Department inspectors visited the property, they found an abundance of wires on the third floor, originally installed by a previous owner, an amateur radio operator who wanted to build a radio center. Anonymous letters to editors of various newspapers accused the conductor of sending prostitutes with venereal diseases to military bases and passing along guns that had been tampered with to American soldiers. Others suspected that Muck had plotted to blow up the birthplace of Henry Wadsworth Longfellow on Cambridge's Brattle Street.[74] The rumors had no end.

Once Muck was gone, other members of the symphony came under suspicion. In June of 1918, after a few had already resigned voluntarily, the orchestra fired another eighteen members, among them all the remaining German and Austrian players, including the assistant conductor, Ernst Schmidt, who had conducted the concerts during Muck's absence. The orchestra then assured the press that the replacement musicians would come from the rank and file of loyal Allied countries. At the end of the season, 29 of the 100 members (17 Germans, 1 Bohemian, four Americans, 3 Belgians, three Frenchmen, and one Italian) had left the orchestra, among them seven of the principals and, of course, the conductor. Heartbroken over the political turmoil within the orchestra that he had guided for thirty-eight years of untiring service, Higginson resigned from his position as patron. A board of nine trustees filed papers for the incorporation of the organization to guarantee the continuation of the concerts.[75]

The issue at the heart of the dispute was whether or not Muck's and Higginson's nineteenth-century ideas about musical universalism and the "Republic of Art" that knew no borders could transcend the nationalized debates of the turn of the twentieth century and the patriotic rhetoric of World War I. Supporters of Muck (and there were many) typically came from the ranks of the upper urban elites. The socialite Isabella Stewart Gardner, for one, left her seat in Symphony Hall in protest of the American flag draped above the stage. While opponents of Muck identified him as a direct representative of the German kaiser, his supporters viewed the

30 After several months of negotiations with candidates in England, Italy, and France, in September 1918, a few weeks prior to the season's opening, the Boston Symphony Orchestra announced that the Parisian conductor and composer Henri Rabaud was to become its seventh conductor; Rabaud stayed with the orchestra until the following year. Photographer: Horner, Boston, 1918. 86.7 f1, Boston Symphony Orchestra Archives. Courtesy of the Boston Symphony Orchestra Archives.

charges against him as a direct attack on the institution of the symphony orchestra per se and all it had done for urban communities.

Incarcerated until April 6 in the East Cambridge Jail, Karl Muck was eventually interned at Fort Oglethorpe in the Appalachian Mountains. It was not the worst place to be: of all the internment camps the United States had erected, Oglethorpe was certainly the "classiest." Its foremost clients were industrialists, doctors, teachers, and artists. Locals in the vicinity of the Georgia-Tennessee border called the camp "the millionaire's club," because it consisted of a former mountain resort, complete with a swimming pool, tennis courts, a croquet lawn, and a former ballroom.[76] Still, Muck had not chosen to live there. And despite the armistice of November 11, 1918, the U.S. government continued to arrest enemy aliens until February 1919.

On August 21, 1919, Muck finally left the country aboard the liner *S.S. Frederick VIII*, bound for Copenhagen with a federal agent looking on from the dock. Muck traveled under his Swiss passport and said that he did not know yet where to go. He even refused to reveal his identity to fellow passengers, then exclaimed: "I am not a German, despite the fact that they said I was. I considered myself an American, but see what America has done to me. I am going over to Denmark now, a man without a flag or a country." He spoke bitterly of the American press and the public mob ruling the United States.[77] Less than two years later, his wife, Anita, died, leaving her husband perpetually broken in spirit.

Back in Germany, Muck tried hard to secure a permanent position, and for years he traveled on the guest conductors' circuit, performing, among others, with the Staatsoper Berlin and the Münchener Festspiele. In 1922, he was appointed conductor of the Hamburg Philharmonic Orchestra, where he became one of the first local supporters of Arnold Schoenberg's music. Muck also regularly appeared at the Bayreuth Festspiele. German politicians, cultural administrators, and musical celebrities never forgot to congratulate him on his birthdays.[78]

It took the United States a long time to forgive—or forget. Though Karl Muck was the first conductor to produce commercial recordings with the Boston Symphony Orchestra, in 1917, most of these were never marketed to the public. His interpretation of Tchaikovsky's "Waltz of the Flowers" was not issued until seventy-five years later, and four of the five discs he had made with RCA Victor never reached the market. However, fragments of test recordings remain in the RCA archives and at Yale University.[79] Thirty years after Muck left the United States, newspapers and encyclopedias continued to claim his culpability, with one notable exception.[80]

Perhaps we will never know if Muck was a spy. On the one hand, there were incidents of German sabotage and espionage. German secret agents were quite active in the United States, notably before it entered World War I. German agents tried to block the supply lines between the United States and the Allies by blowing up U.S. ships anchored in American ports. From undercover headquarters established in the United States, they conducted sabotage in Mexico, Canada, and even India (where they hoped to stir up a revolution against the British colonial power).[81] Excerpts of letters Muck had sent his lover referred numerous times to business conversations with von Bernstorff, coded telegrams sent to the German embassy in Washington, DC, and ominous figures and numbers compiled for "Berlin" as a favor to the ambassador, as well as secret news from Germany, the nature of which Muck did not dare reveal to his lover.[82] On the other hand, the original letters never resurfaced, and there is no guarantee that the *Boston Post* had reproduced them accurately.

Furthermore, it remains open to speculation as to why Muck should have poured out his heart and political plans over pages and pages addressed to a girl who was probably no older than fifteen when he first laid eyes on her.

In the grand scheme of events the charges of espionage, never confirmed, mattered much less than his original musical mission, along with his comments on American culture. As the district attorney's office failed to produce evidence for the charges against Muck, arguing that it was bound by confidentiality, newspapers made much of Muck's personal connections with the kaiser. The German government had sent the conductor to the United States to make Germany popular. Wrote the *Boston Traveller* in March 1918, he "had easy access to people and groups in the United States where a good word for Germany could be counted on to do much good in such an emergency as a world war." Had not Muck himself repeatedly underscored how much the kaiser supported, if not pushed for, his appointment as the conductor of the Boston Symphony Orchestra? "Opening the road for world conquest with such men as Dr. Muck might be credited as a superlative move in international intrigue, even if the great musician himself was ignorant that he was part of the preparation."[83]

The reason for the Boston debacle, marveled a newspaper after Higginson had resigned and a board had taken over the orchestra, lay in the orchestra's isolation from public sentiment and indifference to it. The management (that is, Higginson) "honestly believed that its power and the artistic prestige of the orchestra could maintain through a war against Germany a German conductor at the post he had adorned." In the last analysis, this author concluded, the management of the orchestra had always regarded music and music performance as quintessentially German. Had Higginson rearranged his priorities, told his conductor to play the national anthem from the beginning, waved the flag, and made a patriotic announcement, Muck might never have been arrested. One might say with Bliss Perry that Higginson had no political cunning and was simply an old and confused man. But that is missing the point of the story. Higginson was a man of principles. To him, German art and German politics—or musical universalism and German nationalism—were not even two sides of the same coin. They were as vastly apart from each other as the sun and the moon. And just as politics and art did not mesh in his mind, he could not envision how to reconcile the two simply by soothing the public—the very public that he hoped to educate with the concerts of the Boston Symphony Orchestra. Karl Muck's greatest crime, writes Gayle

Turk in a brilliant essay on the legal battles of 1917–18, was not what he did but who he was and what he stood for: Muck incarnated the peril of Germans earning their fortune and enjoying prestige in the United States while at the same time nurturing anti-American sentiments.[84]

In Cincinnati, the conductor Ernst Kunwald was dismissed under circumstances similar to Muck's in Boston. Son of a court attorney from Vienna, Kunwald had come to the city from the Berlin Philharmonic Orchestra. He was to become the first Austrian enemy alien to be interned in southern Ohio, and possibly in the United States. On 8 December 1917, the *Cincinnati Post* reported that Kunwald had been taken to the Montgomery County Jail in Dayton. He was briefly released on December 9 but rearrested on January 12, 1918, on charges of having made "pro-German statements." Kunwald was subsequently interned in Fort Oglethorpe, and his financial possessions, including his annual income and his jewelry and stock certificates, were confiscated.[85]

The appointment of his successor, Eugen Ysaÿe, constituted a powerful example of the nation's new musical alliance and the Franco-American entente: except for one Brahms and a few Beethoven and Mozart numbers, Ysaÿe avoided Kunwald's repertory. Instead, he presented his audiences with twenty-nine French and Belgian compositions, the largest number of Gallic works in any season of the orchestra's history. Ysaÿe became enormously popular with Cincinnati audiences, not so much from a musical as from an emotional point of view. Having fled the Germans in Belgium, he showed profound concern for the victims of the German invasion and, as a result, organized numerous benefit recitals for relief agencies and charitable institutions.[86]

At the same time, French government officials continued their efforts to win American sympathies for French *civilisation*. In October 1918, under the auspices of the French and the U.S. governments, the eighty members of the Paris Conservatory Orchestra and their conductor, André Messager, traveled on a U.S. warship from an unspecified U.S. naval base in France to the United States, for concerts in Boston, in Washington, DC, at the Metropolitan Opera House in New York City, and as far west as Minneapolis.[87] In November 1919, the French government sponsored the child prodigy Magdeleine Brard, a Parisian pianist, who made her Boston debut. Audiences and critics, including Louis C. Elson, called her a "musical marvel," comparing her to Josef Hofmann and Jascha Heifetz. Even though she may not have grasped the political underpinnings of her sponsorship, Brard did wonder about her sudden international fame. "My government has sent me to America, you know," she confessed.

"They call me their 'representative artist,' though I'm sure I've never earned so proud a title."[88]

American private sponsors, too, made an enormous effort to funnel Americans from Germany to western Europe, notably France and Italy. In the summer of 1917, a society for American fellowships in French universities was founded in order to further the knowledge of French culture and scholarship. The main reason for its initiative, the group stated, "is that American graduates for forty years past have gone to Germany, not to France, and have returned to man the faculties of our universities with exclusive esteem for German culture and a propaganda for German repute." Little did the committee mention that many French universities had once practically barred foreigners, while German institutes of learning had offered education to students from outside their country. Other plans included fellowships at the American Academy in Rome, to enable young American composers to study for up to three years in Italy and reside in the Villa Aurelia. The endowment of the fellowships, named for Horatio Parker, former head of the music department at Yale, and Oscar Hammerstein, were supposed to cover the costs for traveling Americans in southern Europe.[89]

In the United States, the symphony orchestras of Philadelphia, Boston, and New York no longer employed German conductors, but they did retain German-born musicians. In 1921, 40 of the 91 members of the New York Philharmonic were born in the United States, while the rest had been naturalized. Only 14 were originally German or Austrian by birth; the others came from Russia, Italy, Holland, Bohemia, France, Poland, Norway, Denmark, and Belgium. According to the records of the Chicago Symphony Orchestra, in 1935, 50 out of 80 of its members were American-born, and the rest had become American. Thirty-two alone came from Illinois, and 23 from Chicago. In contrast, the New York Philharmonic did not count more than 24 percent of its members as being of American birth, while most of its foreign players (29 percent) came from Russia. The Boston Symphony fared likewise, with only 18 American, 36 French, 15 German, and 9 Russian players. The New York Metropolitan Opera had 18 Americans next to 43 Italians.[90]

Critics and the public soon tired of the orchestras' political correctness. "How many of the Teutonic composers shall be excluded from the programs because of the German barbarities of the last four years?" asked Olin Downes in the *Boston Post* in November 1918.[91] In 1920, when the Boston Symphony Orchestra under Pierre Monteux performed Robert Schumann's *Rheinische* Symphony, Louis Elson marveled whether it was high time to include all German composers, "because there is no symphonic work so thoroughly Teutonic as this outcome of Schumann's dwelling in the beautiful Rhineland!' "[92]

As German restaurants in New York went back to advertising *Frankfurter mit Sauerkraut* and *Berlin Pfannekuchen* as their foremost specialties (while, however, dismissing the *Kaiserschnitzel* forever), German-language programs, including operas, vocal concerts, and theatrical productions, likewise reappeared a few months after the war ended. New York singing societies resumed the performance of German songs as early as 1919. Even Mrs. William Jay announced in the *New York Times* the end of her crusade against the Huns Bach, Mozart, Beethoven, Wagner, Goethe, and Schiller. By 1919, three new German theaters (among those one opera) had been founded. The Metropolitan Opera opened the 1919–20 season with Albert Lortzing's *Zar und Zimmermann* as well as Johann Strauss's *Die Fledermaus* and also announced a Wagner cycle for the spring of 1920.[93]

———

Most German music artists could survive in their posts in the United States if they played according to the rule of the day: if they sang in English, if they played the national anthem, if they rejected ties to the fatherland, and if they declared their intention to become U.S. citizens. And Americans' patriotic zeal did not last for long. Once the war was over, audiences soon tired of "nationalist" concerts. "Even the patriotic hymns of the allied nations aroused little enthusiasm," wrote Philip Hale in the *Herald*, while Edith Wharton wondered how much longer Americans were going to believe that their cultural inferiority originated in their national identity: "It is really too easy a disguise for our shortcomings to dress them up as a form of patriotism!"[94]

World War I was not the great watershed in German-American cultural relations that many historians have made it out to be. The criticism of German music grew out of two decades of debates concerning how American artists could possibly free themselves from the fetters of Teutonization, at a time when many critics and musicians interpreted the beginning of the war in Europe as the dawning of American civilization. And it is true that the period most important for the American composer was no doubt the years between 1914 and 1917. European musicians wrote less, particularly less than American conductors were able to obtain and willing to perform. Royalties skyrocketed. At the same time, the transport of music scores across the Atlantic became increasingly difficult. It was simply infinitely easier and politically correct to perform works by native composers.[95]

Other nations sensed the dawn of a musical liberation as well. French composers and intellectuals discussed at length the necessity to break free from the oppression of the German canon, both before but even more so after the onset of the war. "We have failed to cultivate our garden," scolded Claude Debussy in March of 1915, "but on the other hand we have given a warm welcome to any foreign salesmen who care to come our way. We listened to their patter and bought their worthless wares, and when they laughed at our ways we became ashamed of them."[96] New French music was different and, implicitly, better whenever it did not comport with the German tradition: form, design, melody. In Russia, Igor Stravinsky praised the mature Russian civilization, expressing his hope that after the war a revolution would create a Slavonic United States, free from the fetters of German influences.

What was peculiar about the American case, though, was the rancor critics and the public displayed toward their former popular stars, a rancor that originated in decades of musical frustration. In French and British concert halls, German music, including contemporary compositions, continued to be performed, all wartime activities notwithstanding. The faculty at the Sorbonne even renewed the contract of its leading expert in German literature and language in 1915. Writers like Vernon Lee and Romain Rolland continued to hail the significance of nineteenth-century music as a world language. In contrast, when the United States entered the war in April of 1917, emotions escalated and eventually led to a full-fledged assault on all things German, including German music and artists. Conductors like Karl Muck and Frederick Stock represented leaders of large and seemingly German organizations, but their personal fates differed tremendously. No doubt the rebuttals of Muck, the archetypal nineteenth-century European, were most damaging to his own case. Stock, who refused to speak German after 1914, played his hand best because he had revealed his eager patriotism early on. There were other pitiable cases, including the internment and deportation of Ernst Kunwald of Cincinnati, though most orchestral musicians were not interned and deported. Still, hundreds lost their jobs, experienced public pressure and, occasionally, physical threats, all of which affected their lives, their personal security, and their perception of the United States and its musical culture.[97]

The wartime and postwar tenures of Henri Rabaud Monteux, Ysaÿe, and other French conductors foreshadowed both Allied sympathies and a development that characterized the American music scene for the next decades. As Americans deserted Berlin, Leipzig, and Vienna, they began looking for the greener pastures of France, notably Paris, to discover an innately American voice—and there is no doubt that they succeeded in their quest. But as we shall see, such developments did little to shake up the canon or the elective affinity between Germany and the United States.

# Epilogue

Lieutenant Colonel Harry H. Crosby counts among the most decorated U.S. navigators in World War II. He flew thirty-two combat missions aboard Flying Fortress bombers and was eventually promoted to Group Navigator of the 100th Bombardment Group. A brilliant mathematician, the handsome navigator from Iowa was responsible for one of the most remarkable decisions made during the war.

On the night of August 11, 1943, while listening to a recording of Beethoven's Third and Fifth symphonies, Crosby read on the record's jacket that the composer had been born and educated in Bonn. The next day, the Flying Fortress received orders to bomb that city. From an altitude of twenty-five thousand feet, Crosby spotted a huge building below that he believed could be a school. Remembering the album, he gripped the bombardier and shouted: "We do not attack Bonn," then added that Beethoven received his education there. None of the other officers asked any questions, and the Flying Fortress turned southwest to attack a main railway workshop in Cologne. After the war, Crosby was included in a list of outstanding combat officers serving in the European theater of operations.[1]

It is difficult to double-check the accuracy of Crosby's memories, as they were recorded years after the war. His superiors were certainly not pleased with the diversion of a whole raid on these grounds, but it seems that he was not disciplined. What matters in the context of our story is that he remembered his action in a specific way. Why was this bomber-crew navigator thinking about classical music in the midst of a deadly mission? Why did his love for a

German composer lead him and his men to abandon the set target? How could Beethoven make up for all the horrors of World War II? When years ago I interviewed American soldiers about their wartime experience, they repeatedly moderated their historical antipathy for the Germans by emphasizing that Germany had produced great music. One could say, with Thomas Mann's *Doktor Faustus*, that the best and the worst in German *Kultur* is inextricably intertwined. But Adrian Leverkühn's pact with the devil does not explain the emotional level on which music functions as a transcending force in times of peace or of war.[2]

For all the anti-German hysteria in the United States of 1917–18, the nation's musical canon curiously remained solidified throughout the twentieth century. The banning of German music and the deportation of German musicians did not contribute much to the nationalization of American music. It only opened the door to French, later on Russian, and then Asian and Scandinavian conductors and musicians. To this day, the American symphony scene is dominated by non-American conductors, and its programs consist largely of European-composed music, most of it created before World War I. When a few years ago the Philadelphia Orchestra contemplated dedicating an entire season to twentieth-century music, including numerous American compositions, its marketing department groaned that concert subscribers would cancel their subscriptions by the hundreds.

At first sight, the interwar period almost became a replay of the prewar decades: it reestablished musical ties between both countries. As Reinhold Brinkmann and others have shown, in the 1930s and '40s émigré musicians such as Arnold Schoenberg, Kurt Weill, and Paul Hindemith lived on their prominence as successful artists and on their European pedigree, as did many of the lesser-known refugee artists. A steady influx of German-speaking musicians swamped the American musical landscape. Composers, conductors, soloists, and music educators like Schoenberg, Bruno Walter, Otto Klemperer, Fritz Stiedry, Erich Leinsdorf, Wilhelm Steinberg, Artur Schnabel, Eduard Steuermann, and Rudolf Kilisch all built on the preexisting and continuing German musical heritage in the United States. Based on previously published numbers, Brinkmann estimates that some 470 German and Austrian musicians were admitted into the United States between 1933 and 1941.[3]

Famous even before they left Europe and often familiar with the American concert stage, some of these artists and educators encountered no problems receiving engagements between New York and Los Angeles, riding on the wave of an emotional elective affinity that went back almost a century. Arnold Schoenberg worked at the New School of Social

Research in New York, then taught at the University of California in Los Angeles, where he introduced a generation of eager students to serialism, which then found its way back to Germany in the 1950s. Paul Hindemith taught at Yale University, while Otto Klemperer became conductor of the Los Angeles Philharmonic and founder of the new Pittsburgh Orchestra. Erich Leinsdorf conducted the New York Metropolitan Opera but also worked in Cleveland. Wilhelm Steinberg became the conductor of the NBC Orchestra, then moved on to engagements in Buffalo, Pittsburgh, and Boston. Many exiled composers found a career in composing scores for Hollywood films. Werner Richard Heymann, Franz Waxmann, Erich Korngold, and Ernst Toch, all distinguished composers before 1933, gained additional fame after their arrival in the United States when a generation of young intellectuals, disgusted with American popular culture, turned to European visitors in search of new methods and new meaning.[4] Profiting from the established prestige of German musicians as well as the popularization of music theater in the United States, Kurt Weill became a leading figure in the merger of highbrow music and mass entertainment, thus joining the community of twentieth-century musical stars in the United States.[5]

Music theory and music education formed an even larger avenue for German-speaking musicians on the run from the Nazis. Èmigrés such as Heinrich Schenker, Curt Sachs, Willi Apel, and Leo Schrade literally invented music theory and music studies as a field of scholarship at American universities. More than any other professional group, these émigrés were, in the eyes of the American public, the "good Germans" whose professional career was in no way blocked by the language barrier or by political baggage.

Despite all their efforts to nationalize the American music scene, during World War II Americans welcomed the most famous German musicians with open arms and refrained from identifying German Kultur as behind the evil of the Third Reich. A New York handbook of music presented a canon that listed not only the works of eighteenth- and nineteenth-century German composers but also Richard Strauss, who was at the time the most popular (and controversial) composer alive during the Third Reich.[6] Soldiers and sailors attended concerts of German compositions, and there was no deluge of letters to newspaper editors complaining about "enemy music." In fact, had enemy music been boycotted in World War II, there would not have been much left for American orchestras to play, as they would have been forced to eliminate Italian, Hungarian, and, at least at first, Russian and, perhaps, Norwegian music as well. Some Americans regarded the 1917 hysteria with a grain of pragmatism: "People who are sensitive over enemy music," recommended the *Chicago Sunday Tribune* in 1942, "had better put cotton plugs in their ears and retire to a cave hewn in the living rock for the duration."[7]

This is not to say that World War II bore no traces of the previous anti-German hysteria. Already in 1936, the New York Philharmonic had to cancel the engagement of Wilhelm Furtwängler on account of the massive resistance of the New York City audience to his appointment because the conductor had been vice president of the Reich Chamber for Music. After the war, the Chicago Symphony Orchestra had to withdraw its engagement of Furtwängler as music director and conductor because six soloists and three guest conductors threatened to cancel their appearances with the orchestra should Furtwängler come.[8] Philadelphia's conductor, Eugene Ormandy, emphatically declined any offer to conduct the Philharmonics in Vienna or in Salzburg, since those were filled with "former active Nazis and SS men."[9] In 1949, the conductor of the Vienna state opera, Josef Krips, was arrested by the Immigration and Naturalization Service on his way to Chicago, interned on Ellis Island, and forced to return to Europe because he told immigration officials that "I have never belonged to any party because there is no party to Mozart, Beethoven or Schubert."[10] Still, these incidents remained scant, and they pale in comparison with the wartime hysteria three decades prior.

One of the reasons why the anti-German hysteria subsided so quickly was that during the interwar years, American intellectuals and artists became increasingly convinced that the cultural tide had turned. Music was degenerating in Europe, notably in Austria and Germany, declared the pianist Arthur Shattuck in December 1920: "This is due in a large measure to the rot that the futurist element in the musical world is attempting to foist on the musical public." America, he added, would soon impress the world with great composers, with the interest and support of "the masses" playing an important role in this scenario.[11]

Americans became firmly convinced that their country was destined to become the site of the best of high and modern music.[12] In their travel reports, representatives of American Philharmonics noted the economic dissatisfaction on the part of gifted artists in Europe; they repeatedly commented on the poor performances of European orchestras (including those at Vienna, Berlin, and Milan) and the shortage of funds. "All in all my trip has been a great success for me," concluded one American manager in the 1920s, "Heard quite a few concerts which proved to me that The New York Philharmonic without a doubt is the greatest Orchestra in the World."[13]

World War II further contributed to American hopes for a global shift in the arts. European music was past its peak, Leopold Stokowski declared in the early 1940s. Music was a universal language for people from all walks of life, and America was fast becoming the global center of music, highbrow included. America, he prophesied, would develop its own, synthetic musical style; American instrument manufacturers would improve and reinvent instruments while composers would focus on merging different musical styles. In a curious gesture foreshadowing the visions of cold-war advocates of American jazz, Stokowski expounded that music would transcend nationalism, find a universal expression, and give rise to an American Palestrina and an American Bach. "The next hundred years," he declared, "should see the renaissance and flowering of a truly american [sic] music,"[14] and no act symbolized the conductor's confidence more than his subsequent creation of The All-American Youth Orchestra.

Stokowski, along with many other twentieth-century conductors such as Leonard Bernstein, was convinced that musical universalism now bore an American—more than a German—connotation, giving credit to the post–World War II boom on the concert scene. Their credo entailed that even before the arrival of the American Bach, European music would find its finest expression not in Europe but in the United States. The growth of music education in schools, the temporary use of entire symphony orchestras in movie theaters, the improvement in recording and reproduction techniques, and the availability of phonographs and discs to the average consumer all created a music audience outside the concert hall. Thanks to New Deal governmental programs, in the 1930s more symphony orchestras had been created than during the entire century before. By 1940, their number stood at three hundred, among those sixteen major orchestras that ranked among the best in the world. The five most popular composers in 1940 were Beethoven (20.7 percent of works performed), Brahms (13.1 percent), Tchaikovsky (11.4 percent), Sibelius (6.2. percent), and Mozart (5.9 percent). In 1953, statistics published by the National Music Club indicated that thirty million concertgoers made for a gross revenue of approximately $45 million throughout the United States per year. With the number of symphony orchestras booming, budgets expanding, concert performances multiplying, and foundation grants soaring, music historians often describe those years as America's "cultural explosion," portraying what Joseph Horowitz calls the democratization of high culture.[15] Even American political leaders replaced their previous indifference toward the arts with a competitive quest to create arts councils, endowments, and cultural managers all dedicated to the advancement of music.

None of these developments incurred an end to Americans' emotional elective affinity with "the people of music." Indeed, during the following decades and notably during the early cold war period, touring became a way of reasserting the special cultural relationship between the Federal Republic of Germany and the United States. In 1949, the Philadelphia Orchestra was the first one to hit the transatlantic concert circuit and visit Germany. Boston followed in 1952, New York toured Germany in 1955, Cleveland in 1957, Chicago in 1971, and the San Francisco Symphony Orchestra in 1973.[16]

Sponsored by the West German state, several German orchestras likewise began to visit the United States. In the 1950s, the Bamberg Symphony received central government funding specifically for cultural propaganda overseas.[17] The Berlin Philharmonic was heavily backed by the West Berlin authorities from 1949 onward, and the German chancellor Konrad Adenauer gave personal support to its role as cultural ambassador. Overseas tours were financed by the Auswärtiges Amt, and the orchestra visited the United States in 1955, 1956, 1961, 1965, and 1968.

Similarly, the German Democratic Republic sent its best to the United States: in 1974, Kurt Masur and the Leipzig Gewandhausorchester gave 25 concerts in 22 North American cities. Indeed, as Holger Stunz observed recently, from the perspective of many postwar American music critics, there never was an iron curtain.[18] In 1998, the German Youth Orchestra, also conducted by Masur, toured the United States on a Thank You America Tour to mark the fiftieth anniversary of the Berlin airlift.

In October 2001, just three weeks after the attack on the World Trade Center in New York City, the Berlin Philharmonic opened the season at Carnegie Hall with a concert dedicated to physicians and rescue workers. Only five days after the attack, "to overcome the shock, the speechlessness, through music and thereby to express our friendship and solidarity with our American friends," the Philharmonic recorded, in cooperation with the Orchestra of the German Opera of Berlin as well as the Staatskapelle Berlin, a CD that was subsequently distributed all over the United States by the German Foreign Office. Packaged in a flashy triptych jacket featuring pictures of the New York City skyline and the Brandenburg Gate along with snapshots of leading German politicians, including Gerhard Schröder, Angela Merkel, Joschka Fischer, and Johannes Rau, the CD once again underscored the emotional elective affinity between both nations by offering Americans the core of the canon in their moment of deepest grief: Wagner's *Tristan und Isolde*, Mahler's Symphony no. 9, and Franz Schubert's *Unfinished* Symphony.[19] The Foreign Office commissioned six thousand copies of the CD to be distributed primarily among high-ranking representatives in the United States and at U.S. embassies around the world.[20]

There is no doubt that music features prominently in the United States' special relationship with Germany today, and that the perception of a greater German land of music remains unchanged. On October 3, 2002, National Public Radio/WGBH 95 Boston's popular host, Ron Della Chiesa, reminded his "Classics in the Morning" listeners of the twelfth anniversary of German reunification. To celebrate the event, Della Chiesa announced, the station would play a variety of "German-born composers," adding, "Some of them are Austrian."[21]

———

There are three sides to the story of music and emotions in transatlantic relations that only in tandem render its significance complete: European intentions, the process of transmission, and American reactions. Until World War I, cultural diplomacy was not a concern or a responsibility of the state. In Germany and elsewhere, Foreign Office members felt that the determination and promotion of culture was in their interest but out of their range and beyond their authority. Private initiatives were key to the process of international cultural exchange, even though administrators typically kept those at arm's length. Officials feared that nongovernmental organizations and individuals might not necessarily act in the interest of their governments.

Culture had an impact on transatlantic relations with a dynamic and an interest of its own, and remote from state-directed incentives and goals. Beyond formal ties, symbolic acts, science, and visual arts, German-American cultural relations included museums, craftsmanship, musical instruments, novels, translations, and private art exhibitions. We still know very little about these informal and nongovernmental ties between the two nations, but one thing that has emerged is that German-American cultural relations did not "begin" with the academic exchange, nor can they be characterized as "selective" or even "uncoordinated."[22]

The international debate on music as the language of emotions was highly sophisticated and even scientific. It assigned the origins of "the magic" of music to central Europe and inspired thousands of Americans to cross the Atlantic Ocean to experience and carry home the magical atmosphere of Germany. Simultaneously, individual European artists, "rooted cosmopolitans," migrated across the Atlantic and were instrumental in the creation of a concert scene along with numerous symphony orchestras in the United States, which today rank among the finest in the world. Triggering the process of transmission, these artists were driven by a variety of motives, including personal fame, the search for opportunity, the temporary decline of the European music scene after 1848, and most important, a missionary impulse to spread the music of the Romantics among New World audiences.

European artists' efforts alone would not have sufficed to influence the American music scene; instead, they depended on the cultural openness and susceptibility of Victorian Americans. Moving on to the receiving end of the elective affinity, we may ask why, in an age of antiforeignism, immigration restrictions, and self-proclaimed political isolationism, did Americans become so attracted to foreign artists, valuing them more than native talent? The reason is that Americans, too, saw classical music as a means for providing evidence of culture. In their view, the musicians were bringing into the United States an essential element of Western civilization. At this level of analysis, then, Europeans—Germans and those who were perceived as Germans—and Americans were sharing the same ideology, the same experience, and the same emotions. In a perceptive essay on German ethnic culture in Buffalo, David Gerber has written that middle-class Americans feared that the prize for the United States' economic ascent might be a public culture that would remain barren, flat, and heedless of the people's essential psychic need; in more than one way, German rituals and festivities responded to this awareness and this need.[23] But it was not just a domestic concern that drove these men and women. Without the pro-German bent, the organizational talent, the moral engagement, and the financial support of men like Henry Higginson in Boston and Charles Norman Fay in Chicago as well as countless donors, guarantors, trustees, and subscribers all across the nation, the activities of the musical missionaries would not have met with much success. These sponsors all had an interest in music, high culture at large, social improvement, and, most important, foreign imports. Supporting a symphony created an emotional tie to the country that they perceived as the "cradle of music" endowed with a magical atmosphere.

In an essay on the cosmopolitanism of American domesticity, Kristin Hoganson argues that women's craving for foreign goods did not so much reflect an imperialist practice as "a form of cultural insecurity and receptivity to outside influences." American women, Hoganson explains, demonstrated a profound eagerness to receive cultural imports. In decorating their parlors with foreign artifacts, they sought to retrieve precisely that cultural capital the United States was lacking.[24] The domestic display of material goods revealed a broad-minded, well-read, and well-traveled master of the house. Hoganson's portrayal of upper-middle-class women, along with Dana Cooper's recent study on the tide of Anglo-American marriages, Annie Cohen-Solal's analysis of the American art market, and a host of other works dedicated to the currents of international culture in the United States, all reflect on the cultural openness to the world abroad exhibited by many Americans in the late nineteenth century.

But the case of music shows that there was more to the influx of foreign culture than mere cosmopolitan adornment. The concert-going audience was highly heterogeneous, encompassing visitors from different ethnic groups, the working classes, the lower middle classes, and the fashionable circle. The concert repertory was likewise much more diverse than it is today. Popular performances comprising operatic overtures, Strauss waltzes, and even transcriptions of folk songs were part of a carrot-and-stick scheme to attract audiences from all walks of life, and the resulting rush on symphony concerts proved this strategy right.

Curiously, American critics, observers, and even the public perceived the concert scene as German, referring to an unspecified location that exceeded by far the territorial borders of the German Empire. The reality of the American music scene was far more complex. There was always an abundance of Italian, French, British, and eastern European soloists and musicians touring the United States. It is thus important to distinguish between cultural agents on the one hand, and the content of cultural import on the other. The agents were mostly German expatriates as well as other Europeans often seen as German. The content consisted partly of Romantic and contemporary German music that, as time went by, solidified into the canon.

Although the nineteenth-century American musical landscape was remarkably resourceful, it was German music that first delivered the core of the canon of accredited masterpieces and then became the focus of the nationalization debate. In the late nineteenth-century United States, German Kultur included the artists and composers to whom Americans turned in search of taste and high culture. The passion for Strauss and Wagner, and an array of German-trained performers, seemed to prove that Anglo-American elites favored German over British music.[25]

The gap between taste and the avant-garde may have been one of the starkest ironies of the German-American cultural exchange. Both countries witnessed a search for national art that found itself at odds with common cultural trends. But while many avant-garde Germans—like most Europeans—protested against the content of the old masters, Americans rebelled against the forms in which this culture was played out.

Americans criticized modern German music for failing to meet the standards of the past while dismissing their own recent composers for trying to sound too much like the nineteenth-century German masters.

U.S. cultural nationalism as it then developed before World War I contrasted sharply with the affinity for German classical music. Indeed, it renounced what most audiences and critics had first received as a cosmopolitan cultural product, when many German artists hastened to claim their loyalty to the United States or else found themselves targeted as "enemy aliens." This story, how cosmospolitanism yielded to cultural nationalism, only makes sense if understood in the context of the earlier and longer period of cultural affinity between Germany and the United States, when both countries were willing to exchange common emotions through music.

The long-term repercussions of this change have marked the American symphony scene throughout much of the twentieth century. While orchestras, conductors, radio stations, competition managers, film producers, and the media have increasingly popularized classical music on and off the concert stage, popular music itself has been completely removed from both the canon and the repertories of symphony orchestras. As the largest producers and exporters of classical music in the world today, Germany and the United States have continued to solidify their mutual elective affinity in spite of all political tensions and clashes.

––––––

There seems to be a certain irony in the fact that Europe became a source for American culture after 1850, in an age when U.S. policy makers clung feverishly to the stipulations of the Monroe Doctrine. But when selecting their cultural imports, Americans cared little about political implications, since historically they did not see a connection between culture and politics. In addition to influences in art, architecture, literature, and interior design as well as social and intellectual exchanges, these imports and ideas buttress the notion of Europe as a source in an age of political distance. Cultural relations occasionally overlap with but do not necessarily reflect political realities; instead, they develop a life of their own. The nineteenth and twentieth centuries show the peripheral significance of state involvement for cultural exchange, and how exchanges flourished in the face of diplomatic tensions. World War I is a telling example: while cultural relations mattered very little to the direct outbreak of war—least of all to anticipating or preventing it—the war, in turn, affected these relations very little in the long run.

On that note, I would like to end this book with four propositions: (1) the story of German-American musical relations accentuates the historicism of cultural concepts in that culture means different things to different people; (2) it draws our attention to the significance of informal actors and universalist ideas in the international arena in the nineteenth century at the expense of state-directed initiatives; (3) it underscores the United States' cultural affinity toward Germany, not just as the people of music but as the people who had access to the soul; (4) it revises our understanding of high and popular American culture in an age of self-proclaimed isolationism from Europe and puts its emergence and migration into an international perspective based on the idea of an emotional elective affinity.

1. If anything, on a theoretical level, the story of German music in the United States confirms the historicism of culture. Notions of culture are chronically torn between national and universalistic ways of thinking and thus subjected to cycles. Their meaning and their interaction need to be viewed through historical lenses. Nineteenth-century Americans thought of culture along the lines laid out by the philosopher Matthew Arnold: culture was, quite simply, universal knowledge; it embraced the best that had been thought and known in the world.[26] German Kultur, on the other hand, included knowledge, education, civilization, national genius, and the arts (high culture), all of which expressed the national soul.[27] According to Wilhelm von Humboldt, Kultur—above all music—was deeply rooted in an ideology of soft nationalism wedded to vague territorial roots and universal appeal. Ironically, it often comprised German-language areas outside the territorial borders of the German Empire and appealed to universalists who believed that the exportation of Kultur could not fail to produce both artistic admiration and sympathy for Germany. Because American intellectuals' conception of culture was even less nationally bound than Kultur—after all, the critics' definition of *German* did not correspond to the territorial borders of the German Empire or the pre-imperial state system—and because nineteenth-century German cultural expansion catered to universalistic expectations, it initially encountered little resistance in the United States.

2. The effect of the German cultural export depended on the nature of a cultural artifact: nonverbal pieces of art such as classical music were more readily appreciated than those that had to be expressed in the German language, such as novels, ideas, and poetry. Transatlantic, English-speaking, and Protestant, Victorian culture did not offer easy access to foreign words and ideas. This explains why composers associated with

Germany featured so prominently on the programs of leading symphony orchestras in Chicago, Boston, Philadelphia, and New York City. A similar case can be made for the leverage of French impressionism, while British initiatives, unhindered by linguistic differences, could employ verbal venues.

The success of cultural transfer seemed to grow exponentially with the absence of governmental interference; while German administrators tinkered with academic exchange and international art exhibitions, German musicians, German symphonies, and German musicology literally attempted to trumpet down the walls of Jericho in the United States. This is not to say that Carl Pohlig or Johanna Gadski were dummy artists orchestrated by the kaiser's entourage. To the contrary, they represented unwitting agents and succeeded precisely because they lacked political intention. That they seemed to come on their own lent their cause and mission a sincerity that any state involvement would have compromised.[28]

3. In the nineteenth-century United States, German musicians clearly had a monopoly on the display of emotion, an idea that obsessed Victorians as the century came to a close. Modern sociologists and musicologists have analyzed the interplay of music and ideology, the meaning of music as a language filled with symbols and as a powerful transmitter of emotion and ideas. Eero Tarasti and others have shown that the German type of thematic construction supposedly produced an emotional greatness in music that distinguished it from other European genres.[29] The masculinity of the symphony orchestra coupled with the fact that most of the players were not U.S. citizens legitimized the public display and experience of emotion and, at the same time, underlined the Germans' monopoly not just as the "people of music" but, furthermore, as the "people of emotion." By this interpretation, the performance of pieces like Beethoven's Ninth, then, served several purposes: it established German music as the language of feeling reigning over the hearts of listeners between Boston, Pittsburgh, and San Francisco. Moreover, it conveyed an emotion, filling audiences with awe for the superiority not just of German art but of Germany in general. This link between American hosts, critics, and audiences on the one hand and "German" musicians on the other established what I call an emotional elective affinity.

4. In developing an affinity for classical music, American audiences acted exactly the way imperial administrators would have liked them to act. The creation of a symphony scene in the United States originated in the privately organized importation of European artists and the successive popularization of classical music in the guise of high culture. Americans'

construction of the quintessential German and their invitation of the same underlines the by-now common credo that agents on both sides need to share an interest in cultural transmission.

Equally important, while the efforts of Theodore Thomas and Leopold Damrosch may not have represented a diplomatic act, they clearly had a diplomatic effect. For the art of the three *B*s or Wagner evoked precisely the respect for German greatness, *Heimat*, and emotionalism that Reich officials wanted to convey, and their legacy lasted much longer than the German Kaiserreich. For all the musical nationalism at the turn of the twentieth century—all the interned artists and all the bans on the performance of works by Wagner, Strauss, and others; all the efforts to boast American popular culture against European decadence—in the end, American audiences remained dedicated to the canon of the German Romantics.

The long-term consequences of the musicians' evangelism became visible in the twentieth century. There is a telling contrast between Americans' perception of German music during the two world wars, and it indicates a maturing of U.S. nationalism as well as a growing self-confidence that the center of music had shifted from Europe to the United States. Now it was the turn of American orchestras and musicians to go abroad, promoted by the politics of the cold war. Today, the American landscape is filled with internationally renowned conservatories, symphonies, and opera houses beating the drum for nineteenth-century masters and attracting visitors from all over the world.

In the context of my analysis, the notion of an emotional elective affinity should therefore not necessarily be taken as a model, a factor, or a formula for the "success" of German music or German-American relations. Instead, music functioned as a space within which an affinity could be retraced, derived less of real (that is, family- or interest-oriented) than arbitrary and irrational motivations. Whether this relationship was reciprocally "democratic" in the sense that German audiences also developed an affinity for American music (they eventually did) is irrelevant and not part of my argument. Lovers, including the ones we encounter in Goethe's *Wahlverwandtschaften*, are never democratic, nor do they call for equality, moral or otherwise.[30] Instead, they provide each other with disparate qualities—recognition, character traits, feelings—on the basis of which they then adore each other, though their reasons for doing so may differ profoundly. While Germany, in exporting its music, wooed the United States for political recognition, Americans strove to earn cultural acceptance in the eyes of the Germans. It does not matter to the quality of the relationship that the affair was marked by crises, interruptions, and open conflicts; to the contrary, this is considered "normal."

––––––

Questions remain: is music international, or is it national? Are emotions universal, or are they elective? Is the emotional appeal of music universal, or is it constrained by its specific national or racial origin? Can musical internationalism and nationalism exist side by side in the same country in the same period of time? The story of German music and musicians (and those who were perceived as Germans) in the United States reveals the profound longing for an international aesthetic understanding throughout the nineteenth and the twentieth centuries. At the same time, the longing for universalism with all its global attraction always bore a hint of the impossible. Humboldt believed that Beethoven's ability to suffer and demand was German and therefore universal. According to Humboldt, who was primarily concerned with the development and transfer of humanism, *German* entailed universalism as it embedded a free spirit, an open mind, and no geographical constraint.

When, one hundred years later, Leopold Stokowski claimed in 1943 that music was a universal language, he did more than echo an expression that had been endlessly repeated throughout the nineteenth century. By then the word *universal* had a decisively American component. Stokowski anticipated the Americanization of music in the sense that the torch had been passed to the United States to become the principal site for the production of music. The thinking of Humboldt and Stokowski addressed the unsolvable contradiction in the idea of universalism: according to Humboldt, universalism meant to transcend things German. Stokowski, in turn, believed that universalism meant to transcend things American. Thus, even though music and emotions may be universal, they do receive much of their meaning and their clout through actual circumstances. The connotations as well as the moods by which feelings are raised are culturally conditioned and highly dependent on the listener's as well as the performer's disposition. The ways in which musicians realize and audiences understand musical meanings are linked to the beliefs and attitudes of their respective cultures. Such attitudes are subject to cultural change. Or, to put it differently, what matters about music is not only what is played but what people hear and think while giving or attending a performance.

# Appendix: Conductors of U.S. Symphony Orchestras, 1842–1920

Ureli Corelli Hill, George Frederick Bristow, American; Denis Etienne, Alfred Boucher, French; George Loder, British; Max Maretzek, Austro-Bohemian; Henry C. Timm, William Alpers, Louis Wiegers, German, all 1842–49; Theodore Eisfeld, German, 1849–55, 1856–58 (1854–55 with Henry Timm); Carl Bergmann, German, 1855–56, 1858–76 (1859–65 with Theodor Eisfeld); Theodore Leopold Damrosch, German, 1876–77; Theodore Thomas, German-born, 1877–78, 1879–91; Adolf Neuendorff, German, 1878–79; Anton Seidl, Hungarian, German-trained, 1891–98; Emil Paur, Viennese, 1898–1902; Walter Damrosch, German, 1902–3; Edouard Colonne, French; Gustav Kogel, Frankfurt; Henry Wood, London; Victor Herbert, Irish; Felix Weingartner, Munich; Vassily Safonoff, Moscow; Richard Strauss, Berlin, all guest conductors 1903–4; Kogel, Colonne, Safonoff, Weingartner, and Karl Panzner, Bremen, 1904–5; Safonoff, Herbert, Willem Mengelberg, Amsterdam; Max Fiedler, Hamburg; Ernst Kunwald, Frankfurt; Fritz Steinbach, Cologne, all 1905–6; Vassily Ilyich Safonoff, 1906–9; Gustav Mahler, Bohemian-Austrian, 1909–11 (already guest conductor in two extra concerts during the 1908–9 season); Joseph Stransky, Bohemian, 1911–23

Joseph Otten, Dutch, 1880–94; Alfred Ernst, German, 1894–1907; Max Zach, German, 1907–21; Rudolph Ganz, Swiss, 1921–26

BOSTON SYMPHONY ORCHESTRA, 1881–

Georg Henschel, German-Bohemian, 1881–84; Wilhelm Gericke, German-born, 1884–89, 1898–1906; Arthur Nikisch, Hungarian-born, 1889–93; Emil Paur, Austrian, 1893–98; Karl Muck, Swiss-German, 1906–8, 1912–17; Max Fiedler, German, 1908–12; Henri Rabaud, French, 1918–19; Pierre Monteux, 1919–24

CHICAGO SYMPHONY ORCHESTRA, 1891–

Theodore Thomas, 1891–1905; Friedrich Stock, German, 1905–42

CINCINNATI SYMPHONY ORCHESTRA, 1895–1907, 1909–

Frank van der Stucken, born in Texas of Belgian-German parentage, 1895–1907; Leopold Stokowski, British (claimed to be Pomeranian), 1909–12; Ernst Kunwald, German, 1912–17; Eugene Ysaÿe, Belgian, 1918–22

PITTSBURGH ORCHESTRA, 1896–1910, 1926–

Frederic Archer, British, 1896–98; Victor Herbert, Irish, 1898–1904; Emil Paur, Austrian, 1904–10

PHILADELPHIA ORCHESTRA, 1900–

Fritz Scheel, German, 1900–1907; Carl Pohlig, German, 1907–12; Leopold Stokowski, British, 1912–38

MINNEAPOLIS SYMPHONY ORCHESTRA, 1903–

Emil Oberhoffer, German, 1903–22

SAN FRANCISCO SYMPHONY, 1911–

Henry Hadley, American, 1911–15; Alfred Hertz, German, 1915–30

BALTIMORE SYMPHONY ORCHESTRA, 1916–

Gustav Strube, German, 1917–30

# Abbreviations

AA      Auswärtiges Amt, Berlin
AFL     American Federation of Labor
AFM     American Federation of Musicians
AJA     American Jewish Archives, Cincinnati
BA      Bundesarchiv (Berlin Lichterfelde)
BL      Baker Library Special Collections, Harvard University
BPH     Brandenburg-Preussisches Hausarchiv
BSO     Boston Symphony Orchestra (Archives)
CH      Carnegie Hall Archives, New York City
CHM     Chicago History Museum
CIHS    Cincinnati Historical Society
CISO    Cincinnati Symphony Orchestra
CLP     The Carnegie Library of Pittsburgh
CSO     Rosenthal Archives, Chicago Symphony Orchestra
EOP     Emil Oberhoffer Papers (MNHS)
FBZ     Fanny Bloomfield Zeisler Collection (AJA)
GStA PK   Geheimes Staatsarchiv Preussischer Kulturbesitz
GWC     George Wilson Collection (CLP)
HA      Hauptabteilung (in GStA PK)
HHC     Henry Higginson Collection
MF      Microfilm
MHS     Missouri Historical Society
MNHS    Minnesota Historical Society, St. Paul
MNSO    Minneapolis Symphony Orchestra, Minneapolis
MPD     Museum of Performance & Design, San Francisco
NL      Newberry Library, Chicago
NYP     New York Philharmonic
NYPA    New York Philharmonic Archives
NYPL    New York Public Library
NYSS    New York Symphony Society
NYSSSO    New York Symphony Society & Symphony Orchestra

PIO     Pittsburgh Orchestra
PO      Philadelphia Orchestra
POA     Philadelphia Orchestra Association Archives
SFSO    San Francisco Symphony Orchestra
SLPL    Saint Louis Public Library
SLPS    Saint Louis Philharmonic Society
SLSS    Saint Louis Symphony Society
TTP     Theodore Thomas Papers (NL)
UMN     Performing Arts Archives, University of Minnesota
UPA     University of Pennsylvania Archives, Philadelphia

# Notes

INTRODUCTION

1. Jessica C. E. Gienow-Hecht, "Shame on US? Cultural Transfer, Academics, and the Cold War—A Critical Review," *Diplomatic History* 24 (Summer 2000): 465–94.
2. See Charles S. Maier, *Among Empires: American Ascendancy and Its Predecessors* (Cambridge, MA: Harvard University Press, 2006).
3. *Victorian* describes the middle-class generation in both the United States and Great Britain living through the life and reign of Queen Victoria of England (1837–1901). Anne C. Rose, *Victorian America and the Civil War* (New York: Cambridge University Press, 1992); Christopher Lasch, *The New Radicalism in America, 1889–1963: The Intellectual as a Social Type* (New York: Knopf, 1965), 3–68; T. Jackson Lears, *No Place of Grace: Antimodernism and the Transformation of American Culture, 1880–1920* (New York: Pantheon Books, 1981).
4. Henry James to Thomas Sergeant Perry, 29 September 1867, in *Henry James:* Selected Letters, ed. Leon Edel (Cambridge, MA: Harvard University Press, Belknap Press, 1987), 15; quoted in Mark Rennella, *The Boston Cosmopolitans: International Travel and American Arts and Letters* (New York: Palgrave Macmillan, 2008), 197.
5. Georg Bollenbeck, *Bildung und Kultur: Glanz und Elend eines deutschen Deutungsmusters* (Frankfurt am Main: Insel Verlag, 1994); Franz Rauhut, "Die Herkunft der Worte und Begriffe 'Kultur,' 'Civilisation' und 'Bildung,'" *Germanisch-Romanische Monatsschrift* 3 (April 1953): 81–91; Georg Jäger, *Schule und literarische Kultur* (Stuttgart: J. B. Metzlersche Verlagsbuchhandlung, 1981); Terry Eagleton, *The Idea of Culture* (Oxford: Blackwell, 2000).

6. David Thelen, "Of Audiences, Borderlands, and Comparisons: Toward the Internationalization of American History," *Journal of American History* 79 (1992): 436–62; Thomas Bender, ed., *Rethinking American History in a Global Age* (Berkeley and Los Angeles: University of California Press, 2002); Kevin H. O'Rourke and Jeffrey G. Williamson, *Globalization and History: The Evolution of a Nineteenth-Century Atlantic Economy* (Cambridge, MA: MIT Press, 1999); David Hollinger, *Postethnic America*, rev. ed. (New York: Basic Books, 2000), 116.

7. Akira Iriye, *Global Community: The Role of International Organizations in the Making of the Contemporary World* (Berkeley: University of Berkeley Press, 2002); Jessica C. E. Gienow, "On the Division of Knowledge and the Community of Thought," in *Culture and International History*, ed. Jessica C. E. Gienow-Hecht and Frank Schumacher (New York: Berghahn Books, 2003), 3–11.

8. Akira Iriye, *Cultural Internationalism and World Order* (Baltimore: Johns Hopkins University Press , 1997), 12.

9. See Gienow-Hecht and Schumacher, *Culture and International History*; Wilfried Loth and Jürgen Osterhammel, eds., *Internationale Geschichte: Themen—Ergebnisse—Aussichten* (Munich: Oldenbourg, 2000); Michael Hogan and Thomas Paterson, *Explaining the History of American Foreign Relations*, rev. ed. (Cambridge: Cambridge University Press, 2004), 257–78; Rudolph Muhs, Johannes Paulmann, and Willibald Steinmetz, eds., *Aneignung und Abwehr: Interkultureller Transfer zwischen Deutschland und Grossbritannien im 19. Jahrhundert* (Bodenheim: Philo-Verlag, 1998); Magnus Brechtken, *Scharnierzeit 1895–1907: Persönlichkeitsnetze und internationale Politik in den deutsch-britisch-amerikanischen Beziehungen vor dem ersten Weltkrieg* (Mainz: von Zabern, 2006); Madeleine Herren, *Hintertüren zur Macht: Internationalismus und modernisierungsorientierte Außenpolitik in Belgien, der Schweiz und den USA, 1865–1914* (Munich: Oldenbourg, 2000).

10. Richard T. Arndt, *The First Resort of Kings: American Cultural Diplomacy in the Twentieth Century* (Washington, DC: Potomac Books, 2005), 1–23.

11. Christopher Bayly, *The Birth of the Modern World, 1780–1914: Global Connections and Comparisons* (Malden, MA: Blackwell, 2004); Anthony Hopkins, ed., *Global History: Interactions between the Universal and the Local* (Basingstoke, UK: Palgrave Macmillan, 2006).

12. James T. Campbell, *Songs of Zion: The African Methodist Episcopal Church in the United States and South Africa* (New York: Oxford University Press, 1995); Richard Pells, *Not Like Us: How Europeans Have Loved, Hated, and Transformed American Culture since World War II* (New York: Basic Books, 1997); David Armitage, *The Ideological Origins of the British Empire* (Cambridge: Cambridge University Press, 2000); Volker R. Berghahn, *America and the Intellectual Cold Wars in Europe: Shepard Stone between Philanthropy, Academy, and Diplomacy* (Princeton, NJ: Princeton University Press, 2001); Jessica C. E. Gienow-Hecht, *Transmission Impossible: American Journalism as*

*Cultural Diplomacy in Postwar Germany, 1945–1955* (Baton Rouge: Louisiana State University Press, 1999); Thomas Steven Molnar, *The Emerging Atlantic Culture* (London: Transaction Books, 1994); James T. Kloppenberg, *Uncertain Victory: Social Democracy and Progressivism in European and American Thought, 1870–1920* (New York: Oxford University Press, 1986).

13. Peter Gay, *Schnitzler's Century: The Making of Middle Class Culture, 1815–1914* (New York: Norton, 2002), 4.

14. Daniel T. Rodgers, *Atlantic Crossings: Social Politics in a Progressive Age* (Cambridge, MA: Harvard University Press, Belknap Press, 1998).

15. Iriye, *Global Community*, 9–11.

16. Edward P. Crapol, "Coming to Terms with Empire: The Historiography of Late-Nineteenth-Century American Foreign Relations," *Diplomatic History* 16 (Fall 1992): 573–97; Klaus Hildebrand, *Das vergangene Reich: Deutsche Außenpolitik von Bismarck bis Hitler 1871–1945* (Stuttgart: Deutsche Verlagsanstalt, 1995); Manfred Jonas, *The United States and Germany: A Diplomatic History* (Ithaca, NY: Cornell University Press, 1984).

17. Pierre Bourdieu, *Distinction: A Social Critique of the Judgment of Taste*, trans. Richard Nice (Cambridge, MA: Harvard University Press, 1984).

18. Paul DiMaggio, "Cultural Entrepreneurship in Nineteenth-Century Boston: The Creation of an Organizational Base for High Culture in America," *Media, Culture and Society* 4 (1982): 33–50; DiMaggio, "Cultural Entrepreneurship in Nineteenth-Century Boston, Part II: The Classification and Framing of American Art," *Media, Culture and Society* 4 (1982): 303–22; DiMaggio, *Managers of the Arts: Careers and Opinions of Senior Administrators of U.S. Art Museums, Symphony Orchestras, Resident Theatres, and Local Arts Agencies*, 2nd ed. (Washington, DC: Seven Locks Press, 1987); DiMaggio, ed., *Nonprofit Enterprise in the Arts: Studies in Mission and Constraint* (New York: Oxford University Press, 1986); Lawrence Levine, *Highbrow/Lowbrow: The Emergence of Cultural Hierarchy in America* (Cambridge, MA: Harvard University Press, 1988); Helen Horowitz, *Culture and the City: Cultural Philanthropy in Chicago from the 1880s to 1917* (orig. pub. 1976; reprint, Chicago: University of Chicago Press, 1989); Joseph A. Mussulman, *Music in the Cultured Generation: A Social History of Music in America, 1870–1900* (Evanston, IL: Northwestern University Press, 1971). For a dissenting voice, see Ralph P. Locke and Cyrilla Barr, eds., *Cultivating Music in America: Women Patrons and Activists since 1860* (Berkeley and Los Angeles: University of California Press, 1997).

19. Rennella, *The Boston Cosmopolitans*, 181–82, 185.

20. Joseph Horowitz, *Wagner Nights: An American History* (Berkeley and Los Angeles: University of California Press, 1994), 324–27; Michael Kammen, *Mystic Chords of Memory: The Transformation of American Culture* (New York: Alfred Knopf, 1991).

21. "Art, Labor, and Democracy: The Meaning of Art Work in America, 1860–1940," panel at the 115th annual meeting of the American Historical

Association, Boston, 6 January 2001, with contributions by April F. Masten, Frances K. Pohl, and A. Joan Saab.

22. Thomas Zeiler, *Ambassadors in Pinstripes: The Spalding World Baseball Tour and the Birth of the American Empire* (Lanham, MD: Rowman & Littlefield, 2006); Sayuri Guthrie-Shimizu, "For Love of the Game: Baseball in Early U.S.-Japanese Encounters and the Rise of a Transnational Sporting Fraternity," *Diplomatic History* 28 (November 2004): 637–62; Max M. Edling, *A Revolution in Favor of Government: Origins of the United States and the Making of the American State* (New York: Oxford University Press, 2003); Jane Hunter, *How Young Ladies Became Girls: The Victorian Origins of American Girlhood* (New Haven, CT: Yale University Press, 2002); Mark F. Bernstein, *Football: The Ivy League Origins of an American Obsession* (Philadelphia: University of Pennsylvania Press, 2001); Michael A. Bellesiles, *Arming America: The Origins of a National Gun Culture* (New York: Alfred Knopf, 2000); Donald Miller, *City of the Century: The Epic of Chicago and the Making of America* (New York: Simon and Schuster, 1996).

23. Dominic Strinati, *An Introduction to Theories of Popular Culture* (London: Routledge, 1995), 166; Joseph S. Nye Jr., *Soft Power: The Means to Success in World Politics* (New York: Public Affairs, 2004).

24. David Gramit, *Cultivating Music: The Aspirations, Interests, and Limits of German Musical Culture, 1770–1848* (Berkeley and Los Angeles: University of California Press, 2002).

25. Hoffmann borrowed the idea of an autonomous art from K. Ph. Moritz and applied it to music. However, he did not limit it to the sphere of instrumental music. I am indebted to Matthias Tischer for this point. Albrecht von Massow, "Absolute Musik," in *Handwörterbuch der musikalischen Terminologie*, special vol. 1, *Terminologie der Musik im 20. Jahrhundert*, ed. Hans Heinrich Eggebrecht (Stuttgart: Franz Steiner, 1995), 13–29; Celia Applegate and Pamela Potter, "Germans as the 'People of Music': Genealogy of an Identity," in *Music and German National Identity*, ed. Celia Applegate and Pamela Potter (Chicago: University of Chicago Press, 2002), 13, 15, 31; Daniel Beller-McKenna, "How deutsch a Requiem? Absolute Music, Universality, and the Reception of Brahms's *Ein deutsches Requiem*, op. 45," *Nineteenth-Century Music* 22 (Summer 1998): 3–19; Carl Dahlhaus, *Die Idee der absoluten Musik* (Munich: dtv, 1976).

26. Celia Applegate, "What Is German Music? Reflections on the Role of Art in the Creation of the Nation," in "German Identity," special issue, *German Studies Review* (Winter 1992): 28–29; Celia Applegate, "How German Is It? Nationalism and the Idea of Serious Music in the Early Nineteenth Century," *Nineteenth-Century Music* 21 (Spring 1998): 288, 295.

27. See, e.g., Nikolaus Bacht, *Music, Theatre and Politics in Germany, 1848 to the Third Reich* (Aldershot, UK: Ashgate, 2006).

28. Daniel Beller-McKenna, *Brahms and the German Spirit* (Cambridge, MA: Harvard University Press, 2004), 193; Mark Jon Burford, " 'The Real Ideal-

ism of History': Historical Consciousness, Commemoration, and Johannes Brahms's 'Years of Study'" (Ph.D. diss., Columbia University, 2005).

29. Kwame Anthony Appiah, *The Ethics of Identity* (Princeton, NJ: Princeton University Press, 2005), 271–72. Andrea Albrecht has recently reminded us that the current debate on cosmopolitanism echoes—often unknowingly—earlier discourses originating in the writings of eighteenth-century intellectuals such as Herder and Kant. Andrea Albrecht, *Kosmopolitismus: Weltbürgerdiskurse in Literatur, Philosophie und Publizistik um 1800* (Berlin: Walter de Gruyter, 2005), esp. p. 402.

30. Hans Belting, *Die Deutschen und ihre Kunst: Ein schwieriges Erbe*. (Munich: C. H. Beck, 1992).

31. Wagner quotation is from Applegate and Potter, "Germans as the 'People of Music,'" in Applegate and Potter, *Music and German National Identity*, 33.

32. Thomas Grey, "Wagner's *Die Meistersinger* als National Opera (1868–1945)," in Applegate and Potter, *Music and German National Identity*, 90;

33. Oscar Sonneck, "German Influence on the Musical Life of America," in *Oscar Sonneck and American Music*, ed. William Lichtenwanger (Urbana: University of Illinois Press, 1983), 60–75; Pamela Potter, "Klassische deutsche Musik in den Vereinigten Staaten," trans. Christiane Ferdinand-Gonzales, in *Die USA und Deutschland im Zeitalter des Kalten Krieges: Ein Handbuch*, ed. Detlef Junker, Philipp Gassert, Wilfried Mausbach, and David B. Morris (Stuttgart: DVA, 2001), 1:686–87; Alan Howard Levy, *Musical Nationalism: American Composers' Search for Identity* (Westport, CT: Greenwood Press, 1983), 3–13. A welcome exception is provided in Joseph Horowitz, *Classical Music in America: A History of Its Rise and Fall* (New York: Norton and Norton, 2005).

34. Uta G. Poiger, *Jazz, Rock, and Rebels: Cold War Politics and American Culture in a Divided Germany* (Berkeley and Los Angeles: University of California Press, 2000); Michael H. Kater, *Different Drummers: Jazz in the Culture of Nazi Germany* (New York: Oxford University Press, 1992); Reinhold Wagnleitner, *Coca-Colonization and the Cold War: The Cultural Mission of the United States in Austria after the Second World War*, trans. Diana M. Wolf (Chapel Hill: University of North Carolina Press, 1994); Kasper Maase, *Bravo America: Erkundigungen zur Jugendkultur in der Bundesrepublik in den fünfziger Jahren* (Hamburg: Junius, 1992); Eric Zolov, *Refried Elvis: The Rise of the Mexican Counterculture* (Berkeley and Los Angeles: University of California Press, 1999).

35. Two pioneering studies in this field stem from Joseph Horowitz, a music critic and independent scholar: *Wagner Nights* and *Classical Music in America*.

36. For individual biographies and orchestras, see Ezra Schabas, *Theodore Thomas: America's Conductor and Builder of Orchestra, 1835–1905* (Urbana: University of Illinois Press, 1989); Theodore Thomas, *A Musical Autobiography*, ed. George Upton, 2 vols. (Chicago: A. C. McClurg, 1905); Philip Hart,

*Orpheus in the New World: The Symphony Orchestra as an American Cultural Institution* (New York: Norton, 1973).

37. Katherine K. Preston, *Opera on the Road: Traveling Opera Troupes in the United States, 1825–1860* (Urbana: University of Illinois Press, 1993). For a comparison with Europe, see William Weber, *Music and the Middle Class: The Social Structure of Concert Life in London, Paris and Vienna* (New York: Holmes and Meier, 1975).

38. Leonard B. Meyer, *Emotion and Meaning in Music* (Chicago: University of Chicago Press, 1956), 23, 256–72, quotations are from pp. 14, 256; Susanne K. Langer, *Mind: An Essay on Human Feeling* (Baltimore: Johns Hopkins University Press, 1967, 1985), 1:82–84, 161–64, 231–37; Mechtild Fuchs, *"So pocht das Schicksal an die Pforte": Untersuchungen und Vorschläge zur Rezeption sinfonischer Musik des 19. Jahrhunderts* (Munich: Musikverlag Emil Katzbichler, 1986) 89–117.

39. Antony S. R. Manstead and Agneta H. Fischer, "Beyond the Universality-Specificity Dichotomy," *Cognition and Emotion* 16, no. 1 (2002): 1–9; Paul Ekman, *The Face of Man: Expressions of Universal Emotions in a New Guinea Village* (New York: Garland STPM Press, 1980); Paul Ekman and Richard J. Davison, *The Nature of Emotions: Fundamental Questions* (New York: Oxford University Press, 1994); Amelie v. Griessenbeck, *Kulturfaktor Emotion: Zur Bedeutung von Emotion für das Verhältnis von Individuum, Gesellschaft und Kultur* (Munich: Akademischer Verlag, 1997); Horst Gundlach, *Reiz: Zur Verwendung eines Begriffes in der Psychologie* (Bern: H. Huber, 1976); Gary B. Palmer and Debra J. Occhi, eds., *Languages of Sentiment: Cultural Constructions of Emotional Substrates* (Amsterdam: J. Benjamins, 1999); Klaus Scherrer, *Psychologie der Emotion* (Göttingen: Verlag für Psychologie, 1990); Anna Wierzbicka, *Emotions across Languages and Cultures: Diversity and Universals* (Cambridge: Cambridge University Press; Paris: Editions de la Maison des Sciences de l'Homme, 1999); Heinz-Gunter Vester, *Emotion, Gesellschaft und Kultur: Grundzüge einer soziologischen Theorie der Emotionen* (Opladen: Westdeutscher Verlag, 1991); Paul E. Griffiths, *What Emotions Really Are: The Problem of Psychological Categories* (Chicago: University of Chicago Press, 1997); special issue of *Cognition and Emotion* 16, no. 1 (2002).

40. Kenneth J. Gergen, *Realities and Relationships: Soundings in Social Construction*, 2nd ed. (Cambridge, MA: Harvard University Press, 1997).

41. Joel Pfister and Nancy Schnog, eds., *Inventing the Psychological: Toward a Cultural History of Emotional Life in America* (New Haven, CT: Yale University Press, 1997); Burton Raffel, *American Victorians: Explorations in Emotional History* (Hamden, CT: Archon Books, 1984); Carol Zisowitz Stearns and Peter Stearns, *Anger: The Struggle for Emotional Control in America's History* (Chicago: University of Chicago Press, 1986); Etienne François, Hannes Siegrist, and Jakob Vogel, eds., *Nation und Emotion: Deutschland und Frankreich im Vergleich 19. und 20. Jahrhundert* (Göttingen : Vandenhoeck & Ruprecht, 1995).

42. Peter N. Stearns and Carol Z. Stearns, "Emotionology: Clarifying the History of Emotions and Emotional Standards," *American Historical Review* 90 (October 1985): 813–36; Fabian Hilfrich, "Manliness and 'Realism:' The Use of Gendered Tropes in the Debates on the Philippine-American and on the Vietnam War," in Gienow-Hecht and Schumacher, *Culture and International History*, 60–78; Martina Kessel, "Das Trauma der Affektkontrolle: Zur Sehnsucht nach Gefühlen im 19. Jahrhundert," in *Emotionalität: Zur Geschichte der Gefühle*, ed. Claudia Benthien, Anne Fleig, and Ingrid Kasten (Cologne, Weimar: Böhlau, 2000), 156–77; Benthien et al., "Einleitung," in ibid., 7–20; Anne-Charlott Trepp, "Emotion und bürgerliche Sinnstiftung oder die Metaphysik des Gefühls: Liebe am Beginn des bürgerlichen Zeitalters," in *Der bürgerliche Wertehimmel: Innenansichten des 19. Jahrhunderts*, ed. Manfred Hettling and Stefan-Ludwig Hoffmann (Göttingen: Vandenhoeck & Ruprecht, 2000), 23–56; Peter Stearns and Jan Lewis, eds., *An Emotional History of the United States* (New York: New York University Press, 1998).

43. Petra Goedde, *GIs and Germans: Culture, Gender, and Foreign Relations, 1945–1949* (New Haven, CT: Yale University Press, 2003); Frank Costigliola, "'Unceasing Pressure for Penetration': Gender, Pathology, and Emotion in George Kennan's Formation of the Cold War," *Journal of American History* 83 (March 1997): 1309–39; Emily Rosenberg, *Financial Missionaries to the World: The Politics and Culture of Dollar Diplomacy, 1900–1930* (Cambridge, MA: Harvard University Press, 1999); Stephen P. Rosen, *War and Human Nature* (Princeton, NJ: Princeton University Press, 2005); Jonathan Mercer, "Human Nature and the First Image: Emotion in International Politics," *Journal of International Relations* 9 (2006): 288–303.

44. Stephen Kalberg, *Max Weber's Comparative Historical Sociology* (Chicago: University of Chicago Press, 1994), 102–17; the quotation by Kalberg is from p. 103.

45. Johann Wolfgang von Goethe, *Die Wahlverwandtschaften* (orig. pub. 1809; reprint, Munich: Goldmann, 1956).

46. For the musical culture among ethnic German Americans, see Philip Bohlman and Otto Holzapfel, eds., *Land without Nightingales: Music in the Making of German-America* (Madison: University of Wisconsin Press, 2002).

CHAPTER ONE

1. "Aus einem Briefe des Reichskanzlers an Prof. Lamprecht vom 21. Juni 1913," Friedrich Schmidt-Ott Collection, I. HA, Rep. 92, A 77, Bl. 2, GStA PK.

2. See the essays in Eckhardt Fuchs, ed., *Weltausstellungen im 19. Jahrhundert*, *Comparativ* 9/5–6 (Leipzig: Leipziger Universitätsverlag, 2000); Wolfram Kaiser, "The Great Derby Race: Strategies of Cultural Representation at Nineteenth-Century World Exhibitions," in Gienow-Hecht and Schumacher, *Culture and International History*, 45–59.

3.  Ute Frevert, Heinz-Gerhard Haupt, Bettina Brandt, Franz Becker, Dagmar Günther, and Moritz Föllmer, "Zur Wirkung des Nationalismus im Deutschland des 19. Jahrhunderts," panel at the 42nd Deutsche Historikertag, Frankfurt am Main, 9 September 1998; Henrik Karge, "Architektur und Stadtplanung in Dresden nach 1871: Modernität durch Regionalbezug," paper presented at ibid., 11 September 1998; Alon Confino, *The Nation as a Local Metaphor: Württemberg, Imperial Germany, and National Memory,1871–1918* (Chapel Hill: University of North Carolina Press, 1997).

4.  Jost Dülffer, Martin Kröger, and Rolf-Harald Wippich, eds., *Vermiedene Kriege: Deeskalation von Konflikten der Grossmächte zwischen Krimkrieg und Erstem Weltkrieg* (Munich: Oldenbourg, 1997), 19; Roger Chickering, "Patriotische Vereine im europäischen Vergleich," in *Europa um 1900: Texte eines Kolloquiums*, ed. Fritz Klein and Karl-Otmar v. Aretin (Berlin: Akademie Verlag, 1989), 151–62; Eckart Koester, "'Kultur' versus 'Zivilisation': Thomas Manns Kriegspublizistik als weltanschaulich-ästhetische Standortsuche," in *Kultur und Krieg: Die Rolle der Intellektuellen, Künstler und Schriftsteller im Ersten Weltkrieg*, ed. Wolfgang Mommsen (Munich: Oldenbourg, 1996), 249–58; Wolfgang J. Mommsen, *Bürgerliche Kultur und Künstlerische Avant-garde: Kultur und Politik im deutschen Kaiserreich 1870 bis 1918* (Berlin: Propyläen, 1994).

5.  Nancy Troy, *Modernism and the Decorative Arts in France: Art Nouveau to Le Corbusier* (New Haven, CT: Yale University Press, 1991).

6.  *Le Temps*, 1908; quoted in Gerhard Weidenfeller, *VDA: Verein für das Deutschtum im Ausland: Allgemeiner Deutscher Schulverein 1881–1918: Ein Beitrag zur Geschichte des deutschen Nationalismus und Imperialismus im Kaiserreich* (Frankfurt A.M.: Peter Lang, 1976), 316–19; Maurice Brueziere, *L'alliance française: Histoire d'une institution* (Paris: Hachette, 1983), 10, 28, 42, 50, 76; Frank Trommler, "Inventing the Enemy: German-American Cultural Relations, 1900–1917," in *Confrontation and Cooperation: Germany and the United States in the Era of World War I, 1900–1924*, ed. Hans-Jürgen Schröder (Providence, RI: Berg, 1993), 103.

7.  Anne D. Petersen, *Die Engländer in Hamburg, 1814 bis 1914: Ein Beitrag zur hamburgischen Geschichte* (Hamburg: Von Bockel, 1993).

8.  Peter Grupp, "Vorraussetzungen und Praxis deutscher amtlicher Kulturpropaganda in den neutralen Staaten während des Ersten Weltkrieges," in *Der Erste Weltkrieg: Wirkung, Wahrnehmung und Analyse*, ed. Wolfgang Michalka (Munich: Piper, 1994), 802.

9.  Lois M. Fink, *American Art at the Nineteenth Century Paris Salons* (New York: Cambridge University Press, 1990), 61, 113–15, 130–31, 160; Pierre Miquel, *Art et argent 1800–1900: L'ecole de la nature* (Maurs-La-Jolie: Martinelle, 1987), 6:9–84, 303–410.

10. Lois M. Fink, "French Art in the United States, 1850–1870: Three Dealers and Collectors," *Gazette des Beaux-Arts* (September 1978): 87.

11. See Fink, *American Art at the Nineteenth Century Paris Salons*, 1–6, 29, 37; Fink, "French Art in the United States," 95–97. See also Pierre Rosenberg, *France in the Golden Age: Seventeenth-Century French Paintings in American Collections* (New York: Metropolitian Museum of Art, 1982).

12. Reiner Pommerin, *Der Kaiser und Amerika: Die USA in der Politik der Reichsleitung, 1890–1917* (Cologne: Böhlau, 1986), 292–93; Ekkhard Mai, "Präsentation und Repräsentativität—Interne Probleme deutscher Kunstausstellungen im Ausland (1900–1930)," *Zeitschrift für Kulturaustauch* 31 (1981): 112–13; Fink, *American Art at the Nineteenth Century Paris Salons*, 277–78; Paul Lefort, "Les Écoles Étrangères de la Peinture—États Unis," *Gazette des Beaux-Arts* 43 (1879): 483–85; Fink, "French Art in the United States," 87–100; DeCourcy E. McIntosh, "Demand and Supply: The Pittsburgh Art Trade and M. Knoedler & Co," in *Collecting in the Gilded Age: Art Patronage in Pittsburgh, 1890–1910*, ed. Gabriel P. Weisberg, DeCourcy E. McIntosh, and Alison McQueen (Hanover, NH: University Press of New England, 1997), 107–77. See also Gabriel P. Weisberg, "From Paris to Pittsburgh: Visual Culture and American Taste, 1880–1910," in ibid., 179–297.

13. Miquel, *Art et argent*, 355–60; Annie Cohen-Solal, *Un jour, ils auront des peintres: L'avènement des peintres américains, Paris 1867–New York 1948* (Paris: Editions Gallimard, 2000).

14. Barbara H. Weinberg, Doreen Bolger, and David Park Curry, eds., *American Impressionism and Realism: The Painting of Modern Life, 1885–1915* (New York: Metropolitan Museum of Art, 1994); Jean-Paul Carlhian, "L'Ecole des Beaux-Arts and Its Influence on American Architects and American Architecture, 1886–1936," in *Two Hundred Years of Franco-American Relations: Papers of the Bicentennial Colloquium of the Society for French Historical Studies in Newport, Rhode Island, September 7–10, 1978*, ed. Nancy L. Roelker and Charles K. Warner (N.p., n.d.: Heffernan Press, [1978?]), 185–206; Fink, *American Art at the Nineteenth Century Paris Salons*, 64–65, 93–94, 114, 130–32, 271.

15. Trommler, "Inventing the Enemy," 103; Jacques Portes, "L'européanisation des Etats-Unis vue par les Français (1870–1914)," *Revue française d'études américaines* 12 (1982): 51–64.

16. Robert J. Young, *Marketing Marianne: French Propaganda in America, 1900–1940* (New Brunswick, NJ: Rutgers University Press, 2004).

17. "The Anglo-Saxon Family Tree," *Punch* (18 January 1896); reprinted in Stephanie Schneider, " 'International Siamese Twins'—Die symbolische Repräsentation anglo-amerikanischer Beziehungen in politischen Karikaturen der zweiten Hälfte des 19. Jahrhunderts" (Ph.D. diss., Universität Erfurt, 2003), title page, 73–76, 92, 177–78, 184–85.

18. On Anglo-American relations, see David Dimbleby and David Reynolds, *An Ocean Apart: The Relationship between Britain and America in the Twentieth*

*Century* (London: BBC Books, 1988); William Clark, *Less Than Kin: A Study of Anglo-American Relations* (London: H. Hamilton, 1957); A. E. Campbell, *Great Britain and the United States, 1895–1903* (orig. pub. ca. 1960; reprint, Westport, CT: Greenwood Press, 1974); Henry Cranbrook Allen, *Great Britain and the United States: A History of Anglo-American Relations (1783–1951)* (New York: St. Martin's Press, 1955); Herbert G. Nicholas, *The United States and Great Britain* (Chicago: University of Chicago Press, 1975); Stuart Anderson, *Race and Rapprochement: Anglo-Saxonism and Anglo-American Relations, 1895–1904* (London: Associated University Presses, 1981).

19. Christopher Hitchens, *Blood, Class, and Nostalgia: Anglo-American Ironies* (New York: Farrar, Straus, & Giroux, 1990), 8, 63–65, 76, 113; quotation is from pp. 28–30.

20. Daniel Walker Howe, "Victorian Culture in America," in *Victorian America*, ed. Geoffrey Blodgett et al. (Philadelphia: University of Pennsylvania Press, 1976), 3–28; Robert Weisbuch, *Atlantic Double-Cross: American Literature and British Influence in the Age of Emerson* (Chicago: University of Chicago Press, 1986). Victorianism was "middle class" in a limited sense. England's landed aristocracy was politically at least as influential as the East-Elbian Junker elite in Germany, and retained absolute veto power in the House of Lords until shortly before World War I. I am indebted to Wolfram Kaiser for this observation.

21. Tom Standage, *The Victorian Internet: The Remarkable Story of the Telegraph and the Nineteenth Century's On-Line Pioneers* (orig. pub. 1998; reprint, New York: Walker and Co., 1999); David P. Nickles, *Under Wire: How the Telegraph Changed Diplomacy* (Cambridge, MA: Harvard University Press, 2003).

22. Hitchens, *Blood, Class, and Nostalgia*, 5.

23. Frank Aydelotte, *The American Rhodes Scholarships: A Review of the First Forty Years* (Princeton, NJ: Princeton University Press, 1946); Thomas J. Schaeper and Kathleen Schaeper, *Cowboys into Gentlemen: Rhodes Scholars, Oxford, and the Creation of an American Elite* (New York: Berghahn Books, 1998); Hitchens, *Blood, Class, and Nostalgia*, 298–99; Thomas A. Kohut, *Wilhelm II and the Germans: A Study in Leadership* (New York: Oxford University Press, 1991), 152.

24. Hitchens, *Blood, Class, and Nostalgia*, 120–22; Dana Calise Cooper, "Informal Ambassadors: American Women, Transatlantic Marriages, and Anglo-American Relations, 1865–1945" (Ph.D. diss., Texas Tech University, Lubbock, 2006).

25. Hitchens, *Blood, Class, and Nostalgia*, 134, 162, 174, 358; Otto, Graf zu Stolberg-Wernigerode, *Germany and the United States during the Era of Bismarck* (Reading, PA: Henry Janssen Foundation, 1937), 194–95; Bernhard vom Brocke, "Der deutsch-amerikanische Professorenaustausch: Preussische Wissenschaftspolitik, internationale Wissenschaftsbeziehungen und die Anfänge einer deutschen auswärtigen Kulturpolitik vor dem Ersten Weltkrieg," *Zeitschrift für Kulturaustausch* 31 (1981), 131.

26. "Acta betreffend: Die von auswaertigen Behörden gg. über die dortigseiti-
gen wissenschaftlichen und Kunst Anstalten erhaltenen Nachrichten," I
HA, Rep. 76 Ve, Sekt. 1, Abt. 10, no. 1, Bd. I, Bl. 190–97, GStA PK; W.
Loehr [?], Kaiserlich Deutsches Konsulat, St. Louis, Missouri, 11 Feb. 1907,
R 901/37069, Bl. 81–83, BA.

27. Peter Krüger, "Die Beurteilung der Reichsgründung und der Reichsverfassung von 1871 in den USA," in *Liberalitas: Festschrift für Erich Angermann*,
ed. Norbert Finzsch and Hermann Wellenreuther, *Transatlantische Studien*,
vol. 1 (Stuttgart: Franz Steiner, 1992), 269–76; Stolberg-Wernigerode,
*Germany and the United States*, 3–107; Jeannette Keim, *Forty Years of German-
American Political Relations* (Philadelphia: W. J. Dornan, 1919), 7–35.

28. Luise Schorn-Schütte, *Karl Lamprecht: Kulturgeschichtsschreibung zwischen
Wissenschaft und Politik*, Schriftenreihe der Historischen Kommission bei
der Bayerischen Akademie der Wissenschaften, vol. 22 (Göttingen: Vandenhoeck & Ruprecht, 1984), 277; Konrad Jarausch, "American Students
in Germany, 1815–1914," in *German Influences on Education in the United
States to 1917* (New York: Cambridge University Press, 1995), 195–211; Jörg
Nagler, "From Culture to *Kultur*: Changing American Perceptions of Imperial Germany, 1870–1914," in *Transatlantic Images and Perceptions: Germany
and America since 1776*, ed. David E. Barclay and Elisabeth Glaser-Schmidt
(Washington, DC: German Historical Institute; New York: Cambridge
University Press, 1997), 143; Carl Diehl, *Americans and German Scholarship, 1770–1870* (New Haven, CT: Yale University Press, 1978),
50, 69.

29. Dülffer, Kröger, and Wippich, *Vermiedene Kriege*, 283–314; Paul Kennedy,
*The Samoan Tangle: A Study in Anglo-German-American Relations, 1878–1900*
(Dublin: Irish Unversity Press, 1974). See also Raimund Lammersdorf, *Anfänge einer Weltmacht: Theodore Roosevelt und die transatlantischen Beziehungen der USA, 1901–1909* (Berlin: Academie Verlag, 1994).

30. Thomas A. Bailey, "Dewey and the Germans in Manila Bay," *American
Historical Review* 45 (1938): 59–81.

31. Ragnhild Fiebig-von Hase, *Lateinamerika als Konfliktherd der deutsch-ameri-
kanischen Beziehungen 1890–1903: Vom Beginn der Panamerikapolitik bis
zur Venezuelakrise von 1902/03*, 2 vols., Schriftenreihe der Historischen
Kommission bei der Bayerischen Akademie der Wissenschaften, vol 27
(Göttingen:Vandenhoeck & Ruprecht, 1986); Ragnhild Fiebig-von Hase,
"Großmachkonflikte in der Westlichen Hemisphäre: Das Beispiel der
Venezuelakrise vom Winter 1902/03," in Dülffer, Kröger, and Wippich,
*Vermiedene Kriege*, 527–55; Nancy Mitchell, *The Danger of Dreams: German
and American Imperialism in Latin America* (Chapel Hill: University of North
Carolina Press, 1999); quotation is from Fiebig-von Hase, "Großmachkon-
flikte in der Westlichen Hemisphäre," p. 555.

32. John C. G. Röhl, *Kaiser, Hof und Staat: Wilhelm II. und die deutsche Politik*,
4th ed. (Munich: C. H. Beck, 1995), 17–34. See also Holger Herwig, *Politics*

*of Frustration: The United States in German Naval Planning, 1889–1941* (Boston: Little, Brown, 1976); Ute Mehnert, *Deutschland, Amerika und die "Gelbe Gefahr": Zur Karriere eines Schlagworts in der Großen Politik, 1905–1917* (Stuttgart: Franz Steiner Verlag, 1995).

33. Alfred Vagts, "Hopes and Fears of an American-German War, 1870–1915," *Political Science Quarterly* 54 (1939): 514–35; Alfred Vagts, *Deutschland und die Vereinigten Staaten in der Weltpolitik*, 2 vols. (New York: Macmillan, 1935); Stolberg-Wernigerode, *Germany and the United States*, 194–95, 274–75; Ragnhild Fiebig-von Hase, "Die deutsch-amerikanischen Wirtschaftsbeziehungen, 1890–1914, im Zeichen von Protektionismus und internationaler Integration," *Amerikastudien* 33 (1988): 329–57; Fiebig-von Hase, "Amerikanische Friedensbemühungen in Europa, 1905–1914," in Finzsch and Wellenreuther, *Liberalitas*, 285–318; Fiebig-von Hase, "The United States and Germany in the World Arena, 1900–1917," in Schröder, *Confrontation and Cooperation*, 33–68; Edward P. Crapol, "From Anglophobia to Fragile Rapprochement: Anglo-American Relations in the Early Twentieth Century," in Schröder, *Confrontation and Cooperation*, 13–32; Torsten Oppelland, "Der lange Weg in den Krieg (1900–1918)," in *Deutschland und die USA im 20. Jahrhundert: Geschichte der politischen Beziehungen*, ed. Klaus Larres and Torsten Oppelland (Darmstadt: Wissenschaftliche Buchgesellschaft, 1997), 1–30; Otto Pflanze, "Germany—Bismarck—America," in *Deutschland und der Westen im 19. und 20. Jahrhundert*, vol. 1, *Transatlantische Beziehungen*, ed. Jürgen Elvert and Michael Salewski (Stuttgart: Franz Steiner Verlag, 1993), 67–84; Reinhard R. Doerries, "Empire and Republic: German-American Relations before 1917," in *America and the Germans: An Assessment of a Three-Hundred Year History*, ed. Frank Trommler and Joseph McVeigh, vol. 2 (Philadelphia: University of Pennsylvania Press, 1985), 3–17; Reinhard R. Doerries, *Washington-Berlin 1908/1917: Die Tätigkeit des Botschafters Johann Heinrich Graf von Bernstorff in Washington vor dem Eintritt der Vereinigten Staaten von America in den Ersten Weltkrieg* (Düsseldorf: Pädagogischer Verlag Schwann, 1975).

34. "Marriage in Germany," n.p., n.d., Adelaide Kalkman, music scrapbooks, VI, MHS.

35. Misty D. Rodheaver, "Cultural Flows between the United States and Germany, 1890–1929" (M.A. thesis, West Virginia University, 2005), 34–45.

36. I am indebted to Wolfram Kaiser for this information.

37. Henry Adams, *The Education of Henry Adams: An Autobiography* (orig. pub. 1907; reprint, Boston: Houghton Mifflin; New York: Riverside Press, 1918), 74–80; Trommler, "Inventing the Enemy," 103; Portes, "L'européanisation des Etats-Unis vue par les Français."

38. v. Waetzold, Kaiserlich Deutsches Generalkonsulat, New York, to Reichskanzler von Bülow, 24 July 1907, R 901/37069, Bl. 103–4, BA.

39. Johann Heinrich Graf von Bernstorff, quoted in Ragnhild Fiebig-von Hase, "Die politische Funktionalisierung der Kultur: Der deutsch-amerikanische

Professorenaustausch 1904–1914," in *Zwei Wege in die Moderne: Aspekte der deutsch-amerikanischen Beziehungen 1900–1918*, ed. Ragnhild Fiebig-von Hase and Jürgen Heideking (Trier: Wissenschaftlicher Verlag, 1997), 45; Rüdiger vom Bruch, *Weltpolitik als Kulturmission: Auswärtige Kulturpolitik und Bildungsbürgertum in Deutschland am Vorabend des Ersten Weltkrieges* (Paderborn: F. Schöningh, 1982).

40. Grupp, "Vorraussetzungen und Praxis deutscher amtlicher Kulturpropaganda," 802–3; Jürgen Kloosterhuls, "Deutsche auswärtige Kulturpolitik und ihre Trägergruppen vor dem Ersten Weltkrieg," in *Deutsche auswärtige Kulturpolitik seit 1871: Geschichte und Struktur*, ed. Kurt Düwell and Werner Link (Cologne: Böhlau, 1981), 7–36; Jürgen Kloosterhuls, *Friedliche Imperialisten: Deutsche Auslandsvereine und auswärtige Kulturpolitik, 1906–1918* (New York: Peter Lang, 1994).

41. Bollenbeck, *Bildung und Kultur*, 225; Samuel Huntington, *The Clash of Civilizations and the Remaking of World Order* (New York: Simon and Schuster, 1996), 40–41.

42. Vom Brocke, "Der deutsch-amerikanische Professorenaustausch," 132–34; Pommerin, *Der Kaiser und Amerika*, 256–57. For a general account of the challenges facing German cultural diplomacy in the nineteenth century, see Düwell and Link, *Deutsche auswärtige Kulturpolitik seit 1871*.

43. Pommerin, *Der Kaiser und Amerika*, 256–57; Eckhardt Fuchs, "Schriftenaustausch, Copyright und Dokumentation: Das Buch als Medium der internationalen Wissenschaftskommunikation vor dem Ersten Weltkrieg unter besonderer Berücksichtigung Deutschlands und der Vereinigten Staaten von Amerika," *Leipziger Jahrbuch zur Buchgeschichte* 7 (1997): 129.

44. Pommerin, *Der Kaiser und Amerika*, 286; Stefan H. Rinke, *Zwischen Weltpolitik und Monroe Doktrin: Botschafter Speck von Sternburg und die deutsch-amerikanischen Beziehungen, 1898–1908* (Stuttgart: H.-D. Heinz, 1992), 177.

45. Sigmund Skard, *American Studies in Europe: Their History and Present Organization* (Philadelphia: University of Pennsylvania Press, 1958), 1:209–56; Karl Lamprecht, *Americana: Reiseeindrücke, Betrachtungen, geschichtliche Gesamtansicht* (Freiburg i. B.: Heyfelder, 1906); Willi-Paul Adams, "Die Geschichte Nordamerikas in Berlin," in *Geschichtswissenschaft in Berlin im 19. und 20. Jahrhundert: Persönlichkeiten und Institutionen*, ed. Reimar Hansen and Wolfgang Ribbe (Berlin: Walter de Gruyter, 1992), 614–21; Halvdan Koht, *The American Spirit in Europe* (Philadelphia, University of Pennsylvania Press, 1949), 222–23; Thomas Neville Bonner, *American Doctors and German Universities: A Chapter in International Intellectual Relations, 1870–1914* (Lincoln: University of Nebraska Press, 1963); Jürgen Heideking, Henry Geitz, and Jürgen Herbst, eds., *German Influences on American Education to 1917* (Cambridge: Cambridge University Press, 1995).

46. Between 1870 and 1918, there were 153 professors in the Reichstag in the various parliaments (Reichstag [1871–1918], Preußisches Abgeordnetenhaus und Herrenhaus [1870–1918]). Rüdiger vom Bruch, "Gesellschaftliche

Initiativen in den auswärtigen Kulturbeziehungen Deutschlands vor 1914: Der Beitrag des deutschen Bildungsbürgertums," *Zeitschrift für Kulturaustausch* 31 (1981): 43–67; Fritz Ringer, *The Decline of the German Mandarins: The German Academic Community, 1890–1933* (Cambridge: Cambridge University Press, 1969); Bernhard vom Brocke, "Professoren als Parlamentarier," in *Deutsche Hochschullehrer als Elite, 1815–1945*, ed. Klaus Schwabe, Büdinger Forschungen zur Sozialgeschichte 1983 (Boppard am Rhein: H. Boldt, 1988), 59–62; Rüdiger vom Bruch, "Wissenschaftspolitik, Wissenschaftssystem und Nationalstaat im Deutschen Kaiserreich," in *Wirtschaft, Wissenschaft und Bildung in Preußen: Zur Wirtschafts- und Sozialgeschichte Preußens vom 18. bis zum 20. Jahrhundert*, ed. Karl Heinrich Kaufhold and Bernd Sösemann (Stuttgart: Franz Steiner Verlag, 1998), 73–89.

47. Schorn-Schütte, *Karl Lamprecht*, 289–309. List of guest professors in vom Brocke, "Der deutsch-amerikanische Professorenaustausch," 204, 210; Fiebig-von Hase, "Die politische Funktionalisierung der Kultur," 48; Pommerin, *Der Kaiser und Amerika*, 277; Eckhardt Fuchs, "Die internationale Organisation der edukativen Bewegung: Studien zu Austausch- und Transferprozessen im Aufbruch der Moderne" (Habilitation thesis, Humboldt Universität, Berlin, 2004).

48. Pommerin, *Der Kaiser und Amerika*, 255–71; Franziska von Ungern-Sternberg, *Kulturpolitik zwischen den Kontinenten, Deutschland und Amerika: Das Germanische Museum in Cambridge, Mass.* (Cologne: Böhlau, 1994); Fiebig-von Hase, "Die politische Funktionalisierung der Kultur," 54–55; Pommerin, *Der Kaiser und Amerika*, 271–75; Gerhard A. Ritter, "Internationale Wissenschaftsbeziehungen und auswärtige Kulturpolitik im deutschen Kaiserreich," *Zeitschrift für Kulturaustausch* 31 (1981): 13.

49. C. von Uechtritz, Kgl. professor, to AA, Berlin, 14 February 1903, R 901/37068, Bl. 16–18, BA.

50. Pommerin, *Der Kaiser und Amerika*, 292–93; Mai, "Präsentation und Repräsentativität," 112–13; Peter Paret, "Art and the National Image: The Conflict over Germany's Participation in the St. Louis Exposition," *Central European History* 10 (1978): 175–83.

51. Celia Applegate, *Bach in Berlin: Nation and Culture in Mendelssohn's Revival of the " St. Matthew Passion"* (Ithaca, NY: Cornell University Press, 2005), 45–79; Pamela Potter, *Most German of the Arts: Musicology and Society; From the Weimar Republic to the End of Hitler's Reich* (New Haven, CT: Yale University Press, 1998), ix–xvii.

52. Applegate, "What Is German Music?" 29; Applegate, *Bach in Berlin*, 234–63; quotation is from p. 237; Sanna Pederson, "A. B. Marx, Berlin Concert Life, and German National Identity," *Nineteenth-Century Music* 18 (Fall 1994): 87–107; David B. Dennis, *Beethoven in German Politics, 1870–1989* (New Haven, CT: Yale University Press, 1978), 32–85.

53. Thomas Goodwin, *Sketches and Impressions: Musical, Theatrical, and Social (1799–1885)* (New York: G. P. Putnam's Sons, 1887), 156.

54. Musicologists distinguish between the Mannheim school and the Wiener Klassik. After Beethoven, the symphonic form became decisively freer, less restrained. Strictly speaking, much of the music performed by symphony orchestras not only included symphonies but, in a broader sense, symphonic compositions such as Franz Liszt's *Symphonische Dichtungen* or Felix Mendelssohn-Bartholdy's concert ouvertures. I am indebted to Matthias Tischer for this point. For a nuanced discussion of the rise and decline in symphonic production, see Carl Dahlhaus, *Nineteenth-Century Music*, trans. J. Bradford Robinson (Berkeley and Los Angeles: University of California Press, 1989), 152–60, 236; Mark Evan Bonds, *After Beethoven: Imperatives of Originality in the Symphony* (Cambridge, MA: Harvard University Press, 1996).

55. Harold Schonberg, *The Great Conductors* (New York: Simon and Schuster, 1967), 205.

56. A representative of the Prussian cultural ministry stated in the early 1900s that the Germans had created their unification essentially out of songs (and gymnastics). R. Henning, "Die Nordlandfahrt der Berliner Liedertafel," 30 May 1910, R 901/37857, AA, BA.

57. Dennis, *Beethoven in German Politics*, 3; quotation is from p. 5.

58. To Cosima Wagner, the war of 1870 was one big "Beethoven festival." Esteban Buch, *La neuvième de Beethoven: Une histoire politique* (Paris: Gallimard, 1999), 186.

59. Dennis, *Beethoven in German Politics*, 8–20, 34–42, 52, 67.

60. Applegate, "What Is German Music?" 21, 29; Dennis, *Beethoven in German Politics*, 5, 32–85; A. H. Ehrlich, "Musik-Cultus und allgemeine Bildung," *Die Gegenwart* 2 (7 December 1872): 363–64.

61. Applegate, "What Is German Music?" 28–29; Applegate, "How German Is It?" 288, 295.

62. R 901/37853-60, AA, BA.

63. "In the Realm of Tone," n.p., n.d. [ca. September 1892], CSO scrapbooks, MF Columbia Exposition, CSO.

64. Leichner correspondence with the Foreign Office, 1902–3, R 901/37655, AA, BA.

65. Hermann Möser, Cincinnati, to the German kaiser, 5 December 1902, R 901/37655, AA, BA.

66. Newspaper clippings, reports, and correspondence 1902–3, R 901/37655 and 37656, AA, BA.

67. Timotheus Fabri, Berlin, to Herr Staatsminister (10/20 February 1904); von Studt to Lucanus (9 March 1904), both in R 901/37069, Bl. 75–82, AA, BA.

68. Kgl. Bayer/Gesandtschaft to Staatssekretär Dr. von Kühlmann, Foreign Office, 1 March 1918, Konzertreise der Militärkapelle des Kgl. Bayer. Infanterie-Leibregiments, R 901/71215, AA, BA. Dresdner Philharmonic to Vice Consul Pistor, Foreign Office, 23 February 1918, ibid.

69. Berliner Liedertafel and Reichskanzler, 27 September 1907, R 901/37854, AA, BA.

70. Bezirkspräsident J. W. Kilinger, Straßburg, 16 April 1902, R 901/37853, AA, BA.

71. Zöpfel-Quellenstein, Atlanta, to v. Bethmann-Hollweg, 26 May 1911, R 901/37857, AA, BA.

72. Gustav Bluhm, Hamburg, to Dr. von der Heyde, Sao Paolo, 5 November 1912, R 901/37859, AA, BA.

73. Imperial German Embassy, Tokyo, to von Bethmann Hollweg, 11 January 1913, R 901/37860, AA, BA.

74. Grupp, "Vorraussetzungen und Praxis deutscher amtlicher Kulturpropaganda," 807–8; P. Peters, "Aus Stockholm," *Neue Zeitschrift für Musik*, n.d. [end of May], quoted in Peter Muck, *Einhundert Jahre Berliner Philharmonisches Orchester: Darstellung in Dokumenten*, 3 vols. (Tutzing: Schneider, 1982), 1:454.

## CHAPTER TWO

1. Mariano Luigi Patrizi, *I Reflessi Vascolari Nelle Membra e Nel Cervello Dell'Uomo: Per Vari Stimuli e Per Varie Condizioni Fisiologiche e Sperimentali* (Reggio-Emilia: Stefano Calderini e Figlio, 1897); Patrizi, *Il Tempo di Reazione Semplice: Studiato in Rapporto Colla Curva Pletismografica Cerebrale; Nota Sperimentale* (Reggio-Emilia: Stefano Calderini e Figlio, 1897); "Music and the Cerebral Circulation of Man.—First Experiments," *Music* 11 (December 1896): 232–42; review in the *American Journal of Psychology* 9, no. 2 (January 1898): 242–43.

2. G. Schlotterbeck, "Emotionalism in Our Music," *Pittsburgh Post*, 25 January 1903, PIO scrapbooks, vol. 7, GWC, CLP.

3. Maud Matras, "Music as Medicine," *Monthly Musical Record* 35 (1 September 1905): 168–69. On the age of nervosity, see Joachim Radkau, *Das Zeitalter der Nervosität: Deutschland zwischen Bismarck und Hitler* (Munich: C. Hanser Verlag, 1998).

4. Richard Eastcott, *Sketches of the Origin and Progress of Music, With an Account of the Ancient Bards and Minstrels* (Bath: S. Hazard, 1793).

5. Alice E. Gether, "Music for the Sick," *Music* 7 (January 1895): 254–57; J. Cuthbert Hadden, "Music as a Medicine," *Music* 9 (February 1896): 359–68.

6. A. E. Brand, "The Emotional Basis of Musical Sensibility," *Music* 5 (January 1894): 302–5.

7. M. Carriere, "Das Stoffgebiet der Musik," *Die Gegenwart* 9 (13 May 1876): 308–9; "Über die Ausbildung des musikalischen Gefühls," *Neue Zeitschrift für Musik* 59, no. 19 (11 May 1892): 213–14.

8. John S. Van Cleve, "The Dignity of Music," *Music* 1 (November 1891): 12–16. For more on phrenologists' interest in the arts, see Charles Colbert, *A Measure of Perfection: Phrenology and the Fine Arts in America* (Chapel Hill: University of North Carolina Press, 1997).

9.  "Dr. Helmholtz on Harmony," *Dwight's Journal of Music* 33 (31 May 1873): 29–30.
10. Alfred Fouillee, "The Nature and Evolution of Art," *Music* 11 (December 1896): 141.
11. "A Universal Language," *Dwight's Journal of Music* 1 (18 September 1852): 187; www.ptialaska.net/~srice/solresol/sorsoeng.htm (accessed 1 March 2007).
12. I am indebted to Celia Applegate for this information.
13. R. P. Rider, "The Study of Music," *Music* 2 (May 1892): 32–38.
14. Mrs. John Vance Cheney, "The Relation of Music to Life," *Music* 11 (November 1896): 1–9.
15. Essay, *New York American*, 14 January 1912, NYSSSO scrapbooks, vol. 3, 1910–12, CH.
16. "The Symphony in Human Life," n.p., n.d., MNSO scrapbooks, vol. 136, Archives, 1920 clippings, folder symphony orchestras, newspaper clippings, UMN; "Last Night's Symphony," *Boston Globe*, 30 October 1887, BSO scrapbooks, M.125.5/2, BSO.
17. Marcia Wilson Lebow, "A Systematic Examination of the *Journal of Music and Art* Edited by John Sullivan Dwight: 1852–1881, Boston, Massachusetts" (Ph.D. diss., University of California, Los Angeles, 1969), 23.
18. "German Music," *Dwight's Journal of Music* 13 (24 July 1859): 130. The essay was an excerpt from Sabilla Novello's "Truth about Music and Musicians."
19. "Music and Religion," *Monthly Musical Record* 37 (1 April 1907): 77–78.
20. Quotation from "The Religion of Music," *Dwight's Journal of Music* 34 (19 September 1874): 303; "The Religion of Music," *Dwight's Journal of Music* 34 (3 October 1874): 310; Elizabeth A. Kramer, "The Idea of *Kunstreligion* in German Musical Aesthetics of the Early Nineteenth Century" (Ph.D. diss., University of North Carolina, 2005).
21. John Sullivan Dwight, "Introductory," *Dwight's Journal of Music* 1 (10 April 1852): 4.
22. John Sullivan Dwight, "'The Concerts of Past Winter' and Other Selections (1840–1881)," in *Music in Boston: Readings from the First Three Centuries*, ed. John C. Swan (Boston: Trustees of the Public Library of the City of Boston, 1977), 48.
23. Cited in James M. Doering, "'A Salesman of Fine Music': American Music Manager Arthur Judson, 1900–1940" (Ph.D. diss., Washington University, St. Louis, 1998), 82–83.
24. For more on Finck, see Henry T. Finck, *My Adventures in the Golden Age of American Music* (New York: Funk & Wagnalls, 1926).
25. Karleton [*sic*] Hackett, "Music in the Language of the People," *Music* 10 (June 1896): 125.
26. William L. Tomlins, "The American People and Musical Progress," *Music* 7 (April 1895): 541–48.

27. Edward Baxter Perry, "Music and Nutrition," *Music* 6 (October 1894): 559–67.

28. C. M. Frandrau, "Genius Flees When Optimism Comes In," n.p., n.d., MNSO scrapbooks, vol. 34, St. Paul Season, 1914–15, UMN.

29. "Future American Music," n.p., n.d., MNSO scrapbooks, vol. 136, 1920s clippings, American music, UMN. For more on Damrosch see Walter Damrosch, *My Musical Life* (New York: Charles Scribner's Sons, 1923).

30. Dwight, "'The Concerts of Past Winter,'" 63. See also Mark Grant, *Maestros of the Pen: A History of Classical Music Criticism in America* (Boston: Northeastern University Press, 1998), 39–52.

31. "Music as Art, as Language, and as Prophecy," *Dwight's Journal of Music* 20 (22 March 1862): 409; Lebow, "A Systematic Examination of the *Journal of Music and Art*," 17–63.

32. "Music as Universal Language," *Dwight's Journal of Music* 24 (25 June 1864): 262; Dwight, "'The Concerts of Past Winter,'" 55, 62; "The Religion of Music," *Dwight's Journal of Music* 34 (19 September 1874): 302.

33. "Music Mention," *Cincinnati Times-Star*, n.d., BSO scrapbooks, MF Pres/3, BSO.

34. "A Vast Scheme for Music—Mr. Damrosch's Answer," *Harmony* 1 (June 1900): 1.

35. Frank Damrosch, "Music Education and Music Culture," address at the Convention of the General Federation of Women's Clubs, n.d., folder 29, Frank Damrosch Papers, NYPL.

36. The first secular public concert is dated to 1792 in Boston. Richard Crawford, *America's Musical Life: A History* (New York: W. W. Norton, 2001), 3–136.

37. Louis R. Thomas, "A History of the Cincinnati Symphony Orchestra to 1931" (Ph.D. diss., University of Cincinnati, 1972), 24. See also Paul Landormy, *A History of Music*, trans. Frederick H. Martens (New York: Charles Scribner's Sons, 1923), 364.

38. Michael Broyles, *"Music of the Highest Class": Elitism and Populism in Antebellum Boston* (New Haven, CT: Yale University Press, 1992), 20–26. For a history of the Handel and Haydn Society, see H. Earle Johnson, *Hallelujah, Amen! The Story of the Handel and Haydn Society of Boston* (orig. pub. Boston: Bruce Humphries, 1965; reprint, New York: Da Capo, 1981).

39. Ernst Krohn, *Missouri Music* (orig. pub. St. Louis: Privately Published, 1924; portions reprinted in Krohn, *A Century of Missouri Music*, New York: Da-Capo Press, 1971), 5–12; Irene E. Cortinovis, "The Golden Age of German Song," *Missouri Historical Review* 68 (July 1974): 437–42.

40. Daniel Walker Howe, *Making the American Self: Jonathan Edwards to Abraham Lincoln* (Cambridge, MA: Harvard University Press, 1997), 226–27. The original document is in the Houghton Library at Harvard University.

41. David McCullough, *John Adams* (New York: Simon and Schuster, 2001), 307, 329, 338. I am indebted to Richard Brown for this information.

42. Winton Dean, "Beethoven and Opera," in *The Beethoven Reader*, ed. Denis Arnold and Nigel Fortune (New York: W. W. Norton, 1971), 381; Rudolf Pečman, *Beethovens Opernpläne*, trans. from the Czech by Jan Gruna (Brno: Univerzita J. E. Purkyne, 1981), 78.

43. Oscar Thompson, "Why Not American Themes?" *New York Sun*, 6 April 1940, Philharmonic-Symphony Society of New York records, reel 13, NYPL.

44. Jacques Offenbach, quoted in Schabas, *Theodore Thomas*, 77, from Jacques Offenbach, *Orpheus in America: Offenbach's Diary of His Journey to the New World*, trans. Lander MacClintock (orig. pub. 1877; reprint, New York: Greenwood Press, 1957, 1969).

45. Edward G. Baynham, "The Early Development of Music in Pittsburgh" (Ph.D. diss., University of Pittsburgh, 1944); Minutes of the St. Louis Orchestra Club, 1902–13, 69–71, St. Louis Philharmonic Collection, box 9, MHS; Henry Knorr to the Board of Directors of the Academy of Fine Arts, 9 June 1884, "Germania Orchestra," POA; Thomas Ryan, "Recollections of an Old Musician (New York, 1899)," in Swan, *Music in Boston*, 81.

46. Offenbach, *Orpheus in America*, 154.

47. NYP Board of Directors/Executive Committee minutes, 18 November 1873, NYP.

48. Landormy, *A History of Music*, 364–65; James M. Bergquist, "The Forty-Eighters and the Politics of the 1850s," in *Germany and America: Essays on Problems of International Relations and Immigration*, ed. Hans L. Trefousse (New York: Brooklyn Press, 1980); Frank Trommler, "The Use of History in German-American Politics," in *The German Forty-Eighters in the United States*, ed. Charlotte L. Brancaforte (New York: Peter Lang, 1989), 279–95.

49. "Old Guard of Thomas Orchestra," *Chicago Inter Ocean*, 20 April 1913, CSO scrapbooks, CSO.

50. Henry E. Krehbiel, *The Philharmonic Society of New York: A Memorial* (New York: Novello, Ewer & Co., 1892), 81.

51. Heinrich Ehrlich, "Aus dem Musikleben," *Die Gegenwart* 43 (11 November 1893): 315.

52. Frederic W. Root, "The Point of View," quoted in Florence Ffrench, *Music and Musicians in Chicago* (orig. pub. Chicago: Florence Ffrench, 1899; reprint, New York: DaCapo Press, 1979), 126–28.

53. "Fritz Scheel Returns from European Trip," *Musical America* (6 October 1906), PO scrapbooks, 1907–8, POA.

54. "More Than a Thousand," *Boston Home Journal*, 4 July 1901, BSO scrapbooks, MF pres/19, BSO; William Stowe, *Going Abroad: European Travel in Nineteenth-Century American Culture* (Princeton, NJ: Princeton University Press, 1994); Mark Rennella and Whitney Walton, "Planned Serendipity: American Travellers and the Transatlantic Voyage in the Nineteenth and Twentieth Centuries," *Journal of Social History* 38, no. 2 (2004): 365–83.

55. Louis C. Elson, *European Reminiscences, Musical and Otherwise: Being the Recollections of the Vacation Tours of a Musician in Various Countries* (Philadelphia: T. Presser, 1896); J. Horowitz, *Wagner Nights*, 31–32, 138–39.

56. Elam Douglas Bomberger, "The German Musical Training of American Students, 1850–1900," (Ph.D. diss., University of Maryland, 1991), i, 55.

57. Harold Schonberg, *The Lives of the Great Composers*, 3rd ed. (New York: W. W. Norton, 1997), 331; Henry Fry to Richard Willis, 8 February 1854, reprinted in *Dwight's Journal of Music* 3 (4 February 1854): 141.

58. Amy Fay, *Music-Study in Germany: The Classic Memoir of the Romantic Era* (orig. pub. 1880; reprint, New York: Dover Publications, 1965), 159, 170; "An American Student At Leipsic," *Music* 6 (January 1895): 299.

59. S. Margaret W. McCarthy, "Amy Fay: The American Years," *American Music* 3 (Spring 1985): 57. *Allgemeine deutsche Musiker-Zeitung*, October 1884, quoted in Muck, *Einhundert Jahre Berliner Philharmonisches Orchester*, 1:60.

60. Alice James to William James, 4 November 1888, quoted in Jean Strouse, *Alice James: A Biography* (orig. pub. 1980; reprint, Cambridge: Harvard University Press, 1999), 1.

61. *New York Times*, 7 June 1918, p. 9, citation in Craig H. Roell, *The Piano in America, 1890–1940* (Chapel Hill: University of North Carolina Press, 1989), 327.

62. "American Music Is Best, Says Freund," *Minneapolis Journal*, 22 October 1915, MNSO scrapbooks, vol. 38, Home Season, 1915–16, UMN. These numbers vary depending on the criteria. A New York paper estimated in 1907 that every year Americans spent about $3 million on musical training at European conservatories. Quoted in F. O. A., "Der Dollar und die Kunst," *Der Tag* (Berlin), 10 December 1907, PO scrapbooks, 1907–8, POA.

63. M. D. Taylor, "Music in Germany," *Music* 6 (September 1894): 516.

64. "Editorial Bric-a-Brac," *Music* 8 (August 1895): 402.

65. Hobart H. Burr, "American Women-Musicians," *Cosmopolitan* (August 1901), FBZ, X186–A, AJA.

66. "American's Great Violinist," n.p., n.d., BSO scrapbooks, M.125.5/6, BSO; "Leonora Jackson," *Musical Courier*, 3 January 1900, BSO scrapbooks, M.125.5/6, BSO.

67. Eugene Crawford, "Vienna to Honor Leschetizky's Grave," *Chicago Daily News*, 25 September 1926, FBZ, 2/28, AJA.

68. "A Musical Editor in Europe," *Music* 1 (December 1891): 174.

69. Janice Wenger, "William Henry Pommer: His Life and Works" (Ph.D. diss., University of Missouri, Kansas City, 1987), 12–22.

70. Dietmar Schenk, *Die Hochschule für Musik zu Berlin: Preußens Konservatorium zwischen romantischem Klassizismus und Neuer Musik, 1869–1932/33* (Stuttgart: Franz Steiner, 2003); Stephan Schmitt, ed., *Geschichte der Hochschule für Musik und Theater München von den Anfängen bis 1945* (Tutzing: H. Schneider, 2005); Yvonne Wasserloos, *Das Leipziger Konservatorium für Musik*

*im 19. Jahrhundert: Anziehungs- und Ausstrahlungskraft eines musikpädago-gischen Modells auf das internationale Musikleben* (Hildesheim: Olms, 2004).

71. "Die von dem Prof. Dr. A. B. Marx zu Berlin beantragte Gründung eines Conservatoriums für Musik," I, HA, Rep. 100, no. 1597/1, GStA PK.

72. V. Roon and v. Mühler to Wilhelm I, Berlin, 14 February 1870, I. HA, Rep. 89, no. 20390, GHStA PK, Bl. 43.

73. Abschrift, Ausgaben des Staats für Musikzwecke, Friedrich Schmidt-Ott Papers, I. HA, Rep. 92, A 11, GStA PK, Bl. 176–8.

74. Heinrich Ehrlich, "Aus dem Musikleben," *Die Gegenwart* 43 (21 October 1893): 261–62.

75. Wasserloos, *Leipziger Konservatorium*, 64, 68.

76. Annual reports, Hochschule für Musik, 1 October 1907–1 October 1908, Friedrich Schmidt-Ott Papers, I. HA, Rep. 92, A 12, GStA PK.

77. "Die Ausländer der Kgl. akademischen Hochschule für Musik in Berlin," *Berliner Neueste Nachrichten*, 22 February 1914, Friedrich Schmidt-Ott Papers, I. HA, Rep. 92, A 11, GStA PK, Bl. 171–72.

78. Dr. Kretzschmar, 6 March 1914, Friedrich Schmidt-Ott Papers, I. HA, Rep. 92, A 11, GStA PK, Bl. 175.

79. Wasserloos, *Leipziger Konservatorium*, 74–75.

80. A. Fay, *Music-Study*, xiv.

81. Fay's letters appeared in the *Atlantic Monthly* in 1874, then as a book. S. M. McCarthy, "Amy Fay," 52–61.

82. A. Fay, *Music-Study*, 123, 122.

83. Ibid., x, 215, 218, 219, 222, 227, 352; on Liszt's master classes in Weimar, see Bomberger, "German Musical Training," 253–79.

84. Richard Gipson, *The Life of Emma Thursby, 1845-1931* (New York: New York Historical Society, 1940), 88–89, 259–66.

85. "Letter from Leipzig," *Dwight's Journal of Music* 7 (14 July 1855); "'Coals to Newcastle'—American Singers in Europe," *Dwight's Journal of Music* 33 (20 January 1874): 156.

86. *Philadelphia Ledger*, quoted in Arthur M. Kennedy, ed., *A History of the Orpheus Club of Philadelphia* (Philadelphia: Orpheus Club of Philadelphia/ Allen, Lane & Scott, 1936), 56.

87. "Unfledged Prima Donna," *Dwight's Journal of Music* 33 (7 March 1874): 187.

88. "Biography of Frank Damrosch," folder 1, Frank Damrosch Papers, NYPL; on Joachim's teaching skills, see also Ellen Knight, *Charles Martin Loeffler: A Life Apart in American Music* (Urbana: University of Illinois Press, 1993), 15–16.

CHAPTER THREE

1. "Der [sic] Orchester," SLPS records, 1860–1930, box 1/8, MHS.

2. Appiah, *Ethics of Identity*, 213–72.

3. Preston, *Opera on the Road*.

4. R. Crawford, *America's Musical Life*, 283–84.

5. Henry Albrecht, *Skizzen aus dem Leben der Musik-Gesellschaft Germania* (Philadelphia: King and Baird, 1869), trans. Nancy Newman in Newman, "Gleiche Rechte, gleiche Pflichten, und gleiche Genüsse: Henry Albrecht's Utopian Vison of the Germania Musical Society," *Yearbook of German-American Studies* 34 (1999): quotations are from pp. 91, 107; Nancy Newman, "Good Music for a Free People: The Germania Musical Society and Transatlantic Musical Culture of the Mid-Nineteenth Century" (Ph.D. diss., Brown University, 2002).

6. "The Germania Musical Society," *Chronicle*, 26 April 1852, Charles Chauncey Mellor scrapbooks 2, CLP; Newman, "Gleiche Rechte, gleiche Pflichten," 83–111.

7. A. Willhartitz to A. E. Kroeger, *St. Louis Republican*, 27 October 1875, SLPS, box 1/4, MHS; Heinrich Börnstein in *Anzeiger des Westens*, reprinted in *Dwight's Journal of Music* 3 (9 July 1853), quoted in Newman, "Gleiche Rechte, gleiche Pflichten," 108.

8. John Sullivan Dwight, quoted in Newman, "Gleiche Rechte, gleiche Pflichten," 102.

9. Essay, *New York American*, 14 January 1912, NYSSO scrapbooks, vol. 3, 1910–12, CH.

10. Norman Lebrecht, *The Maestro Myth: Great Conductors in Pursuit of Power* (New York: Birch Lane Press, 1991), 12; Martin Wolschke, *Von der Stadtpfeiferei zu Lehrlingskapelle und Sinfonieorchester* (Regensburg: Gustav Bosse Verlag, 1981), 17–120; Schonberg, *Lives of the Great Composers*, 24–25.

11. Newspaper clipping, *Boston Home Journal*, 1 March 1903, M.125.5/7, BSO scrapbooks, BSO.

12. Schonberg, *Great Conductors*, 15–24; Lebrecht, *Maestro Myth*, 2, 4, 10.

13. Applegate, *Bach in Berlin*, 255–56.

14. J. Horowitz, *Classical Music*, 113, 147; J. Horowitz, *Wagner Nights*, 81–85.

15. On Seidl in the United States, see Henry T. Finck, ed., *Anton Seidl: A Memorial by His Friends* (New York: C. Scribner's Sons, 1899), 28–80; quoted in J. Horowitz, *Wagner Nights*, 87–88.

16. J. Horowitz, *Wagner Nights*, 11–18, 96, 124–25, 127, 129–31, 168–70; Finck, *Anton Seidl*, 180.

17. Katherine Gladney Wells, *Symphony and Song: The St. Louis Symphony Orchestra; The First Hundred Years, 1880–1980* (Taftsville, VT: Countryman Press, 1980; reprint, Tucson, AZ: Patrice Press, 1993), 6.

18. J. Horowitz, *Wagner Nights*, 255; Schonberg, *Lives of the Great Composers*, 190.

19. L. Thomas, "History of the Cincinnati Symphony Orchestra," 20, 24, 26–27; quotation is from pp. 26–27.

20. Glessner Journals, 17 January 1897, box 4, CHM.

21. Frederick Stock, handwritten manuscripts, n.d. [1918], trustees, general records, general correspondence, box 1, 1/33, CSO; Charles N. Fay, "Theodore Thomas," Program of the 50th Season, 1940–41, PR, conductors: Thomas, misc., CSO.

22. Schabas, *Theodore Thomas*, 63.

23. Rose Fay Thomas's guest book, TTP, box 5, NL; *William Vocke: Aus seinem Leben und Wirken* (Chicago: Deutscher Republikanischer Central-Verein, n.d.), PR, conductors, box 2: Thomas Papers, biographies, correspondence, CSO.

24. Correspondence in Thomas Papers, box 1, NL; photocopies in PR, conductors: Thomas, correspondence, CSO.

25. Manuscript by Vera Wolfe, PR, conductors: F. Stock, CSO; Stock, Berlin, to his daughter Vera, 23 July 1926, Stock Papers, 1/38, CSO; Donald Herbert Berglund, "A Study of the Life and Work of Frederick Stock during the Time He Served as Musical Director of the Chicago Symphony Orchestra, with Particular Reference to His Influence on Music Education" (Ph.D. diss, Northwestern University, 1955), 34, 54; "Friedrich Wilhelm August Stock," Stock Papers, 1/21, CSO; Stock to Vera, summer 1926, Stock Papers, 1/28, 1/38, CSO.

26. Emil Scaria, Vienna, to Thomas, 25 January 1884, TTP, box 2, NL.

27. Phylo Adams Otis, *The Chicago Symphony Orchestra: Its Organization, Growth and Development 1891–1924* (Chicago: Clayton F. Summy O., 1924), 178.

28. *New York Press* quotation in Schabas, *Theodore Thomas*, 225; Thomas, Chicago, to Mrs. Twombly, TTP, box 3, NL.

29. Quotations in PR, conductors: F. Stock, CSO; and in *Biography of an Orchestra: An Affectionate Look Back at Eighty Years of Music and Life in Chicago* (Chicago: R. R. Donnelly and Sons, [1971?]), 2; Otis, *Chicago Symphony Orchestra*, 26.

30. Thomas, New York, to George Ward, 27 March 1877, Felsengarten Collection, CSO; J. Horowitz, *Wagner Nights*, 54; quotations from newspaper clipping, PR, conductors: Thomas, books and articles, CSO; quotation from Henry Van Dyke, "The Master of Music," PR, conductors: Thomas, books and articles, CSO.

31. "Hinter den Kulissen," *Berliner Börsen-Courier*, 19 February 1908 and 16 June 1912, "Karl Muck," BPH Rep. 119, Generalintendanz des Preußischen Staatstheater, no. 3052, GStA PK, 411.

32. Volbach, who was known as an expert of the German song, ultimately did not sign on with the Cincinnati Symphony Orchestra, because the trustees were unable to pay him more than $3,000. Felix Volbach, Mainz, to "Madam" [Taft?], 14 July 1894, Wulsin Family Papers, series 1, box 24, folder 1, CIHS; "Schreiben an den Kaiser," 23 September 1903, HA, Rep. 89, no. 19917, GHStA PK, Bl. 327–9; "Fritz Volback," *Musikalisches Wochenblatt* 40 (3 June 1909): 162. In 1907, Volbach tried his luck again and applied at the Saint Louis Symphony Orchestra. SLSS minutes, 29 April 1907, box 2, MHS.

33. "Kunwald in Cincinnati," *Cincinnati Post*, 6 June 1912, CISO scrapbooks, vol. 10,CHM; J. Horowitz, *Wagner Nights*, 14, 211.

34. Goodwin, *Sketches and Impressions*, 153–56, 192–94, 199; "'Education' in Musical Taste," *New York Times*, 9 November 1902.

35. Schabas, *Theodore Thomas*, 32.

36. Newspaper clipping, *New York Mail*, 4 December 1909, Gustav Mahler/Mail, NYP press clippings, 1909–10, NYPA; J. Horowitz, *Wagner Nights*, 155; Louis Engel, obituary, *London World*, 4 March 1885, Philharmonic-Symphony Society of New York Records, MF/21, NYPL.

37. "Biography of Frank Damrosch," folder 1, Frank Damrosch Papers, NYPL.

38. J. Horowitz, *Wagner Nights*, 78–79. For a comprehensive account of the Damrosch family, see George W. Martin, *The Damrosch Dynasty: America's First Family of Music* (Boston: Houghton Mifflin, 1983).

39. Article, n.p., n.d., Philharmonic-Symphony Society of New York records, reel 21, NYPL.

40. Schabas, *Theodore Thomas*, 252–53.

41. J. Horowitz, *Wagner Nights*, 246–52; Finck, *Anton Seidl*, 71–83.

42. Peter Tchaikovsky to Vladimir Davidov, 30 April 1891, in Elkhonon Yoffe, ed., *Tchaikovsky in America: The Composer's Visit in 1891*, trans. Lidya Yoffe (New York: Oxford University Press, 1986), 62–63; Marc A. De Wolfe Howe, *The Boston Symphony Orchestra, 1881–1931* (Boston: Houghton Mifflin, 1931), 54.

43. J. Horowitz, *Wagner Nights*, 115, 116. For more on Lehmann, see also Lilli Lehmann, *My Path through Life*, trans. Alice Benedict Seligman (New York: G. P. Putnam's Sons, 1914).

44. Schonberg, *Lives of the Great Composers*, 446–49; William J. McGrath, *Dionysian Art and Populist Politics in Austria* (London: Yale University Press, 1974), 12; quotation cited in Jonathan Carr, *Mahler: A Biography* (Woodstock, NY: Overlook Press, 1997), 165. See also Frank Berger, *Gustav Mahler: Vision und Mythos; Versuch einer geistigen Biographie* (Stuttgart: Verlag Freies Geistesleben, 1993); Hermann Danuser, ed., *Gustav Mahler* (Darmstadt: Wissenschaftliche Buchgesellschaft, 1992); Karen Painter, ed., *Mahler and His World* (Princeton, NJ: Princeton University Press, 2002); Karen Painter, "The Sensuality of Timbre: Responses to Mahler and Modernity at the Fin de siècle," *Nineteenth-Century Music* 18 (Spring 1995): 236–56; Henning Böke, "Gustav Mahler und das Judentum," *Archiv für Musikwissenschaft* 54 (1992): 1–21; Jonathan Koehler, "Gustav Mahler: A Study of Cultural Identity in the Austro-Hungarian Empire," (honors thesis, University of California, Davis, 1998).

45. "Orchestra Players and Their Earning Powers," *Musical Leader*, 17 April 1913, MNSO scrapbooks, vol. 136, Archives, 1920 clippings, folder "Symphony Orchestras," newspaper clippings, UMN.

46. F. O. A., "Der Dollar und die Kunst," *Der Tag* (Berlin), 10 December 1907, PO scrapbooks, 1907–8, POA.

47. NYP Board of Directors/Executive Committee minutes, 17 April and 8 May 1898, NYPA; Richard James Wolfe, "A Short History of the Pittsburgh Orchestra" (M.A. thesis, Carnegie Institute of Technology, 1954), 51; W. L. Elliot, "Mr. Higginson as Benefactor," n.p., 24 September 1889, BSO scrapbooks, M.125.5/3, BSO.

48. "List of Soloists Proposed for the Season 1899–1900," PIO correspondence, vol. 3, CLP; NYP Board of Directors/Executive Committee minutes, 9 September 1898, NYPA; Records of Proceedings of The Orchestra Association Company, 8 October 1903, 3 April 1906, CISO; SLSS minutes, 29 October 1912, Executive Committee, box 1/5, MHS.

49. Krehbiel, *Philharmonic Society of New York*, 14.

50. During the 1899–1900 season, Pittsburgh orchestral musicians earned between $25 and $60 a week, with the highest amount paid to the concertmaster and the lowest to a member of the second violins section. A violist at the Philadelphia Orchestra made between $25 and $40 per week for a 22-week season in the early 1900s, while a horn player could make up to $80. In 1913, the U.S. dollar was worth approximately four German mark. List of BSO players, 1883–84, weekly salaries, Higginson correspondence, 1883–84, oversize material, box 3, BSO; "What Some Musicians Earn," n.p., n.d. [September 1893], BSO scrapbooks, M.125.5/4, BSO; Wolfe, "A Short History of the Pittsburgh Orchestra," 47, 204–6; Minutes of the Board of Directors, POA, 23 March 1909, vol. 2, S 104, POA.

51. Before World War I, German vocalists connected with opera houses rarely made $10,000 or more per annum, while $1,500 was considered a fair income, even for the leading partsl. Chorus singers, dancers, and solo dancers earned between $450 and $750 a year. Nachricht der General-Intendantur der kgl. Schauspiele Zerbst, 18 January 1898, BPH, Rep. 119 neu, no. 4100, GStA PK; Dienstvertrag für Herrn Franz Schalk, 12 March 98, ibid., no. 3547; Dienstvertrag Hans Vanseil, 2 November 1894, ibid., no. 3898; article from *Reich-Arbeitsblatt* quoted in "Pay of Musicians in Germany," n.p., n.d., MNSO scrapbooks, vol. 136, Archives, 1920 clippings, folder "Symphony Orchestras," newspaper clippings, UMN.

52. Walter Damrosch, New York, to George Wilson, 14 March 1903, George Wilson personal scrapbooks, vol. 2, GWC, CLP.

53. "How the Hammer That Lost Its Head," *Minneapolis Journal*, 1 June 1924, MNSO scrapbooks, vol. 70, 21st Home Season, 1923–24, UMN.

54. L. Thomas, "History of the Cincinnati Symphony Orchestra," 177.

55. George Seltzer, *The Professional Symphony Orchestra in the United States* (Metuchen, NJ: Scarecrow Press, 1975), 21–22. The number of 1,500 may well be hyperbole, as Nancy Newman argues in "Good Music for a Free People," 286–87.

56. L. Thomas, "History of the Cincinnati Symphony Orchestra," 247.

57. "The Symphony Concerts," n.p., n.d. [January 1885], M.125.5/1, BSO scrapbooks, BSO; Wilhelm Gericke Papers, Houghton Library, Harvard University.

58. Born in Czernovitz, Austria, in 1865, Paur entered the Vienna Conserva-
    tory at age 11; there he studied violin with Hellmesberg and composition
    with Dessoff. He also studied piano with Hans von Bulow and began his
    conducting career at age 21 with an orchestra in Cassel. He went on to
    Königsberg, Mannheim (1880), where he directed the Court Opera, and
    then to Leipzig, where he conducted the Leipzig Stadttheater. In 1891, Paur
    and his wife, Marie, sailed for America, where he had received an appoint-
    ment as conductor of the Boston Philharmonic Orchestra. He subsequently
    was appointed as Seidl's successor at the Met and, in the early 1900s, as
    Victor Herbert's successor in Pittsburgh. "Emil Paur, as a Pittsburger at
    Home," *Pittsburg Dispatch*, 21 October 1904, PIO scrapbooks, 9, GWC,
    CLP; "Musical Matter," *Herald*, 8 October 1893, BSO scrapbooks, M.125.
    5/4, BSO.
59. Philip Hale, "About Music," n.p., n.d. [ca. 3 May 1896], BSO scrapbooks,
    M.125.5/5, BSO; "The Chatterer," "Cynicism," n.p., n.d. [Summer 1893],
    BSO scrapbooks, M.125.5/4, BSO.
60. "The Waltz—Lanner—Strauss," *Dwight's Journal of Music* 32 (5 October
    1872): 315; "We Hurry Too Much to Produce Tenors," n.p. [*Pittsburg
    Dispatch*?], 3 April 1910, George Wilson personal scrapbooks, vol. 17,
    CLP; "Three of World's Greatest Pianists," *Daily News*, 11 September 1915,
    MNSO scrapbooks, vol. 38, 13th Home Season, newspaper clippings, UMN;
    "Fires of Genius Make a Hot Time Over a Concert," newspaper clipping,
    n.p., 31 January 1910, NYP press clippings, 1909–10, Gustav Mahler/Mis-
    cellaneous, NYPA; "With the Musicians," *Pittsburgh Post*, 16 January 1897,
    PIO scrapbooks, vol. 1, GWC, CLP; "Two Great Soloists for the Symphony
    Concerts," *Cincinnati Star*, 9 February 1904, CISO scrapbooks, vol. 2, CIHS;
    "Soloist Likes American Girls: So, Girls, There's a Chance," *Cincinnati Post*,
    12 March 1904, CISO scrapbooks, vol. 2, CIHS.
61. "Maker of Music," n.p. [St. Paul], 28 April 1896, CSO scrapbooks, MF/1,
    1894–1904, CSO. On Herbert's youth in Germany, see Edward N. Waters,
    *Victor Herbert: A Life in Music* (New York: MacMillan Co., 1955), 5–25.
62. "Victor Herbert Presented with Bust of Beethoven," *Atlanta Gazette*, 9 Feb-
    ruary 1901, George Wilson personal scrapbooks, vol. 18, CLP; "When the
    Band Plays in Private," *Pittsburgh Leader*, 19 January 1902, PIO scrapbooks,
    vol. 6, GWC, CLP.
63. Joseph Horowitz, *Understanding Toscanini: How He Became an American Cul-
    ture-God and Helped Create a New Audience for Old Music* (New York: Knopf,
    1987), 37–38, 41.
64. Carl Pohlig (his first name also has been spelled with a *K*) toured Germany,
    Austria, Russia, Scandinavia, and Italy, and then became Kapellmeister in
    Graz. He was also associated with Mahler at the Opera in Hamburg and
    spent time at Covent Garden and Bayreuth, where he trained artists for the
    Wagner Festival. Pohlig appeared as symphony conductor in Coburg, Berlin,
    Frankfurt, Munich, and finally Stuttgart. "Pohlig, New Leader, Here Ready

for Duties," *Philadelphia Press*, 15 September 1907, PO scrapbooks, 1907–8, POA.

65. "Music in Boston," n.p., 20 March 1882, M.125.5/1, BSO scrapbooks, BSO.

66. "Biography of Frank Damrosch," folder 1, Frank Damrosch Papers, NYPL.

67. "Dr. Kunwald," *Cincinnati Volksblatt*, 26 April 1912, CISO scrapbooks, vol. 10, CHM; newspaper clipping, *Cincinnati Enquirer*, 5 May 1912, ibid; "Berlin," *Musical Courier*, 25 May 1912, ibid; "Kunwald in Cincinnati," *Cincinnati Post*, 6 June 1912, ibid; L. Thomas, "History of the Cincinnati Symphony Orchestra," 373; Muck, *Einhundert Jahre Berlin Philharmonisches Orchester*, 1:337.

68. Frances Anne Wister, *Twenty-Five Years of the Philadelphia Orchestra, 1900–1925* (Philadelphia: Edward Stern & Co., 1925), 25–28.

69. Newspaper clippings, ads, September 1893 to October 1894, PO Conductors, Biographical Files: Fritz Scheel, San Francisco Years (1895 [*sic*]–99), POA.

70. "Laud Debut Symphony's Leader," newspaper clipping, n.p., n.d., M.125.5/8, BSO scrapbooks, BSO.

71. H. T. P., "The Symphony Concerts," *Boston Transcript*, 19 September 1908, M.125.5/8, BSO scrapbooks, BSO.

72. "Dr. Fiedler Wins Audience," *Boston Globe*, 11 October 1908, M.125.5/8, BSO scrapbooks, BSO.

73. "The creative instinct of the musical artist is aroused by emotion and to the emotion he speaks through the sensation of tone." G. Schlotterbeck, "Emotionalism in Our Music," *Pittsburgh Post*, 25 January 1903, PIO scrapbooks, vol. 7, GWC, CLP.

74. "Playing upon Human Minds Like Strings," *Philadelphia North American*, 28 February 1909, "Carl Pohlig," PO Conductors, Biographical Files, POA.

75. "Mark Hambourg Coming to Pittsburgh," *Pittsburgh Gazette Times*, 17 November 1907, PIO scrapbooks, vol. 13, GWC, PIO; "The Symphony Concert," *Boston Transcript*, 19 April 1913, M.125.5/10, BSO; Brand, "The Emotional Basis of Musical Sensibility."

76. "Symphony Concert Is Conservative," *Boston Advertiser*, 31 March 1917, BSO scrapbooks, M.125.5/11, BSO; undated manuscript,ca. 1900, PO scrapbooks, 1900–1901, POA.

77. Warren Davenport, "Mr. Gericke Goes Backward," *Boston Herald*, 24 March 1901, M.125.5/6, BSO scrapbooks, BSO.

78. Henry Krehbiel, "Compliments for Mr. Nikisch," n.p. [*Boston Evening Transcript?*], 16 October 1889, BSO scrapbooks, M.125.5/3, BSO.

79. "In Musical Circles," *Chicago Journal and Press*, 21 December 1895, CSO scrapbooks, MF/1, 1894–1904, CSO.

80. Newspaper clipping, n.p., n.d. [29 March 1903], BSO scrapbooks, MF Pres/9, BSO.

81. "Hans von Buelow," *Dwight's Journal of Music* (27 November 1875); "Mr. Fiedler in New York," *Boston Transcript*, 6 November 1908, BSO scarpbooks, M.125.5/8.

82. Schabas, *Theodore Thomas*, 127.
83. Arthur Warren, "Celebrities Here and There," *Boston Home Journal*, n.d. [ca. 17 October 1886], M.125.5/2, BSO scrapbooks, BSO; newspaper clipping, n.p., n.d. [1880s], M.125.5/2, BSO scrapbooks, BSO; newspaper clipping, ca. 16 March 1902, M.125.5/6, BSO scrapbooks, BSO.
84. "New Conductor's Characteristics," *New York Times*, 7 December 1902, POA scrapbooks, 1902–3, POA.
85. Richard E. Mueller, "The St. Louis Symphony Orchestra, 1931–1958" (Ph.D. diss., St. Louis University, 1976), 11.
86. Louis C. Elson, "Dr. Hans Richter," n.p. [*Boston Home Journal?*], n.d. [ca. 14 April 1893], BSO scrapbooks, M.125.5/4, BSO.
87. "Will Richter Come?, n.p. [*Boston Transcript?*], n.d. [ca. 17 April 1893], BSO scrapbooks, M.125.5/4, BSO.
88. Ludwig August Frankl, quoted in Heinrich Eduard Jacob, *Johann Strauss und das 19. Jahrhundert: Die Geschichte einer musikalischen Weltherrschaft (1819–1917)* (Amsterdam: Querido Verlag, 1937), 91; Schonberg, *Lives of the Great Composers*, 317.
89. Wolfe, "A Short History of the Pittsburgh Orchestra," 109.
90. Charles Menees, ed., *The St. Louis Symphony Orchestra* (St. Louis: Menelle Print, 1955).
91. "The Chatterer," "Cynicism," n.p., n.d. [Summer 1893], BSO scrapbooks, M.125.5/4, BSO; "Music and Drama," *Boston Transcript*, ca. 3 November 1895, BSO scrapbooks, M.125.5/5, BSO; quotation from "The Boston Symphony Concerts," n.p., n.d. [December 1881], M.125.5/1, BSO scrapbooks, BSO.
92. "The History of the Orchestra," in *St. Louis Symphony Orchestra: Diamond Jubilee Souvenir Program*, ed. Charles Menees (St. Louis: Mendle Print, 1995). Saint Louis Symphony Society Records, box 4.
93. Lebrecht, *Maestro Myth*, 34–35.
94. Wolfe, "A Short History of the Pittsburgh Orchestra," 426–27; Robert Schmalz, "Paur and the Pittsburgh: Requiem for an Orchestra," *American Music* 12 (Summer 1994): 125–47; "Emil Paur, as a Pittsburger at Home," *Pittsburg Dispatch*, 21 October 1904, PIO scrapbooks, 9, GWC, CLP.
95. "Mr. Walter Damrosch and the New York Symphony Orchestra," PIO correspondence, vol. 1, CLP; Hans von Bülow, Hamburg, to Walter Damrosch, 13 February 1887, Damrosch Collection, Carnegie Hall, New York; "How Mr. Damrosch Became Conductor," *New York Times*, 14 March 1910, NYSSSO scrapbooks, vol. 2, 1909–10, CH.
96. Mary Lawton, ed., *Schumann-Heink: The Last of the Titans* (New York: Macmillan, 1928), 205.
97. Victor Herbert, Morningside, NY, to George Wilson, 16 July 1901, PIO correspondence, vol. 3, CLP; "Symphony Players Back," *Boston Herald*, 17 September 1909, M.125.5/9, BSO scrapbooks, BSO.

98. Newspaper clipping, *Music Zeitung*, n.d., Philharmonic-Symphony Society of New York records, scrapbooks, 31st season, 1872–73, extracts from newspapers, MF/21. NYPL.

99. "Music," *Pittsburgh Press*, 20 November 1898, PIO scrapbooks, vol. 3, GWC, CL. Rose Fay Thomas, *Memoirs of Theodore Thomas* (New York: Moffat, Yard and Co., 1911), 117.

100. Levine, *Highbrow/Lowbrow*, 104–42, 219; Yoffe, *Tchaikovsky in America*, vii; Schonberg, *Lives of the Great Composers*, 317.

101. Schonberg, *Lives of the Great Composers*, 170, 238; personnel file Richard Strauss, BPH, Rep. 19 neu, no. 3810, GStA PK; "Richard Strauss' Konzerte im Warenhaus," newspaper clipping, n.p., n.d., personnel file Richard Strauss, BPH, Rep. 119 neu, No. 3810, GStA PK; Richard Aldrich, *Concert Life in New York, 1902–1923* (New York: G. B. Putnam's Sons, 1941), 696–97.

102. Tchaikovsky, Maidanovo, to Vladimir Napravnik, 29 May 1891, quoted in Yoffe, *Tchaikovsky in America*, 160.

103. Harold Schonberg, *The Great Pianists* (New York: Simon and Schuster, 1963), 285–91.

104. Newspaper clipping, n.p., n.d. [ca. September 1899], BSO scrapbooks, M125.5/6, BSO.

105. Schonberg, *Great Pianists*, 253–63.

106. Ibid., 299; "Newest Hair, Music and Mesmerig [*sic*] Idol—Paderewski Has Fallen!" n. p. [ca. 8 November 1898], BSO scrapbooks, M.125.5/5, BSO; "The Chatterer," *Boston Herald*, n.d. [January 1899], BSO scrapbooks, M.125.5/6, BSO; "Sauer Will Return," *News*, n.d. [ca. 15 January 1899], BSO scrapbooks, MF Pres/7, BSO.

107. Schabas, *Theodore Thomas*, 52.

108. Victor Thrane, New York, to Anna Millar, Chicago, 11 November 1899, Manager's Files, A. Millar, 1/19, CSO; newspaper clipping, n.p., n.d. [ca. 21 January 1893], BSO scrapbooks, M.125.5/4, BSO.

109. Philip Hale, "Esclarmonde," n.p., n.d. [October 1900], BSO scrapbooks, M.125.5/6, BSO.

110. General correspondence 1896, box 1, folder 1/4, general records, Board of Directors/Trustees, CSO.

111. "Buelow in Baltimore," *Dwight's Journal of Music* 35 (25 December 1875): 147; Schonberg, *Great Pianists*, 26.

112. Heinrich Röckner, "Moderne Musik und Volksthümlichkeit," *Die Gegenwart* 45 (13 January 1894), 25.

113. John K. Sherman, *Music and Maestros: The Story of the Minneapolis Symphony Orchestra* (Minneapolis: University of Minnesota Press, 1952), 100; newspaper clipping, *Journal*, 1 March 1903, M.125.5/7, BSO scrapbooks, BSO; "Philip Hale: Selections from His Columns in the *Boston Home Journal*, 1889–91," in Swan, *Music in Boston*, 93; Louis Moreau Gottschalk, *Notes of*

*a Pianist* (orig. pub. Philadelphia, 1888; reprint, Philadelphia, 1979), 127, quoted in J. Horowitz, *Wagner Nights*, 34.

114. J. Horowitz, *Wagner Nights*, 36; Krehbiel, *Philharmonic Society of New York*, 42, 45, 76.

115. "German/Austrian Musicians," database, CSO.

116. "Old Guard of Thomas Orchestra," *Chicago Inter Ocean*, 20 April 1913, CSO scrapbooks, MF/4, 1912–17, CSO.

117. Elsa Müller, New York, to Higginson, 25 April 1882, Higginson correspondence, 1882–83 season (3), box 1, BSO; "Frisky Lambs," *Musical Courier* (June 1898), PIO scrapbooks, vol. 2, CLP; "Will Lead the Violins," n.p., n.d., PIO correspondence, vol. 1, CLP.

118. "Suicide by Gas of Symphony Musicians," *Boston Herald*, 8 April 1910 [1909?], BSO scrapbooks, MF Pres/13, BSO; "Mrs. Hess Dies Abroad," ibid., 26 February 1909; "Revenge on Elopers Cost Lenom $2000," *Post*, n.d. [ca. 20 March 1903], BSO scrapbooks, MF Pres/13, BSO;"Henri Merck Mysteriously Leaves City," *Pittsburgh Sun*, 4 February 1910, George Wilson personal scrapbooks, vol. 16, CLP; quotation from Wolfe, "A Short History of the Pittsburgh Orchestra," 399; "Kings, Queens, Princes Decorate Bramsen," *Pittsburgh Leader*, 7 January 1906, PIO scrapbooks, vol. 11, GWC, CLP.

119. William B. Scott and Peter M. Rutkoff, *New York Modern: The Arts and the City* (Baltimore: Johns Hopkins University Press, 1999), 19; Sherman, *Music and Maestros*, 92; photocopy of dictionary entry, Artist Files: Theodore Thomas, POA.

120. Mueller, "St. Louis Symphony Orchestra," 12.

121. Minneapolis Real Estate Board to "Dayton, Ohio," 21 February 1916, MNSO scrapbooks, vol. 41, Winter Tour 1915, UMN.

122. Wister, *Twenty-Five Years of the Philadelphia Orchestra*, 40; Sherman, *Music and Maestros*, 40, 95–96, 97; quotation is from p. 96.

123. "Biography of Frank Damrosch," folder 1, Frank Damrosch Papers, NYPL.

124. Sherman, *Music and Maestros*, 116, 311–15; "Musical Invasion of Eastern Cities Starts Tonight," *Minneapolis Journal*, 8 March 1913, MNSO scrapbooks, vol. 10, Home Season, 1911–12, UMN; MNSO scrapbooks, vol. 38, 13th Home Season, newspaper clippings, UMN.

125. Minutes of the Meetings of The Philadelphia Orchestra Association and the Board of Directors thereof, The Philadelphia Orchestra, POA.

126. Sherman, *Music and Maestros*, 104, 107.

127. "Archer on the Orchestra," *Pittsburgh Leader*, 13 May 1901, PIO scrapbooks, vol. 5, GWC, CLP; M. Howe, *Boston Symphony Orchestra*, 76–77; Schonberg, *Great Pianists*, 26; "Scheel and His Orchestra," *Reading (PA) Herald*, 20 November 1900, PO scrapbooks, POA; Lawton, *Schumann-Heink*, 287; "Had a Slim House," *Dubuque (Iowa) Telegraph*, 27 April 1895, CSO scrapbooks, MF/1, 1894–1904, CSO.

128. L. Thomas, "History of the Cincinnati Symphony Orchestra," 342.

129. Catherine Rodman, Pittsburgh, to James Buchanan, Pittsburgh, 5 November 1907, PIO correspondence, vol. 5, CLP; list of players, n.d. [1907–8 season?], PIO correspondence, vol. 5, CLP; Parsons, Akron, to George Wilson, 21 August 1900, PIO correspondedce, vol. 4, CLP. On the drinking problem, see also David Gerber, " 'The Germans Take Care of Our Celebrations': Middle-Class Americans Appropriate German Ethnic Culture in Buffalo in the 1850s," in *Hard at Play: Leisure in America, 1840–1940*, ed. Kathryn Grover (Amherst, MA: University of Amherst Press, 1992).

CHAPTER FOUR

1. William Foster Apthorp, "Musical Reminiscences of Boston Thirty Years Ago," in Swan, *Music in Boston*, 78.
2. Charles N. Fay, New York, to the Trustees of the Orchestral Association, Chicago, 10 March 1913, trustees, general correspondence, general records, 1/30, CSO.
3. Henry E. Krehbiel, *An Account of the Fourth Musical Festival Held at Cincinnati May 18, 19, 20 & 21, 1880* (Cincinnati: Aldine Printing Worlds, 1880), 8.
4. Armand Mattelart and Ariel Dorfman, *Para leer al pato Donald* (La Habana: Editorial de Ciencias Sociales, 1971) (translated edition: *How To Read Donald Duck: Imperialist Ideology in Disney Comic* [New York: International General, 1975]), 10, 95 (page references are to the translated edition); Arturo Torrecilla, "Cultural Imperialism, Mass Media and Class Struggle: An Interview with Armand Mattelart," *Insurgent Sociologist* 9, no. 4 (Spring 1990): 69–79; Armand Mattelart and Peter Jehle, "Neue Horizonte der Kommunikation: Die Rückkehr zur Kultur," *Argument* 35, no. 5 (September-October 1993): 689–706; Christine Mangala Frost, "30 Rupees for Shakespeare: A Consideration of Imperial Theatre in India," *Modern Drama* 35 (1992): 90–100.
5. Sherman, *Music and Maestros*, 20.
6. John Francis Marion, *Within These Walls: A History of the Academy of Music in Philadelphia* (Philadelphia: Academy of Music, 1984); William G. Bruce, ed., *History of Milwaukee, City and County* (Chicago: S. J. Clarke, 1922), 1: 675–83; L. Thomas, "History of the Cincinnati Symphony Orchestra," 50.
7. M. Howe, *Boston Symphony Orchestra*, 91–107; Ethel Peyser, *The House That Music Built: Carnegie Hall* (New York: Robert M. McBride, 1936); Richard Schickel and Michael Walsh, *Carnegie Hall: The First One Hundred Years* (New York: H. N. Abrams, 1987).
8. Timeline in Weisberg, McIntosh, and McQueen, *Collecting in the Gilded Age*, n.p.
9. Wolfe, "A Short History of the Pittsburgh Orchestra," 6–7.
10. Between 1830 and 1860, European municipalities, including smaller cities, began to organize public concerts. These occasions then grew into a popular site for middle-class citizens who a generation earlier had little if

any access to concert music. These are the years when virtuoso celebrities like Fréderic Chopin and Franz Liszt came into their own, sometimes as popular stars. See Gay, *Schnitzler's Century*, 229.

11. It is important to distinguish between the formal name of an orchestra and the formal name of its governing organization: in Chicago, the symphony is called the Chicago Symphony Orchestra, while its governing body is called the Orchestral Association. This distinction is particularly important in the case of New York: the 1842 symphony was called the New York Philharmonic, while the governing organization was called the New York Philharmonic Society. As a membership organization, the Philharmonic constituted a group of musicians that administered itself. The board consisted of orchestra members who were elected by common vote of all players; business meetings included everybody. Consequently, the organization had a constitution, violations were penalized promptly, and artists were at the same time businessmen. In contrast, the organizing body of the New York Symphony Orchestra, founded several decades later, was named the New York Symphony Society. Minutes of Business Meetings, 25 May 1877, New York Philharmonic Society, NYPA; NYP Annual Report 1857–58, NYPA; Howard Shanet, *Philharmonic: A History of New York's Orchestra* (New York: Doubleday, 1975), 491.

12. NYP Society Minutes of the Business Meetings, 5 May 1874, NYPA.

13. Newspaper clipping from *New Bedford (MA) Standard*, n.d. [March 1882], HHC, MF/1, BL.

14. M. Howe, *Boston Symphony Orchestra*, 17–18.

15. Higginson to Ward Cotton Burton, Deephaven, MN, 18 May 1903, Henry Higginson correspondence, 1903 oversize materials, box 3, BSO.

16. Throughout this text, I refer to the original orchestra as the Chicago Symphony Orchestra, even though the organization changed its name several times. After Theodore Thomas's death in 1905, the trustees voted to rename the orchestra the Theodore Thomas Orchestra. In 1912/13, the trustees were advised to rename the orchestra Chicago Symphony Orchestra before some other group tried to take that title. Programs and ads varied until about 1915, when the name change finally appeared consistently in print.

17. Otis, *Chicago Symphony Orchestra*, 25–27.

18. Sherman, *Music and Maestros*, 49–51.

19. David Schneider, *The San Francisco Symphony: Music, Maestros and Musicians* (Novato, CA: Presidio Press, 1983), 5–6.

20. Menees, *St. Louis Symphony Orchestra*; Mueller, "St. Louis SymphonyOrchestra," 6.

21. Four of the twenty-one original guarantors of conductor Van der Stucken's salary were of Jewish descent. L. Thomas, "Cincinnati Symphony Orchestra," 160–65.

22. Minutes of the Board of Trustees, 9 October 1894, Board of Directors/Trustees, box 1, vol. 1, p. 22, CSO.

23. Robert D. King, "Primary Study for Boston Symphony Orchestra: Personnel and Repertoire," typewritten manuscript (1994), BSO.

24. Treasurer's Report, 20 December 1917, Board of Trustees, The Orchestral Association, minutes, vol. 2, box 1, p. 41, CSO.

25. SLSS minutes, 1897–99, Executive Committee, box 1/1–2, MHS.

26. SLSS minutes, March 1916, Executive Committee, box 1/5, MHS.

27. Wister, *Twenty–Five Years of the Philadephia Orchestra*, 47–61.

28. "Women Take Up Orchestra Work," *Pittsburgh Gazette-Times*, 3 March 1910, George Wilson personal scrapbooks, vol. 16, CLP.

29. Krehbiel, *Philharmonic Society of New York*, 62–63.

30. Memoranda, Ladies Musical Club, (1893) Orchestra Association, 1894–1924, Mss qXL155, CIHS.

31. Over the next few years, the membership rose to fifty women. They held biweekly social and musical meetings, and debated and voted on everything, from the hiring of conductors, soloists, and musicians to the concert fee to be paid, although the conductors' recommendations were typically followed. Records of Proceedings of The Orchestra Association Company, 11 April 1894, CISO; L. Thomas, "History of the Cincinnati Symphony Orchestra," 88–159; Records of Proceedings of The Orchestra Association Company, 1 June 1909, CISO; L. Thomas, "History of the Cincinnati Symphony Orchestra," 357, 369.

32. Financial Statement of The Orchestral Organization Season, 1907–1908, correspondence 1907–10, Edward Chenery Gale Papers, MNHS.

33. Bliss Perry, ed., *Life and Letters of Henry Lee Higginson* (Boston: Atlantic Monthly Press, 1921), 293; M. Howe, *Boston Symphony Orchestra*, 7–14.

34. "To the Patrons of the Chicago Orchestra," n.d. [ca. 1898], CSO Finance Department, General Ledgers, Building Subscriptions, CSO.

35. Minutes of the Board of Trustees, 9 December 1913, Board of Directors/Trustees, box 1, vol. 1, pp. 249–50, CSO.

36. Annual report of the president, 1911–12, SLSS minutes, Executive Committee, box 1/5, MHS. The fund-raising committee in Pittsburgh embarked on a desperate attempt to raise $50,000 in 1910. Falling short of this goal, the orchestra committee of the Art Society decided to suspend the orchestra for one year; the suspension eventually led to dissolution. It was sixteen years before the city managed to form a new orchestra. Similarly, the Cincinnati Symphony Orchestra went through a one-year adjournment filled by several guest orchestras because it was considered too expensive. Wolfe, "A Short History of the Pittsburgh Orchestra," 550–51.

37. L. Thomas, "History of the Cincinnati Symphony Orchestra," 31, 39, 40. See also Mona Mender, *Extraordinary Women in Support of Music* (Lanham, MD: Scarecrow Press, 1997); Kathleen D. McCarthy, *Women's Culture:*

*American Philanthropy and Art, 1830–1930* (Chicago: University of Chicago Press, 1991).

38. L. Thomas, "History of the Cincinnati Symphony Orchestra," 92–100, 119; for background on the ladies, see 107–8.

39. Arthur Meeker, *Prairie Avenue* (New York: Alfred A. Knopf, 1949).

40. Albert Nelson Marquis, *The Book of Chicagoans: A Biographical Dictionary of Leading Living Men of the City of Chicago* (Chicago: A. N. Marquis, 1911), 108, 405, 437, 519; "Bryan Lathrop, Pioneer, Dies Suddenly," *Chicago Herald*, 14 May 1916, PR File, Trustees, CSO.

41. Trustees of the Chicago Orchestra Association, database, CSO.

42. John Glessner Lee, "Introduction to the Glessner Journals,"CHM.

43. Mrs. John Jacob Glessner Journals, 4 March 1893, box 3, CHM.

44. Otis, *Chicago Symphony Orchestra*, 228, 281, 303; Philo A. Otis, *The Hymns You Ought to Know* (Chicago: Clayton F. Summy, 1928).

45. Wolfe, "A Short History of the Pittsburgh Orchestra," 40.

46. Perry, *Life and Letters of Henry Lee Higginson*, 66.

47. Ibid., 37, 45–48, 54, 66–67; quotations are from 105–6, 121–24.

48. Higginson to Muck, 20 and 25 March 1912, HHC, MF BSO/4, BL.

49. Higginson to Charles A. Ellis, London, 3 May 1906, HHC, MF BSO/4, BL.

50. "Bryan Lathrop," *Herald*, 14 May 1916; "Bryan Lathrop Dies," News, 13 May 1916, CSO scrapbooks, MF/4, 1912–17, CSO.

51. Jeffrey N. Hyson, "Urban Jungles: Zoos and American Society" (Ph.D. diss., Cornell University, 1999).

52. L. Thomas, "History of the Cincinnati Symphony Orchestra," 3, 44; Sherman, *Music and Maestros*, 3–116.

53. "Why the Visiting Orchestra Cannot Supplant the Permanent Local Orchestra in Cultural Value," *Musical America* (19 September 1914), MNSO scrapbooks, vol. 34, St. Paul Season, 1914–15, UMN.

54. "Boston Symphony Orchestra," *Musical Courier*, n.d. [February 1887], BSO scrapbooks, M125.5/2, BSO.

55. Minutes of the Board of Trustees, January–February 1905, Board of Directors/Trustees, box 1, vol. 1, p. 121, CSO. New York appears to have been an exception, as a group of wealthy German Americans there even sponsored American Composers' Concerts. Elam Douglas Bomberger, *"A Tidal Wave of Encouragement": American Composers' Concerts during the Gilded Age* (Westport, CT: Praeger, 2002), 32.

56. Guest list for Orchestra Hall Fundraising Dinner, 14 March 1910, trustees, general correspondence, general records, box 1, folder 1/14, CSO.

57. H. Horowitz, *Culture and the City*, 111.

58. "Significant Facts in the History of the Saint Louis Symphony Society," manuscript, St. Louis, 1927, Mary McKittrick Markham Collection, box 3, MHS; L. Thomas, "History of the Cincinnati Symphony Orchestra," 10.

59. I am indebted to Frank Trommler for this point.

60. Ernst Kroeger, "On the Condition of Musical Affairs in St. Louis," *St. Louis Republic*, n.d. [ca. 1902], Ernst Kroeger scrapbooks, 1902–8, MHS. On German Festkultur, see Gerber, "The Germans Take Care of Our Celebrations," 39–60; Heike Bungert, "Feste und das ethnische Gedächtnis: Die Festkultur der DeutschAmerikaner im Spannungsfeld zwischen deutscher und amerikanischer Identität, 1848–1914" (Habilitation thesis, Universität Köln, 2004).

61. SLSS minutes, 23 March 1916, Executive Committee, box 1/5, MHS.

62. J. Horowitz, *Classical Music*, 247.

63. "Fred C. M. Lautz Has Passed Away," newspaper clipping, n.p., n.d., Buffalo, PIO correspondence, vol. 5, CLP.

64. "Joseph W. Drexel Dead," *New York Times*, 26 March 1888, p. 1; *National Cyclopedia of American Biography*, vol. 2 (1921), 366.

65. Higginson to William Gair Rathbone, London, 20 June 1906, HHC, MF BSO/4, BL.

66. Higginson to Ellis, 24 May 1906, HHC, MF BSO/4, BL; Higginson to Milka Ternina, Munich, 18 March 1906, ibid.; Higginson to William Gair Rathbone, London, 20 June 1906, ibid.

67. Bliss, *Life and Letters of Henry Lee Higginson*, 321.

68. Lucien Wulsin, Cincinnati, to Franz Wullner, Kapellmeister, Cologne, 15 May 1894, Wulsin Family Papers, series 1, box 24, folder 1, CIHS.

69. Lucien Wulsin to Otto Floersheim, Berlin, 15 May 1894, Wulsin Family Papers, series 5, box 182, folder 5, p. 365, CIHS.

70. Eventually they settled on Frank Van der Stucken as a compromise, owing to a lack of funds. Born to a Belgian father and a German mother in the German community of Fredericksburg, Texas, as a child Van der Stucken had received his training in Belgium and Leipzig before visiting Franz Liszt in Weimar, where he presented his own works in 1883. Records of Proceedings of The Orchestra Association Company, 15 June–9 October 1894, 9 April 1895, CIHS; Bomberger, *"A Tidal Wave of Encouragement,"* 30.

71. NYP Society Minutes of the Business Meetings, 2 April 1890, NYPA.

72. I am indebted to William Weber for this point. See also William Weber, *The Great Transformation of Musical Taste: Concert Programming from Haydn to Brahms* (New York: Cambridge University Press, 2008). On genteel critics in the late nineteenth century, see Mussulman, *Music in the Cultured Generation*; Grant, *Maestros of the Pen*, esp. pp. 58–132.

73. Leon Botstein, "Listening through Reading: Musical Literacy and the Concert Audience," *Nineteenth-Century Music* 16 (1992): 129–45.

74. "Index," *Dwight's Journal of Music*, vols. 13–14 (1858–59): iv. For a comparison, see "Correspondenzen," *Neue Zeitschrift für Musik* 67 (1871): 4–6.

75. J. Horowitz, *Wagner Nights*, 41, 346; quotation is from p. 43.

76. Finck had studied music at Harvard with John K. Paine. When he graduated in 1876, he immediately borrowed money to go to Bayreuth. Ibid., 330; Grant, *Maestros of the Pen*, 100.

77. "Music Loses a Critic of Commanding Influence," n.p., n.d. [ca. end of March 1923], Wulsin Family Papers, series 1, 24/12, CIHS; Henry E. Krehbiel, *Afro-American Folksongs: A Study in Racial and National Music*, 4th ed. (Portland, ME: Longwood Press, 1976); J. Horowitz, *Wagner Nights*, 4–5; Grant, *Maestros of the Pen*, 80–86.

78. Aldrich, *Concert Life in New York*, ix–x.

79. Felix Borowski, biographical information, accession files, NL; Otis, *Chicago Symphony Orchestra*, 200.

80. "Death Takes Louis C. Elson," *Boston Globe*, 16 February 1920, BSO scrapbooks, M.125.5/12, BSO; Grant, *Maestros of the Pen*, 94–99.

81. "Philip Hale," in Swan, *Music in Boston*, 87; Bomberger, "German Musical Training," 130–33; Grant, *Maestros of the Pen*, 74–80.

82. POA program books, 1902–3, 557; W. J. Henderson, *Richard Wagner: His Life and His Dramas* (New York: G. P. Putnam's Sons, 1901); W. J. Henderson, *What Is Good Music? Suggestions to Persons Desiring to Cultivate a Taste in Musical Art* (New York: C. Scribner's Sons, 1898, 1922); Finck, *My Adventures in the Golden Age of American Music*.

83. Program books of the CSO, CSO; BSO program books, 1904–8, BSO.

84. Lebow, "A Systematic Examination of the *Journal of Music and Art*," 17–63.

85. Dwight, " 'The Concerts of Past Winter,' " 45–47.

86. "What the Leipzig Journal Thinks of Music in America," *Dwight's Journal of Music* 15 (11 June 1859).

87. "Enter Herr Richard Straus," *New York Sun*, 25 February 1904, Philharmonic-Symphony Society of New York Records, reel 10, NYPL.

88. Victor Nilsson, "Fire Hose Ready for Music Bombs," *Minneapolis Journal*, 2 November 1916, MNSO scrapbooks, vol. 45, 14th Home Season, 1916–17, newspaper clippings, UMN.

89. Albert G. Browne, New York, to Higginson, 23 March 1886, HHC, MF/1, BL.

90. When the Romantics went out of vogue, many critics found it difficult to adjust their cultural preferences. J. Horowitz, *Wagner Nights*, 283–94; Grant, *Maestros of the Pen*, 91–94.

91. "Musical Notes," *Journal of Fine Arts* 10 (15 December 1899), PR Anna Millar, CSO.

CHAPTER FIVE

1. G. Schlotterbeck, "Outlook for the Pittsburg Orchestra," *Pittsburgh Post*, 1 November 1903, PIO scrapbooks, vol. 8, GWC, CLP.

2. F. O. A., "Der Dollar und die Kunst," *Der Tag* (Berlin), 10 December 1907, PO scrapbooks, 1907–8, POA; "Many Millions for Music," *Cincinnati Times Star*, 19 June 1913, CISO scrapbooks, vol. 11, CIHS.

3. "Is Called Symphony Hall," *Boston Transcript*, [16 September?] 1900, BSO scrapbooks, M.125.5/6, BSO.

4. Francis A. Wister, "Facts about the Philadelphia Orchestra and other Permanent Orchestras" (Philadelphia: Women's Committee for the Philadelphia Orchestra, May 1905), PIO, vol. 5, CLP; Treasurer's Report, 20 December 1917, Board of Trustees, The Orchestral Association, minutes, vol. 2, box 1, p. 39, CSO.

5. Henry James, *The Bostonians: A Novel* (London: Macmillan, 1886); Edith Wharton, *The Age of Innocence* (New York: D. Appleton and Co., 1920). For New York music life, see Vera Brodsky Lawrence, *Strong on Music: The New York Muscial Scene in the Days of George Templeton Strong, 1836–1875*, 3 vols. (New York: Oxford University Press, 1988–99).

6. "Music Patrons," *Brooklyn Citizen*, 12 October 1895, BSO scrapbooks, MF Pres/5, BSO; "Society Attends Concerts," *Minneapolis Daily News*, 8 October 1910, MNSO scrapbooks, vol. 5, Home, newspaper clippings 1910–11, UMN; Krehbiel, *Philharmonic Society of New York*, 177–83; Patrons of the CSO, Finance Department, General Ledgers, Building Subscriptions, CSO; correspondence, general, 1896, ibid., 1/4; Trustees, correspondence to Mrs. Glessner, ibid., 1/8.

7. Peggy Perkins, "Costly Gowns, Rich Gems and Pretty Women Fill Boxes at Music Festival," *Denver Daily News*, 20 April 1910, MNSO scrapbooks, vol. 1, Spring Tours, newspaper clippings, 1910–11, UMN.

8. Sherman, *Music and Maestros*, 16; minutes, 29 October 1912, Executive Committee, box 1/5, SLSS, MHS; "Average attendance with prices paid season 1900–1901," Manager's Files, F. Wessels, 1/21, Rosenthal Archives, CSO; "A Complete Success," *Boston Herald*, 21 October 1900, BSO scrapbooks, M.125.5/6, BSO.

9. SLSS minutes, 29 October 1912, Executive Committee, box 1/5, MHS; "Estimated Income and Expenses," Manager's Files, F. Wessels, 1/28, CSO; "Average attendance with prices paid season 1900–1901," Manager's Files, F. Wessels, 1/21, CSO; "Average attendance with prices paid season 1900–1901," Manager's Files, F. Wessels, 1/21, CSO; Wolfe, "A Short History of the Pittsburgh Orchestra," 63, 74.

10. I am indebted to Joseph Kett for this point.

11. Letters to Oberhoffer in EOP, folder 1, MNHS; annual report 1911–12, SLSS minutes, box 1/5, MHS.

12. "Oh! So Delightful," *Boston Daily Globe*, 15 October 1892, BSO scrapbooks, MF Pres/4, BSO.

13. "Dress Suits among Gallery Gods, Patches in Orchestra Seats at Symphony," n.p., 27 August 1922, MNSO scrapbooks, vol. 26, Spring Tour Reviews, 1912–13, newspaper clippings, UMN.

14. June Sawyers, "Way We Were," n.p., n.d., PR, conductors: Thomas, articles, books, CSO.

15. Rev. C. M. Southgate, Dedham, MA, to Higginson, 17 March 1882, HHC, MF/1, BL; letter to the editor, 4 January 1884, reprinted in *Boston Herald*, n.d., BSO scrapbooks, M.125.5/1, BSO.

16. Kathy Peiss, *Cheap Amusements: Working Women and Leisure in Turn-of-the-Century New York* (Philadelphia: Temple University Press, 1986), 144–46.

17. Hart, *Orpheus in the New World*, 29; "Musical Comments and Current Events," *Pittsburgh Post*, 26 November 1911, MNSO scrapbooks, vol. 6, Tours 1910-11-12, newspaper clippings, UMN; "Children to Hear Symphony Concert," *Minneapolis Journal*, 27 September 1911, MNSO scrapbooks, vol. 7, Home Season, 1911–12, newspaper clippings, UMN; "Last Children's Concert History," *Minneapolis Journal*, 2 March 1912, MNSO scrapbooks, vol. 10, Home Season, 1911–12, UMN; "Police Call for Symphony Crowd," 11 February 1913, MNSO scrapbooks, vol. 13, Home Season, 1912–15, UMN; "More Than 2,000 Students Will Attend Festival," n.p., n.d., MNSO scrapbooks, vol. 35, Spring Tour 1915, programs, reviews, UMN.

18. "Free Musical Concerts," *New York Evening Post*, 17 February 1910, NYP press clippings, 1909–10, Gustav Mahler/Evening Post, NYPA.

19. Wister, *Twenty-Five Years of the Philadelphia Orchestra*, 143–60; Board of the Musical Fund Society, to "Madam," 1 October 1895, Edward Garret McCollin Papers, UPA.

20. Rudolph Ganz, Birmingham, AL, to his wife, Mary, 10 December 1911, Ganz Papers, box 8/5/ 10, NL.

21. Oswald Harrison Villard, New York, to Higginson, Boston, 12 January 1914, HHC, MF/2, BL.

22. NYP Annual Report, 1855–56, NYP.

23. "Their Vigil Ended," *Pittsburgh Leader*, 20 October 1898, PIO scrapbooks, vol. 3, GWC, CLP; "Lined Up for a Long Wait Are Boys Who Are Holding Places for Orchestra Buyers," *Pittsburg Dispatch*, 23 October 1901, PIO scrapbooks, vol. 6, GWC, CLP.

24. "We Aint No Weak'ners, See!," n.p., n.d. [Fall 1889], BSO scrapbooks, M.125.5/3, BSO; "Bound to Be the First in Line," n.p., n.d., ibid.

25. Goodwin, *Sketches and Impressions*, 158; Krehbiel, *Philharmonic Society of New York*, 29.

26. Oscar Sonneck, quoted in Wister, *Twenty-Five Years of the Philadelphia Orchestra*, 152.

27. "Theaters and Concerts," n.p., n.d. [ca. 1882], BSO scrapbooks, M.125.5/1, BSO.

28. "Resenting an Insult to His Wife," *New York Sun*, n.d. [ca. February 1882], BSO scrapbooks, M.125.5/1, BSO.

29. Rudolph Ganz, San Francisco, to his wife, Mary, 7 May 1904, Ganz Papers, box 5/2/10, NL.

30. Wm. Clayton, Ann Arbor, to Mr. Wilson, 12 November 1900, PIO correspondence, vol. 3, CLP.

31. O. W. Norton, to Frances Glessner, n.d. [ca. January 1896], Glessner Journals, box 4,CHM.

32. "Symphony Audiences," n.p. [*Boston Advertiser?*], 22 October 1906, BSO scrapbooks, M.125.5/8, BSO.

33. For more on the cult of manliness and character building, see Gail Bedermann, *Manliness and Civilization: A Cultural History of Gender and Race in the United States, 1880–1917* (Chicago: University of Chicago Press, 1995); David I. Macleod, *Building Character in the American Boy: The Boy Scouts, the YMCA, and Their Forerunners, 1870–1920* (Madison: University of Wisconsin Press, 1983); Kara Anne Gardner, "Living by the Ladies' Smiles: The Feminization of American Music and the Modernist Reaction" (Ph.D. diss., Stanford University, 1999); Richard Leppert, *Music and Image: Domesticity, Ideology and Socio-Cultural Formation in Eighteenth-Century England* (Cambridge: Cambridge University Press, 1988), 11–27, 107–46.

34. I am indebted to William Weber for this information. Weber, *Music and the Middle Class.*

35. "Thousand Women Unable to Hear Symphony Rehearsal," *Boston Globe,* 14 October 1907, BSO scrapbooks, M.125.5/8, BSO; Louis Madison, "At the 'Symphony Rehearsal,'" *Boston Gazette,* n.d. [ca. 14/15 February 1886], BSO scrapbooks, M.125.5/2, BSO.

36. "The Rehearsal Girl," *Boston Globe,* 20 October 1900, BSO scrapbooks, M.125.5/6, BSO; "The Symphony Rush," *Boston Transcript,* 26 October 1896, BSO scrapbooks, M.125.5/5, BSO.

37. Musikverein (ed.), *Der Musikverein von Milwaukee, 1850–1900: Eine Chronik* (Milwaukee: Herold, 1900), 8–10.

38. "The Boston Girl," *Boston Daily Evening Traveller,* 17 November 1884, BSO scrapbooks, M.125.5/1, BSO.

39. Arthur Warren, "Celebrities Here and There," *Boston Home Journal,* n.d. [ca. 17 October 1886], M.125.5/2, BSO scrapbooks, BSO; Fanny Raymond Ritter, "Berlioz, Liszt, Wagner," *Dwight's Journal of Music* 5 (February 1876): 1; Apollo, "Musical Matters at the Hub," n.p., n.d. [January 1881], M.125.5/1, BSO scrapbooks, BSO; "Stokovski to Be Disappointment to Matinee Idol-Worshipping Girls," *Cincinnati Post,* 31 May 1909, CISO scrapbooks, vol. 5, CIHS.

40. "Newest Hair, Music and Mesmerig [*sic*] Idol—Paderewski Has Fallen!" n. p., n.d. [ca. 8 November 1898], BSO scrapbooks, M.125.5, reel 5, BSO.

41. "Soloist Likes American Girls: So, Girls, There's a Chance," *Cincinnati Post,* 12 March 1904, CISO scrapbooks, vol. 2, CIHS.

42. Rudolph Ganz to his wife, Mary, 18 December 1907, Ganz Papers, box 7/4/4, NL.

43. J. Horowitz, *Wagner Nights,* 11–17, 217, 221, 226.

44. "Arthur Nikisch," n.p., n.d. [ca. 23 April 1893], BSO scrapbooks, M.125.5/4, BSO.

45. R. Crawford, *America's Musical Life,* 139–55, 225–71. Publishers and manufacturers included national and foreign enterprises in Frankfurt am Main, Leipzig, Gotha, and Vienna.

46. Roell, *The Piano in America*, 8, 108, 186, 188; Thorstein Veblen, *The Theory of the Leisure Class* (New York: Macmillan, 1899, 1945).

47. Roell, *The Piano in America*, 88, 216, 293.

48. "Die Musik der Metropole," *New York Evening Staatszeitung*, 25 March 1911, BSO scrapbooks, MF Pres/14, BSO.

49. John K. Paine, ed., *Famous Composers and Their Works* (Boston: J. B. Millet, 1891); John W. Moore, *Complete Encyclopaedia of Music, Elementary, Technical, Historical, Biographical, Vocal, and Instrumental* (Boston: John P. Jewett & Co., 1854).

50. "Our Girls and Other Girls," reprinted in the *Monthly Musical Record* 9 (1 February 1897): 24–25.

51. Van Cleve, "The Dignity of Music," 11–12.

52. Newman, "Good Music for a Free People," 273–76; Preston, *Opera on the Road*, 307, 309, 316.

53. I am indebted to Marianne Betz for this point.

54. Hart, *Orpheus in the New World*, 59.

55. W. Weber, "The History of Musical Canon," in *Rethinking Music*, ed. Nicholas Cook and Mark Everist (Oxford: Oxford University Press, 1999), 349, 352.

56. Schonberg, *Lives of the Great Composers*, 217; Werner Oehlmann, *Das Berliner Philharmonische Orchester, 1901–1985*, 2nd ed. (Kassel: Bärenreiter, 1975), 14–16.

57. J. Horowitz, *Wagner Nights*, 56.

58. "Performers in Thomas Orchestra 'Living Music' Benefit as They Will Appear on Stage," *Chicago Record-Herald*, 6 January 1908, CSO scrapbooks, MF/2, 1904–8, CSO.

59. "Philadelphia Orchestra to Give Beethoven Cycle," *Philadelphia North American*, 15 March 1903, PO scrapbooks, 1902–3, POA; J. Horowitz, *Wagner Nights*, 304.

60. J. Horowitz, *Wagner Nights*, 30, 76, 96, 123, 125–26, 153–54, 156, 241, 245. On the seven-year run of German opera at the Met, see Irving Kolodin, *The Metropolitan Opera, 1883–1966: A Candid History*, 4th ed. (New York: A. A. Knopf, 1966), 87–105.

61. King, "Primary Study for Boston Symphony Orchestra."

62. Sherman, *Music and Maestros*, 71.

63. James Huneker, *The Philharmonic Society of New York and Its Seventy-fifth Anniversary: A Retrospect* (New York, 1917).

64. "Symphonic Season Gloriously Opened," *Minneapolis Journal*, 25 October 1913, MNSO scrapbooks, vol. 21, 11th Home Season, 1913–14, newspaper clippings, UMN.

65. PO program book, 5 and 7 March 1903–4, pp. 233–34, POA; "The Symphony Concert," n.p., n.d. [February 1896], BSO scrapbooks, M.125.5/5, BSO; C. L. Capen, "Symphony Concert," n.p., n.d. [February 1896], ibid.

66. John Ardoin, ed., *The Philadelphia Orchestra: A Century of Music* (Philadelhia: Temple University Press, 1999), 45.

67. The meaning of the term *modern music*, of course, depended on the time. In 1840, Beethoven was novel, as were Mendelssohn, Schubert, and Schumann. In 1870, all three had entered the canon; Wagner, Brahms, and Liszt were new. In 1910, all six constituted part of the canon, while Bartok, Strauss, and Reger were considered modern.

68. In Germany, Joseph Gungl's Privatorchester was one of the first to present such concerts in Berlin; later on, Gungl took his band to New York, Washington, DC, and Baltimore. In Europe, the programs of serious orchestras typically featured two to three symphonies performed in the formal setting of a concert hall. Popular orchestras, in contrast, played in more informal settings, such as big public beer halls. At Benjamin Bilse's concerts in Berlin in the 1880s, families would group around tables and have their supper; women would often knit, men would drink beer, and the hall where the event took place would be turned into "a sort of matrimonial bureau," with young men and women wooing and being wooed over plates loaded with roast and gravy. "Pops," *Journal*, 11 May 1897, BSO scrapbooks, MF Pres/6, BSO.

69. Menees, *St. Louis Symphony Orchestra*; Sherman, *Music and Maestros*, 3–4.

70. D. Schneider, *The San Francisco Symphony*, 5–6.

71. In Philadelphia, Fritz Scheel refused to play waltzes during his regular concerts, while Pittsburgh's Frederic Archer lamented that at pop concerts audiences "drink pop, eat ice cream and smoke stogies while the band renders waltz tunes, 'The Old Folks at Home,' and the like." Minneapolis's Oberhoffer flatly declared all such "musical comedy" simply as "punk." Ardoin, *Philadelphia Orchestra*, 31; Wister, *Twenty-Five Years of the Philadelphia Orchestra*, 34; "Archer on the Orchestra," *Pittsburgh Leader*, 13 May 1901, PIO scrapbooks, vol. 5, GWC, CLP; Margaret Tobin, "Musical Comedy Is 'Punk' in Eyes of Eml Oberhoffer," *South Bend (IN) Times*, 10 May 1913, MNSO scrapbooks, vol. 26, Spring Tour Reviews 1912–13, UMN.

72. In 1905, some 1,670 Philadelphians cast their ballots to select a program: the leading symphonies were Tchaikovsky's *Pathétique* (606 votes), Strauss's *Sinfonia Domestica* (330) and Dvorak's *From the New World* (132). The list of overtures was headed by Wagner's *Tannhäuser* (405), Beethoven's *Leonore* (292), and Goldmark's *Sakuntula* (261). Among the items on the miscellaneous list, Wagner's "Good Friday Spell" from *Parsifal* won (290) before Von Weber's *Invitation to the Dance* (277) and Galzounow's *Scènes de Ballet* (258). "Patrons of the Philadlephia Orchestra Will Choose by Vote the Program for the Final Concert," *Philadelphia North American*, 16 March 1902, PO scrapbooks, 1901–2, POA; "Vote for Favorite Orchestra Music," *Philadelphia North American*, 15 March 1905, PO scrapbooks, 1904–5, POA.

73. Gay, *Schnitzler's Century*, 238–39; Grant, *Maestros of the Pen*, 79.

74. For the rare exception among the clientele of the Metropolitan Opera, see J. Horowitz, *Wagner Nights*, 325–36.

75. NYP Board of Directors/Executive Committee minutes, 9 September 1865, 16 Feb. 1872, 5 October 1875, 20 December 1899, 1903–12 (no date noted), NYPA.

CHAPTER SIX

1. Louis Elson, quoted in M. Howe, *Boston Symphony Orchestra*, 54, 82.
2. Robert Schmalz, "Personalities, Politics, and Prophecy: Frederic Archer and the Birth of the Pittsburgh Symphony Orchestra," *American Music* 5 (Fall 1967): 311–12, 313.
3. Alan Howard Levy, "The Search for Identity in American Music, 1890–1920," *American Music* 2 (Summer 1984): 74.
4. The movement rose in the 1880s, climaxed around 1890, and then subsided quickly. Bomberger, *"A Tidal Wave of Encouragement,"* xiii.
5. But during their lifetimes, the Yankee composers led an existence artistically and economically isolated from the American mainstream; missing recognition by the public at large, most of them fell back on visions of immortality in the distant future. Macdonald Smith Moore, *Yankee Blues: Musical Culture and American Identity* (Bloomington: Indiana University Press, 1985), 1–63; Levy, *Musical Nationalism*, 105.
6. J. Horowitz, *Wagner Nights*, 167.
7. "A Biographical Sketch of Frank Damrosch Appearing in the London Musical Times," 1 December 1904, folder 40, Frank Damrosch Papers, NYPL; quotation is from "Biography of Frank Damrosch," folder 1, ibid.
8. Eric J. Hobsbawm, *Nations and Nationalism since 1780: Programme, Myth, Reality*, 2nd ed. (Cambridge: Cambridge University Press, 1992).
9. Ernest Gellner, *Nations and Nationalism* (Ithaca, NY: Cornell University Press, 1983).
10. Jörg Echternkamp, *Der Aufstieg des deutschen Nationalismus, 1770–1840* (Frankfurt A.M.: Campus, 1998); Jörg Echternkamp and Sven Oliver Müller, eds., *Die Politik der Nation: Deutscher Nationalismus in Krieg und Krisen, 1760–1960* (Munich: Oldenbourg, 2002); Svenja Goltermann, *Körper der Nation: Habitusformierung und die Politik des Turnens 1860–1890* (Göttingen: Vandenhoeck & Ruprecht, 1998); Manfred Hettling and Paul Nolte, eds., *Nation und Gesellschaft in Deutschland: Historische Essays* (Munich: C. H. Beck, 1996); Confino, *The Nation as a Local Metaphor*; Celia Applegate, *A Nation of Provincials: The German Idea of* Heimat (Berkeley and Los Angeles: University of California Press, 1990).
11. Marsha Siefert, "Remastering the Past: Musical Heritage, Sound Recording and the Nation in Hungary and Russia," in *National Heritage—National Canon*, Proceedings of the Focus Group "Humanities in Historical and Comparative Perspective: Roots and Margins of the European Tradition and Reactions to It," Collegium Budapest, 1999/2000, 247–76.

12. "English Musical Art," *Monthly Musical Record* 22 (1 October 1892): 262; Otto Viktor Maeckel, "Musik und Künstler des feindlichen Ausländers," *Neue Zeitschrift für Musik* 81 (12 November 1914): 533–34. Quotation is from Maud Matras, "Nationality and Music," *Monthly Musical Record* 37 (1 June 1907): 126–27.

13. "An Tonsetzer aller Nationalitäten," *Neue Zeitschrift für Musik* 78 (14 September 1911): 514–16.

14. Ottmar Rutz, *Sprache, Gesang und Körperhaltung: Handbuch zur Typenlehre* (Munich: O. Beck, 1911).

15. M. Howe, *Boston Symphony Orchestra*, 120.

16. "Russian Program to Be Played by Orchestra This Afternoon," *Minneapolis Tribune*, 18 December 1910, MNSO scrapbooks, vol. 5, Home, newspaper clippings, 1910–11, UMN.

17. Jean Moos, "The Origin and Growth of National Music," *Music* 1 (April 1892): 531–43.

18. "Concert and Lyceum," n.p., n.d. [ca. 9/10 February 1890], BSO scrapbooks, M.125.5/3, BSO; "Nationalism Feature of Music Played by Symphony at Its Twelfth Rehearsal," *Boston Monitor*, 25 January 1915, BSO scrapbooks, MF Pres/16, BSO.

19. "About Music," *Journal*, 2 May 1897, BSO scrapbooks, M.125.5/5, BSO; review of season, *Chicago Tribune*, 21 April 1912, quoted in Berglund, "A Study of the Life and Work of Frederick Stock," 238.

20. Newspaper clipping, n.p., n.d. [January 1901], BSO scrapbooks, M.125.5/6, BSO; Dwight's valedictory in the final issue of *Journal of Music* (September 1881), quoted in Bliss, *Life and Letters of Henry Lee Higginson*, 392.

21. Letters to the editors, March 16–27, *Boston Transcript*, n.d., BSO scrapbooks, M.125.5/8, BSO.

22. Louis C. Elson, "Musical Matters," *Boston Advertiser*, 5 February 1906, 7 January 1901, BSO scrapbooks, M.125.5/6, BSO.

23. M. Howe, *Boston Symphony Orchestra*, 72–73.

24. "Music," *Boston Gazette*, n.d. [September 1895], BSO scrapbooks, M.125.5/5, BSO; Stanford, quoted in "The Orchestra," n.p., n.d., MNSO scrapbooks, vol. 136, Archives, 1920 clippings, folder symphony orchestras, newspaper clippings, UMN. The New York critic James Huneker was probably the first of the great Gilded Age critics to hail the music of the European "moderns." Grant, *Maestros of the Pen*, 119–24.

25. R. Crawford, *America's Musical Life*, 127–31.

26. Betty E. Chmaj, "Fry versus Dwight: American Music's Debate over Nationality." *American Music* 3 (Spring 1985): 63–64.

27. Defenders of a national culture could be found in the arena of public politics as well. In the 1840s and 1850s, various secret nativist societies reacted with fierce hostility to the great wave of Irish and German immigrants. The most powerful of these was the Order of the Star-Spangled Banner (1850),

whose members acquired the moniker Know-Nothings because they an-swered all questions about their society with "I know nothing." Emerging between 1853 and 1856 as a major political force, the American Party, the Know-Nothings are best remembered for opposition to officeholding by immigrants (and Catholics) and for their desire to make naturalization more difficult; but they also crusaded against the overwhelming prepon-derance of German musicians. Promoters of Know-Nothingism sharply criticized the number of German musicians in the initial makeup of the New York Philharmonic Society, even though by then the German staff accounted for less than 50 percent of the group. Henry Krehbiel, "The National Anthem at Orchestral Concerts," *New York Tribune*, 4 November 1917, NYSS scrapbooks, vol. 5, 1915–18, CH.

28. Giustizia, New York, letter to the editor, 20 September 1852, reprinted in "Germano-Phobia," *Dwight's Journal of Music* 2 (9 October 1852): 4–5; "Musi-cal Talent of the Americans," *Dwight's Journal of Music* 7 (16 June 1855).

29. Henry Fry, quoted in Chmaj, "Fry versus Dwight," 65, 72.

30. Henry Fry, letter to the editor, reprinted in *Dwight's Journal of Music* 3 (28 January 1854): 139–40.

31. Correspondence between Henry Fry and Richard Willis of the *New York Musical World and Times*, in *Dwight's Journal of Music* 3 (26 January 1854): 139–40; (4 February 1854): 146–47; (8 February 1854): 151; (25 February 1854): 163–64; (4 March 1845): 171–73.

32. Newspaper clipping, n.p., n.d. [ca. November 1911], BSO scrapbooks, M.125.5/9, BSO.

33. Bomberger, "German Musical Training," 82–201, 315–504; "Victor Her-bert," *Hamilton's Monthly*, Pittsburgh, October 1900, PIO scrapbooks, vol. 5, GWC, CLP; "Concertmeister Is Here," *Pittsburgh Post*, 20 September 1897, PIO scrapbooks, vol. 2, GWC, CLP; newspaper clipping, no title, n.p. [*Pittsburg Dispatch?*], 20 September 1897, ibid.; Wolfe, "A Short History of the Pittsburgh Orchestra," 121.

34. H. T. P., "Mr. Chadwick as a True Composer," transcript, Boston, 10 Febru-ary 1908, BSO scrapbooks, MF M.125.5/8, BSO.

35. Ibid.

36. "Mr. Gericke's Mistake," n.p., n.d., BSO scrapbooks, M.125.5/2, BSO; Dis-senter, Boston, letter to the editor of *Musical Courier*, 15 November 1903, BSO scrapbooks, M.125.5/7, BSO.

37. "A German Conductor Who Speaks English," *New York Morning Telegraph*, n.d., BSO scrapbooks, MF Pres/13, BSO; Warren Davenport, "Miss Lang's Overture," n.d. [April 1893], BSO scrapbooks, M.125.5/4, BSO.

38. Berglund, "A Study of the Life and Work of Frederick Stock," 216. Stock scheduled his first all-American program in 1912, but the orchestra had already presented an all-American program in 1892, with works by Paine, Chadwick, Gleason, and Shelley. "A Plea for an American Composer," *Chi-*

*cago Evening Post*, 17 December 1907, quoted in ibid., 233; Herbert J. Gans, *Popular Culture and High Culture: An Analysis and Evaluation of Taste*, rev. ed. (New York : Basic Books, 1999).

39. "Future American Music," n.p., n.d., MNSO scrapbooks, vol. 136, 1920s clippings, American music, UMN; Stokowski to Judson, 8 July 1918, Administrative Files, series 1—Leopold Stokowski correspondence, POA; Judson to Stokowski, Seal Harbor, 18 July 1918, ibid.

40. Newspaper clipping, n.p. [San Francisco], 16 August 1903, PO Conductors, Biographical Files: Fritz Scheel, POA; John V. Sears, "Art, Painting, Music, the Drama in Today's News," *Evening Telegraph* [Philadelphia?], 11 July 1904, PO scrapbooks, 1904-5, POA.

41. Schmalz, "Personalities, Politics, and Prophecy," 311-12, 313.

42. Subscriber, Boston, letter to the editor of the *Musical Courier*, 16 January 1903, BSO scrapbooks, M.125.5/7, BSO.

43. "The Men Who Play," *Boston Transcript*, 16 March 1907, BSO scrapbooks, M.125.5/8, BSO.

44. Blumenberg, "By the Editor," *Musical Courier*, 15 December 1909, 22, NYP press excerpts, 1909-10, Gustav Mahler/*Musical Courier*, NYPA.

45. Frederic W. Root, "A Program of American Compositions," *Music* 2 (May 1892): 4-5.

46. Herbert J. Krum, "Americanism Musically," *Music* 6 (September 1894): 547.

47. Hackett, "Music in the Language of the People," 125-33.

48. Krehbiel, Hamburg, to Lucien Wulsin, 2 September 1886, Wulsin Family Papers, series 1, 24/11, CIHS.

49. Editorial quotation from Doering, "'A Salesman of Fine Music,'" 82-83; "American Music Is Best, Says Freund," *Minneapolis Journal*, 22 October 1915, MNSO scrapbooks, vol. 38, Home Season, 1915-16, UMN.

50. "America Outranks Europe in Music," *Philadelphia Telegraph*, 19 August 1911, PO scrapbooks, 1911-12, POA.

51. Eric Delamarter, "British Symphonic Music," *Chicago Inter Ocean*, 10 January 1914, CSO scrapbooks, MF/4, 1912-17, CSO.

52. H. F. P., "Discover Wealth of Folk Music among Primitive Mountain People in South," *Musical America* (9 September 1916), MNSO scrapbooks, vol. 136, 1920 clippings, American music, UMN.

53. *Vogue*, 1 May 1917; http://pike.services.brown.edu/bamco/bamco .php?eadid-mswyman (accessed 4 February 2009).

54. Jean Moos, "The Origin and Growth of National Music," *Music* 2 (April 1892): 531.

55. Homer Moore, "How Can American Music Be Developed," *Music* 1 (February 1891): 331-32.

56. Offenbach, *Orpheus in America*, 70-71.

57. Henry Louis Reginald de Koven, quoted in "Leading Musicians in New Movement," *Brooklyn (NY) Standard Union*, 22 July 1917, FBZ, AJA.

58. "Directors," HHC, MF/1, BL; Emanuel Rubin, "Jeannette Meyers Thurber and the National Conservatory of Music," *American Music* 8, no. 3 (Autumn 1990): 294–325.

59. Ludmila Bradová, "Antonin Dvorák, 1841–1904," in *Abroad in America: Visitors to the New Nation, 1776–1914*, ed. Marc Pachter and Frances Wein (Reading, MA: Addison-Wesley Publishing Co., 1976), 229. See also John Clapham, "Dvorák on the American Scene," *Nineteenth-Century Music* 5 (Summer 1981): 16–23.

60. Bradová, "Antonin Dvorák," 228–37; quotation from Philip Hale, "About Music: The Hunting Expedition of Antonin Dvorak," n.p., n.d. [ca. January 1894], BSO scrapbooks, M.125.5/4, BSO. Dvorak's idea to build American music on African-American songs was not new. Twenty years earlier, the Fisk Jubilee Singers, a group of about a dozen African-American students from Fisk University, a school for former slaves, had toured the United States and Europe to raise funds for their university. Their repertory consisted largely of spirituals, which they introduced as one of the great American music forms. Later on, celebrated white singers such as Mme. Schumann-Heink included several African-American songs in their repertory. "History of the American Negro as Expressed in His Music," *Musical Leader*, 30 September 1930, MNSO scrapbooks, vol. 136, 1920 clippings, American music, UMN; Andrew Ward, *Dark Midnight When I Rise: The Story of the Jubilee Singers Who Introduced the World to the Music of Black America* (New York: Farrar, Straus & Giroux, 2000).

61. Levy, "Search for Identity in American Music," 77.

62. "Music of the Week," *Chicago Times*, 28 October 1894, CSO scrapbooks, MF/1, 1894–1904, CSO.

63. Philip Hale, "About Music: The Hunting Expedition of Antonin Dvorak," n.p., n.d. [ca. January 1894], BSO scrapbooks, M.125.5/4, BSO.

64. Glessner Journals, 4 November 1894, box 3,CHM; H. T. P., "Mr. Chadwick As a True American Composer," *Boston Transcript*, 10 February 1908, BSO scrapbooks, M.125.5/8, BSO; Huneker quotation is from Philip Hale, "About Music: The Hunting Expedition of Antonin Dvorak," n.p., n.d. [ca. January 1894], BSO scrapbooks, M.125.5/4, BSO; "Music," *Pittsburg Dispatch*, 31 March 1895, CSO scrapbooks, MF/1, 1894–1904, CSO. The only thing most everybody seemed to agree on was a common dismissal of African-American influences on Dvorak's famous symphony, even though the composer had explicitly favored these harmonies. "Negro airs," wrote Philip Hale, "tint slightly two or three passages of the New World Symphony without injuring its Czech character." Added Henry T. Finck from New York: "Nothing could be more ridiculous than the attempts that have been made to find anything black or red in the glorious soulful melody which opens the [largo] movement. . . . Nothing could be more white. . . . Only a genius could have written it." Levy, "Search for Identity in American Music," 73.

65. John Tibbett, "The Missing Title Page: Dvorak and the American National Song," in *Music and Culture in America, 1861–1918*, ed. Michael Saffle (New York: Garland Publishing, 1998), 343–65; quotation is from p. 352.

66. Charles E. Rose, "The American Federation of Musicians and Its Effect on Black Musicians in St. Louis in the Twentieth Century" (B.A. thesis, University of Missouri–Columbia, 1978), 8–9.

67. Cincinnati Musicians' Protective Association no. 1 to Mrs. C. R. Holmes, CIO Association, March 1907, Wulsin Family Papers, series 1, box 24/3, CIHS.

68. M. Howe, *Boston Symphony Orchestra*, 60–61.

69. Newspaper clippings, *Press*, 28 July 1907, PIO scrapbooks, vol. 13, GWC, CLP.

70. Fink, "French Art in the United States," 92.

71. Fink, *American Art at the Nineteenth Century Paris Salons*, 131–33.

72. "Music," *Boston Home Journal*, n.d. [1885–89], BSO scrapbooks, M.125.5/2, BSO.

73. J. G. Carlisle to Alexander Bremer. President, Musical Mutual Protective Union, New York, 29 March 1893, HHC, MF/1, BL.

74. Otis, *Chicago Symphony Orchestra*, 244.

75. "The Philadelphia Orchestra," n.p., 25 April 1902, Labor General, PO Labor Relations, POA.

76. "Closed Shop Rules For Leader Pohlig," *Philadelphia Public Ledger*, 18 October 1907, POA scrapbooks, 1907–8, POA.

77. Wolfe, "A Short History of the Pittsburgh Orchestra," 99–101; "Imported Artists Barred by Union," *Pittsburg Dispatch*, 12 October 1904, PIO scrapbooks, vol. 9, GWC, CLP; Schmalz, "Paur and the Pittsburgh," 140–42.

78. L. Thomas, "History of the Cincinnati Symphony Orchestra," 79, 138, 142.

79. Ibid., 178–90, 258–87.

80. Charles Norman Fay, Cambridge, "Orchestra and Union," n.p., n.d. [ca. 3 April 1920], BSO scrapbooks, M.125.5/12, BSO; Fay to Higginson, 22 June 1905, MF BSO/2, HHC, BL.

81. M. Howe, *Boston Symphony Orchestra*, 90; "The Nikisch Matter," *American Musician*, 29 September 1889, BSO scrapbooks, M.125.5/3, BSO.

82. J. G. Carlisle, Treasury Department, to Sherman Hoar, Washington, 5 April 1893, HHC, MF/1, BSO, BL.

83. Treasury Department to Higginson, 29 May and 2 June 1900, Higginson correspondence, MF/2, BSO, BL.

84. Gienow-Hecht, "Shame on US?" 466–79; D. H. Lawrence, *Studies in Classic American Literature* (orig. pub. Thomas Seltzer, 1923; reprint, New York: Viking Press, 1950), 9–21; Adolf Halfeld, *Amerika und der Amerikanismus: Kritische Betrachtungen eines Deutschen und Europäers* (Jena: E. Diederichs, 1927); Mary Nolan, *Visions of Modernity: American Business and the Modernization of Germany* (New York: Oxford University Press, 1994), 26, 113–14; Frank Costigliola, *Awkward Dominion: American Political, Economic, and*

*Cultural Relations with Europe, 1919–1933* (orig. pub. 1984; reprint, Ithaca, NY: Cornell University Press, 1987), 19ff., 167–83, 264ff.; Alexander Schmidt, *Reisen in die Moderne: Der Amerika-Diskurs des deutschen Bürgertums vor dem Ersten Weltkrieg im europäischen Vergleich* (Berlin: Akademie Verlag, 1997), 163–69.

## CHAPTER SEVEN

1. Lawton, *Schumann-Heink*, 264–65.
2. Trommler, "Inventing the Enemy," 115–16; Elliot Shore, "The Kultur Club," in Schröder, *Confrontation and Cooperation*, 127–33.
3. Gayle Turk, "The Case of Dr. Karl Muck: Anti-German Hysterian and Enemy Alien Internment during World War I" (undergraduate thesis, Harvard University, 1994), 23, 24; Charles Elllis, Munich, to Higginson, 9 August 1914, HHC, MF BSO/3, BL; Higginson to Otto Braunfels, Frankfurt/M., ibid.; Charles Ellis, Rotterdam, to Higginson, HHC, 12-15; 26-8-191+, BL.
4. "How Great War Hits Famous Violinists," *Boston Sunday Post*, 6 December 1914, BSO scrapbooks, MF Pres/16, BSO; "Violinist Kreisler Tells of His Experiences in the War How He Killed a Cossack," *Evening Record*, 24 November 1914, ibid.
5. "Musicians of World Fame Ruined by War," *Minneapolis Journal*, 30 September 1914, MNSO scrapbooks, vol. 29, 12th Home Season, 1914–15, UMN.
6. "Thibaud Found That Trench Life Had Not Interfered with Talent," *Pioneer Press*, 19 November 1916, MNSO scrapbooks, vol. 47, St. Paul Concerts, 1916–18, UMN. For a general survey on the impact of the war, see John Keegan, *The First World War* (New York: A. Knopf, 1999); Walter Laqueur and George L. Mosse, eds., *1914: The Coming of the First World War* (New York: Harper & Row, 1966); Paul Fussell, *The Great War and Modern Memory* (New York: Oxford University Press, 1975); Jay M. Winter, *Sites of Memory, Sites of Mourning: The Great War in European Cultural History* (Cambridge: Cambridge University Press, 1995); Samuel Lynn Hynes, *A War Imagined: The First World War and English Culture* (New York: Atheneum, 1991; Maxwell Macmillan International, 1990); John Frederick Macdonald, *Two Towns—One City: Paris—London* (New York: Dodd, Mead and Company, n.d. [1918?]).
7. "Daughter of Opera Singer for Germany," *Duluth Morning Tribune*, 18 November 1915, MNSO scrapbooks, vol. 38, 13th Home Season, newspaper clippings, UMN.
8. "European Musical Life Paralyzed by War," *Musical America* (8 August 1914), Fritz Kreisler Collection, 17/17, Library of congress, Washington, DC.
9. E. W. Sloenm, Brooklyn, to Higginson, Boston, 3 September 1914, HHC, MF BSO/3, BL; Dodge Macknight, East Sandwich, to Isabella Stewart Gardner, 14 June 1915, ibid.

10. Jörg Nagler, *Nationale Minoritäten im Krieg: "Feindliche Ausländer" und die amerikanische Heimatfront während des Ersten Weltkriegs* (Hamburg: Hamburger Edition, 2000), 99–108.

11. Julius Gugler, "Anklage," in "Program des Wohltätigkeits-Basar zum Besten der Kriegsnotleidenden in Deutschland, Österreich und Ungarn, abgehalten vom 2.–7. März 1916 im Auditorium, Milwaukee, Wisc.," Dorothea Library, Wisconsin Conservatory of Music, Milwaukee.

12. Higginson to Eva Blomberg, Boston, 4 May 1915, HHC, MF BSO/4, BL; Higginson, proposed article for *Herald* not sent, 18 July 1919, HHC, 12-22; 18-7-19, misc., BL; Higginson to Richard Guinness, 27 August 1914, quoted in Bliss, *Life and Letters of Henry Lee Higginson*, 466.

13. Higginson to Weeks, 3 August 1914, to J. P. Morgan (the younger), 5 August 1914, and to Eliot, 8 May 1915, quoted in Bliss, *Life and Letters of Henry Lee Higginson*, 464, 474.

14. Higginson, Boston, to Lodge, Washington, 27 November 1914, 15-3, p. 165, and 16 March 1915, 15-3, pp. 244–46, correspondence, HHC, BL; Lodge, Nahant, to Higginson, Boston, 3 September 1915, 12-1, 3/9/1915, p. 1, and 10 February 1918, 12-20, 10/2/17, ibid.; Lodge, Washington, to Higginson, Boston, 10 February 1918, 12-20, 10/2/17, 20 February 1915, 12-17, 2/23/15, ibid.

15. Higginson to Muck, 20 March 1912, HHC, MF BSO/4, BL.

16. Nagler, "From Culture to Kultur," 139–41; A. Maynard Butler, London, to Secretary of State John Hay, 24 January 1903, John Hay Collection, Library of Congress, Washington, DC, courtesy of Scott Snyder.

17. Reinhard R. Doerries, *Imperial Challenge: Ambassador Count Berstorff and German-American Relations, 1908–1917*, trans. Christa D. Shannon (Chapel Hill: University of North Carolina Press, 1989), 41, 260; John Cowper Powys, *The War and Culture: A Reply to Professor Münsterberg* (New York: G. A. Shaw, 1914); Hugo Münsterberg, *The War and America* (Leipzig: Bernhard Tauchnitz, 1915); Gustavus Ohlinger, *Their True Faith and Allegiance* (New York: Macmillan, 1916); John Cowper Powys, *The Menace of German Culture* (New York: W. W. Norton, 1914); James Watson Gerard, *Face to Face with Kaiserism* (New York: George H. Doran Company, 1918), 129–42; Trommler, "Inventing the Enemy," 117; Fiebig-von Hase, "Die politische Funktionalisierung der Kultur," 71–72.

18. Rudyard Kipling, "Kultur More Barbararous Phase of Thuggee," 14 April 1918, *St. Louis Post-Dispatch* newspaper clippings, SLPL; "An Appeal by American Brewers to the American People," advertisement, 23 September 1918, ibid.

19. "Boston Symphony Orchestra Disproves Slur of Germans," n.p., n.d. [ca. December 1918], BSO scrapbooks, MF Pres/18, BSO; "Dr. Muck's Tears," *Literary Digest*, 4 May 1918, ibid; newspaper clipping, n.d., ibid; Kolodin, *Metropolitan Opera*, 269.

20. Committee on Public Information, quoted in J. Horowitz, *Understanding Toscanini*, 79.

21. Nagler questions whether such broad arrests were necessary; after all, there were only five acts of (provable) sabotage and in only one could the investigators hold three German enemy aliens responsible. Nagler, *Nationale Minoritäten im Krieg*, 687–90. See also Katja Wüstenbecker, *Deutsch-Amerikaner im Ersten Weltkrieg: US-Politik und nationale Identitäten im Mittleren Westen* (Stuttgart: Franz Steiner, 2007).

22. "Staunton, Ill., Celebrates Its 'Americanization,'" *St Louis Post*-Dispatch, 14 February 1918, *St. Louis Post-Dispatch* newspaper clippings, SLPL; Glenn Watkins, *Proof through the Night: Music and the Great War* (Berkeley and Los Angeles: University of California Press, 2003), 252; Nagler, *Nationale Minoritäten im Krieg*, 384–403, 694–95.

23. "Mystery of Pretzel-Loss Pops Solved," *Boston Daily Evening Traveller*, 3 May 1918, BSO scrapbooks, MF Pres/18, BSO.

24. Karleton Hackett, "Teuton Music Plots Exposed," *Chicago Post*, 16 September 1918, CSO scrapbooks, MF/6, 1917–24, CSO.

25. Lawton, *Schumann-Heink*, 236.

26. "Musical Celebrities Bring Joy to Troops in the Far Western Camps," *Musical America* (11 May 1918), FBZ, box X-186.

27. 13/14 December 1917, NYP program book, 1917–18, NYP; "Symphony Orchestra to Give Concert," *Fort Sheridan Reveille*, 17 October 1917, CSO scrapbooks, MF/6, 1917–24, CSO; "Camp Dix Gives Ovation to Stokowski Forces," *Musical America* (19 January 1918), PO scrapbooks, 1917–18, POA.

28. "Damrosch at Camp Upton," n.p., n.d. [December 1917], NYSS scrapbooks, vol. 3, CH.

29. Walter Anthony, "San Francisco Has Successful Symphony Year," n.p., n.d. [1918], SFSO archives, PR loose press clippings, MPD.

30. "Loyalty Pledge Is Part of the Contract," *St. Paul Daily News*, 25 August 1918, MNSO scrapbooks, vol. 59, St. Paul Concerts, 1919–22, UMN.

31. Doering, "'A Salesman of Fine Music,'" 153–68. For more on Stokowski, see Abram Chasins, *Leopold Stokowski: A Profile* (New York: Hawthorn Books, 1979).

32. "Alien Enemy Ban Cuts Boston and Philadelphia Orchestra," *Philadelphia Public Ledger*, 2 December 1917, PO scrapbooks, 1917–18, POA; "Orchestra to be 'All-American,'" *Musical Leader*, 13 December 1917, WWI activities, POA.

33. "Pittsburgh Cuts Out German Composers," *Philadelphia Public Ledger*, 9 November 1917, PO scrapbooks, 1917–18, POA.

34. "Bar Phila Orchestra from Playing German Music," *Philadelphia North American*, 13 March 1918, PO scrapbooks, 1917–18, POA.

35. Glessner Journals, 1 November 1896, box 4, CHM; Wolfe, "A Short History of the Pittsburgh Orchestra," 267–75.

36. Sherman, *Music and Maestros*, 113, 136–40.

37. Lawton, *Schumann-Heink*, 272–73.

38. Hitchens, *Blood, Class, and Nostalgia*, 175; Kevin Phillips, *The Cousins' Wars: Religion, Politics, and the Triumph of Anglo-America* (New York: Basic Books, 1999), 564.

39. "Chicago's Alien Enemy Women in Registration," *Chicago Post*, 17 June 1918, CSO scrapbooks, MF/6, 1917–24, CSO; "Enemy Women under U.S. Eye," *Chicago Journal*, 17 June 1918, ibid.

40. Turk, "The Case of Dr. Karl Muck," 48–51; "World War One Document Archive," http://www.lib.byu.edu/~rdh/wwi/ (accessed 6 August 2008).

41. Typewritten manuscript, n.d., trustees, general records, general correspondence, box 1, 1/33, CSO.

42. Frederick Stock, handwritten manuscript, n.d. [1918], trustees, general records, general correspondence, box 1, 1/33, CSO.

43. Milwaukee Orchestral Association to F. J. Wessels, Milwaukee, 20 February 1918, Manager's Files, F. Wessels, 1/13, CSO; Wm. C. White to A. Story Goodrich, Milwaukee, 21 February 1918, ibid.; William White, Milwaukee, to Wessels, Chicago, 23 April 1918, ibid.

44. "Stock Is Loyal, Is Declaration of F. J. Wessel," *Chicago Post*, 23 April 1918, CSO scrapbooks, MF/6, 1917–24, CSO.

45. Frederick Stock, handwritten manuscript, n.d. [1918], trustees, general records, general correspondence, box 1, 1/33, CSO.

46. "Fred'k Stock Forced to Quit," *Chicago Journal*, 16 August 1918; "Union Ousts Germans from Orchestra," n.p., n.d. [ca. August 1918], trustees, general records, general correspondence, box 1, 1/33, CSO.

47. "Disloyalists in Orchestra Soon Will Be Named," *Chicago Post*, 22 August 1918, CSO scrapbooks, MF/6, 1917–24, CSO; "Kaiser Lovers in Orchestra under Probe," *Chicago Journal*, 8 August 1918, ibid.

48. The spelling of Steindel's name varies; in this text, I follow the spelling listed in the CSO database. Orchestra members (1891–1930), database, CSO; "Only Great Artist May Punch Critics," *Chicago Examiner*, 5 March 1909, CSO scrapbooks, MF/2, 1904–8, CSO.

49. "Bruno Steindl in U.S. Inquiry," *Herald*, 10 August 1918, CSO scrapbooks, MF/6, 1917–24, CSO; "More Symphony Players Hear[d] in Loyalty Quiz," *Chicago Tribune*, 13 August 1918, ibid.; "Steindl Stills Cello," *Chicago Daily News*, 13 August 1918, CSO scrapbooks, MF/6, 1917–24, CSO; "Steindel in Federal Net," *Chicago Journal*, 3 October 1918, ibid.; "Union Ousts Four Symphony Players," *Chicago Herald*, 11 October 1918, ibid.; Horace Oakley to "Charles," confidential note, 2 August 1927, Horace S. Oakley Papers, Outgoing, 1917–29, folder 1927, NL; Robert D. Leiter, *The Musicians and Petrillo* (New York: Bookman Associates, 1953).

50. "Symphony Members Pledge Loyalty Publicly to the U.S.," *Chicago Tribune*, 17 August 1918, CSO scrapbooks, MF/6, 1917–24, CSO; "Alien Members of Symphony Drop Kaiser," *Chicago American*, 17 August 1918, ibid.

51. Stock, Merrill, New York, to Trustees of the Orchestral Association, Chicago, 17 August 1918, Minutes, Board of Trustees, 1 October 1918, box 1, vol. 2, CSO.

52. H. E. Krehbiel, "Theoretic [sic] and Applied Patiotism and Music," *New York Tribune*, 8/9 June 1918, BSO scrapbooks, MF Pres/18, BSO.

53. "German Emperor Lends Boston His Conductor," *New York World*, 7 April 1907, BSO scrapbooks, MF Pres/12, BSO; "To Honor Dr. Karl Muck," n.p., 4 February 1908, BSO scrapbooks, M.125.5/8, BSO. For more on Muck, see Peter Muck, *Karl Muck: Ein Dirigentenleben in Briefen und Dokumenten* (Tutzing: H. Schneider, 2003).

54. "Karl Muck," BPH Rep. 119, Generalintendanz des Preußischen Staatstheater, nr. 3052, GStA PK, 1–6, 9, 24–25, 59, 98, 129, 162, 190, 191, 205, 263, 408.

55. Schonberg, *Great Conductors*, 221.

56. Higginson to Charles A. Ellis, 3 September 1914, quoted in Bliss, *Life and Letters of Henry Lee Higginson*, 470; Higginson's address to the orchestra at the first rehearsal, 12 October 1914, ibid., 471.

57. King, "Primary Study for Boston Symphony Orchestra ." These numbers correlate loosely but not entirely. Higginson claimed that when the United States entered World War I, of the 100 players in the BSO, 51 were American citizens (17 native-born), 22 were Germans (9 had taken out their first naturalization papers), 8 Austrians, 2 Italians, 2 British, 6 Dutch, 2 Russians, 3 Frenchmen, 2 Belgians, and 2 Bohemians. Bliss, *Life and Letters of Henry Lee Higginson*, 484.

58. "Art and War," *Providence (RI) Tribune*, 23 May 1915, BSO scrapbooks, MF Pres/16, BSO; "Same Men under Muck," *Washington Post*, n.d. [ca. September 1915], ibid.

59. "The Symphony Concert," *Boston Transcript*, 7 April 1917, BSO scrapbooks, M.125.5/11, BSO; "Example from Cambridge for Boston to Outdo," ibid., 30 April 1917; "Symphony Season Ends Brilliantly," *Boston Globe*, 5 May 1917, ibid.

60. Bliss, *Life and Letters of Henry Lee Higginson*, 480–81.

61. Higginson to Eliot, 9 July 1917, quoted in ibid., 483.

62. The *Providence Journal*, October 17, 1917, quoted in Turk, "The Case of Dr. Karl Muck," 6, 7. See also Barbara L. Tischler, "One Hundred Percent Americanism and Music in Boston during World War I," *American Music* 4, no. 2 (Summer 1986): 164–76.

63. Fourth Programme, Boston Symphony Orchestra Programmes, 1917–18, BSO.

64. "Damrosch Backs Muck in Stand," *New York Morning Telegraph*, 2 November 1917; "Dr. Muck Resigns, Then Plays Anthem," *New York Times*, 3 November 1917; BSO scrapbooks, MF Pres/17, BSO.

65. In the *New York Evening Sun*, 1 November 1917, quoted in Turk, "The Case of Dr. Karl Muck," 14; "Will Not Play Anthem in New York, Says Muck," *American*, 1 November 1917, BSO scrapbooks, MF Pres/17, BSO.

66. "Music and Patriotism," *Outlook* (14 November 1917), BSO scrapbooks, MF Pres/17, BSO.

67. "Cheer Wafield [*sic*] and Hiss Name of Muck," *Baltimore News*, 7 November 1917, BSO scrapbooks, MF Pres/17, BSO.

68. "May Bar All Music of German Masters for Duration of War," *Traveler*, 3 November 1917, BSO scrapbooks, MF Pres/17, BSO; "Hiss Name of Muck at Baltimore," *Post*, 7 November 1917, ibid.; "Mucks Bild in Chicago Zerfetzt," *New York Evening Staatszeitung*, 11 November 1917, ibid.

69. "'Star Spangled' Banner Row as Musicians Analyze It," *New York Sun*, 11 November 1917, BSO scrapbooks, MF Pres/17, BSO.

70. Mrs. William Jay, quoted in Turk, "The Case of Dr. Karl Muck," 16, 17.

71. Irving Lowens, "L'affaire Karl Muck: A Study in War Hysteria (1917–18)," *Musicology* 1 (1947): 272; Applegate, *Bach in Berlin*, 255–56.

72. Turk, "The Case of Dr. Karl Muck," 30–31, 39.

73. Quoted in ibid., 58, 59–60.

74. Ibid., 45; J. Horowitz, *Understanding Toscanini*, 80.

75. Turk, "The Case of Dr. Karl Muck," 65; "Germans Drop From Orchestra," *Monitor*, 2 June 1918, BSO scrapbooks, MF Pres/18, BSO; "Higginson's Withdrawal," *Musical America* (4 May 1918), ibid.; King, "Primary Study for Boston Symphony Orchestra ."

76. Turk, "The Case of Dr. Karl Muck," 20–21, 48–51; "Muck Says U.S. Accorded Him Square Deal," n.p., n.d. [November 1919], BSO scrapbooks, M.125.5/12, BSO; "Report Dr. Muck Will Be Deported," *Traveler*, 14 February 1919, BSO scrapbooks, M.125.5/12, BSO.

77. "Muck Finally Bids Adieu to America," n.p., n.d., MNSO scrapbooks, vol. 136, 1920 clippings, "Muck," UMN.

78. "Adlerschild für Generalmusikdirektor Dr. Karl Muck," *Kleine Kunst-B.Z.*, 22 October 1929 [1939], "Karl Muck," BPH, Rep. 119, Generalintendanz der Preussischen Staatstheater, no. 3052, GStA PK, Bl. 475; H. H. Stuckenschmidt, *Zum Hören geboren: Ein Leben mit der Musik unserer Zeit* (Munich: Piper, 1979), 67.

79. *Classical Performances with Richard Knisely*, WGBH Boston, 89.7, 4 October 1917, 1:00 p.m.

80. Lowens, "L'affaire Karl Muck."

81. Doerries, *Washington-Berlin 1908/1917*, 165–217.

82. See reprints in *Boston Post*, 16, 19, 22, and 24 November 1919, BSO scrapbooks, MF Pres/19, BSO.

83. "Suspect Kaiser Had Object in Sending Dr. Muck to U.S.," *Boston Traveller*, 27 March 1918, BSO scrapbooks, MF Pres/18, BSO.

84. "New Horizons for the Symphony Orchestra," n.p., n.d. [ca. mid-1918], BSO scrapbooks, M.125.5/11, BSO; quoted in Perry, *Life and Letters of Henry Lee Higginson*, 135; Turk, "The Case of Dr. Karl Muck," 92.

85. Jessica C. E. Gienow-Hecht, "Music and Emotions in German-American Relations" (Habilitation thesis, Martin-Luther-Universität Halle-Wittenberg, 2003), 390–94.

86. L. Thomas, "History of the Cincinnati Symphony Orchestra," 449–96. For more on Ysaÿe, see Antoine Ysaÿe and Bertram Radcliffe, *Ysaÿe: His Life, Work and Influence* (London: William Heinemann Ltd., 1947).

87. "Move to Encourage French Learning," *New York Herald*, 9 July 1917, HHC, Society for American Fellowships in French Universities, 12–20, BL.

88. "Hail Girl of 16 as Musical Marvel," *Boston Advertiser*, 23 November 1919, BSO scrapbooks, M.125.5/12, BSO; Whitney Walton, "Internationalism and the Junior Year Abroad: American Students in France in the 1920s and 1930s," *Diplomatic History* 29, no. 2 (April 2005): 255–79.

89. "9th Concert by Symphony," *Herald*, 31 December 1918, BSO scrapbooks, M.125.5/12, BSO; Aldrich, *Concert Life in New York*, 567–70, 629–33.

90. J. Horowitz, *Wagner Nights*, 311; "From Strauss to Wagner at Auditorium," *Sunday Tribune*, 15 May 1921, MNSO scrapbooks, vol. 67, Audience Attractions, UMN; Manager's Files, H. Voegeli, 1/50, CSO.

91. "Boston Symphony's Director Far Excels Muck, Says Olin Downes," *Boston Post*, 10 November 1918, BSO scrapbooks, M.125.5/12, BSO.

92. Louis C. Elson, "American Work in Symphony Concert," *Boston Advertiser*, 15 February 1920, BSO scrapbooks, M.125.5/12, BSO.

93. Alfons M. Nuese, "Deutsches Kunsterwachen in New York," *Vossische Zeitung*, 19 August 1919 (evening edition), R 901/72721, AA.

94. "9th Concert by Symphony," *Herald*, 31 December 1918, BSO scrapbooks, M.125.5/12, BSO; Edith Wharton, in a letter dated 19 July 1919, quoted in Watkins, *Proof through the Night*, 333.

95. Berglund, "A Study of the Life and Work of Frederick Stock," 256.

96. Watkins, *Proof through the Night*, 120, 252; Debussy quotation is from pp. 101–2.

97. Patrick Wright, *Iron Curtain: From Stage to Cold War* (Oxford: Oxford University Press, 2007), 85–87, 389–90.

EPILOGUE

1. Volker Thomalla, "Der Tag an dem Beethoven Bonn rettete," letter to the editor, *Generalanzeiger*, 27 October 2003. See also Edward Jablonski, *Flying Fortress: The Illustrated Biography of the B-17s and the Men Who Flew Them* (Garden City, NY: Doubleday, 1965); http://www.nasm.si.edu/getinvolved/membership/pevents/rall-crosby.htm (accessed 22 July 2004).

2. Thomas Mann, *Doktor Faustus: Das Leben des deutschen Tonsetzers Adrian Leverkühn, erzählt von einem Freunde* (Stockholm: Bermann-Fischer Verlag, 1947).

3. Reinhold Brinkmann, "Reading a Letter," in *Driven into Paradise: The Musical Migration from Nazi Germany to the United States*, ed. Reinhold Brinkmann and Christoph Wolff (Berkeley and Los Angeles: University of California Press, 1999), 18.

4. Bryan Gilliam, "A Viennese Opera Composer in Hollywood: Korngold's Double Exile in America," in Brinkmann and Wolff, *Driven into Paradise*, 225–32. Carol J. Oja, "The USA, 1918–45," in *Modern Times: FromWorld War I to the Present*, ed. Robert P. Morgan (Englewood Cliffs, NJ: Prentice Hall, 1993), 206–30; Joseph Horowitz, *Artists in Exile: How Refugees from 20th Century War and Revolution Transformed the American Performing Arts* (New York: Harper Collins, 2007).

5. Kim H. Kowalke, "Kurt Weill's America," in *Amerikanismus, American-ism, Weill: Die Suche nach kultureller Identität in der Moderne*, ed. Hermann Danuser and Hermann Gottschewski (Schliengen: Edition Argus, 2003), 9–15.

6. Potter, "Klassische deutsche Musik," 686–95.

7. "Advance, Music, to Be Recognized," *Chicago Sunday Tribune*, 19 July 1942, Henry Voegeli Papers,CHM.

8. Wilhelm Furtwängler, Ain Shams, 27 March 1936, to Charles Triller, NYP conductors files, 010-13/16, NYP; details of the Furtwängler controversy, from the CSO Archives, database of trustee minutes and correspondence, 1948–49, CSO.

9. Eugene Ormandy to Arthur Judson, NYC, 8 March 1950, NYP conductors files, 011-01/23, NYP.

10. Joseph Krips, *Erinnerungen: Ohne Liebe kann man keine Musik machen*, ed. Harietta Krips (Vienna: Böhlau, 1994), 229.

11. "Music Degenerating in Europe," *Evening Tribune*, 2 December 1920, MNSO scrapbooks, vol. 63, 18th Home Season, 1920–21, UMN.

12. Carol J. Oja, *Making Music Modern: New York in the 1920s*. New York: Oxford University Press, 2000.

13. "Van Praag's Report for Mr. Mackay," n.d. [ca. 1926], NYP conductors files, 011-01/11, NYP.

14. "Leopold Stokowski, Who Opens Philharmonic-Symphony Centennial Sea-son Tomorrow, Discusses Music of Next Hundred Years," press release by the Philharmonic-Symphony Society of New York, 10/6/41, NYP Conduc-tors Files, 011-11-01-5, folder 25, NYPA. "Music is a universal language," Stokowski observed in *Music for All of Us*, in 1943; quoted in Ardoin, *Phila-delphia Orchestra*, 48. Ironically, advocates of popular music, such as Louis Armstrong, cited the same reasons for the export of jazz: "Music is stronger than nations," *Newsweek* magazine quoted Satchmo as saying in Decem-ber 1955. Quoted in Penny Von Eschen, *Satchmo Blows Up the World: Jazz Ambassadors Play the Cold War* (Cambridge, MA: Harvard University Press, 2004), 11.

15. J. Horowitz, *Understanding Toscanini*, 399; Margaret Grant and Herman S. Hettinger, *America's Symphony Orchestras and How They Are Supported* (New York: W. W. Norton & Co., 1940), 46–64, 233, 272.

16. Potter, "Klassische deutsche Musik," 694. For more on the link between music and cold-war propaganda, see Mark Carrol, *Music and Ideology in*

*Cold War Europe* (Cambridge: Cambridge University Press, 2003); Frances Stonor Saunders, *Who Paid the Piper? The CIA and the Cultural Cold War* (London: Granta Books, 1999), 117; Giles Scott-Smith, "The 'Masterpieces of the Twentieth Century' Festival and the Congress for Cultural Freedom: Origins and Consolidation, 1947–52," *Intelligence and National Security* 15 (Spring 2000): 121, 136. On the significance of classical music during the U.S. occupation after Worled War II, see David Monod, *Settling Scores: German Music, Denazification, and the Americans, 1945–1953* (Chapel Hill: University of North Carolina Press, 2005); Toby Thacker, *Music after Hitler, 1945–1955* (Aldershot, UK: Ashagte, 2007); Elizabeth Janik, *Recomposing German Music: Politics and Tradition in Cold War Berlin* (Leiden: Brill, 2005).

17. For example, in 1954–55, the Bamberg Symphony played in Mexico City, Havana, New York, Brussels, Lisbon, Paris, The Hague, and Belgrade, with "a purely German program." I am indebted to Toby Thacker for this information.

18. Potter, "Klassische deutsche Musik," 694; Jürgen Grosse, *Amerikapolitik und Amerikabild in der DDR, 1974–1989* (Bonn: Bouvier, 1999), 145–46; Holger Stunz, presentation at the Heidelberg Center for American Studies, 2004.

19. "In Friendship and Solidarity," 16 September 2001; broadcasting live concert, DVD recording.

20. I am indebted to Barbara May from the German Foreign Office for this information.

21. Ron Della Chiesa on *Classics in the Morning*, WGBH Boston, 89.7, approx. 8:12 a.m. The program began with "Six German Dances" by Mozart, then ranged from Richard Strauss, Schubert, Wagner (*Tannhäuser*), Samuel Barber, Fritz Kreisler ("Liebeslied"), Haydn (Quartet in D Major, op. 76, no. 3, the model composition for the *Deutschlandlied*), to excerpts from Bach's *Weihnachtsoratorium*.

22. I am indebted to Eckhard Fuchs for this suggestion.

23. Gerber, "The Germans Take Care of Our Celebrations," 48.

24. Kristin Hoganson, "Cosmopolitan Domesticity: Importing the American Dream," *American Historical Review* 107 (February 2002): 77. See also Kristin L. Hoganson, *Consumers' Imperium: The Global Production of American Domesticity, 1865–1920* (Chapel Hill: University of North Carolina Press, 2007); for a twentieth-century perspective, see Richard Pells, "American Culture Goes Global, or Does It?" *Chronicle of Higher Education*, 12 April 2002, pp. B7–9.

25. Karen Ahlquist, "Mrs. Potiphar at the Opera: Satire, Idealism, and Cultural Authority in Post–Civil War New York," in Saffle, *Music and Culture in America*, 29–52.

26. Matthew Arnold, "The Function of Criticism at the Present Time," in Arnold, *Essays and Criticism* (London: Macmillan and Co., 1865), 1–41. See

also Matthew Arnold, *Culture and Anarchy: An Essay in Political and Social Criticism* (London: Smith, Elder & Co, 1869).

27. Max Weber, "Die 'Objektivität' sozialwissenschaftlicher und sozialpolitischer Erkenntnis," in *Gesammelte Aufsätze zur Wissenschaftslehre* (Tübingen: Mohr, 1988), 146–214; Ute Daniel, "'Kultur' und 'Gesellschaft': Überlegungen zum Gegenstandsbereich der Sozialgeschichte," *Geschichte und Gesellschaft* 19 (1993): 69–99; Friedrich Jaeger, "Der Kulturbegriff im Werk Max Webers und seine Bedeutung für eine moderne Kulturgeschichte," *Geschichte und Gesellschaft* 18 (1992): 371–93.

28. Jessica Gienow-Hecht, "Trumpeting Down the Walls of Jericho: The Politics of Art, Music and Emotion in German-American Relations, 1870–1920," *Journal of Social History* 36, no. 3 (Spring 2003): 585–613.

29. Eero Tarasti, *Myth and Music: A Semiotic Approach to the Aesthetics of Myth in Music, Especially That of Wagner, Sibelius and Stravinsky* (The Hague: Mouton, 1979).

30. See also Appiah, *Ethics of Identity*, 227–28.

# Bibliography

## Primary Sources

### Archives

GERMANY

Bundesarchiv Berlin Lichterfelde
- R 901 Auswärtiges Amt des Deutschen Reiches
  Rechtsabteilung
    Innere Verwaltung
    Kunst und Wissenschaft
    Nachrichtenabteilung
    Abteilung Deutschland
    Kulturpropaganda
    Politische Propaganda
  Nachrichten- und Presseabteilung
  Zentralstelle für Auslandsdienst
  Kulturpolitische Abteilung
  Politische Abteilung

Geheimes Staatsarchiv, Preußischer Kulturbesitz, Berlin Dahlem (GStPK)
- I. HA Rep. 76 Ministerium der geistlichen, Unterrichts- und Medizinal-Angelegenheiten
- I. HA Rep. 89 Geheimes Zivilkabinett
- I. HA Rep. 92 Nachlässe
  Nl Schmidt-Ott
- I. HA Rep. 209 Staatliche Akademische Hochschule für Musik in Berlin
- III. HA Ministerium des Auswärtigen III
- Brandenburg-Preussisches Hausarchiv
    Rep. 119 neue Generalintendanz der Preußischen Staatstheater

## BIBLIOGRAPHY

### UNITED STATES

#### BOSTON

Boston Symphony Orchestra Archives
- Boston Symphony Orchestra scrapbooks (MF), **M.125.5
- Boston Symphony Orchestra scrapbooks MF Pres. 56
- Programs, 1881–1930
- Robert D. King, "Primary Study for Boston Symphony Orchestra: Personnel and Repertoire," typewritten manuscript (1994)
- Henry Higginson Papers
- SH 198, Symphony Hall program scrapbooks

#### CAMBRIDGE, MASSACHUSSETTS

Baker Library Special Collections, Harvard Business School
- Henry Lee Higginson Collection

Houghton Library, Harvard College Library, Harvard University
- Wilhelm Gericke Papers

#### CHICAGO

Chicago History Museum
- Glessner Journals
- Henry Voegeli Collection
- Julia Gerstenberg Collection

Chicago Symphony Orchestra, Rosenthal Archives
- Inmagic records of the Chicago Symphony, 1890–1920
    Board of Directors/Trustees
        Minutes of the Board of Trustees, 1890–1935
        General records
            General correspondence, 1894–1927, box 1
- Manager's files
    Henry E. Voegeli Papers
    Frederick Wessels Papers
- Public relations
    Music directors, series 1
        Frederick Stock Papers
        Theodore Thomas Papers
        Max Bendix Papers
    Former musicians
    Trustees
- Felsengarten Collection
- Marketing and communications

Conductors
Frederick Stock
- CSO scrapbooks, MF
- Program books, 1891–1920

Newberry Library
- Theodore Thomas Papers
- Frederick Stock Papers
- Felix Borowski Papers
- Fanny Bloomfeld Zeisler Papers
- Rudolf Ganz Papers
- Horace Sweeney Oakley Papers (MS 67-1963)
- Joseph Joachim Correspondence

CINCINNATI

American Jewish Archives
- Fanny Bloomfield Zeisler Papers

Cincinnati Symphony Orchestra
- Cincinnati Symphony Orchestra Association
  Cincinnati Symphony Orchestra Board of Directors minutes
  Cincinnati Symphony Orchestra Board of Trustees minutes
  Cincinnati Symphony Orchestra Executive Committee minutes
  Cincinnati Symphony Orchestra program books
  Scrapbooks

Cincinnati Historical Society
- Cincinnati Musical Festival Association records
- Cincinnati Symphony Orchestra scrapbooks, 1902–64 (86 vols.)
- Cincinnati Symphony Orchestra Association
- Alien property custodian legal records pertaining to Ernst Kunwald (1922)
- Memoranda, Ladies Musical Club, 1893/Orchestra Association, 1894–1924, MSS qXL155
- Wulsin Family Papers, 1820–1981, MSS 844
  Manuscript relating to the Wulsin family

MILWAUKEE

Dorothea Library, Wisconsin Conservatory of Music
- Pamphlets pertaining to 1917–18

MINNEAPOLIS

Minnesota Historical Society
- Emil Oberhoffer Papers (1867–1933)

- Edward Chenery Gale Papers (1862–1943)

University of Minnesota, Archive for the Performing Arts
- Minnesota Orchestra Collection
  Minneapolis Symphony Orchestra scrapbooks, 1908–75
  Minneapolis Symphony Orchestra programs, 1908–71
  Publicity and publications

### NEW YORK CITY

Carnegie Hall
- Symphony Society and Symphony Orchestra scrapbooks
- Concert record scrapbooks
- Damrosch Collection, 1876–1946 (originals in Library of Congress, Music Division)

New York Philharmonic-Symphony Society
- Records of the New York Philharmonic Society
  Orchestra member files
  Conductor files
  Minutes of the business meetings, to 1903
  Board of Directors files
    Files, Box 006-04
    Minutes, since 1850
    Biographical, other directors
  Presidential files
  Board minutes
  Annual reports
  Press clippings
  Program books
  NYP Programs Database, New York Philharmonic
  Conductor's Committee minutes
- Records of the Symphony Society of New York
  Conductors, 1878–1928

New York Historical Society
- George Templeton Strong Diaries
- William Steinway Diaries
- Emma C. Thursby Papers

New York Public Library
- Frank Damrosch Papers
- New York Philharmonic–Symphony Society scrapbooks
  Executive Committee of the Board of Directors minutes
- New York Symphony Society records (Walter Damrosch)

PHILADELPHIA

Academy of Music
· Philadelphia Orchestra member biographical files
· Artist files
· Administrative files, series 1 (Conductors)
  Fritz Scheel
  Carl Pohlig
  Leopold Stokowski
· Richard Strauss file (1904, 1921)
· scrapbooks
· programs
· Minutes of the Meetings of The Philadelphia Orchestra Association and the Board of Directors
· Minutes of the Trustees of The Philadelphia Orchestra Association
· Correspondence by Stokowski

University of Pennsylvania Archives
· Edward Garrett McCollin Papers (1877–1951)
  Scrapbooks, Germania Orchestra


PITTSBURGH

The Carnegie Library of Pittsburgh
· George Wilson Collection
  Records relating to the Pittsburgh Orchestra
    Programs of the afternoon and evening concerts
    Programs of the out-of-town and extra concerts
    Scrapbooks, 1896–1910 (21 vols.)
    Correspondence, 1897–1903 (23 vols.)
    Files, 1896–1910
· Pittsburgh Symphony Orchestra
  Minutes of the Executive Committee, 1910
· Charles Chauncey Mellor scrapbooks


SAN FRANCISCO

Museum of Performance & Design
· San Francisco Symphony Archives Collection
· Musical Association (since 1909)
· Gustav Hinrichs Collection
· Fritz Scheel Papers
· Anton Seidl Papers
· San Francisco Symphony programs, 1909–18
· San Francisco Symphony Society, *Music* (pamphlet)

· San Francisco Philharmonic Society

ST. LOUIS

Missouri Historical Society
· Adelaide Kalkman music scrapbooks
· Mary McKittrick Markham Collection
· Ernest R. Kroeger scrapbooks
· Music papers
· W. H. Pommer Papers
· St. Louis Philharmonic Society Collection (1860–1922)
  Programs, 1911–62
  Scrapbooks
  Official records
  Minute books
· St. Louis Symphony Society Collection (1897–1982)
  Minutes, Executive Committee
  Minutes, Board of Directors
  Scrapbooks, useless
  Printed programs
  Correspondence files
  "An Informal History of the St. Louis Symphony Society," compiled for
    George D. Markham

St. Louis Public Library
· *St. Louis Post-Dispatch*

WASHINGTON, DC

Library of Congress, Music Division
· Fritz Kreisler Collection
· Victor Herbert Collection
· Damrosch-Blaine Collection
· Damrosch-Te-Van Collection
· Lilli Lehmann Collection
· Loeffler Collection
· Music—Department of State

## Published Sources

Adams, Henry. *The Education of Henry Adams: An Autobiography*. Orig. pub. 1907.
    Reprint, Boston: Houghton Mifflin; New York: Riverside Press, 1918.
Albrecht, Henry. *Skizzen aus dem Leben der Musik-Gesellschaft Germania*. Philadel-
    phia: King and Baird, 1869.

Aldrich, Richard. *Concert Life in New York, 1902–1923*. New York: G. B. Putnam's Sons, 1941.

Damrosch, Walter. *My Musical Life*. New York: Charles Scribner's Sons, 1923.

Eastcott, Richard. *Sketches of the Origin and Progress of Music, With an Account of the Ancient Bards and Minstrels*. Bath: S. Hazard, 1793.

Edel, Leon, ed. *Henry James: Selected Letters*. Cambridge, MA: Harvard University Press, Belknap Press, 1987.

Elson, Louis C. *European Reminiscences, Musical and Otherwise. Being the Recollections of the Vacation Tours of a Musician in Various Countries*. Philadelphia: T. Presser, 1896.

Fay, Amy. *Music-Study in Germany: The Classic Memoir of the Romantic Era*. Orig. pub. 1880. Reprint, New York: Dover Publications, 1965.

Finck, Henry T., ed. *Anton Seidl: A Memorial by His Friends*. New York: C. Scribner's Sons, 1899.

———. *My Adventures in the Golden Age of American Music*. New York: Funk & Wagnalls, 1926.

Ffrench, Florence. *Music and Musicians in Chicago*. Orig. pub. Chicago: Florence Ffrench, 1899. Reprint, New York: Da Capo Press, 1979.

Gerard, James Watson. *Face to Face with Kaiserism*. New York: George H. Doran Company, 1918.

Gottschalk, Louis Moreau. *Notes of a Pianist*. Orig. pub. Philadelphia, 1888. Reprint, Philadelphia, 1979.

Henderson, William James. *Richard Wagner: His Life and His Dramas*. New York: G. P. Putnam's Sons, 1901.

———. *What Is Good Music? Suggestions to Persons Desiring to Cultivate a Taste in Musical Art*. New York: C. Scribner's Sons, 1898, 1922.

Huneker, James. *The Philharmonic Society of New York and Its Seventy-fifth Anniversary: A Retrospect*. New York, 1917.

James, Henry. *The Bostonians: A Novel*. London: Macmillan, 1886.

Krehbiel, George H. "A Short History of the Cincinnati May Festival." *Saxby's* 19 (May 1908): 55–58.

Krehbiel, Henry E. *An Account of the Fourth Musical Festival Held at Cincinnati May 18, 19, 20 & 21, 1880*. Cincinnati: Aldine Printing Worlds, 1880.

———. *Afro-American Folksongs: A Study in Racial and National Music*. 4th ed. Portland, ME: Longwood Press, 1976.

———. *The Philharmonic Society of New York: A Memorial*. New York: Novello, Ewer & Co., 1892.

Lamprecht, Karl. *Americana: Reiseeindrücke, Betrachtungen, geschichtliche Gesamtansicht*. Freiburg i. B.: H. Heyfelder, 1906.

Lawrence, D. H. *Studies in Classic American Literature*. Orig. pub. Thomas Seltzer Inc., 1923. Reprint, New York: Viking Press, 1950.

Lawton, Mary, ed. *Schumann-Heink: The Last of the Titans*. New York: Macmillan, 1928.

Lefort, Paul. "Les Écoles Étrangères de la Peinture—États Unis." *Gazette des Beaux-Arts* 43 (1879): 483–85.

Lehmann, Lilli. *My Path through Life.* Translated by Alice Benedict Seligman. New York: G. P. Putnam's Sons, 1914.

Moore, John W. *Complete Encyclopaedia of Music, Elementary, Technical, Historical, Biographical, Vocal, and Instrumental.* Boston: John P. Jewett & Co., 1854.

Münsterberg, Hugo. *The War and America.* Leipzig: Bernhard Tauchnitz, 1915.

Offenbach, Jacques. *Orpheus in America: Offenbach's Diary of His Journey ot the New World.* Translated by Lander MacClintock. Orig. pub. 1877. Reprint, New York: Greenwood Press, 1957, 1969.

Ohlinger, Gustavus. *Their True Faith and Allegiance.* New York: Macmillan, 1916.

Otis, Philo A. *The Hymns You Ought to Know.* Chicago: Clayton F. Summy, 1928.

Paine, John K., ed. *Famous Composers and Their Works.* Boston: J. B. Millet, 1891.

Patrizi, Mariano Luigi. *I Reflessi Vascolari Nelle Membra e Nel Cervello Dell'Uomo: Per Vari Stimuli e Per Varie Condizioni Fisiologiche e Sperimentali.* Reggio-Emilia: Stefano Calderini e Figlio, 1897.

———. *Il Tempo di Reazione Semplice: Studiato in Rapporto Colla Curva Pletismografica Cerebrale. Nota Sperimentale.* Reggio-Emilia: Stefano Calderini e Figlio, 1897.

Powys, John Cowper. *The Menace of German Culture.* New York: W. W. Norton, 1914.

———. *The War and Culture: A Reply to Professor Münsterberg.* New York: G. A. Shaw, 1914.

Rutz, Ottmar. *Sprache, Gesang und Körperhaltung: Handbuch zur Typenlehre.* Munich: O. Beck, 1911.

Sonneck, Oscar. "German Influence on the Musical Life of America." In Lichtenwanger, *Oscar Sonneck and American Music,* 60–75.

Stokowski, Leopold. *Music for All of Us.* New York: Simon and Schuster, 1943.

Swan, John C., ed. *Music in Boston: Readings from the First Three Centuries.* Boston: Trustees of the Public Library of the City of Boston, 1977.

Thomas, Rose Fay. *Memoirs of Theodore Thomas.* New York: Moffat, Yard, 1911.

Thomas, Theodore. *A Musical Autobiography.* Edited by George Upton. 2 vols. Chicago: A. C. McClurg, 1905.

Veblen, Thorstein. *The Theory of the Leisure Class.* New York: Macmillan, 1899, 1945.

Wharton, Edith. *The Age of Innocence.* New York: D. Appleton and Co., 1920.

## Secondary Sources

Adams, Willi-Paul. "Die Geschichte Nordamerikas in Berlin." In *Geschichtswissenschaft in Berlin im 19. und 20. Jahrhundert: Persönlichkeiten und Institutionen,* edited by Reimar Hansen and Wolfgang Ribbe, 597–631. Berlin: Walter de Gruyter, 1992.

Ahlquist, Karen. "Mrs. Potiphar at the Opera: Satire, Idealism, and Cultural Authority in Post–Civil War New York." In Saffle, *Music and Culture in America*, 29–52.

Albrecht, Andrea. *Kosmopolitismus: Weltbürgerdiskurse in Literatur, Philosophie und Publizistik um 1800*. Berlin: Walter de Gruyter, 2005.

Allen, Henry Cranbrook. *Great Britain and the United States: A History of Anglo-American Relations (1783–1951)*. New York: St. Martin's Press, 1955.

Anderson, Stuart. *Race and Rapprochement: Anglo-Saxonism and Anglo-American Relations, 1895–1904*. London: Associated University Presses, 1981.

Appiah, Kwame Anthony. *The Ethics of Identity*. Princeton, NJ: Princeton University Press, 2005.

Applegate, Celia. *Bach in Berlin: Nation and Culture in Mendelssohn's Revival of the "St. Matthew Passion."* Ithaca, NY: Cornell University Press, 2005.

———. "How German Is It? Nationalism and the Idea of Serious Music in the Early Nineteenth Century." *Nineteenth-Century Music* 21 (Spring 1998): 274–96.

———. *A Nation of Provincials: The German Idea of* Heimat. Berkeley and Los Angeles: University of California Press, 1990.

———. "What Is German Music? Reflections on the Role of Art in the Creation of the Nation." "German Identity," special issue, *German Studies Review* (Winter 1992): 21–32.

Applegate, Celia, and Pamela Potter, eds. *Music and German National Identity*. Chicago: University of Chicago Press, 2002.

Ardoin, John, ed. *The Philadelphia Orchestra: A Century of Music*. Philadelphia: Temple University Press, 1999.

Arndt, Richard T. *The First Resort of Kings: American Cultural Diplomacy in the Twentieth Century*. Washington, DC: Potomac Books, 2005.

Arnold, Denis, and Nigel Fortune. *The Beethoven Reader*. New York: W. W. Norton, 1971.

Arnold, Matthew. "The Function of Criticism at the Present Time." In Arnold, *Essays and Criticism*, 1–41. London: Macmillan and Co., 1865.

"Art, Labor, and Democracy: The Meaning of Art Work in America, 1860–1940." Panel at the 115th annual meeting of the American Historical Association, Boston, 6 January 2001, with contributions by April F. Masten, Frances K. Pohl, and A. Joan Saab.

Aydelotte, Frank. *The American Rhodes Scholarships: A Review of the First Forty Years*. Princeton, NJ: Princeton University Press, 1946.

Bacht, Nikolaus. *Music, Theatre and Politics in Germany, 1848 to the Third Reich*. Aldershot, UK: Ashgate, 2006.

Bailey, Thomas A. "Dewey and the Germans in Manila Bay." *American Historical Review* 45 (1938): 59–81.

Barclay, David E., and Elisabeth Glaser-Schmidt, eds. *Transatlantic Images and Perceptions: Germany and America since 1776*. Washington, DC: German Historical Institute; New York: Cambridge University Press, 1997.

Bayly, Christopher. *The Birth of the Modern World, 1780–1914: Global Connections and Comparisons*. Malden, MA: Blackwell, 2004.

Baynham, Edward G. "The Early Development of Music in Pittsburgh." Ph.D. diss., University of Pittsburgh, 1944.

Bedermann, Gail. *Manliness and Civilization: A Cultural History of Gender and Race in the United States, 1880–1917*. Chicago: University of Chicago Press, 1995.

Beller-McKenna, Daniel. *Brahms and the German Spirit*. Cambridge, MA: Harvard University Press, 2004.

———. "How deutsch a Requiem? Absolute Music, Universality, and the Reception of Brahms's *Ein deutsches Requiem*, op. 45." *Nineteenth-Century Music* 22 (Summer 1998): 3–19.

Bellesiles, Michael A. *Arming America: The Origins of a National Gun Culture*. New York: Alfred Knopf, 2000.

Belting, Hans. *Die Deutschen und ihre Kunst: Ein schwieriges Erbe*. Munich: C. H. Beck, 1992. Translated edition: *The Germans and Their Art: A Troublesome Relationship*, translated by Scott Kleager. New Haven, CT: Yale University Press, 1998.

Bender, Thomas, ed. *Rethinking American History in a Global Age*. Berkeley and Los Angeles: University of California Press, 2002.

Benthien, Claudia, Anne Fleig, and Ingrid Kasten, eds. *Emotionalität: Zur Geschichte der Gefühle*. Cologne: Böhlau, 2000.

Berger, Frank. *Gustav Mahler: Vision und Mythos; Versuch einer geistigen Biographie*. Stuttgart: Verlag Freies Geistesleben, 1993.

Berghahn, Volker R. *America and the Intellectual Cold Wars in Europe: Shepard Stone between Philanthropy, Academy, and Diplomacy*. Princeton, NJ: Princeton University Press, 2001.

Berglund, Donald Herbert. "A Study of the Life and Work of Frederick Stock during the Time He Served as Musical Director of the Chicago Symphony Orchestra, with Particular Reference to His Influence on Music Education." Ph.D. diss., Northwestern University, 1955.

Bergquist, James M. "The Forty-Eighters and the Politics of the 1850s." In *Germany and America: Essays on Problems of International Relations and Immigration*, edited by Hans L. Trefousse, 111–21. New York: Brooklyn Press, 1980.

Bernstein, Mark F. *Football: The Ivy League Origins of an American Obsession*. Philadelphia: University of Pennsylvania Press, 2001.

*Biography of an Orchestra: An Affectionate Look at Eighty Years of Music and Life in Chicago*. Chicago: R. R. Donnelly & Sons, [1971?].

Blodgett, Geoffrey et al., eds. *Victorian America*. Philadelphia: University of Pennsylvania Press, 1976.

Bohlman, Philip, and Otto Holzapfel, eds. *Land without Nightingales: Music in the Making of German-America*. Madison: University of Wisconsin Press, 2002.

Böke, Henning. "Gustav Mahler und das Judentum." *Archiv für Musikwissenschaft* 54 (1992): 1–21.

Bollenbeck, Georg. *Bildung und Kultur. Glanz und Elend eines deutschen Deutungsmuster*. Frankfurt am Main: Insel Verlag, 1994.

Bomberger, Elam Douglas. "The German Musical Training of American Students, 1850–1900." Ph.D. diss., University of Maryland, 1991.

———. "A Tidal Wave of Encouragement": American Composers' Concerts during the Gilded Age. Westport, CT: Praeger, 2002.

Bonds, Mark Evan. After Beethoven: Imperatives of Originality in the Symphony. Cambridge, MA: Harvard University Press, 1996.

Bonner, Thomas Neville. American Doctors and German Universities: A Chapter in International Intellectual Relations, 1870–1914. Lincoln: University of Nebraska Press, 1963.

Botstein, Leon. "Listening through Reading: Musical Literacy and the Concert Audience." Nineteenth-Century Music 16 (1992): 129–45.

Bourdieu, Pierre. Distinction: A Social Critique of the Judgment of Taste. Translated by Richard Nice. Cambridge, MA.: Harvard University Press, 1984.

Bradová, Ludmila. "Antonin Dvorák, 1841–1904." In Pachter and Wein, Abroad in America, 228–37.

Brancaforte, Charlotte L., ed. The German Forty-Eighters in the United States. New York: Peter Lang, 1989.

Brechtken, Magnus. Scharnierzeit 1895–1907: Persönlichkeitsnetze und internationale Politik in den deutsch-britisch-amerikanischen Beziehungen vor dem ersten Weltkrieg. Mainz: Von Zabern, 2006.

Brinkmann, Reinhold, and Christoph Wolff, eds. Driven into Paradise: The Musical Migration from Nazi Germany to the United States. Berkeley and Los Angeles: University of California Press, 1999.

Brocke, Bernhard vom. "Der deutsch-amerikanische Professorenaustausch: Preussische Wissenschaftspolitik, internationale Wissenschaftsbeziehungen und die Anfänge einer deutschen auswärtigen Kulturpolitik vor dem Ersten Weltkrieg." Zeitschrift für Kulturaustausch 31 (1981): 128–82.

———. "Professoren als Parlamentarier." In Schwabe, Deutsche Hochschullehrer als Elite, 55–68.

Broyles, Michael. "Music of the Highest Class": Elitism and Populism in Antebellum Boston. New Haven, CT: Yale University Press, 1992.

Bruce, William G., ed. History of Milwaukee, City and County. Vol. 1. Chicago: S. J. Clarke, 1922.

Bruch, Rüdiger vom. "Gesellschaftliche Initiativen in den auswärtigen Kulturbeziehungen Deutschlands vor 1914: Der Beitrag des Bürgertums." Zeitschrift für Kulturaustausch 31 (1981): 43–67.

———. Weltpolitik als Kulturmission: Auswärtige Kulturpolitik und Bildungsbürgertum in Deutschland am Vorabend des Ersten Weltkrieges. Paderborn: F. Schöningh, 1982.

———. "Wissenschaftspolitik, Wissenschaftssystem und Nationalstaat im Deutschen Kaiserreich." In Wirtschaft, Wissenschaft und Bildung in Preußen: Zur Wirtschafts- und Sozialgeschichte Preußens vom 18. bis zum 20. Jahrhundert, edited by Karl Heinrich Kaufhold and Bernd Sösemann, 73–89. Stuttgart: Franz Steiner Verlag, 1998.

Brueziere, Maurice. *L'alliance française: Histoire d'une institution*. Paris: Hachette, 1983.

Buch, Esteban. *La neuvième de Beethoven: Une histoire politique*. Paris: Gallimard, 1999.

Buchholz, Werner, Kyra T. Inachin, Ernst Schubert, Henrik Karge, Katharina Weigand, and Hans-Michael Körner. "Nationalstaat und regionale Selbst- behauptung: Kulturpolitik in den deutschen Staaten des 19. Jahrhunderts." Panel at the 42nd Deutsche Historikertag, Frankfurt am Main, 11 September 1998.

Bungert, Heike. "Feste und das ethnische Gedächtnis: Die Festkultur der Deutsch- Amerikaner im Spannungsfeld zwischen deutscher und amerikanischer Identität, 1848–1914." Habilitation thesis, Universität Köln, 2004.

Burford, Mark Jon. " 'The Real Idealism of History': Historical Consciousness, Commemoration, and Johannes Brahms's 'Years of Study.' " Ph.D. diss., Columbia University, 2005.

Campbell, A. E. *Great Britain and the United States, 1895–1903*. Orig. pub. ca. 1960. Reprint, Westport, CT: Greenwood Press, 1974.

Campbell, James T. *Songs of Zion: The African Methodist Episcopal Church in the United States and South Africa*. New York: Oxford University Press, 1995.

Carlhian, Jean-Paul. "L'École des Beaux-Arts and Its Influence on American Archi- tects and American Architecture, 1886–1936." In Roelker and Warner, *Two Hun- dred Years of Franco-American Relations*, 185–206. N.p.: Heffernan Press, [1978?].

Carr, Jonathan. *Mahler: A Biography*. Woodstock, NY: Overlook Press, 1997.

Carrol, Mark. *Music and Ideology in Cold War Europe*. Cambridge: Cambridge University Press, 2003.

Chasins, Abram. *Leopold Stokowski: A Profile*. New York: Hawthorn Books, 1979.

Chickering, Roger. "Patriotische Vereine im europäischen Vergleich." In *Europa um 1900: Texte eines Kolloquiums*, edited by Fritz Klein and Karl-Otmar v. Aretin, 151–62. Berlin: Akademie Verlag, 1989.

Chmaj, Betty E. "Fry versus Dwight: American Music's Debate over Nationality." *American Music* 3 (Spring 1985): 63–84.

Clapham, John. "Dvorák on the American Scene." *Nineteenth-Century Music* 5 (Summer 1981): 16–23.

Clark, William. *Less than Kin: A Study of Anglo-American Relations*. London: H. Hamilton, 1957.

Cohen-Solal, Annie. *Un jour, ils auront des peintres: L'avènement des peintres améri- cains, Paris 1867–New York 1948*. Paris: Editions Gallimard, 2000.

Colbert, Charles. *A Measure of Perfection: Phrenology and the Fine Arts in America*. Chapel Hill: University of North Carolina Press, 1997.

Confino, Alon. *The Nation as a Local Metaphor: Württemberg, Imperial Germany, and National Memory, 1871–1918*. Chapel Hill: University of North Carolina Press, 1997.

Cook, Nicholas, and Mark Everist, eds. *Rethinking Music*. Oxford: Oxford Univer- sity Press, 1999.

Cooper, Dana Calise. "Informal Ambassadors: American Women, Transatlantic Marriages, and Anglo-American Relations, 1865–1945." Ph.D. diss., Texas Tech University, Lubbock.

Cortinovis, Irene E. "The Golden Age of German Song," *Missouri Historical Review* 68 (July 1974): 437–42.

Costigliola, Frank. *Awkward Dominion: American Political, Economic, and Cultural Relations with Europe, 1919–1933*. Orig. pub. 1984. Reprint, Ithaca, NY: Cornell University Press, 1987.

———. "'Unceasing Pressure for Penetration': Gender, Pathology, and Emotion in George Kennan's Formation of the Cold War." *Journal of American History* 83 (March 1997): 1309–39.

Crapol, Edward P. "Coming to Terms with Empire: The Historiography of Late-Nineteenth-Century American Foreign Relations." *Diplomatic History* 16 (Fall 1992): 573–97.

———. "From Anglophobia to Fragile Rapprochement: Anglo-American Relations in the Early Twentieth Century." In Schröder, *Confrontation and Cooperation*, 13–32.

Crawford, Richard. *America's Musical Life: A History*. New York: W. W. Norton, 2001.

Dahlhaus, Carl. *Die Idee der absoluten Musik*. Munich: dtv, 1976.

———. *Nineteenth-Century Music*. Translated by J. Bradford Robinson. Berkeley and Los Angeles: University of California Press, 1989.

Daniel, Ute. "'Kultur' und 'Gesellschaft': Überlegungen zum Gegenstandsbereich der Sozialgeschichte." *Geschichte und Gesellschaft* 19 (1993): 69–99.

Danuser, Hermann, ed. *Gustav Mahler*. Darmstadt: Wissenschaftliche Buchgesellschaft, 1992.

Danuser, Hermann, and Hermann Gottschewski, eds. *Amerikanismus, Americanism, Weill: Die Suche nach kultureller Identität in der Moderne*. Schliengen: Edition Argus, 2003.

Dean, Winton. "Beethoven and Opera." In Arnold and Fortune, *The Beethoven Reader*, 331–86.

Dennis, David B. *Beethoven in German Politics, 1870–1989*. New Haven, CT: Yale University Press, 1996.

Diehl, Carl. *Americans and German Scholarship, 1770–1870*. New Haven, CT: Yale University Press, 1978.

DiMaggio, Paul. "Cultural Entrepreneurship in Nineteenth-Century Boston: The Creation of an Organizational Base for High Culture in America." *Media, Culture and Society* 4 (1982): 33–50.

———. "Cultural Entrepreneurship in Nineteenth-Century Boston, Part II: The Classification and Framing of American Art." *Media, Culture and Society* 4 (1982): 303–22.

———. *Managers of the Arts: Careers and Opinions of Senior Administrators of U.S. Art Museums, Symphony Orchestras, Resident Theatres, and Local Arts Agencies*. 2nd ed. Washington, DC: Seven Locks Press, 1987.

———, ed. *Nonprofit Enterprise in the Arts: Studies in Mission and Constraint.* New York: Oxford University Press, 1986.

Dimbleby, David, and David Reynolds. *An Ocean Apart: The Relationship between Britain and America in the Twentieth Century.* London: BBC Books, 1988.

Doering, James M. "'A Salesman of Fine Music': American Music Manager Arthur Judson, 1900–1940." Ph.D. diss., Washington University, St. Louis, 1998.

Doerries, Reinhard R. "Empire and Republic: German-American Relations Before 1917." In Trommler and McVeigh, *America and the Germans,* 2:3–17.

———. *Imperial Challenge: Ambassador Count Berstorff and German-American Relations, 1908–1917.* Translated by Christa D. Shannon. Chapel Hill: University of North Carolina Press, 1989.

———. *Washington-Berlin 1908/1917: Die Tätigkeit des Botschafters Johann Heinrich Graf von Bernstorff in Washington vor dem Eintritt der Vereinigten Staaten von America in den Ersten Weltkrieg.* Düsseldorf: Pädagogischer Verlag Schwann, 1975.

Douglas, Ann. *The Feminization of American Culture.* New York: Knopf, 1977.

———. *Terrible Honesty: Mongrel Manhattan in the 1920s.* New York: Farrar, Straus & Giroux, 1995.

Dülffer, Jost, Martin Kröger, and Rolf-Harald Wippich, eds. *Vermiedene Kriege: Deeskalation von Konflkten der Grossmächte zwischen Krimkrieg und Erstem Weltkrieg.* Munich: Oldenbourg, 1997.

Düwell, Kurt, and Werner Link, eds. *Deutsche auswärtige Kulturpolitik seit 1871: Geschichte und Struktur.* Cologne: Böhlau, 1981.

Eagleton, Terry. *The Idea of Culture.* Oxford: Blackwell, 2000.

Echternkamp, Jörg. *Der Aufstieg des deutschen Nationalismus, 1770–1840.* Frankfurt am Main: Campus, 1998.

Echternkamp, Jörg, and Sven Oliver Müller, eds. *Die Politik der Nation: Deutscher Nationalism in Krieg und Krisen, 1760–1960.* Munich: Oldenbourg, 2002.

Edling, Max M. *A Revolution in Favor of Government: Origins of the United States and the Making of the American State.* New York: Oxford University Press, 2003.

Ekman, Paul. *The Face of Man: Expressions of Universal Emotions in a New Guinea Village.* New York: Garland STPM Press, 1980.

Ekman, Paul, and Richard J. Davison. *The Nature of Emotions: Fundamental Questions.* New York: Oxford University Press, 1994.

Elson, Louis C. *European Reminiscences, Musical and Otherwise: Being the Recollections of the Vacation Tours of a Musician in Various Countries.* Philadelphia: T. Presser, 1896.

Elvert, Jürgen, and Michael Salewski, eds. *Deutschland und der Westen im 19. und 20. Jahrhundert.* Vol. 1: *Transatlantische Beziehungen.* Stuttgart: Franz Steiner Verlag, 1993.

Fiebig-v. Hase, Ragnhild. "Amerikanische Friedensbemühungen in Europa, 1905–1914." In Finzsch and Wellerreuther, *Liberalitas,* 285–318.

———. "Die deutsch-amerikanischen Wirtschaftsbeziehungen, 1890–1914, im Zeichen von Protektionismus und internationaler Integration." *Amerikastudien* 33 (1988): 329–57.

———. "Großmachtkonflikte in der Westlichen Hemisphäre: Das Beipspiel der Venezuelakrise vom Winter 1902/03." In Dülffer, Kröger, and Wippich, *Vermiedene Kriege*, 527–55. Munich: Oldenbourg, 1997.

———. *Lateinamerika als Konfliktherd der deutsch-amerikanischen Beziehungen 1890–1903: Vom Beginn der Panamerikapolitik bis zur Venezuelakrise von 1902/03.* 2 vols. Schriftenreihe der Historischen Kommission bei der Bayerischen Akademie der Wissenschaften, vol. 27. Göttingen:Vandenhoeck & Ruprecht, 1986.

———. "Die politische Funktionalisierung der Kultur: Der deutsch-amerikanische Professorenaustausch 1904–1914." In *Zwei Wege in die Moderne, Aspekte der deutsch-amerikanischen Beziehungen 1900–1918*, edited by Ragnhild Fiebig-von Hase and Jürgen Heideking, 45–88. Trier: Wissenschaftlicher Verlag, 1997.

———. "The United States and Germany in the World Arena, 1900–1917." In Schröder, *Confrontation and Cooperation*, 33–68.

Finck, Henry T., ed. *Anton Seidl: A Memorial by His Friends.* New York: C. Scribner's Sons, 1899.

Fink, Lois M. *American Art at the Nineteenth Century Paris Salon.* New York: Cambridge University Press, 1990.

———. "French Art in the United States, 1850–1870: Three Dealers and Collectors." *Gazette des Beaux-Arts* (September 1978): 87–100.

Finzsch, Norbert, and Hermann Wellenreuther, eds. *Liberalitas: Festschrift für Erich Angermann. Transatlantische Studien.* Vol. 1. Stuttgart: Franz Steiner, 1992.

François, Etienne, Hannes Siegrist, and Jakob Vogel, eds. *Nation und Emotion: Deutschland und Frankreich im Vergleich 19. und 20. Jahrhundert.* Göttingen: Vandenhoeck & Ruprecht, 1995.

Frevert, Ute, Heinz-Gerhard Haupt, Bettina Brandt, Franz Becker, Dagmar Günther, and Moritz Föllmer. "Zur Wirkung des Nationalismus im Deutschland des 19. Jahrhunderts." Panel at the 42nd Deutsche Historikertag, Frankfurt am Main, 9 September 1998.

Frost, Christine Mangala. "30 Rupees for Shakespeare: A Consideration of Imperial Theatre in India." *Modern Drama* 35 (1992): 90–100.

Fuchs, Eckhardt. "Die internationale Organisation der edukativen Bewegung: Studien zu Austausch- und Transferprozessen im Aufbruch der Moderne." Habilitation thesis, Humboldt-Universität, Berlin.

———. "Schriftenaustausch, Copyright und Dokumentation: Das Buch als Medium der internationalen Wissenschaftskommunikation vor dem Ersten Weltkrieg unter besonderer Berücksichtigung Deutschlands und der Vereinigten Staaten von Amerika." *Leipziger Jahrbuch zur Buchgeschichte* 7 (1997): 125–68.

———, ed. *Weltausstellungen im 19. Jahrhundert, Comparativ* 9/5–6. Leipzig: Leipziger Universitätsverlag, 2000.

Fuchs, Mechtild. *"So pocht das Schicksal an die Pforte": Untersuchungen und Vorschläge zur Rezeption sinfonischer Musik des 19. Jahrhunderts.* Munich: Musikverlag Emil Katzbichler, 1986.

Fussell, Paul. *The Great War and Modern Memory*. New York: Oxford University Press, 1975.

Gardner, Kara Anne. "Living by the Ladies' Smiles: The Feminization of American Music and the Modernist Reaction." Ph.D. diss., Stanford University, 1999.

Gatzke, Hans Wilhelm. *Germany and the United States: "A Special Relationship?"* Cambridge, MA: Harvard University Press, 1980.

Gay, Peter. *Schnitzler's Century: The Making of Middle Class Culture, 1815–1914*. New York: Norton, 2002.

Gellner, Ernest. *Nations and Nationalism*. Ithaca, NY: Cornell University Press, 1983.

Gerber, David A. "The Germans Take Care of Our Celebrations: Middle-Class Americans Appropriate German Ethnic Culture in Buffalo in the 1850s." In Grover, *Hard At Play*, 39–60.

Gergen, Kenneth J. *Realities and Relationships: Soundings in Social Construction*. 2nd ed. Cambridge, MA: Harvard University Press, 1997.

Gienow-Hecht, Jessica C. E. "Music and Emotions in German-American Relations." Habilitation thesis, Martin-Luther-Universität Halle-Wittenberg, 2003.

———. "On the Division of Knowledge and the Community of Thought." In Gienow-Hecht and Schumacher, *Culture and International History*, 3–26.

———. "Shame on US? Academics, U.S. Cultural Transfer, and the Cold War." *Diplomatic History* 24 (Summer 2000): 465–94.

———. *Transmission Impossible: American Journalism as Cultural Diplomacy in Postwar Germany, 1945-1955*. Baton Rouge: Louisiana State University Press, 1999.

———. "Trumpeting Down the Walls of Jericho: The Politics of Art, Music and Emotion in German-American Relations, 1870–1920." *Journal of Social History* 36, no. 3 (Spring 2003): 585–613.

Gienow-Hecht, Jessica C. E., and Frank Schumacher. *Culture and International History*. Oxford: Berghahn Books, 2003.

Gilliam, Bryan. "A Viennese Opera Composer in Hollywood: Korngold's Double Exile in America." In Brinkmann and Wolff, *Driven into Paradise*, 223–42.

Gipson, Richard. *The Life of Emma Thursby, 1845–1931*. New York: New York Historical Society, 1940.

Goedde, Petra. *GIs and Germans: Culture, Gender, and Foreign Relations, 1945–1949*. New Haven, CT: Yale University Press, 2003.

Goethe, Johann Wolfgang von. *Die Wahlverwandtschaften*. Orig. pub. 1809. Reprint, Munich: Goldmann, 1956.

Goltermann, Svenja. *Körper der Nation: Habitusformierung und die Politik des Turnens 1860–1890*. Göttingen: Vandenhoeck & Ruprecht, 1998.

Goodwin, Thomas. *Sketches and Impressions: Musical, Theatrical, and Social (1799–1885)*. New York: G. P. Putnam's Sons, 1887.

Gramit, David. *Cultivating Music: The Aspirations, Interests, and Limits of German Musical Culture, 1770–1848*. Berkeley and Los Angeles: University of California Press, 2002.

Grant, Margaret, and Herman S. Hettinger. *America's Symphony Orchestras and How They Are Supported*. New York: W. W. Norton & Co., 1940.

Grant, Mark. *Maestros of the Pen: A History of Classical Music Criticism in America*. Boston: Northeastern University Press, 1998.

Grey, Thomas S. "Wagner's *Die Meistersinger* als National Opera (1868–1945)." In Applegate and Potter, *Music and German National Identity*, 78–104.

Griessenbeck, Amelie v. *Kulturfaktor Emotion: Zur Bedeutung von Emotion für das Verhältnis von Individuum, Gesellschaft und Kultur*. Munich: Akademischer Verlag, 1997.

Griffiths, Paul E. *What Emotions Really Are: The Problem of Psychological Categories*. Chicago: University of Chicago Press, 1997.

Grosse, Jürgen. *Amerikapolitik und Amerikabild in der DDR, 1974–1989*. Bonn: Bouvier, 1999.

Grover, Kathryn, ed. *Hard At Play: Leisure in America, 1840–1940*. Amherst, MA: University of Amherst Press, 1992.

Grupp, Peter. "Vorraussetzungen und Praxis deutscher amtlicher Kulturpropaganda in den neutralen Staaten während des Ersten Weltkrieges." In *Der Erste Weltkrieg: Wirkung, Wahrnehmung und Analyse*, edited by Wolfgang Michalka, 799–824. Munich: Piper, 1994.

Gundlach, Horst. *Reiz: Zur Verwendung eines Begriffes in der Psychologie*. Bern: H. Huber, 1976.

Guthrie-Shimizu, Sayuri. "For Love of the Game: Baseball in Early U.S.-Japanese Encounters and the Rise of a Transnational Sporting Fraternity." *Diplomatic History* 28 (November 2004): 637–62.

Halfeld, Alfred. *Amerika und der Amerikanismus: Kritische Betrachtungen eines Deutschen und Europäers*. Jena: E. Diederichs, 1927.

Hart, Philip. *Orpheus in the New World: The Symphony Orchestra as an American Cultural Institution*. New York: Norton, 1973.

Heideking, Jürgen, Henry Geitz, and Jürgen Herbst, eds. *German Influences on American Education to 1917*. Cambridge: Cambridge University Press, 1995.

Herren, Madeleine. *Hintertüren zur Macht: Internationalismus und modernisierungsorientierte Außenpolitik in Belgien, der Schweiz und den USA, 1865–1914*. Munich: Oldenbourg, 2000.

Herwig, Holger. *Politics of Frustration: The United States in German Naval Planning, 1889–1941*. Boston: Little, Brown, 1976.

Hettling, Manfred, and Stefan-Ludwig Hoffmann, eds. *Der bürgerliche Wertehimmel: Innenansichten des 19. Jahrhunderts*. Göttingen: Vandenhoeck & Ruprecht, 2000.

Hettling, Manfred, and Paul Nolte, eds. *Nation und Gesellschaft in Deutschland: Historische Essays*. Munich: C. H. Beck, 1996.

Hildebrand, Klaus. *Das vergangene Reich: Deutsche Außenpolitik von Bismarck bis Hitler 1871–1945*. Stuttgart: Deutsche Verlagsanstalt, 1995.

Hilfrich, Fabian. "Manliness and 'Realism': The Use of Gendered Tropes in the Debates on the Philippine-American and on the Vietnam War." In Gienow-Hecht and Schumacher, *Culture and International History*, 60–78.

Hitchens, Christopher. *Blood, Class, and Nostalgia: Anglo-American Ironies*. New York: Farrar, Straus & Giroux, 1990.

Hobsbawm, Eric J. "Kultur als Ghetto." In *"Kultur-Zerstörung"? 10. Römer-berggespräche in Frankfurt a.M.*, edited by Hilmar Hoffmann, 60–69. König-stein/Ts.: Athenäum, 1983.

———. *Nations and Nationalism since 1780: Programme, Myth, Reality*. 2nd ed. Cambridge: Cambridge University Press, 1992.

Hogan, Michael, and Thomas Paterson, eds. *Explaining the History of American Foreign Relations*. Rev. ed. Cambridge: Cambridge University Press, 2004.

Hoganson, Kristin L. *Consumers' Imperium: The Global Production of American Domesticity, 1865–1920*. Chapel Hill: University of North Carolina Press, 2007.

———. "Cosmopolitan Domesticity: Importing the American Dream." *American Historical Review* 107 (Feburary 2002): 55–83.

Hollinger, David. *Postethnic America*. Rev. ed. New York: Basic Books, 2000.

Hopkins, Anthony, ed. *Global History: Interactions between the Universal and the Local*. Basingstoke, UK: Palgrave Macmillan, 2006.

Horowitz, Helen L. *Culture and the City: Cultural Philanthropy in Chicago from the 1880s to 1917*. Orig. pub. 1976. Reprint, Chicago: University of Chicago Press, 1989.

Horowitz, Joseph. *Artists in Exile: How Refugees from 20th Century War and Revolution Transformed the American Performing Arts*. New York: Harper Collins, 2007.

———. *Classical Music in America: A History of Its Rise and Fall*. New York: Norton and Norton, 2005.

———. *Understanding Toscanini: How He Became an American Culture-God and Helped Create a New Audience for Old Music*. New York: Knopf, 1987.

———. *Wagner Nights: An American History*. Berkeley and Los Angeles: University of California Press, 1994.

Howe, Daniel Walker. *Making the American Self: Jonathan Edwards to Abraham Lincoln*. Cambridge, MA: Harvard University Press, 1997.

———. "Victorian Culture in America." In Blodgett et al., *Victorian America*, 3–28.

Howe, Marc A. De Wolfe. *The Boston Symphony Orchestra, 1881–1931*. Boston: Houghton Mifflin, 1931.

Hunter, Jane. *How Young Ladies Became Girls: The Victorian Origins of American Girlhood*. New Haven, CT: Yale University Press, 2002.

Huntington, Samuel. *The Clash of Civilizations and the Remaking of World Order*. New York: Simon and Schuster, 1996.

Hynes, Samuel Lynn. *A War Imagined: The First World War and English Culture*. New York: Atheneum, 1991; Maxwell Macmillan International, 1990.

Iriye, Akira. *Cultural Internationalism and World Order*. Baltimore: Johns Hopkins University Press, 1997.

———. "Culture." *Journal of American History* 77, no. 1 (June 1990): 99–107.

———. *Global Community: The Role of International Organizations in the Making of the Contemporary World*. Berkeley and Los Angeles: University of California Press, 2002.

Jablonski, Edward. *Flying Fortress: The Illustrated Biography of the B-17s and the Men Who Flew Them.* Garden City, NY: Doubleday, 1965.

Jacob, Heinrich Eduard. *Johann Strauss und das 19. Jahrhundert: Die Geschichte einer musikalischen Weltherrschaft (1819–1917).* Amsterdam: Querido Verlag, 1937.

Jaeger, Friedrich. "Der Kulturbegriff im Werk Max Webers und seine Bedeutung für eine moderne Kulturgeschichte." *Geschichte und Gesellschaft* 18 (1992): 371–93.

Janik, Elizabeth. *Recomposing German Music: Politics and Tradition in Cold War Berlin.* Leiden: Brill, 2005.

Jarausch, Konrad. "American Students in Germany, 1815–1914." In *German Influences on Education in the United States to 1917*, 195–211. New York: Cambridge University Press, 1995.

Johnson, H. Earle. *Hallelujah, Amen! The Story of the Handel and Haydn Society of Boston.* Orig. pub. Boston: Bruce Humphries, 1965. Reprint, New York: Da Capo, 1981.

Jonas, Manfred. *The United States and Germany: A Diplomatic History.* Ithaca, NY: Cornell University Press, 1984.

Junker, Detlef, Philipp Gassert, Wilfried Mausbach, and David B. Morris, eds. *Die USA und Deutschland im Zeitalter des Kalten Krieges: Ein Handbuch.* 2 vols. Stuttgart: DVA, 2001.

Kaiser, Wolfram. "The Great Derby Race: Strategies of Cultural Representation at Nineteenth-Century World Exhibitions." In Gienow-Hecht and Schumacher, *Culture and International History*, 45–59.

Kalberg, Stephen. *Max Weber's Comparative Historical Sociology.* Chicago: University of Chicago Press, 1994.

Kammen, Michael. *Mystic Chords of Memory: The Transformation of American Culture.* New York: Alfred Knopf, 1991.

Kater, Michael H. *Different Drummers: Jazz in the Culture of Nazi Germany.* New York: Oxford University Press, 1992.

Keegan, John. *The First World War.* New York: A. Knopf, 1999.

Keim, Jeannette. *Forty Years of German-American Political Relations.* Philadelphia: W. J. Dornan, 1919.

Kennedy, Arthur M., ed. *A History of the Orpheus Club of Philadelphia.* Philadelphia: Orpheus Club of Philadelphia/Allen, Lane & Scott, 1936.

Kennedy, Paul. *The Samoan Tangle: A Study in Anglo-German-American Relations, 1878–1900.* Dublin: Irish University Press, 1974.

Kessel, Martina. "Das Trauma der Affektkontrolle: Zur Sehnsucht nach Gefühlen im 19. Jahrhundert." In Benthien, Fleig, and Kasten, *Emotionalität*, 156–77.

Kloosterhuls, Jürgen. "Deutsche auswärtige Kulturpolitik und ihre Trägergruppen vor dem Ersten Weltkrieg." In Düwell and Link, *Deutsche auswärtige Kulturpolitik seit 1871*, 7–36.

———. *Friedliche Imperialisten: Deutsche Auslandsvereine und auswärtige Kulturpolitik, 1906–1918.* New York: Peter Lang, 1994.

Kloppenberg, James T. *Uncertain Victory: Social Democracy and Progressivism in European and American Thought, 1870–1920*. New York: Oxford University Press, 1986.

Knight, Ellen. *Charles Martin Loeffler: A Life Apart in American Music*. Urbana: University of Illinois Press, 1993.

Koehler, Jonathan. "Gustav Mahler: A Study of Cultural Identity in the Austro-Hungarian Empire." Honors thesis, University of California, Davis, 1998.

Koester, Eckart. " 'Kultur' versus 'Zivilisation': Thomas Manns Kriegspublizistik als weltanschaulich-ästhetische Standortsuche." In Mommsen, *Kultur und Krieg*, 249–58.

Koht, Halvdan. *The American Spirit in Europe*. Philadelphia: University of Pennsylvania Press, 1949.

Kohut, Thomas A. *Wilhelm II and the Germans: A Study in Leadership*. New York: Oxford University Press, 1991.

Kolodin, Irving. *The Metropolitan Opera, 1883–1966: A Candid History*. 4th ed. New York: A. A. Knopf, 1966.

Kowalke, Kim H. "Kurt Weill's America." In *Amerikanismus, Americanism, Weill: Die Suche nach kultureller Identität in der Moderne*, edited by Hermann Danuser and Hermann Gottschewski, 9–15. Schliengen: Edition Argus, 2003.

Kramer, Elizabeth A. "The Idea of *Kunstreligion* in German Musical Aesthetics of the Early Nineteenth Century." Ph.D. diss., University of North Carolina, Chapel Hill, 2005.

Krips, Joseph. *Erinnerungen: Ohne Liebe kann man keine Musik machen*. Edited by Harietta Krips. Vienna: Böhlau, 1994.

Krohn, Ernst C. *Missouri Music*. Orig. pub. St. Louis: Privately published, 1924. Portions reprinted in Krohn, *A Century of Missouri Music*. New York: DaCapo Press, 1971.

Krüger, Peter. "Die Beurteilung der Reichsgründung und der Reichsverfassung von 1871 in den USA." In Finzsch and Wellenreuther, *Liberalitas*, 263–83. Transatlantische Studien, vol. 1. Stuttgart: Franz Steiner, 1992.

Lammersdorf, Raimund. *Anfänge einer Weltmacht: Theodore Roosevelt und die transatlantischen Beziehungen der USA, 1901–1909*. Berlin: Akademie Verlag, 1994.

Landormy, Paul. *A History of Music*. Translated by Frederick H. Martens. New York: Charles Scribner's Sons, 1923.

Langer, Susanne K. *Mind: An Essay on Human Feeling*. 3 vols. Baltimore: Johns Hopkins University Press, 1967, 1985.

Laqueur, Walter, and George L. Mosse, eds. *1914: The Coming of the First World War*. New York: Harper & Row, 1966.

Larres, Klaus, and Torsten Oppelland. *Deutschland und die USA im 20. Jahrhundert: Geschichte der politischen Beziehungen*. Darmstadt: Wissenschaftliche Buchgesellschaft, 1997.

Lasch, Christopher. *The New Radicalism in America, 1889–1963: The Intellectual as a Social Type*. New York: Knopf, 1965.

Lawrence, Vera Brodsky. *Strong on Music: The New York Muscial Scene in the Days of George Templeton Strong, 1836–1875.* 3 vols. New York: Oxford University Press, 1988–99.

Lears, T. Jackson. *No Place of Grace: Antimodernism and the Transformation of American Culture, 1880–1920.* New York: Pantheon Books, 1981.

Lebow, Marcia Wilson. "A Systematic Examination of the *Journal of Music and Art* Edited by John Sullivan Dwight: 1852–1881, Boston Massachusetts." Ph.D. diss., University of California, Los Angeles, 1969.

Lebrecht, Norman. *The Maestro Myth.* New York: Birch Lane, 1991.

Leiter, Robert D. *The Musicians and Petrillo.* New York: Bookman Associates, 1953.

Leppert, Richard. *Music and Image: Domesticity, Ideology and Socio-Cultural Formation in Eighteenth-Century England.* Cambridge: Cambridge University Press, 1988.

Levine, Lawrence. *Highbrow/Lowbrow: The Emergence of Cultural Hierarchy in America.* Cambridge, MA: Harvard University Press, 1988.

Levy, Alan Howard. *Musical Nationalism: American Composers' Search for Identity.* Westport, CT: Greenwood Press, 1983.

———. "The Search for Identity in American Music, 1890–1920." *American Music* 2 (Summer 1984): 70–81.

Lichtenwanger, William. *Oscar Sonneck and American Music.* Urbana, IL: University of Illinois Press, 1983.

Locke, Ralph P., and Cyrilla Barr, eds. *Cultivating Music in America: Women Patrons and Activists since 1860.* Berkeley and Los Angeles: University of California Press, 1997.

Loth, Wilfried, and Jürgen Osterhammel, eds. *Internationale Geschichte: Themen, Ergebnisse, Aussichten.* Munich: Oldenbourg, 2000.

Lowens, Irving. "L'affaire Karl Muck: A Study in War Hysteria (1917–18)." *Musicology* 1 (1947): 265–74.

Maase, Kasper. *Bravo America: Erkundigungen zur Jugendkultur in der Bundesrepublik in den fünfziger Jahren.* Hamburg: Junius, 1992.

Macdonald, John Frederick. *Two Towns—One City: Paris—London.* New York: Dodd, Mead and Company, [1918?].

Macleod, David I. *Building Character in the American Boy: The Boy Scouts, the YMCA, and Their Forerunners, 1870–1920.* Madison: University of Wisconsin Press, 1983.

Mai, Ekkehard. "Präsentation und Repräsentativität—Interne Probleme deutscher Kunstausstellungen im Ausland (1900–1930)." *Zeitschrift für Kulturaustausch* 31 (1981): 107–23.

Maier, Charles S. *Among Empires: American Ascendancy and Its Predecessors.* Cambridge, MA: Harvard University Press, 2006.

Mann, Thomas. *Doktor Faustus: Das Leben des deutschen Tonsetzers Adrian Leverkühn, erzählt von einem Freunde.* Stockholm: Bermann-Fischer Verlag, 1947.

Manstead, Antony S. R., and Agneta Fischer. "Beyond the Universality-Specificity Dichotomy." *Cognition and Emotion* 16 (January 2002): 1–9.

Marion, John Francis. *Within These Walls: A History of the Academy of Music in Philadelphia*. Philadelphia: Academy of Music, 1984.

Marquis, Albert Nelson. *The Book of Chicagoans: A Biographical Dictionary of Leading Living Men of the City of Chicago*. Chicago: A. N. Marquis, 1911.

Martin, George W. *The Damrosch Dynasty: America's First Family of Music*. Boston: Houghton Mifflin, 1983.

Massow, Albrecht von. "Absolute Musik." In *Handwörterbuch der musikalischen Terminologie*, special vol. 1, *Terminologie der Musik im 20. Jahrhundert*, edited by Hans Heinrich Eggebrecht, 13–29. Stuttgart: Franz Steiner, 1995.

Mattelart, Armand, and Ariel Dorfman. *Para leer al pato Donald*. Havana: Editorial de Ciencias Sociales, 1971. Translated edition: *How To Read Donald Duck: Imperialist Ideology in Disney Comic*. New York: International General, 1975.

Mattelart, Armand, and Peter Jehle. "Neue Horizonte der Kommunikation: Die Rückkehr zur Kultur." *Argument* 35, no. 5 (September–October 1993): 689–706.

McCarthy, Kathleen D. *Women's Culture: American Philanthropy and Art, 1830–1930*. Chicago: University of Chicago Press, 1991.

McCarthy, S. Margaret W. "Amy Fay: The American Years." *American Music* 3 (Spring 1985): 52–61.

McCullough, David. *John Adams*. New York: Simon and Schuster, 2001.

McGrath, William J. *Dionysian Art and Populist Politics in Austria*. London: Yale University Press, 1974.

McIntosh, DeCourcy E. "Demand and Supply: The Pittsburgh Art Trade and M. Knoedler & Co." In Weisberg, McIntosh, and McQueen, *Collecting in the Gilded Age*, 107–77.

Meeker, Arthur. *Prairie Avenue*. New York: Alfred A. Knopf, 1949.

Mehnert, Ute. *Deutschland, Amerika und die "Gelbe Gefahr": Zur Karriere eines Schlagworts in der Großen Politik, 1905–1917*. Stuttgart: Franz Steiner Verlag, 1995.

Mender, Mona. *Extraordinary Women in Support of Music*. Landham, MD, 1997.

Menees, Charles, ed. *The St. Louis Symphony Orchestra*. St. Louis: Mendle Print, 1955.

Mercer, Jonathan. "Human Nature and the First Image: Emotion in International Politics." *Journal of International Relations* 9 (2006): 288–303.

Meyer, Leonard B. *Emotion and Meaning in Music*. Chicago: University of Chicago Press, 1956.

Miller, Donald. *City of the Century: The Epic of Chicago and the Making of America*. New York: Simon and Schuster, 1996.

Miquel, Pierre. *Art et argent 1800–1900: L'école de la nature*. Vols. 5, 6. Maurs-La-Jolie: Martinelle, 1986, 1987.

Mitchell, Nancy. *The Danger of Dreams: German and American Imperialism in Latin America*. Chapel Hill : University of North Carolina Press, 1999.

Molnar, Thomas Steven. *The Emerging Atlantic Culture*. London: Transaction Books, 1994.

Mommsen, Wolfgang J. *Bürgerliche Kultur und Künstlerische Avant-garde: Kultur und Politik im deutschen Kaiserreich 1870 bis 1918*. Berlin: Propyläen, 1994.

———, ed. *Kultur und Krieg: Die Rolle der Intellektuellen, Künstler und Schriftsteller im Ersten Weltkrieg*. Schriften des Historischen Kollegs, Kolloquien 34. Munich: Oldenbourg, 1996.

Monod, David. *Settling Scores: German Music, Denazification, and the Americans, 1945–1953*. Chapel Hill: University of North Carolina Press, 2005.

Moore, Macdonald Smith. *Yankee Blues: Musical Culture and American Identity*. Bloomington: Indiana University Press, 1985.

Morgan, Robert P. "Ives and Mahler: Mutual Responses at the End of an Era." *Nineteenth-Century Music* 2 (July 1978): 72–81.

Muck, Peter. *Einhundert Jahre Berliner Philharmonisches Orchester: Darstellung in Dokumenten*. 3 vols. Tutzing: Schneider, 1982.

———. *Karl Muck: Ein Dirigentenleben in Briefen und Dokumenten*. Tutzing: H. Schneider, 2003.

Mueller, Richard E. *A Century of the Symphony*. St. Louis: Knight Publishing Co., 1979.

———. "The St. Louis Symphony Orchestra, 1931–1958." Ph.D. diss., St. Louis University, 1976.

Muhs, Rudolph, Johannes Paulmann, and Willibald Steinmetz, eds. *Aneignung und Abwehr: Interkultureller Transfer zwischen Deutschland und Grossbritannien im 19. Jahrhundert*. Bodenheim: Philo-Verlag, 1998.

Musikverein, ed. *Der Musikverein von Milwaukee, 1850–1900: Eine Chronik*. Milwaukee: Herold, 1900.

Mussulman, Joseph A. *Music in the Cultured Generation: A Social History of Music in America, 1870–1900*. Evanston, IL: Northwestern University Press, 1971.

Nagler, Jörg. "From Culture to *Kultur*: Changing American Perceptions of Imperial Germany, 1870–1914." In Barclay and Glaser-Schmidt, *Transatlantic Images and Perceptions*, 131–54.

———. *Nationale Minoritäten im Krieg: "Feindliche Ausländer" und die amerikanische Heimatfront während des Ersten Weltkriegs*. Hamburg: Hamburger Edition, 2000.

National Task Force for the American Orchestra, An Initiative for Change. *Americanizing the American Orchestra: Report of the National Task Force for the American Orchestra. An Intitative for Change, June 1893*. Washington, DC: American Symphony Orchestra League, 1993.

Newman, Nancy. "Gleiche Rechte, gleiche Pflichten, und gleiche Genüsse: Henry Albrecht's Utopian Vision of the Germania Musical Society." *Yearbook of German-American Studies* 34 (1999): 83–111.

———. "Good Music for a Free People: The Germania Musical Society and Transatlantic Musical Culture of the Mid-Nineteenth Century." Ph.D. diss., Brown University, 2002.

Nicholas, Herbert G. *The United States and Great Britain*. Chicago: University of Chicago Press, 1975.

Nickles, David P. *Under Wire: How the Telegraph Changed Diplomacy.* Cambridge, MA: Harvard University Press, 2003.

Nolan, Mary. *Visions of Modernity: American Business and the Modernization of Germany.* New York: Oxford University Press, 1994.

Nye, Joseph S. Jr. *Soft Power: The Means to Success in World Politics.* New York: Public Affairs, 2004.

Oehlmann, Werner. *Das Berliner Philharmonische Orchester, 1901–1985.* 2nd ed. Kassel: Bärenreiter, 1975.

Oja, Carol J. *Making Music Modern: New York in the 1920s.* New York: Oxford University Press, 2000.

———. "The USA, 1918–45." In *Modern Times: From World War I to the Present,* edited by Robert P. Morgan, 206–30. Englewood Cliffs, NJ: Prentice Hall, 1993.

Oppelland, Torsten. "Der lange Weg in den Krieg (1900–1918)." In Larres and Oppelland, *Deutschland und die USA im 20. Jahrhundert,* 1–30.

O'Rourke, Kevin H., and Jeffrey G. Williamson. *Globalization and History: The Evolution of a Nineteenth-Century Atlantic Economy.* Cambridge, MA: MIT Press, 1999.

Otis, Philo Adams. *The Chicago Symphony Orchestra: Its Organization, Growth and Development, 1891–1924.* Chicago: Clayton F. Summy O., 1924.

Pachter, Marc, and Frances Wein, eds. *Abroad in America: Visitors to the New Nation, 1776–1914.* Reading, MA: Addison-Wesley Publishing Co., 1976.

Painter, Karen, ed. *Mahler and His World.* Princeton, NJ: Princeton University Press, 2002.

———. "The Sensuality of Timbre: Responses to Mahler and Modernity at the Fin de siècle." *Nineteenth-Century Music* 18 (Spring 1995): 236–56.

Palmer, Gary B., and Debra J. Occhi, eds. *Languages of Sentiment: Cultural Constructions of Emotional Substrates.* Amsterdam: J. Benjamins, 1999.

Paret, Peter. "Art and the National Image: The Conflict over Germany's Participation in the St. Louis Exposition." *Central European History* 10 (1978): 175–83.

Pečman, Rudolf. *Beethovens Opernpläne.* Translated from the Czech by Jan Gruna. Brno: Univerzita J. E. Purkyne, 1981.

Pederson, Sanna. "A. B. Marx, Berlin Concert Life, and German National Identity." *Nineteenth-Century Music* 18 (Fall 1994): 87–107.

Peiss, Kathy. *Cheap Amusements: Working Women and Leisure in Turn-of-the-Century New York.* Philadelphia: Temple University Press, 1986.

Pells, Richard. "American Culture Goes Global, or Does It?" *Chronicle of Higher Education,* 12 April 2002, pp. B7–9.

———. *Not Like Us: How Europeans Have Loved, Hated, and Transformed American Culture since World War II.* New York: Basic Books, 1997.

Perry, Bliss. *Life and Letters of Henry Lee Higginson.* Boston: Atlantic Monthly, 1921.

Petersen, Anne D. *Die Engländer in Hamburg, 1814 bis 1914: Ein Beitrag zur hamburgischen Geschichte.* Hamburg: Von Bockel, 1993.

Peyser, Ethel. *The House That Music Built: Carnegie Hall*. New York: Robert M. McBride,1936.

Pfister, Joel, and Nancy Schnog, eds. *Inventing the Psychological: Toward a Cultural History of Emotional Life in America*. New Haven, CT: Yale University Press, 1997.

Pflanze, Otto. "Germany—Bismarck—America." In Elvert and Salewski, *Deutschland und der Westen*, 1:67–84.

Phillips, Kevin. *The Cousins' Wars: Religion, Politics, and the Triumph of Anglo-America*. New York: Basic Books, 1999.

Poiger, Uta G. *Jazz, Rock, and Rebels: Cold War Politics and American Culture in a Divided Germany*. Berkeley and Los Angeles: University of California Press, 2000.

Pommerin, Reiner. *Der Kaiser und Amerika: Die USA in der Politik der Reichsleitung, 1890–1917*. Cologne: Böhlau, 1986.

Portes, Jacques. "L'européanisation des Etats-Unis vue par les Français (1870–1914)." *Revue française d'études américaines* 12 (1982): 51–64.

Potter, Pamela M. "Klassische deutsche Musik in den Vereinigten Staaten." Translated by Christiane Ferdinand-Gonzales. In Junker et al., *Die USA und Deutschland im Zeitalter des Kalten Krieges*, 1:686–95.

———. *Most German of the Arts: Musicology and Society; From the Weimar Republic to the End of Hitler's Reich*. New Haven, CT: Yale University Press, 1998.

Preston, Katherine K. *Opera on the Road: Traveling Opera Troupes in the United States, 1825–1860*. Urbana: University of Illinois Press, 1993.

Radkau, Joachim. *Das Zeitalter der Nervosität: Deutschland zwischen Bismarck und Hitler*. Munich: C. Hanser Verlag, 1998.

Raffel, Burton. *American Victorians: Explorations in Emotional History*. Hamden, CT: Archon Books, 1984.

Rauhut, Franz. "Die Herkunft der Worte und Begriffe 'Kultur,' 'Civilisation' und 'Bildung.'" *Germanisch-Romanische Monatsschrift* 3 (April 1953): 81–91.

Rennella, Mark. *The Boston Cosmopolitans: International Travel and American Arts and Letters*. New York: Palgrave Macmillan, 2008.

Rennella, Mark, and Whitney Walton. "Planned Serendipity: American Travellers and the Transatlantic Voyage in the Nineteenth and Twentieth Centuries." *Journal of Social History* 38, no. 2 (2004): 365–83.

Ringer, Fritz. *The Decline of the German Mandarins: The German Academic Community, 1890–1933*. Cambridge, MA: Cambridge University Press, 1969.

Rinke, Stefan H. *Zwischen Weltpolitik und Monroe Doktrin: Botschafter Speck von Sternburg und die deutsch-amerikanischen Beziehungen, 1898–1908*. Stuttgart: H.-D. Heinz, 1992.

Ritter, Gerhard A. "Internationale Wissenschaftsbeziehungen und auswärtige Kulturpolitik im deutschen Kaiserreich." *Zeitschrift für Kulturaustausch* 31 (1981): 5–16.

Rodgers, Daniel T. *Atlantic Crossings: Social Politics in a Progressive Age*. Cambridge, MA: Harvard University Press, Belknap Press, 1998.

Rodheaver, Misty D. "Cultural Flows between the United States and Germany, 1890–1929." M.A. thesis, West Virginia University, 2005.

Roelker, Nancy L., and Charles K. Warner, eds. *Two Hundred Years of Franco-American Relations: Papers of the Bicentennial Colloquium of the Society for French Historical Studies in Newport, Rhode Island, September 7–10, 1978*. N.p.: Heffernan Press, [1978?].

Roell, Craig H. *The Piano in America, 1890–1940*. Chapel Hill: University of North Carolina Press, 1989.

Röhl, John C. G. *Kaiser, Hof und Staat: Wilhelm II. und die deutsche Politik*. 4th ed. Munich: C. H. Beck, 1995.

Rose, Anne C. *Victorian America and the Civil War*. New York: Cambridge University Press, 1992.

Rose, Charles E. "The American Federation of Musicians and Its Effect on Black Musicians in St. Louis in the Twentieth Century." B.A. thesis, University of Missouri, Columbia, 1978.

Rosen, Stephen P. *War and Human Nature*. Princeton, NJ: Princeton University Press, 2005.

Rosenberg, Emily. *Financial Missionaries to the World: The Politics and Culture of Dollar Diplomacy, 1900–1930*. Cambridge, MA: Harvard University Press, 1999.

Rosenberg, Pierre. *France in the Golden Age: Seventeenth-Century French Paintings in American Collections*. New York: Metropolitian Museum of Art, 1982.

Roth, Günther. " 'Americana': Bildungsbürgerliche Ansichten und auswärtige Kulturpolitik im wilhelminischen Deutschland." In Roth, *Politische Herrschaft und persönliche Freiheit*, 175–200. Frankfurt: Suhrkamp, 1987.

Rubin, Emanuel. "Jeannette Meyers Thurber and the National Conservatory of Music." *American Music* 8, no. 3 (Autumn 1990): 294–325.

Saffle, Michael, ed. *Music and Culture in America, 1861–1918*. New York: Garland Publishing, 1998.

Saunders, Frances Stonor. *Who Paid the Piper? The CIA and the Cultural Cold War*. London: Granta Books, 1999.

Schabas, Ezra. *Theodore Thomas: America's Conductor and Builder of Orchestra, 1835–1905*. Urbana: University of Illinois Press, 1989.

Schaeper, Thomas J., and Kathleen Schaeper. *Cowboys into Gentlemen: Rhodes Scholars, Oxford, and the Creation of an American Elite*. New York: Berghahn Books, 1998.

Schenk, Dietmar. *Die Hochschule für Musik zu Berlin: Preußens Konservatorium zwischen romantischem Klassizismus und Neuer Musik, 1869–1932/33*. Stuttgart: Franz Steiner, 2003.

Scherrer, Klaus. *Psychologie der Emotion*. Göttingen: Verlag für Psychologie, 1990.

Schickel, Richard, and Michael Walsh. *Carnegie Hall: The First One Hundred Years*. New York: H. N. Abrams, 1987.

Schmalz, Robert. "Paur and the Pittsburgh: Requiem for an Orchestra." *American Music* 12 (Summer 1994): 125–47.

———. "Personalities, Politics, and Prophecy: Frederic Archer and the Birth of the Pittsburgh Symphony Orchestra." *American Music* 5 (Fall 1987): 305–16.

Schmidt, Alexander. *Reisen in die Moderne: Der Amerika-Diskurs des deutschen Bürgertums vor dem Ersten Weltkrieg im europäischen Vergleich*. Berlin: Akademie-Verlag, 1997.

Schmitt, Stephan, ed. *Geschichte der Hochschule für Musik und Theater München von den Anfängen bis 1945*. Tutzing: H. Schneider, 2005.

Schneider, David. *The San Francisco Symphony: Music, Maestros, and Musicians*. 2nd ed. Novato, CA: Presidio Press, 1983.

Schneider, Stephanie. "'International Siamese Twins'—Die symbolische Repräsentation anglo-amerikanischer Beziehungen in politischen Karikaturen der zweiten Hälfte des 19. Jahrhunderts." Ph.D. diss., Universität Erfurt, 2003.

Schonberg, Harold. *The Great Conductors*. New York: Simon and Schuster, 1967.

———. *The Great Pianists*. New York: Simon and Schuster, 1963.

———. *The Lives of the Great Composers*. 3rd ed. New York: W. W. Norton, 1997.

Schorn-Schütte, Luise. *Karl Lamprecht: Kulturgeschichtsschreibung zwischen Wissenschaft und Politik*. Schriftenreihe der Historischen Kommission bei der Bayerischen Akademie der Wissenschaften, vol. 22. Göttingen: Vandenhoeck & Ruprecht, 1984.

Schröder, Hans-Jürgen, ed. *Confrontation and Cooperation: Germany and the United States in the Era of World War I, 1900–1924*. Providence, RI: Berg, 1993.

Schwabe, Klaus, ed. *Deutsche Hochschullehrer als Elite, 1815–1945*. Büdinger Forschungen zur Sozialgeschichte 1983. Boppard am Rhein: H. Boldt, 1988.

Scott, William B., and Peter M. Rutkoff. *New York Modern: The Arts and the City*. Baltimore: Johns Hopkins University Press, 1999.

Scott-Smith, Giles. "The 'Masterpieces of the Twentieth Century' Festival and the Congress for Cultural Freedom: Origins and Consolidation, 1947–52." *Intelligence and National Security* 15 (Spring 2000): 121–43.

Seltzer, George. *The Professional Symphony Orchestra in the United States*. Metuchen, NJ: Scarecrow Press, 1975.

Shanet, Howard. *Philharmonic: A History of New York's Orchestra*. New York: Doubleday, 1975.

Sherman, John K. *Music and Maestros: The Story of the Minneapolis Symphony Orchestra*. Minneapolis: University of Minnesota Press, 1952.

Shore, Elliott. "The Kultur Club." In Schröder, *Confrontation and Cooperation*, 127–33.

Siefert, Marsha. "Remastering the Past: Musical Heritage, Sound Recording and the Nation in Hungary and Russia." In *National Heritage—National Canon*, Proceedings of the Focus Group "Humanities in Historical and Comparative Perspective: Roots and Margins of the European Tradition and Reactions to It," Collegium Budapest, 1999/2000, pp. 247–76.

Skard, Sigmund. *American Studies in Europe: Their History and Present Organization*. 2 vols. Philadelphia: University of Pennsylvania Press, 1958.

Standage, Tom. *The Victorian Internet: The Remarkable Story of the Telegraph and the Nineteenth Century's On-Line Pioneers.* Orig. pub. 1998. Reprint, New York: Walker and Co., 1999.

Stearns, Carol Zisowitz, and Peter Stearns. *Anger: The Struggle for Emotional Control in America's History.* Chicago: University of Chicago Press, 1986.

Stearns, Peter, and Jan Lewis, eds. *An Emotional History of the United States.* New York: New York University Press, 1998.

Stearns, Peter, and Carol Z. Stearns. "Emotionology: Clarifying the History of Emotions and Emotional Standards." *American Historical Review* 90 (October 1985): 813–36.

Stolberg-Wernigerode, Otto, Graf zu. *Germany and the United States during the Era of Bismarck.* Reading, PA: Henry Janssen Foundation, 1937.

Stowe, William. *Going Abroad: European Travel in Nineteenth-Century American Culture.* Princeton, NJ: Princeton University Press, 1994.

Strinati, Dominic. *An Introduction to Theories of Popular Culture.* London: Routledge, 1995.

Strouse, Jean. *Alice James: A Biography.* Orig, pub. 1980. Reprint, Cambridge, MA: Harvard University Press, 1999.

Stuckenschmidt, H. H. *Zum Hören geboren: Ein Leben mit der Musik unserer Zeit.* Munich: Piper, 1979.

Tarasti, Eero. *Myth and Music: A Semiotic Approach to the Aesthetics of Myth in Music, Especially That of Wagner, Sibelius and Stravinsky.* The Hague: Mouton, 1979.

Thacker, Toby. *Music after Hitler, 1945–1955.* Aldershot, UK: Ashgate, 2007.

Thelen, David. "Of Audiences, Borderlands, and Comparisons: Toward the Internationalization of American History." *Journal of American History* 79 (1992): 436–62.

Thomas, Louis R. "A History of the Cincinnati Symphony Orchestra to 1931." Ph.D. diss., University of Cincinnati, 1972.

Tibbett, John. "The Missing Title Page: Dvorak and the American National Song." In Saffle, *Music and Culture in America*, 343–65.

Tischler, Barbara L. "One Hundred Percent Americanism and Music in Boston during World War I." *American Music* 4, no. 2 (Summer 1986): 164–76.

Torrecilla, Arturo. "Cultural Imperialism, Mass Media and Class Struggle: An Interview with Armand Mattelart." *Insurgent Sociologist* 9, no. 4 (Spring 1990): 69–79.

Trepp, Anne-Charlott. "Emotion und bürgerliche Sinnstiftung oder die Metaphysik des Gefühls: Liebe am Beginn des bürgerlichen Zeitalters." In Hettling and Hoffmann, *Der bürgerliche Wertehimmel*, 23–56.

Trommler, Frank. "Inventing the Enemy: German-American Cultural Relations, 1900–1917." In Schröder, *Confrontation and Cooperation*, pp. 99–125.

———. "The Use of History in German-American Politics." In Brancaforte, *The German Forty-Eighters in the United States*, 279–95.

Trommler, Frank, and Joseph McVeigh. *America and the Germans: An Assessment of a Three-Hundred Year History.* 2 vols. Philadelphia: University of Pennsylvania Press, 1985.

Turk, Gayle. "The Case of Dr. Karl Muck: Anti-German Hysteria and Enemy Alien Internment during World War I." Undergraduate thesis, Harvard University, 1994.

Ungern-Sternberg, Franziska von. *Kulturpolitik zwischen den Kontinenten, Deutschland und Amerika: Das Germanische Museum in Cambridge, Mass.* Cologne: Böhlau, 1994.

Vagts, Alfred. *Deutschland und die Vereinigten Staaten in der Weltpolitik.* 2 vols. New York: Macmillan, 1935.

———. "Hopes and Fears of an American-German War, 1870–1915." *Political Science Quarterly* 54 (1939): 514–35.

Vester, Heinz-Gunter. *Emotion, Gesellschaft und Kultur: Grundzüge einer soziologischen Theorie der Emotionen.* Opladen: Westdeutscher Verlag, 1991.

Von Eschen, Penny. *Satchmo Blows Up the World: Jazz Ambassadors Play the Cold War.* Cambridge, MA: Harvard University Press, 2004.

Wagnleitner, Reinhold. *Coca-Colonization and the Cold War: The Cultural Mission of the United States in Austria after the Second World War.* Translated by Diana M. Wolf. Chapel Hill: University of North Carolina Press, 1994.

Walton, Whitney. "Internationalism and the Junior Year Abroad: American Students in France in the 1920s and 1930s." *Diplomatic History* 29, no. 2 (April 2005): 255–79.

Ward, Andrew. *Dark Midnight When I Rise: The Story of the Jubilee Singers Who Introduced the World to the Music of Black America.* New York: Farrar, Straus & Giroux, 2000.

Wasserloos, Yvonne. *Das Leiziger Konservatorium für Musik im 19. Jahrhundert: Anziehungs- und Ausstrahlungskraft eines musikpädagogischen Modells auf das internationale Musikleben.* Hildesheim: Olms, 2004.

Waters, Edward N. *Victor Herbert: A Life in Music.* New York: MacMillan Co., 1955.

Watkins, Glenn. *Proof through the Night: Music and the Great War.* Berkeley and Los Angeles: University of California Press, 2003.

Weber, Max. "Die 'Objektivität' sozialwissenschaftlicher und sozialpolitischer Erkenntnis." In Weber, *Gesammelte Aufsätze zur Wissenschaftslehre,* 146–214. Tübingen: Mohr, 1988.

Weber, Rolf, ed. *Land ohne Nachtigall: Deutsche Emigranten in Amerika, 1777–1886.* Berlin: Buchverlag Der Morgen, 1981.

Weber, William. *The Great Transformation of Musical Taste: Concert Programming from Haydn to Brahms.* New York: Cambridge University Press, 2008.

———. "The History of Musical Canon." In Cook and Everist, *Rethinking Music,* 336–55.

———. *Music and the Middle Class: The Social Structure of Concert Life in London, Paris and Vienna.* New York: Holmes and Meier, 1975.

Weidenfeller, Gerhard. *VDA: Verein für das Deutschtum im Ausland: Allgemeiner Deutscher Schulverein 1881–1918; Ein Beitrag zur Geschichte des deutschen Nationalismus und Imperialismus im Kaiserreich.* Frankfurt am Main: Peter Lang, 1976.

Weinberg, H. Barbara, Doreen Bolger, and David Park Curry, eds. *American Impressionism and Realism: The Painting of Modern Life, 1885–1915*. New York: Metropolitan Museum of Art, 1994.

Weisberg, Gabriel P. "From Paris to Pittsburgh: Visual Culture and American Taste, 1880–1910." In Weisberg, McIntosh, and McQueen, *Collecting in the Gilded Age*, 179–297.

Weisberg, Gabriel P., DeCourcy E. McIntosh, and Alison McQueen, eds. *Collecting in the Gilded Age: Art Patronage in Pittsburgh, 1890–1910*. Lebanon, NH: University Press of New England, 1997.

Weisbuch, Robert. *Atlantic Double-Cross: American Literature and British Influence in the Age of Emerson*. Chicago: University of Chicago Press, 1986.

Wells, Katherine Gladney. *Symphony and Song: The St. Louis Symphony Orchestra; The First Hundred Years, 1880–1980*. Taftsville, VT: Countryman Press, 1980. Reprint, Tucson, AZ: Patrice Press, 1993.

Wenger, Janice. "William Henry Pommer: His Life and Works." Ph.D. diss., University of Missouri, Kansas City, 1987.

Wierzbicka, Anna. *Emotions across Languages and Cultures: Diversity and Universals*. Cambridge: Cambridge University Press; Paris: Editions de la Maison des Sciences de l'Homme, 1999.

Winter, Jay M. *Sites of Memory, Sites of Mourning: The Great War in European Cultural History*. Cambridge: Cambridge University Press, 1995.

Wister, Frances Anne. *Twenty-Five Years of the Philadephia Orchestra, 1900–1925*. Philadelphia: Edward Stern & Co., 1925.

Wolfe, Richard James. "A Short History of the Pittsburgh Orchestra, 1896–1910." M.A. thesis, Carnegie Institute of Technology, 1954.

Wolschke, Martin. *Von der Stadtpfeiferei zu Lehrlingskapelle und Sinfonieorchester*. Regensburg: Gustav Bosse Verlag, 1981.

Wright, Patrick. *Iron Curtain: From Stage to Cold War*. Oxford: Oxford University Press, 2007.

Wüstenbecker, Katja. *Deutsch-Amerikaner im Ersten Weltkrieg: US-Politik und nationale Identitäten im Mittleren Westen*. Stuttgart: Franz Steiner, 2007.

Yoffe, Elkhonon, ed. *Tchaikovsky in America: The Composer's Visit in 1891*. Translated by Lidya Yoffe. New York: Oxford University Press, 1986.

Young, Robert J. *Marketing Marianne: French Propaganda in America, 1900–1940*. New Brunswick, NJ: Rutgers University Press, 2004.

Ysaÿe, Antoine, and Bertram Ratcliffe. *Ysaÿe: His Life, Work and Influence*. London: William Heinemann, 1947.

Zeiler, Thomas. *Ambassadors in Pinstripes: The Spalding World Baseball Tour and the Birth of the American Empire*. Lanham, MD: Rowman & Littlefield, 2006.

Zolov, Eric. *Refried Elvis: The Rise of the Mexican Counterculture*. Berkeley and Los Angeles: University of California Press, 1999.

Zwerdling, Alex. *Improvised Europeans: American Literary Expatriates and the Siege of London*. New York: Basic Books, 1998.

# Index

*Note: Italicized page numbers indicate illustrations.*